LAND O LAKES®
TREASURY OF
COUNTRY
RECIPES

CREDITS:

Published 1992 by
Tormont Publications Inc.
338 Saint Antoine St. East
Montreal, Canada   H2Y 1A3
Tel. (514) 954-1441
Fax (514) 954-1443

Recipes developed and tested by the Land O'Lakes Test Kitchens,
with assistance from Robin Krause and Barbara Strand.

Design, photography and production by Cy DeCosse Incorporated.

ISBN 2-89429-165-5
Printed in Canada

LAND O LAKES®
TREASURY OF
COUNTRY
RECIPES

TORMONT

LAND O LAKES®
TREASURY OF
COUNTRY
RECIPES

The heritage of the country has long been cherished at Land O'Lakes. Founded as a rural dairy cooperative in the early 1920s, Land O'Lakes has maintained a deep understanding and appreciation for the ways of the country.

With this *LAND O LAKES® Treasury of Country Recipes,* the rich heritage of country cooking has been preserved for your eating pleasure. These traditional country-style recipes have been updated yet kept unchanged in their simplicity and hearty goodness.

Home economists in the Land O'Lakes Test Kitchens developed these recipes to showcase the wholesome appeal of country foods while keeping in mind contemporary cooking and eating styles. The recipes were tested extensively to ensure easy preparation and excellent results every time you use them. Beautiful color photos of the completed recipes plus step-by-step photos show you just what to expect.

We hope that you will enjoy using this treasury of great recipes to bring the fresh, wholesome tastes of country cooking home to your family and friends.

Contents

APPETIZERS, SNACKS & BEVERAGES

On a beautiful day, the best place for a party is the porch or patio. The fresh-mown grass and the beds of brightly colored flowers create a lovely backdrop for entertaining, whether it's a birthday celebration, an anniversary or just a long overdue get-together of good neighbors.

Your guests will enjoy the chance to be outdoors. Games for the children. Perhaps a croquet match for the grown-ups. And lots of time to catch up on what's new, what's important in each other's lives.

The occasion calls for your very best nibbles and beverages, from old family favorites to enticing new creations. Start with tall glasses of icy-cold lemonade or fresh fruit juices. Then treat your guests to a bountiful tray of appetizers and snacks. Butter-rich pastry turnovers wrapped around a creamy filling. Crumb-coated chicken bites with a savory sauce for dipping. Fresh vegetable kabobs to admire and devour. A tangy spread to serve with hard rolls or a robust rye bread.

These treats are just as tantalizing when served indoors for a holiday open house or a casual weekend evening in the family room. They're also great take-alongs for someone else's party. But most important, they're good because you made them to share.

Country Chicken Nuggets

30 to 40 nuggets
30 minutes

*Buttery crumb-coated chicken bites
dipped in a sour cream-mustard sauce.*

75 g	(*3 oz*) cornflakes, crushed
7 ml	(*1 1/2 tsp*) oregano leaves
7 ml	(*1 1/2 tsp*) thyme leaves
2	whole boneless chicken breasts, skinned, cut into 2.5-cm (*1-in*) pieces
125 g	(*4 oz*) butter or margarine, melted

Sauce

250 ml	(*8 fl oz*) sour cream
30 ml	(*2 tbsp*) country-style Dijon mustard
15 ml	(*1 tbsp*) milk

Heat oven to 220 °C (*425 °F*) mark 7. In small bowl stir together cornflake crumbs, oregano and thyme. Dip chicken pieces in melted butter, then coat with crumb mixture. Place chicken 1 cm (*1/2 in*) apart on 40 x 25 x 2.5-cm (*15 x 10 x 1-in*) Swiss roll tin. Bake for 10 to 15 min. or until fork tender and crisp. Meanwhile, in small bowl stir together all sauce ingredients. Serve nuggets with sauce.

Tip: Nuggets can be baked ahead of time and reheated at 180 °C (*350 °F*) mark 4 for 10 min.

Microwave Directions: In 1-litre (*1 3/4-pt*) casserole place chicken pieces. Cover; microwave on HIGH, stirring twice, until fork tender (3 to 4 min.). In small bowl stir together cornflake crumbs, oregano and thyme. In small bowl melt butter on HIGH (70 to 80 sec.). Dip half of chicken pieces in melted butter, then coat with crumb mixture. On 23-cm (*9-in*) serving plate place chicken pieces 1 cm (*1/2 in*) apart around outside edge. Cover with paper towel; microwave on HIGH, turning plate 1/4 turn after 1 min. of time, until heated through (1 1/2 to 2 min.). Repeat with remaining chicken pieces.

Lemon Vegetable Kabobs

8 servings
30 minutes

This light, nutritious appetizer has a fresh summer taste.

1	whole boneless chicken breast, skinned, cut into 10 x 1-cm (*4 x 1/2-in*) strips
8	cherry tomatoes
1	med. green pepper, cut into 2.5-cm (*1-in*) pieces
15 ml	(*1 tbsp*) chopped fresh parsley
2 ml	(*1/2 tsp*) thyme leaves

1 ml	(*1/4 tsp*) salt
	Pinch of pepper
30 ml	(*2 tbsp*) lemon juice
4	(1-cm) (*1/2-in*) slices lemon, cut in fourths
8	(13 x 20-cm) (*5 to 8-in*) skewers

In medium bowl stir together all ingredients *except* lemon slices and skewers. Marinate 10 min. Meanwhile, heat grill. On each skewer place 1 piece lemon. Alternate threading chicken strips and vegetables on each skewer; end with lemon. Brush with marinade; grill 5 to 10 cm (*2 to 4 in*) from heat, turning once, until chicken is fork tender (3 to 5 min.).

Tip: Kabobs can be grilled over ash white coals. Grill for 20 to 30 min., turning occasionally, or until chicken is fork tender.

Microwave Directions: Use large size cherry tomatoes and bamboo or wooden skewers. Proceed as directed left *except* cut chicken into 5 x 1-cm (*2 x 1/2-in*) strips. Place filled skewers on microwave-safe roasting rack. Brush with marinade; microwave on HIGH, turning rack 1/4 turn and turning kabobs over after 4 min., until chicken is fork tender (7 to 8 min.).

Country Chicken Nuggets (top)
Lemon Vegetable Kabobs (bottom)

30 turnovers
60 minutes

Creamy Chicken-Filled Turnovers

A filled butter pastry that can be made ahead, frozen and baked as needed.

Filling

30 g	(*1 oz*) butter or margarine
30 ml	(*2 tbsp*) finely chopped onion
200 g	(*7 oz*) cooked, shredded chicken
75 g	(*3 oz*) cream cheese
1 ml	(*1/4 tsp*) salt
1 ml	(*1/4 tsp*) thyme leaves
1 ml	(*1/4 tsp*) pepper
45 ml	(*3 tbsp*) white wine or chicken stock

Pastry

200 g	(*7 oz*) plain flour
2 ml	(*1/2 tsp*) salt
2 ml	(*1/2 tsp*) paprika
125 g	(*4 oz*) butter or margarine
30 to 60 ml	(*2 to 4 tbsp*) cold water

In 25-cm (*10-in*) frying pan melt butter; add onion. Cook over med. heat until softened (4 to 5 min.). Stir in remaining filling ingredients. Continue cooking, stirring occasionally, until cream cheese is melted and heated through (2 to 3 min.). Set aside. Heat oven to 190 °C (*375 °F*) mark 5. In medium bowl combine all pastry ingredients *except* butter and water. Cut in butter until crumbly. Stir in water; shape into ball. On lightly floured surface roll out dough to 1.5-mm (*1/16-in*) thickness. Cut with floured 6-cm (*2 1/2-in*) round cookie cutter. Place 5 ml (*1 tsp*) filling on one half of circle; fold other half over. Press edges with fork to seal. Place on baking sheets; repeat with remaining pastry and filling. Bake for 15 to 20 min. or until golden brown.

Microwave Directions: Filling: Cut cream cheese into 6 pieces. In 1-litre (*1 3/4-pt*) casserole melt butter on HIGH (40 to 50 sec.). Stir in onion; microwave on HIGH until softened (1 1/2 to 1 3/4 min.). Stir in cream cheese and remaining filling ingredients. Microwave on HIGH, stirring after 1 min., until heated through (2 to 2 1/2 min.). Continue as directed left.

Creamy Chicken-Filled Turnovers

Deviled Chicken (top)
Chicken Wings With Pineapple Sauce (bottom)

Chicken Wings With Pineapple Sauce

Horseradish adds spark to these tender chicken wings.

30 pieces
420 ml (*14½ fl oz*)
2 hours 30 minutes

Marinade

45 ml	(*3 tbsp*) cider vinegar
30 ml	(*2 tbsp*) soy sauce
75 ml	(*5 tbsp*) reserved pineapple juice
30 ml	(*2 tbsp*) vegetable oil
10 ml	(*2 tsp*) prepared horseradish
5 ml	(*1 tsp*) crushed fresh garlic

1.2 kg	(*2½ lb*) chicken wings, jointed (reserve tips for use in soups)

Sauce

450 g	(*16 oz*) crushed canned pineapple, drained, reserve juice for marinade
125 ml	(*4 fl oz*) honey
15 ml	(*1 tbsp*) cornflour

In large bowl stir together all marinade ingredients and jointed chicken wings. Marinate at least 1 hr. Heat oven to 220 °C (*425 °F*) mark 7. Place chicken wings and marinade on 40 x 25 x 2.5-cm (*15 x 10 x 1-in*) Swiss roll tin. Bake, stirring occasionally, for 50 to 60 min. or until browned and fork tender. In 2-litre (*3½-pt*) saucepan combine all sauce ingredients. Cook over med. high heat, stirring occasionally, until slightly thickened and heated through (3 to 5 min.).

Microwave Directions: Marinate as directed left. Meanwhile, in small bowl stir together all sauce ingredients. Microwave on HIGH, stirring twice during last half of time, until mixture is slightly thickened and heated through (4½ to 5 min.). Set aside. On 23-cm (*9-in*) round serving dish place half of chicken wings spoke fashion, spaced at least 1 cm (*½ in*) apart. Cover with waxed paper; microwave on HIGH, turning dish ¼ turn twice, until fork tender (8 to 9 min.). Repeat with remaining wings.

Deviled Chicken

6 servings
45 minutes

A tangy, buttery appetizer spread that goes well with French bread or a hearty rye bread.

300 g	(*11 oz*) cooked, shredded chicken
125 ml	(*4 fl oz*) mayonnaise
45 g	(*1½ oz*) butter or margarine, melted
30 ml	(*2 tbsp*) country-style Dijon mustard
	Pinch of cayenne pepper

130 g	(*4½ oz*) fresh breadcrumbs
50 ml	(*4 tbsp*) chopped fresh parsley
30 g	(*1 oz*) butter or margarine, melted

French bread, sliced

Heat oven to 200 °C (*400 °F*) mark 6. In medium bowl stir together chicken, mayonnaise, 45 g (*1½ oz*) butter, mustard and pepper. Spread into 25-cm (*10-in*) flan dish or 23-cm (*9-in*) pie dish. In small bowl stir together breadcrumbs, parsley and 30 g (*1 oz*) butter. Sprinkle over top of chicken mixture. Bake for 20 to 25 min. or until golden brown and heated through. Serve spread on French bread.

Microwave Directions: In small bowl stir together breadcrumbs and 30 g (*1 oz*) melted butter; microwave on HIGH, stirring every 30 seconds, until crumbs are toasted (3 to 4 min.). Stir in parsley; set aside. In 25-cm (*10-in*) flan dish or 23-cm (*9-in*) pie dish melt 45 g (*1½ oz*) butter on HIGH (40 to 50 sec.). Stir in chicken, mayonnaise, mustard and pepper. Microwave on MEDIUM (50% power), stirring every 2 min., until heated through (8 to 10 min.). Sprinkle with toasted breadcrumbs. Microwave on MEDIUM (50% power) until heated through (1 min.).

about 350 g (*12 oz*)
2 hours 30 minutes

Chicken Liver Spread

Serve this flavourful spread with sliced rye bread or wheat crackers.

Spread

45 g	(*1½ oz*) butter or margarine
225 g	(*8 oz*) chicken livers
5 ml	(*1 tsp*) crushed fresh garlic
30 ml	(*2 tbsp*) country-style Dijon mustard
1 ml	(*¼ tsp*) salt
	Pinch of pepper

Frosting

75 g	(*3 oz*) cream cheese, softened
30 to 45 ml	(*2 to 3 tbsp*) single cream
10 ml	(*2 tsp*) chopped fresh chives

In 25-cm (*10-in*) frying pan melt butter; add chicken livers and garlic. Cook over med. high heat, stirring occasionally, until liver is fork tender (6 to 8 min.). Stir in remaining spread ingredients. Continue cooking until heated through (1 to 2 min.). Spoon into blender container or food processor. Blend or process until smooth. Press liver mixture into greased 450-ml (*¾-pt*) mould or soup bowl. Chill until firm (1 to 2 hr.). In small bowl stir together all frosting ingredients. Unmould liver spread onto serving plate. Frost and decorate liver spread.

Microwave Directions: Spread: Cut chicken livers in half. In 1-litre (*1¾-pt*) casserole melt butter on HIGH (40 to 50 sec.). Stir in chicken livers and garlic. Cover; microwave on HIGH, stirring every min., until liver is fork tender (5 to 6 min.). Stir in remaining spread ingredients. Microwave on HIGH until mixture just comes to a boil (45 to 60 sec.). Continue as directed left. Frosting: In small bowl microwave cream cheese on MEDIUM (50% power), stirring once after half the time, until softened (1 to 1¼ min.). Continue as directed left.

To Serve Spread:

1. Unmould liver spread onto serving plate.

2. Frost and decorate liver spread.

Chicken Liver Spread

Garden-Stuffed Mushrooms

Bacon-Wrapped Chicken Livers

20 appetizers
45 minutes

Bacon adds hearty smoked flavour and almonds add crunch to chicken livers.

225 to 350 g	(*8 to 12 oz*) chicken livers, quartered
20	whole blanched almonds
10	rashers of bacon, cut in half

Sauce

30 ml	(*2 tbsp*) soy sauce
15 ml	(*1 tbsp*) sherry
5 ml	(*1 tsp*) crushed fresh garlic

Heat oven to 200 °C (*400 °F*) mark 6. Place 1 chicken liver and 1 almond on top of ½ rasher bacon. Roll up; secure with wooden pick. Repeat with remaining ingredients. In medium bowl stir together sauce ingredients. Add chicken livers; marinate 10 min. Place chicken livers and sauce on 40 x 25 x 2.5-cm (*15 x 10 x 1-in*) Swiss roll tin. Bake for 10 to 15 min. or until liver is fork tender.

Microwave Directions: On microwave-safe roasting rack microwave bacon on MEDIUM (50% power), turning rack after half the time, until partially cooked (12 to 14 min.). Continue as directed left *except* place wrapped liver pieces on microwave-safe roasting rack. Microwave on HIGH, rearranging pieces after half the time, until liver is fork tender (6 to 8 min.).

Garden-Stuffed Mushrooms

16 appetizers
45 minutes

Carrot and green pepper add colour and crunch to these tasty stuffed mushrooms.

65 g	(*2½ oz*) dried crumbly style herb seasoned stuffing, crushed
50 g	(*2 oz*) butter or margarine, melted
50 ml	(*4 tbsp*) finely chopped carrot
50 ml	(*4 tbsp*) finely chopped green pepper

	Pinch of pepper
30 ml	(*2 tbsp*) finely chopped onion
16	(5-cm) (*2-in*) mushrooms, stems removed

Heat oven to 180 °C (*350 °F*) mark 4. In small bowl stir together all ingredients *except* mushrooms. Stuff each mushroom cap with 15 ml (*1 tbsp*) filling. Place in buttered 33 x 23-cm (*13 x 9-in*) baking dish. Bake for 20 to 25 min. or until tender.

Microwave Directions: Prepare mushrooms as directed left. Place in buttered 30 x 20-cm (*12 x 8-in*) baking dish. Cover; microwave on HIGH, turning dish after half the time, until tender (8 to 9 min.).

Pepper Swiss Cheese Ball

about 650 g (*23 oz*)
20 minutes

Smoked Salmon Cracker Spread

This hearty cracker spread is great for entertaining.

225 g	(*8 oz*) cream cheese, softened
2 ml	(*1/2 tsp*) salt
15 ml	(*1 tbsp*) lemon juice
10 ml	(*2 tsp*) finely chopped onion
5 ml	(*1 tsp*) liquid smoke
2 ml	(*1/2 tsp*) prepared horseradish

450 g	(*16 oz*) canned salmon, drained, bones removed, flaked
	Chopped pecans
	Chopped fresh parsley

In small mixer bowl beat cream cheese at med. speed, scraping bowl often, until light and fluffy (2 to 3 min.). Add salt, lemon juice, onion, liquid smoke and horseradish. Continue beating until well mixed (1 to 2 min.). By hand, stir in salmon. Spoon into serving bowl. If desired, garnish with pecans and parsley. Serve with crackers. Store refrigerated.

1 cheese ball
2 hours

Pepper Swiss Cheese Ball

Pepper complements the nutty flavour of Swiss cheese.

175 g	(*6 oz*) cream cheese, softened
125 ml	(*4 fl oz*) sour cream
1 ml	(*1/4 tsp*) garlic salt
175 g	(*6 oz*) shredded Swiss cheese

30 ml	(*2 tbsp*) chopped fresh parsley
30 to 45 ml	(*2 to 3 tbsp*) coarsely ground pepper

In small mixer bowl beat cream cheese on med. speed, scraping bowl often, until smooth (1 to 2 min.). Add sour cream and garlic salt; continue beating until well mixed. By hand, stir in cheese and parsley. Refrigerate at least 2 hr. Shape into flattened cheese ball or log. Roll in pepper to coat. Store refrigerated.

Cheese & Bacon Pinwheels

28 appetizers
30 minutes

Hearty rye bread pairs up with bacon and cheese for a quick, crowd-pleasing appetizer.

100 g	(*4 oz*) shredded Cheddar cheese
25 g	(*1 oz*) crisply cooked, crumbled bacon
50 g	(*2 oz*) butter or margarine, softened

30 ml	(*2 tbsp*) sliced 3 mm (*⅛ in*) spring onions
7	slices rye bread, crusts removed

In small bowl stir together all ingredients *except* bread. Flatten each bread slice with rolling pin. Spread each bread slice with 25 ml (*1½ tbsp*) cheese mixture. Roll up Swiss roll fashion beginning with short side. With serrated knife slice each roll into 4 pinwheels; secure each with wooden pick. Place on baking sheet. Heat grill. Grill 13 cm (*5 in*) from heat for 1½ to 2½ min. or until lightly browned and cheese is melted. Remove from baking sheet; serve immediately.

To Prepare Pinwheels:

1. Flatten each bread slice with rolling pin.

2. With serrated knife slice each roll into 4 pinwheels; secure each with wooden pick.

Cheese & Bacon Pinwheels

10 to 12 servings
30 minutes

Cheese & Bacon Potato Wedges

A hearty appetizer or late night snack.

675-g	(*24-oz*) pkg. frozen potato wedges	100 g	(*4 oz*) crisply cooked, crumbled bacon
225 g	(*8 oz*) shredded Cheddar cheese	50 ml	(*4 tbsp*) sliced spring onions
			Sour cream

Heat oven according to pkg. directions. Place potatoes in single layer on baking sheet. Bake according to pkg. directions. Immediately sprinkle with cheese, bacon and onions; continue baking for 1 to 2 min. or until cheese is melted. Serve warm. If desired, serve with sour cream.

Microwave Directions: Place potatoes in single layer on large plate or microwave-safe baking sheet. Microwave on HIGH, rearranging potatoes after half the time, until potatoes are hot (10 to 12 min.). Immediately sprinkle with cheese, bacon and onions. Microwave on HIGH until cheese is melted (1 to 2 min.).

500 ml (*17 fl oz*)
2 hours 15 minutes

Home-Style Vegetable Dip

Fresh chopped vegetables add a spark of colour and flavour to this dip.

250 ml	(*8 fl oz*) sour cream	1 ml	(*1/4 tsp*) garlic powder
125 ml	(*4 fl oz*) mayonnaise		
50 ml	(*4 tbsp*) chopped green pepper		Carrot sticks, broccoli or cauliflower
50 g	(*2 oz*) canned diced pimento, drained		flowerets, celery sticks, mangetout,
15 ml	(*1 tbsp*) chopped spring onion		cherry tomatoes, mushrooms
5 ml	(*1 tsp*) seasoned salt		

In medium bowl stir together all ingredients *except* vegetables. Cover; refrigerate at least 2 hr. Serve with vegetables.

Home-Style Vegetable Dip

Festive Stuffed Mangetout

50 appetizers
45 minutes

*Cheese and coarsely ground pepper add flavour and colour
to the cream cheese filling in these extra special appetizers.*

225 g	(*8 oz*) (approx. 50) mangetout		50 g	(*2 oz*) shredded Cheddar cheese
225 g	(*8 oz*) cream cheese, softened		2 ml	(*½ tsp*) coarsely ground pepper

In 2-litre (*3½-pt*) saucepan bring 500 ml (*17 fl oz*) water to a full boil. Add mangetout; cook 1 min. Drain well; plunge into ice water. Drain well. Cut stems off mangetout. Cut seam on side of mangetout forming pocket; set aside. In small mixer bowl combine cream cheese, Cheddar cheese and pepper. Beat at med. speed, scraping bowl often, until well mixed (1 to 2 min.). Spoon or pipe cheese mixture into pocket of each mangetout. Refrigerate until ready to serve.

To Prepare Stuffed Mangetout:

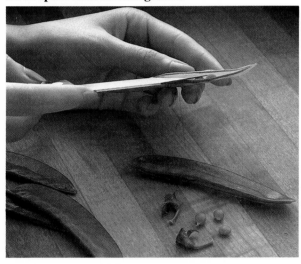

1. Cut stems off mangetout. Cut seam on side of mangetout forming pocket; set aside.

2. Spoon or pipe cheese mixture into pocket of each mangetout.

Festive Stuffed Mangetout

about 250 g *(9 oz)*
15 minutes

Buttery Pecan Date Spread

Serve this tasty spread at your next brunch or on bran muffins at breakfast.

75 g   *(3 oz)* butter or margarine, softened
75 g   *(3 oz)* cream cheese, softened
50 ml   *(4 tbsp)* finely chopped dates

50 ml   *(4 tbsp)* chopped pecans
15 ml   *(1 tbsp)* sherry or apple juice

In small mixer bowl combine butter and cream cheese. Beat at med. speed, scraping bowl often, until well mixed (1 to 2 min.). By hand, stir in remaining ingredients. Serve with crackers or nut bread. Store refrigerated.

450 ml *(¾ pt)*
2 hours

Sunshine Fruit Dip

This sunny fruit dip can be a light refreshing dessert too!

500 ml   *(17 fl oz)* sour cream
30 ml   *(2 tbsp)* firmly packed brown sugar
15 ml   *(1 tbsp)* orange juice

15 ml   *(1 tbsp)* grated orange rind

Fresh fruit, cut up

In medium bowl stir together all ingredients *except* fruit. Cover; refrigerate at least 2 hr. Serve with fresh fruit.

Sunshine Fruit Dip

Orange & Cinnamon Spiced Nuts

about 1 kg (*2¼ lb*)
1 hour 20 minutes

One taste of these subtly spiced nuts and the dish will soon be empty.

300 g	(*11 oz*) whole blanched almonds			Pinch of salt
175 g	(*6 oz*) pecan halves		2	egg whites
200 g	(*7 oz*) filberts		15 ml	(*1 tbsp*) grated orange rind
225 g	(*8 oz*) sugar		125 g	(*4 oz*) butter or margarine
1 ml	(*¼ tsp*) cinnamon			
1 ml	(*¼ tsp*) nutmeg			

Heat oven to 160 °C (*325 °F*) mark 3. Spread nuts in 40 x 25 x 2.5-cm (*15 x 10 x 1-in*) Swiss roll tin. Bake, stirring occasionally, for 20 to 25 min. or until lightly toasted. In small bowl stir together sugar, cinnamon, nutmeg and salt. In small mixer bowl beat egg whites at high speed, scraping bowl often, until soft peaks form (1 to 2 min.). Continue beating, gradually adding sugar mixture, until stiff peaks form (1 to 2 min.). By hand, fold in nuts and orange rind. In same Swiss roll tin melt butter in oven (4 to 6 min.). Spread nut mixture over butter. Bake, stirring every 10 min., for 25 to 30 min. or until nuts are brown and no butter remains. Cool completely. Store in airtight container.

Microwave Directions: Spread nuts in 30 x 20-cm (*12 x 8-in*) baking dish. Microwave on HIGH, stirring every 2 min., until lightly browned (10 to 12 min.). In small bowl stir together sugar, cinnamon, nutmeg and salt. In small mixer bowl beat egg whites at high speed, scraping bowl often, until soft peaks form (1 to 2 min.). Continue beating, gradually adding sugar mixture, until stiff peaks form (1 to 2 min.). By hand, fold in nuts and orange rind. In same baking dish melt butter on HIGH (70 to 80 sec.). Spread nut mixture over butter. Microwave on HIGH, stirring twice during the time, until nuts are brown and no butter remains (9 to 11 min.). Cool completely. Store in airtight container.

Chewy Maple Oat Clusters

about 1 kg (*2¼ lb*)
2 hours

A chewy snack for home, work or school.

130 g	(*4½ oz*) old-fashioned rolled oats		90 g	(*3½ oz*) raisins
30 g	(*1 oz*) crisp rice cereal		225-g	(*8-oz*) pkg. diced dried fruit mix
50 g	(*2 oz*) bran flakes		50 g	(*2 oz*) butter or margarine, melted
50 g	(*2 oz*) pecan halves, cut in half		375 ml	(*13 fl oz*) pure maple syrup or maple flavoured syrup
75 g	(*3 oz*) sunflower nuts			

Heat oven to 160 °C (*325 °F*) mark 3. In 33 x 23-cm (*13 x 9-in*) baking dish spread rolled oats. Bake, stirring occasionally, for 20 to 30 min. or until light golden brown. Stir in crisp rice cereal, bran flakes, pecans and sunflower nuts. Continue baking for 14 to 16 min. or until lightly toasted. Remove from oven; stir in raisins and dried fruit. In small bowl stir together butter and maple syrup; pour over cereal mixture. Stir to coat well. Continue baking, stirring occasionally, for 45 to 50 min. or until mixture clumps together and is golden brown. Spread on waxed paper. Cool completely; break into pieces.

Microwave Directions: In 30 x 20-cm (*12 x 8-in*) baking dish spread rolled oats. Microwave on HIGH, stirring every min., until light golden brown (5 to 8 min.). Stir in crisp rice cereal, bran flakes, pecans and sunflower nuts. Microwave on HIGH, stirring every min., until lightly toasted (2 to 4 min.). Stir in raisins and dried fruit. In small bowl stir together butter and maple syrup; pour over cereal mixture. Stir to coat well. Microwave on HIGH, stirring every 2 min., until mixture clumps together and is golden brown (6 to 8 min.). Spread on waxed paper. Cool completely; break into pieces.

Chewy Maple Oat Clusters (top)
Orange & Cinnamon Spiced Nuts (bottom)

29

Party Popcorn

about 250 to 450 g (*9 to 16 oz*)
15 minutes

Party Popcorn

Four specialty popcorns — great for your next party.

125 g   (*4 oz*) popped popcorn
75 g   (*3 oz*) butter or margarine

In large bowl place popcorn. In 1-litre (*1¾-pt*) saucepan melt butter over low heat (2 to 3 min.). Follow directions for desired variation. Serve immediately.

Variations:

TexMex Popcorn: Stir 1 ml (*¼ tsp*) hot pepper sauce into melted butter. Drizzle over popcorn; toss to evenly coat. In small bowl combine 5 ml (*1 tsp*) chilli powder and 1 ml (*¼ tsp*) garlic salt. Sprinkle over popcorn; toss to evenly coat.

Savoury Popcorn: Stir 10 ml (*2 tsp*) Worcestershire sauce into melted butter. Drizzle over popcorn; toss to evenly coat. In small bowl combine 5 ml (*1 tsp*) paprika, 2 ml (*½ tsp*) seasoned salt, 1 ml (*¼ tsp*) basil leaves, 1 ml (*¼ tsp*) marjoram leaves, 1 ml (*¼ tsp*)

thyme leaves and 1 ml (*¼ tsp*) garlic powder. Sprinkle over popcorn; toss to evenly coat.

Parmesan Italian Popcorn: Drizzle melted butter over popcorn; toss to evenly coat. In small bowl combine 30 ml (*2 tbsp*) grated Parmesan cheese, 5 ml (*1 tsp*) basil leaves, 2 ml (*½ tsp*) oregano leaves and 1 ml (*¼ tsp*) garlic powder. Sprinkle over popcorn; toss to evenly coat.

Praline Pecan Popcorn: Increase butter to 125 g (*4 oz*). Stir 90 g (*3½ oz*) firmly packed brown sugar and 5 ml (*1 tsp*) cinnamon into melted butter. Cook over med. heat, stirring occasionally, until mixture comes to a full boil (3 to 5 min.). Boil, stirring constantly, 7 min. Remove from heat; stir in 90 g (*3½ oz*) chopped pecans. Slowly pour over popcorn; stir to evenly coat. Cool 10 min.; break apart.

4 dozen
30 minutes

Crispy Snack Crackers

These savoury rye crackers are easy to make and fun to serve for a snack or with soups and salads.

½   loaf (24 slices) cocktail sandwich bread
75 g   (*3 oz*) butter or margarine
15 ml   (*1 tbsp*) sesame seed

2 ml   (*½ tsp*) thyme leaves
    Pinch of pepper
2 ml   (*½ tsp*) crushed fresh garlic

Heat oven to 180 °C (*350 °F*) mark 4. Cut each bread slice in half diagonally. In 40 x 25 x 2.5-cm (*15 x 10 x 1-in*) Swiss roll tin melt butter in oven (3 to 5 min.). Stir in remaining ingredients *except* bread slices. Place bread slices in butter mixture; turn

to coat. Bake 10 min.; stir crackers. Continue baking for 5 to 10 min. or until crackers are crisp.

Tip: Cocktail sandwich bread can be cut out with small (5-cm) (*2-in*) cookie cutters.

Old-Fashioned Hot Buttered Rum (right)
Orange Mint Coffee (left)

16 servings
15 minutes

Old-Fashioned Hot Buttered Rum

Chase away those winter chills with this traditional hot beverage.

225 g	(*8 oz*) sugar	Rum or rum extract
175 g	(*6 oz*) firmly packed brown sugar	Boiling water
225 g	(*8 oz*) butter	Nutmeg
500 ml	(*17 fl oz*) vanilla ice cream, softened	

In 2-litre (*3¹⁄₂-pt*) saucepan combine sugar, brown sugar and butter. Cook over low heat, stirring occasionally, until butter is melted (6 to 8 min.). In large mixer bowl combine cooked mixture with ice cream; beat at med. speed, scraping bowl often, until smooth (1 to 2 min.). Store refrigerated up to 2 weeks or frozen up to 1 month. For each serving, fill mug with 50 ml (*4 tbsp*) mixture, 30 ml (*1 oz*) rum or 1 ml (*¹⁄₄ tsp*) rum extract and 200 ml (*7 fl oz*) boiling water; sprinkle with nutmeg.

6 servings
3 hours

Orange Mint Coffee

Poured over mint and orange, this pleasing coffee is delicious, iced or hot.

Iced Coffee

6	sprigs fresh mint
6	orange slices
2.5 litres	(*4¹⁄₄ pt*) fresh brewed coffee
625 ml	(*1 pt*) vanilla ice cream

For Iced Coffee: Place mint and orange slices into large heat-proof pitcher; add fresh brewed coffee. Let cool 1 hr. Cover; refrigerate until chilled (about 2 hr.). Into each of 6 glasses scoop 125 ml (*4 fl oz*) ice cream; pour chilled coffee over ice cream.

Hot Coffee

6	sprigs fresh mint
6	orange slices
2.5 litres	(*4¹⁄₄ pt*) fresh brewed coffee
	Sweetened whipped cream

For Hot Coffee: Place 1 sprig of mint and 1 orange slice in each of 6 cups. Pour fresh brewed coffee into each cup. Serve with sweetened whipped cream. If desired, refill cups with additional coffee.

Hot Spiced Punch

1.5 litres (*2¾ pt*)
4 hours 45 minutes

Serve this spicy punch with a spoon so no one misses
the raisins and almonds at the bottom of the cup.

1 litre	(*1¾ pt*) apple cider	6	strips 7 x 1 cm (*3 x ½ in*) orange rind
500 ml	(*17 fl oz*) grape juice or dry red wine	1	cinnamon stick
30 ml	(*2 tbsp*) chopped crystallized ginger	100 g	(*4 oz*) raisins
8	whole cloves	100 g	(*4 oz*) slivered almonds

In 3-litre (*5-pt*) saucepan combine all ingredients *except* raisins and almonds. Let stand at room temperature for 4 hr. Cook over med. heat until mixture just comes to a boil (15 to 20 min.). Reduce heat to low; simmer for 15 min. Strain; discard spice mixture. Return to saucepan. Add raisins and almonds. Continue cooking over low heat until raisins are tender (10 to 15 min.). Serve hot with a spoon in each mug.

Sunny Apple Cider

4 litres (*7 pt*)
20 minutes

A traditional cold weather chaser with a splash of orange juice.

4 litres	(*7 pt*) apple cider	3	whole cloves
178-ml	(*6½-oz*) carton frozen orange juice concentrate	2	cinnamon sticks

In large flameproof casserole combine all ingredients. Cook over med. heat until heated through and flavours are blended (about 15 min.).

Tip: To keep cider warm, hold in crockery cooker on low temperature.

Hot Spiced Punch (left)
Sunny Apple Cider (right)

Rich 'n Creamy Hot Chocolate (left)
Old-Fashioned Creamy Eggnog (right)

2 litres (*3½ pt*)
30 minutes

Rich 'n Creamy Hot Chocolate

Enjoy a heartwarming mugful of this rich, creamy all-time favourite.

90 g	(*3½ oz*) semi-sweet real chocolate chips
100 g	(*4 oz*) sugar
125 ml	(*4 fl oz*) water
	Pinch of salt
1.4 litres	(*2½ pt*) milk
500 ml	(*17 fl oz*) double cream
10 ml	(*2 tsp*) vanilla

Liqueurs
Sweetened whipped cream
Grated chocolate
Grated lemon rind
Grated orange rind
Cinnamon
Nutmeg

In 3-litre (*5-pt*) saucepan melt chocolate chips over low heat, stirring constantly. Stir in sugar, water and salt. Cook over med. heat, stirring constantly with wire whisk, until mixture comes to a full boil (4 to 5 min.). Boil, stirring constantly, 2 min. Stir in milk and whipping cream. Continue cooking over med. heat, stirring occasionally, until heated through (12 to 15 min.). DO NOT BOIL. Add vanilla. Beat with wire whisk or rotary beater until frothy. Pour into mugs. If desired, add 15 to 30 ml (*1 to 2 tbsp*) liqueur to each serving. Top each serving with a dollop of sweetened whipped cream. If desired, garnish with one of the following: grated chocolate, grated lemon rind, grated orange rind, cinnamon or nutmeg.

Microwave Directions: In 3-litre (*5-pt*) bowl combine chocolate chips, sugar, water and salt. Microwave on HIGH, stirring every min., until chocolate chips are melted and mixture comes to a full boil (3 to 4 min.). Microwave on HIGH 2 min. Stir in milk and whipping cream. Microwave on HIGH, stirring after half the time, until heated through (8 to 10 min.). DO NOT BOIL. Add vanilla. Beat with wire whisk or rotary beater until frothy. Pour into mugs. If desired, add 15 to 30 ml (*1 to 2 tbsp*) liqueur to each serving. Top each serving with a dollop of sweetened whipped cream. If desired, garnish with one of the following: grated chocolate, grated lemon rind, grated orange rind, cinnamon or nutmeg.

1.3 litres (*2¼ pt*)
25 minutes

Old-Fashioned Creamy Eggnog

Fresh cream makes this warmed eggnog extra rich — perfect for holiday gatherings!

50 g	(*2 oz*) icing sugar
4	eggs
1 ml	(*¼ tsp*) salt
2 ml	(*½ tsp*) vanilla

1 litre	(*1¾ pt*) double cream or milk

Rum
Sweetened whipped cream
Nutmeg

In 1.3-litre (*2¼-pt*) blender container combine icing sugar, eggs, salt and vanilla. Cover; blend at high speed until well blended (15 to 20 sec.). In 2-litre (*3½-pt*) saucepan place 500 ml (*17 fl oz*) double cream. Cook over med. heat until thermometer reaches 60 °C (*140 °F*) (5 to 6 min.). While blending at med. speed, slowly add warm double cream to egg mixture. Continue blending until frothy (15 to 20 sec.).

* In same 2-litre (*3½-pt*) saucepan stir together egg mixture and remaining 500 ml (*17 fl oz*) double cream. Cook over med. heat, stirring occasionally, until thermometer reaches 60 °C (*140 °F*) (5 to 6 min.). If desired, add 15 to 30 ml (*1 to 2 tbsp*) rum to each serving; top with sweetened whipped cream and nutmeg.

*Mixture can be stored refrigerated 2 to 3 days.

4 litres (*7 pt*)
15 minutes

Lime Cream Cooler

A creamy, refreshing punch that's just right for your next special party.

1 litre   (*1¾ pt*) vanilla ice cream, slightly softened

1 litre   (*1¾ pt*) lime sherbet, slightly softened

1 litre   (*1¾ pt*) milk

178-ml   (*6¼-oz*) carton frozen lemonade concentrate

178-ml   (*6¼-oz*) carton frozen limeade concentrate

500 ml   (*17 fl oz*) water

1 litre   (*1¾ pt*) ginger ale

In large punch bowl stir together ice cream, sherbet and milk. In 1-litre (*1¾-pt*) pitcher stir together lemonade concentrate, limeade concentrate and water.

Pour over ice cream mixture. Add ginger ale; stir until slightly mixed.

1.2 litres (*2 pt*)
15 minutes

Ice Cream Parlour Chocolate Malt

A traditional malt with four mouth-watering variations.

175 ml   (*6 fl oz*) milk

50 ml   (*4 tbsp*) natural instant malted milk

1 litre   (*1¾ pt*) chocolate ice cream

In 1.3-litre (*2¼-pt*) blender container combine milk and instant malted milk. Blend at med. speed, stopping blender frequently to scrape sides, until instant malted milk is dissolved (30 to 40 sec.). Add ice cream; continue blending, stopping blender frequently to scrape sides, until smooth (30 to 40 sec.). Serve immediately.

Variations:

Chocolate Raspberry: Prepare chocolate malt as directed above. By hand, stir in 130 g (*4½ oz*) sweetened raspberries.

Chocolate Mint Cookie Malt: Prepare chocolate malt as directed above. Blend in 12 crushed chocolate mint sandwich cookies.

Peanut Butter Chocolate Malt: Prepare chocolate malt as directed above. Blend in 275 g (*10 oz*) peanut butter.

Chocolate Almond Malt: Prepare chocolate malt as directed above. Blend in 5 ml (*1 tsp*) almond extract. By hand, stir in 175 g (*6 oz*) mini semi-sweet chocolate chips.

Lime Cream Cooler (right)
Ice Cream Parlour Chocolate Malt (left)

3 litres (*5 pt*)
10 minutes

Apple Orchard Punch

This quick and easy punch would be delightful at a country wedding or any celebration.

1-litre	(*1¾-pt*) bottle apple juice, chilled		250 ml	(*8 fl oz*) orange juice
341-ml	(*12-oz*) carton frozen cranberry cocktail concentrate		1.5 litres	(*2¾ pt*) ginger ale or champagne, chilled
			1	red apple, do not core

In large punch bowl combine apple juice, cranberry cocktail concentrate and orange juice. Stir to dissolve. Slowly add ginger ale or champagne. Vertically, thinly slice apple forming whole apple slices. Float apple slices on top of punch.

1.5 litres (*2¾ pt*)
40 minutes

Sparkling Pink Lemonade

Spending a hot day on the front porch is just not the same without homemade lemonade — especially when it's sparkling pink!

300 g	(*11 oz*) sugar
6	lemons freshly squeezed
1 litre	(*1¾ pt*) club soda, chilled*
20 ml	(*4 tsp*) grenadine syrup**

15-cm (*6-in*) wooden skewers
Fresh fruit pieces (strawberries, melon balls, pineapple chunks, etc.)

In 2-litre (*3½-pt*) pitcher combine sugar and lemon juice. Stir well; refrigerate at least 30 min. Just before serving, add club soda. Stir in grenadine syrup.

*1 litre (*1¾ pt*) water can be substituted for club soda.

On 15-cm (*6-in*) wooden skewers, thread fruit pieces to make kabobs. Place kabobs in glasses; add ice. Pour in lemonade.

**4 to 6 drops red food colouring can be substituted for grenadine syrup.

Apple Orchard Punch

BREADS

Bread baking in the oven. It fills the air with an aroma so tantalizing that you can hardly wait for your first taste. Finally, the bread has cooled enough to eat. The butter begins to melt as you spread it on the warm, thick slice of bread. Topped with your favorite strawberry jam, it's every bit as good as dessert.

Fresh bread has an appeal that's hard to match. Spicy-sweet muffins warm from the oven. Homemade doughnuts and crisp, flaky pastries. They're made to be enjoyed around the kitchen table for a leisurely weekend breakfast or when friends stop by to catch up on the news of your household.

For lunch and dinner, too, homemade bread adds so much. Moist and tender cornbread, served with honey butter, to enjoy with hearty soup. Big, flaky buttermilk biscuits for a country-style supper. And loaves of hearty wheat bread, so good for sandwiches.

Homemade bread keeps the house full of good smells and tastes. And it's possibly the most welcome gift you can give to those who gather in your kitchen.

Honey-Moist Cornbread

6 servings
30 minutes

Moist and tender cornbread, even better served with butter.

150 g	(*5 oz*) plain flour	250 ml	(*8 fl oz*) double cream
150 g	(*5 oz*) yellow cornmeal	50 ml	(*4 tbsp*) vegetable oil
50 g	(*2 oz*) sugar	50 ml	(*4 tbsp*) honey
15 ml	(*1 tbsp*) baking powder	2	eggs, slightly beaten
2 ml	(*1/2 tsp*) salt		

Heat oven to 200 °C (*400 °F*) mark 6. In medium bowl stir together flour, cornmeal, sugar, baking powder and salt. Stir in remaining ingredients just until moistened. Pour into greased 23-cm (*9-in*) sq. cake tin. Bake for 20 to 25 min. or until wooden pick inserted in centre comes out clean.

Microwave Directions: Mix cornbread as directed left. Pour into greased 1.5-litre (*2¾-pt*) microwave ring mould. Microwave on HIGH, turning dish every 3 min., until cornbread pulls away from sides of mould and is dry on top (7 to 9 min.). Let stand 3 min.

Flaky Buttermilk Biscuits

8 biscuits
25 minutes

Warm, flaky, melt-in-your-mouth biscuits.

300 g	(*11 oz*) plain flour	150 g	(*5 oz*) shortening
20 ml	(*4 tsp*) baking powder	180 ml	(*6 fl oz*) buttermilk
2 ml	(*1/2 tsp*) salt		

Heat oven to 220 °C (*425 °F*) mark 7. In large bowl combine flour, baking powder and salt. Cut in shortening until crumbly. Stir in buttermilk just until moistened. Turn dough onto lightly floured surface; knead until smooth (1 min.). Roll out dough to 2-cm (*¾-in*) thickness. Cut into 8 (5-cm) (*2-in*) biscuits; place 2.5 cm (*1 in*) apart on baking sheet. Bake for 10 to 14 min. or until lightly browned.

Honey-Moist Cornbread (left)
Flaky Buttermilk Biscuits (right)

Parmesan Butter Tin Biscuits

*Parmesan and basil make the difference
in these country-style tin biscuits.*

75 g	(*3 oz*) butter or margarine		20 ml	(*3¹/₂ tsp*) baking powder
350 g	(*12 oz*) plain flour		5 ml	(*1 tsp*) basil leaves
30 ml	(*2 tbsp*) grated Parmesan cheese		15 ml	(*1 tbsp*) chopped fresh parsley
15 ml	(*1 tbsp*) sugar		250 ml	(*8 fl oz*) milk

Heat oven to 200 °C (*400 °F*) mark 6. In 23-cm (*9-in*) sq. cake tin melt butter in oven (3 to 5 min.). Meanwhile, in medium bowl combine all ingredients *except* milk. Stir in milk just until moistened. Turn dough onto lightly floured surface; knead 10 times or until smooth. Roll dough into 30 x 10-cm (*12 x 4-in*) rectangle. Cut into 12 (2.5-cm) (*1-in*) strips. Dip each strip into melted butter. Place in same tin. Bake for 20 to 25 min. or until lightly browned.

To Prepare Biscuits:

1. Roll dough into 30 x 10-cm (*12 x 4-in*) rectangle. Cut into 12 (2.5-cm) (*1-in*) strips.

2. Dip each strip into melted butter. Place in same tin.

Parmesan Butter Tin Biscuits

Nutmeg Streusel Muffins

1 dozen
30 minutes

Nutmeg Streusel Muffins

Enjoy these nutmeg muffins fresh from the oven.

Streusel Mixture
200 g	*(7 oz)* plain flour
175 g	*(6 oz)* firmly packed brown sugar
125 g	*(4 oz)* butter or margarine, softened

Muffins
100 g	*(4 oz)* plain flour
7 ml	*(1½ tsp)* baking powder

7 ml	*(1½ tsp)* nutmeg
2 ml	*(½ tsp)* bicarbonate of soda
2 ml	*(½ tsp)* salt
150 ml	*(¼ pt)* buttermilk
1	egg

Heat oven to 200 °C (*400 °F*) mark 6. In large bowl combine 200 g (*7 oz*) flour and brown sugar; cut in butter until crumbly. Reserve ⅙ of mixture for streusel topping. In same bowl add all muffin ingredients to streusel mixture. Stir just until moistened. Spoon into greased muffin tins. Sprinkle with reserved streusel mixture. Bake for 18 to 22 min. or until lightly browned. Let stand 5 min.; remove from tins.

Microwave Directions: Mix muffins as directed left. Spoon ⅓ of batter into 6 paper-lined microwave-safe muffin tins, filling ½ full. Microwave on HIGH 1 min. Sprinkle with ⅓ of streusel mixture; turn. Microwave on HIGH until muffins are dry on top (1½ to 2½ min.). Repeat with remaining batter.   18 muffins.

---

1 dozen
30 minutes

Spiced Pumpkin Muffins

*During the fall harvest enjoy tender pumpkin muffins
subtly spiced with cinnamon and ginger.*

300 g	*(11 oz)* plain flour
125 g	*(4 oz)* firmly packed brown sugar
65 g	*(2½ oz)* sugar
15 ml	*(1 tbsp)* baking powder
5 ml	*(1 tsp)* salt
5 ml	*(1 tsp)* cinnamon

1 ml	*(¼ tsp)* bicarbonate of soda
1 ml	*(¼ tsp)* ginger
125 g	*(4 oz)* butter or margarine, melted
125 g	*(4 oz)* cooked pumpkin
75 ml	*(5 tbsp)* buttermilk
2	eggs, slightly beaten

Heat oven to 200 °C (*400 °F*) mark 6. In large bowl stir together all ingredients *except* butter, pumpkin, buttermilk and eggs. In medium bowl stir together remaining ingredients. Add to flour mixture; stir just until moistened. Spoon batter into greased 12 muffin tins. Bake for 15 to 20 min. or until lightly browned. Let stand 5 min.; remove from tins.

Microwave Directions: Mix muffins as directed left. Spoon ⅓ of batter into 6 paper-lined microwave-safe muffin tins, filling ½ full. Microwave on HIGH, turning after half the time, until muffins are dry on top (2½ to 3½ min.). Repeat with remaining batter. 18 muffins.

16 scones
30 minutes

Cheddar Dill Scones

The irresistible aroma of this quick bread will fill the kitchen and tempt the appetite.

375 g	(*13 oz*) plain flour
100 g	(*4 oz*) shredded Cheddar cheese
50 ml	(*4 tbsp*) chopped fresh parsley
15 ml	(*1 tbsp*) baking powder
10 ml	(*2 tsp*) dill weed

2 ml	(*½ tsp*) salt
175 g	(*6 oz*) butter or margarine
2	eggs, slightly beaten
120 ml	(*4 fl oz*) single cream

Heat oven to 200 °C (*400 °F*) mark 6. In medium bowl combine all ingredients *except* butter, eggs and cream. Cut in butter until crumbly. Stir in eggs and cream just until moistened. Turn dough onto lightly floured surface; knead until smooth (1 min.). Divide dough in half; roll each half into 20-cm (*8-in*) circle. Cut each circle into 8 pie-shaped wedges. Place 2.5 cm (*1 in*) apart on baking sheets. Bake for 15 to 20 min. or until lightly browned.

To Prepare Cheddar Dill Scones:

1. Stir in eggs and cream just until moistened. Turn dough onto lightly floured surface; knead until smooth (1 min.).

2. Divide dough in half; roll each half into 20-cm (*8-in*) circle. Cut each circle into 8 pie-shaped wedges.

Cheddar Dill Scones

Tender Popovers

Popovers that pop up and over the tin to provide old-fashioned goodness.

6 popovers
55 minutes

3	eggs, room temperature
300 ml	(*1/2 pt*) milk, room temperature
175 g	(*6 oz*) plain flour
1 ml	(*1/4 tsp*) salt

Heat oven to 230 °C (*450 °F*) mark 8. In small mixer bowl beat eggs at med. speed, scraping bowl often, until light yellow (1 to 2 min.). Add milk; continue beating for 1 min. to incorporate air. By hand, stir in remaining ingredients. Pour batter into greased 6 popover tins or 6 ramekin dishes. Bake for 15 min.; reduce temperature to 180 °C (*350 °F*) mark 4. *Do not open oven door.* Bake for 25 to 30 min. or until golden brown. Insert knife in popovers to allow steam to escape. Serve immediately.

Tip: Eggs and milk should be at room temperature (22 °C) (*72 °F*) to help ensure successful popovers.

To Prepare Popovers:

1. Pour batter into greased 6 popover tins or 6 ramekin dishes.

2. Insert knife in popovers to allow steam to escape.

Tender Popovers

Crackling Bacon Corn Cakes

Crackling Bacon Corn Cakes

6 corn cakes
25 minutes

Savoury griddle cakes that taste great with sausage, eggs and maple syrup.

6	rashers of bacon, cut into 1-cm (*¹/2-in*) pieces	175 ml	(*6 fl oz*) milk
50 g	(*2 oz*) chopped onion	1	egg, slightly beaten
150 g	(*5 oz*) plain flour	15 ml	(*1 tbsp*) vegetable oil
30 ml	(*2 tbsp*) chopped fresh chives	175 g	(*6 oz*) canned sweetcorn, drained
5 ml	(*1 tsp*) baking powder	50 g	(*2 oz*) shredded Cheddar cheese
2 ml	(*¹/2 tsp*) salt		
	Pinch of cayenne pepper		Maple syrup or maple flavoured syrup, warmed

In 25-cm (*10-in*) frying pan cook bacon and onion over med. high heat until bacon is browned (7 to 9 min.). Meanwhile, in medium bowl combine flour, chives, baking powder, salt and cayenne pepper. Stir in milk, egg and oil just until moistened. Stir in bacon and onion and remaining ingredients *except* maple syrup. Heat griddle to 180 °C (*350 °F*) mark 4 or until drops of water sizzle. For each corn cake pour 75 ml (*5 tbsp*) batter onto greased griddle. Cook until corn cakes are golden brown (3 to 4 min. on each side). Serve warm with maple syrup.

Courgette Harvest Bread

2 loaves
1 hour 30 minutes

Cinnamon fills the air with its tantalizing aroma as this quick bread bakes.

450 g	(*1 lb*) plain flour	5 ml	(*1 tsp*) bicarbonate of soda
350 g	(*12 oz*) sugar	1 ml	(*¹/4 tsp*) baking powder
90 g	(*3¹/2 oz*) firmly packed brown sugar	1 ml	(*¹/4 tsp*) nutmeg
225 g	(*8 oz*) butter or margarine, softened	1 ml	(*¹/4 tsp*) cloves
3	eggs	15 ml	(*1 tbsp*) vanilla
15 ml	(*1 tbsp*) cinnamon	2	med. unpeeled, shredded courgettes
5 ml	(*1 tsp*) salt	65 g	(*2¹/2 oz*) chopped walnuts

Heat oven to 180 °C (*350 °F*) mark 4. In large mixer bowl combine all ingredients *except* courgettes and walnuts. Beat at low speed, scraping bowl often, until well mixed (2 to 3 min.). By hand, stir in courgettes and nuts. Spread into 2 greased 450-g (*1-lb*) loaf tins. Bake for 50 to 65 min. or until wooden pick inserted in centre comes out clean. Cool 10 min.; remove from tins. Cool completely; store refrigerated.

Crispy Cracker Bread

4 cracker breads
45 minutes

While soup is simmering, prepare this thin, crisp bread.

7-g	(*¼-oz*) pkg. active dry yeast
250 ml	(*8 fl oz*) warm water (40 ° to 46 °C)
	(*105 ° to 115 °F*)
10 ml	(*2 tsp*) sugar
5 ml	(*1 tsp*) salt
45 g	(*1½ oz*) butter or margarine, melted

375 to 450 g	(*13 to 16 oz*) plain flour
1	egg, slightly beaten
	Coarse salt*
	Coarse pepper*
	Sesame seed

Heat oven to 200 °C (*400 °F*) mark 6. In large bowl dissolve yeast in warm water. Stir in sugar, 5 ml (*1 tsp*) salt and butter. Gradually stir in flour, 150 g (*5 oz*) at a time, using enough flour to make dough easy to handle. Turn dough onto lightly floured surface; knead until smooth (5 min.). Divide dough into 4 equal portions; shape into balls. Let rest 10 min.; roll each ball into 30-cm (*12-in*) circle.

Place on greased baking sheets. Brush with beaten egg; sprinkle with salt, pepper or sesame seed. Bake for 10 to 15 min. or until lightly browned. Cool completely on wire rack. (Bread will be irregular in shape and browning.) To serve, break into pieces.

*Table salt and pepper can be substituted for coarse salt and coarse pepper.

To Prepare Crispy Cracker Bread:

1. Divide dough into 4 equal portions; shape into balls. Let rest 10 min.; roll each ball into 30-cm (*12-in*) circle.

2. Place on greased baking sheets. Brush with beaten egg; sprinkle with salt, pepper or sesame seed.

Crispy Cracker Bread

6 slices
15 minutes

Pan-Toasted Garlic Bread

Bread is toasted with garlic butter and topped with a sprinkling of Mozzarella cheese.

75 g	(*3 oz*) butter or margarine	6	(2.5-cm) (*1-in*) slices French bread
0.5 ml	(*⅛ tsp*) cayenne pepper	50 g	(*2 oz*) shredded Mozzarella cheese
5 ml	(*1 tsp*) crushed fresh garlic		

In 25-cm (*10-in*) frying pan melt butter until sizzling. Stir in cayenne pepper and garlic. Dip both sides of *each* bread slice in melted butter; place in same frying pan. Cook over med. heat, watching closely, until bread is lightly browned (2 to 3 min.). Reduce heat to low. Turn bread slices over; sprinkle each slice with about 15 ml (*1 tbsp*) cheese. Cover; continue cooking until cheese is melted (1 to 2 min.). Serve immediately.

To Prepare Pan-Toasted Garlic Bread:

1. Dip both sides of *each* bread slice in melted butter; place in same frying pan. Cook over med. heat, watching closely, until bread is lightly browned (2 to 3 min.). Reduce heat to low.

2. Turn bread slices over; sprinkle each slice with about 15 ml (*1 tbsp*) cheese. Cover; continue cooking until cheese is melted (1 to 2 min.).

Pan-Toasted Garlic Bread

Homemade Bread

2 loaves
4 hours

Serve this delicious bread warm from the oven and smothered with butter.

500 ml	(*17 fl oz*) milk	825 to 975 g	(*1¾ to 2¼ lb*) plain flour
15 g	(*½ oz*) butter or margarine	30 ml	(*2 tbsp*) sugar
7-g	(*¼-oz*) pkg. active dry yeast	10 ml	(*2 tsp*) salt
50 ml	(*2 fl oz*) warm water (40 ° to 46 °C)		Butter or margarine, softened
	(*105 ° to 115 °F*)		

In 1-litre (*1¾-pt*) saucepan scald milk; stir in butter until melted. Cool to lukewarm (40 ° to 46 °C) (*105 ° to 115 °F*). In large mixer bowl dissolve yeast in warm water. Add milk mixture, 450 g (*1 lb*) flour, sugar and salt to yeast. Beat at med. speed, scraping bowl often, until smooth (1 to 2 min.). By hand, stir in enough remaining flour to make dough easy to handle. Turn dough onto lightly floured surface; knead until smooth and elastic (about 10 min.). Place in greased bowl; turn greased side up.Cover; let rise in warm place until double in size (about 1½ hr.). Dough is ready if indentation remains when touched. Punch down dough; divide in half. Shape each half into loaf. Place loaves in 2 greased 450-g (*1-lb*) loaf tins. Cover; let rise until double in size (about 1 hr.). Heat oven to 200 °C (*400 °F*) mark 6. Bake for 25 to 35 min. or until loaves sound hollow when tapped. Remove from tins immediately. If desired, brush tops of loaves with butter.

Hearty Honey Wheat Bread

2 loaves
4 hours

This whole grain bread fills the kitchen with its tempting aroma.

250 ml	(*8 fl oz*) milk	300 g	(*11 oz*) whole-wheat flour
45 g	(*1½ oz*) butter or margarine	75 ml	(*5 tbsp*) honey
2	(*7-g*) (*¼-oz*) pkg. active dry yeast	2	eggs
250 ml	(*8 fl oz*) warm water (40 ° to 46 °C)	15 ml	(*1 tbsp*) salt
	(*105 ° to 115 °F*)	5 ml	(*1 tsp*) sugar
700 to 875 g	(*1½ to 2 lb*) plain flour		Butter or margarine, softened

In 1-litre (*1¾-pt*) saucepan combine milk and butter. Cook over med. heat until butter is melted (3 to 4 min.). Cool to lukewarm (40 ° to 46 °C) (*105 ° to 115 °F*). In large mixer bowl dissolve yeast in warm water. Add milk mixture, 300 g (*11 oz*) flour, whole-wheat flour, honey, eggs, salt and sugar to yeast. Beat at med. speed, scraping bowl often, until smooth (1 to 2 min.). By hand, stir in enough remaining flour to make dough easy to handle. Turn dough onto lightly floured surface; knead until smooth and elastic (about 10 min.). Place in greased bowl; turn greased side up. Cover; let rise in warm place until double in size (about 1½ hr.). Dough is ready if indentation remains when touched. Punch down dough; divide in half. Shape each half into loaf. Place loaves in 2 greased 450-g (*1-lb*) loaf tins. Cover; let rise until double in size (about 1½ hr.). Heat oven to 180 °C (*350 °F*) mark 4. Bake for 25 to 35 min. or until loaves sound hollow when tapped. Remove from tins immediately. If desired, brush tops of loaves with butter.

Homemade Bread (right)
Hearty Honey Wheat Bread (left)

Oatmeal Molasses Rolls

4 dozen
3 hours

Grandma's Dinner Rolls

Old-fashioned goodness, perfect for any occasion.

500 ml	(*17 fl oz*) boiling water	1.3 to 1.5 kg	(*2³/4 to 3¹/4 lb*) plain flour
125 g	(*4 oz*) butter or margarine, softened	100 g	(*4 oz*) sugar
2	(7-g) (*¹/4-oz*) pkg. active dry yeast	3	eggs
125 ml	(*4 fl oz*) warm water (40 ° to 46 °C)	7 ml	(*¹/2 tsp*) salt
	(*105 ° to 115 °F*)		

Butter or margarine, softened

In medium bowl stir together boiling water and butter until butter is melted. Cool to warm (40 ° to 46 °C) (*105 ° to 115 °F*). In large mixer bowl dissolve yeast in warm water. Add butter mixture, 450 g (*1 lb*) flour, sugar, eggs and salt to yeast. Beat at med. speed, scraping bowl often, until smooth (1 to 2 min.). By hand, stir in enough remaining flour to make dough easy to handle. Turn dough onto lightly floured surface; knead until smooth and elastic (about 10 min.). Place in greased bowl, turn greased side up.

Cover; let rise in warm place until double in size (about 1 hr). Dough is ready if indentation remains when touched. Punch down dough; divide in half. With floured hands shape each half into 24 rounds. Place in 2 greased 33 x 23-cm (*13 x 9-in*) baking tins. Cover; let rise until double in size (about 1 hr.). Heat oven to 200 °C (*400 °F*) mark 6. Bake for 20 to 25 min. or until golden brown. If desired, brush tops of rolls with butter.

3 dozen
3 hours

Oatmeal Molasses Rolls

Homemade dinner rolls that are tender and slightly sweet.

175 g	(*6 oz*) old-fashioned rolled oats	175 g	(*6 oz*) firmly packed brown sugar
375 ml	(*13 fl oz*) boiling water	75 ml	(*5 tbsp*) light molasses
50 g	(*2 oz*) butter or margarine	2	eggs
2	(7-g) (*¹/4-oz*) pkg. active dry yeast	7 ml	(*1¹/2 tsp*) salt
125 ml	(*4 fl oz*) warm water (40 ° to 46 °C)		
	(*105 ° to 115 °F*)		
950 g to 1 kg	(*2 to 2¹/4 lb*) plain flour		

Butter or margarine, softened

In medium bowl stir together oats, boiling water and butter until butter is melted. Cool to warm (40 ° to 46 °C) (*105 ° to 115 °F*). In large mixer bowl dissolve yeast in warm water. Add oat mixture, 300 g (*11 oz*) flour, brown sugar, molasses, eggs and salt to yeast. Beat at med. speed, scraping bowl often, until smooth (1 to 2 min.). By hand, stir in enough remaining flour to make dough easy to handle. Turn dough onto lightly floured surface; knead until smooth and elastic (about 10 min.). Place in greased bowl, turn greased side up.

Cover; let rise in warm place until double in size (about 1¹/2 hr.). Dough is ready if indentation remains when touched. Punch down dough; divide in half. With floured hands shape each half into 18 rounds. Place in 2 greased 33 x 23-cm (*13 x 9-in*) baking tins. Cover; let rise until double in size (about 1 hr.). Heat oven to 190 °C (*375 °F*) mark 5. Bake for 20 to 25 min. or until golden brown. If desired, brush tops of rolls with butter.

Double Caramel-Raisin Rolls

18 rolls
3 hours

All-time favourite caramel rolls or the goodness of frosted orange rolls — both from the same recipe.

Dough*

675 to 750 g	(1½ to 1¾ lb) plain flour
65 g	(2½ oz) sugar
250 ml	(8 fl oz) warm milk (49 ° to 54 °C)
	(120 ° to 130 °F)
125 g	(4 oz) butter or margarine,melted
7-g	(¼-oz) pkg. active dry yeast
2	eggs
2 ml	(½ tsp) salt
125 g	(4 oz) raisins

Filling

200 g	(7 oz) firmly packed brown sugar
175 g	(6 oz) butter or margarine, melted
45 ml	(3 tbsp) light corn syrup
7 ml	(1½ tsp) cinnamon

In large mixer bowl combine 300 g (11 oz) flour, sugar, milk, 125 g (4 oz) butter, yeast, eggs and salt. Beat at med. speed, scraping bowl often, until smooth (1 to 2 min.). By hand, stir in raisins and enough remaining flour to make dough easy to handle. Turn dough onto lightly floured surface; knead until smooth and elastic (3 to 5 min.). Place in greased bowl; turn greased side up. Cover; let rise in warm place until double in size (about 1 to 1½ hr.). Dough is ready if indentation remains when touched. Punch down dough. In medium bowl stir together all filling ingredients *except* cinnamon. Spread ½ of filling on bottom of greased 33 x 23-cm (13 x 9-in) baking tin. Stir cinnamon into remaining filling. On lightly floured surface roll dough into 45 x 23-cm (18 x 9-in) rectangle; spread with remaining filling. Roll up Swiss roll fashion beginning with 45-cm (18-in) side. Pinch edge of dough into roll to seal well. Cut into 2.5-cm (1-in) slices; place slices in prepared tin. Cover; let rise until double in size (about 1 hr.). Heat oven to 190 °C (375 °F) mark 5. Bake for 25 to 30 min. or until golden brown. Immediately invert tin onto serving platter; remove tin.

Glazed Orange Rolls: Prepare dough as directed left except omit raisins. Omit filling. To prepare orange filling: In small bowl stir together 75 ml (5 tbsp) melted butter, 200 g (7 oz) sugar, 15 ml (1 tbsp) light corn syrup and 15 ml (1 tbsp) grated orange rind. On lightly floured surface roll dough into 45 x 23-cm (18 x 9-in) rectangle; spread with orange filling. Roll up Swiss roll fashion beginning with 45-cm (18-in) side. Pinch edge of dough into roll to seal well. Cut into 2.5-cm (1-in) slices; place slices in greased 33 x 23-cm (13 x 9-in) baking tin. Cover; let rise until double in size (about 1 hr.). Heat oven to 190 °C (375 °F) mark 5. Bake for 25 to 30 min. or until golden brown. Immediately invert tin onto wire rack; remove tin. Invert rolls onto serving platter (top sides up). To prepare glaze: In small bowl stir together 225 g (8 oz) icing sugar, 50 ml (4 tbsp) orange juice and 5 ml (1 tsp) grated orange rind. Glaze top of warm rolls.

*2 (450-g) (1-lb) loaves frozen bread dough can be substituted for dough recipe. Let frozen dough thaw according to pkg. directions. If preparing Double Caramel-Raisin Rolls, knead 125 g (4 oz) raisins into dough. Prepare filling and continue as directed left.

Double Caramel-Raisin Rolls

10 servings
3 hours

Glazed Lemon Daisy Bread

Take some time to shape this tender bread to look like a daisy.

Dough

100 g	(*4 oz*) sugar
125 g	(*4 oz*) butter or margarine
175 ml	(*6 fl oz*) milk
7-g	(*1/4-oz*) pkg. active dry yeast
650 to 700 g	(*1 1/2 lb*) plain flour
3	eggs
2 ml	(*1/2 tsp*) salt
15 ml	(*1 tbsp*) grated lemon rind
5 ml	(*1 tsp*) vanilla

Filling

50 g	(*2 oz*) butter or margarine, softened
2 ml	(*1/2 tsp*) ground cloves

Glaze

100 g	(*4 oz*) sugar
125 ml	(*4 fl oz*) sour cream
50 g	(*2 oz*) butter or margarine
30 ml	(*2 tbsp*) lemon juice

In 1-litre (*1 3/4-pt*) saucepan combine 110 g (*4 oz*) sugar, 125 g (*4 oz*) butter and milk. Cook over med. heat until butter is melted (3 to 5 min.). Pour into large bowl; cool to warm (40 ° to 46 °C) (*105 ° to 115 °F*). Stir in yeast until dissolved. Add 450 g (*1 lb*) flour and remaining dough ingredients; stir until well mixed. Stir in remaining flour, 75 g (*3 oz*) at a time, until soft dough forms. Turn dough onto lightly floured surface; knead until smooth and elastic (3 to 5 min.). Place in greased bowl; turn greased side up. Cover; let rise in warm place until doubled in size (1 to 1 1/2 hr.). Dough is ready if indentation remains when touched. Punch down dough; let rest 10 min. On lightly floured surface roll dough into 45-cm (*18-in*) circle. Spread with softened 50 g (*2 oz*) butter; sprinkle with cloves. Place

beverage tumbler in centre; make 4 cuts at equal intervals from outside of circle to beverage tumbler. Cut each wedge into 5 wedges. Twist every two wedges together tightly, making 10 twists; pinch ends of twists together. Coil twists toward centre, making daisy design; remove beverage tumbler. Coil one twist for centre. Place on greased large baking sheet; reshape design, if necessary. Cover; let rise about 45 min. Heat oven to 180 °C (*350 °F*) mark 4. Bake for 20 to 30 min. or until golden brown. In 2-litre (*3 1/2-pt*) saucepan combine all glaze ingredients. Cook over med. heat, stirring occasionally, until mixture comes to a full boil (5 to 6 min.); boil 3 min. Pour warm glaze over warm bread.

To Prepare Bread:

1. Place beverage tumbler in centre; make 4 cuts at equal intervals from outside of circle to beverage tumbler. Cut each wedge into 5 wedges. Twist every two wedges together tightly, making 10 twists; pinch ends of twists together.

2. Coil twists toward centre, making daisy design; remove beverage tumbler. Coil one twist for centre.

Glazed Lemon Daisy Bread

1 coffee cake
3 hours 40 minutes

Raisin'n Nut Pull-Apart Coffee Cake

Perfect for a potluck or family gathering,
this old-fashioned pull-apart sweetbread will serve a crowd.

250 ml	(*8 fl oz*) milk
50 g	(*2 oz*) butter or margarine
7-g	(*1/4-oz*) pkg. active dry yeast
50 ml	(*2 fl oz*) warm water (40 ° to 46 °C)
	(*105 ° to 115 °F*)
525 to 600 g	(*18 oz to 1 1/4 lb*) plain flour
50 g	(*2 oz*) sugar

1	egg
2 ml	(*1/2 tsp*) salt
225 g	(*8 oz*) sugar
65 g	(*2 1/2 oz*) chopped pecans
7 ml	(*1 1/2 tsp*) cinnamon
125 g	(*4 oz*) butter or margarine, melted
90 g	(*3 1/2 oz*) golden raisins

In 1-litre (*1 3/4-pt*) saucepan scald milk; stir in 50 g (*2 oz*) butter until melted. Cool to warm (40 ° to 46 °C) (*105 ° to 115 °F*). In large mixer bowl dissolve yeast in warm water. Add cooled milk mixture, 300 g (*11 oz*) flour, 55 g (*2 oz*) sugar, egg and salt. Beat at med. speed, scraping bowl often, until smooth (1 to 2 min.). By hand, stir in enough remaining flour to make dough easy to handle. Turn dough onto lightly floured surface; knead until smooth and elastic (about 10 min.). Place in greased bowl, turn greased side up. Cover; let rise in warm place until double in size (about 1 1/2 hr.). Dough is ready if indentation remains when touched. Punch down dough; divide in half. With floured hands shape each half into 24 balls. In

small bowl stir together 225 g (*8 oz*) sugar, pecans and cinnamon. Dip balls first in melted butter, then in sugar mixture. Place 24 balls in bottom of greased 25-cm (*10-in*) tubular cake tin. (If removable bottom tubular tin, line with aluminum foil.) Sprinkle with raisins. Top with remaining 24 balls. Cover; let rise until double in size (about 45 min.). Heat oven to 190 °C (*375 °F*) mark 5. Bake for 35 to 40 min. or until coffee cake sounds hollow when tapped. (Cover with aluminum foil if coffee cake browns too quickly.) Immediately invert tin on heat-proof serving plate. Let tin stand 1 min. to allow sugar mixture to drizzle over cake. Remove tin; serve warm.

To Prepare Coffee Cake:

1. With floured hands shape each half into 24 balls. In small bowl stir together 225 g (*8 oz*) sugar, pecans and cinnamon. Dip balls first in melted butter, then in sugar mixture. Place 24 balls in bottom of greased 25-cm (*10-in*) tubular cake tin.

2. Immediately invert tin on heat-proof serving plate. Let tin stand 1 min. to allow sugar mixture to drizzle over cake. Remove tin; serve warm.

Raisin'n Nut Pull-Apart Coffee Cake

Honey-Glazed Raised Donuts

2 dozen
4 hours

*These old-fashioned donuts satisfy hungry appetites
with their hearty yeast bread-like texture and allspice flavour.*

Donuts

225 g	(*8 oz*) sugar
175 g	(*6 oz*) butter or margarine, cut into pieces
375 ml	(*13 fl oz*) milk
15 ml	(*1 tbsp*) allspice
7 ml	(*1½ tsp*) salt
125 ml	(*4 fl oz*) warm water (40 ° to 46 °C) (*105 ° to 115 °F*)
3	(7-g) (*¼-oz*) pkg. active dry yeast
4	eggs
1 to 1.2 kg	(*2 to 2½ lb*) plain flour
	Vegetable oil

Glaze

300 g	(*11 oz*) icing sugar
50 ml	(*2 fl oz*) water
30 ml	(*2 tbsp*) honey

In 2-litre (*3½-pt*) saucepan combine sugar, butter, milk, allspice and salt. Cook over med. heat until butter melts (3 to 4 min.). Cool to warm (40 ° to 46 °C) (*105 ° to 115 °F*). Meanwhile, in large mixer bowl combine 125 ml (*4 fl oz*) water and yeast. Add milk mixture, eggs and 600 g (*1¼ lb*) flour. Beat at low speed, scraping bowl often, until moistened. Increase to med. speed; continue beating 3 min. By hand, stir in enough remaining flour to form a soft dough. Turn dough onto lightly floured surface; knead until smooth and elastic (5 to 10 min.). Place in greased bowl; turn greased side up. Cover; let rise in warm place until double in size (1 to 1½ hr.). Dough is ready if indentation remains when touched. Punch down dough; divide in half. On lightly floured surface roll each half to 1-cm (*½-in*) thickness. With lightly floured 8-cm (*3-in*) donut cutter cut out donuts. Place donuts on greased baking sheets. Cover; let rise in warm place until double in size (30 to 45 min.). Heat 8 cm (*3 in*) oil in deep-fat fryer or heavy-based pan to 190 °C (*375 °F*). Place donuts into hot oil. Fry until golden brown (30 to 45 sec. on each side). Remove from oil; drain on paper towels. In small bowl stir together all glaze ingredients. Dip warm donuts in glaze; place on waxed paper. Serve warm.

Tip: To reheat donuts in microwave, microwave one donut on HIGH 5 to 6 seconds.

To Prepare Honey-Glazed Raised Donuts:

1. Heat 8 cm (*3 in*) oil in deep-fat fryer or heavy-based pan to 190 °C (*375 °F*). Place donuts into hot oil. Fry until golden brown (30 to 45 sec. on each side).

2. Dip warm donuts in glaze; place on waxed paper.

Honey-Glazed Raised Donuts

Bake Shop Krispies

2 dozen
3 hours 20 minutes

Bake Shop Krispies

A homemade recipe for a bake shop favourite — also known as elephant ears.

Dough

560 to 650 g	(*1¼ to 1½ lb*) plain flour
7-g	(*¼-oz*) pkg. active dry yeast
50 g	(*2 oz*) sugar
300 ml	(*½ pt*) milk
50 g	(*2 oz*) butter or margarine
5 ml	(*1 tsp*) salt
1	egg

Filling

225 g	(*8 oz*) sugar
50 g	(*2 oz*) butter or margarine, melted
2 ml	(*½ tsp*) cinnamon

Topping

50 g	(*2 oz*) butter or margarine, melted
225 g	(*8 oz*) sugar
5 ml	(*1 tsp*) cinnamon
65 g	(*2½ oz*) chopped pecans

In large mixer bowl combine 300 g (*11 oz*) flour and yeast. In 1-litre (*1¾-pt*) saucepan combine 55 g (*2 oz*) sugar, milk, 50 g (*2 oz*) butter and salt. Cook over med. heat, stirring constantly, until warm (46 ° to 49 °C) (*115 ° to 120 °F*). Add to flour mixture; add egg. Beat at low speed, scraping bowl often, until well mixed (1 to 2 min.). Beat at high speed, scraping bowl often, 3 min. By hand, stir in enough remaining flour to make dough easy to handle. Turn dough onto lightly floured surface; knead until smooth and elastic (about 5 min.). Place in greased bowl; turn greased side up. Cover; let rise in warm place until double in size (about 1½ hr.). Dough is ready if indentation remains when touched. Punch down dough; divide in half. Roll each half into 30-cm (*12-in*) sq. In medium bowl stir together filling ingredients. Spread half over each 30-cm (*12-in*) sq. Roll each 30-cm (*12-in*) sq. up Swiss roll fashion; pinch to seal seams well. Cut each

into 12 rolls. Place on greased baking sheets 7 to 10 cm (*3 to 4 in*) apart (about 6 rolls per baking sheet). Cover with waxed paper. With rolling pin flatten each roll to about 7 cm (*3 in*) in diameter. Do not remove waxed paper; let rise in warm place 30 min. Heat oven to 200 °C (*400 °F*) mark 6. With rolling pin flatten to 3-mm (*⅛-in*) thickness; remove waxed paper. Brush rolls with 50 ml (*4 tbsp*) melted butter. In small bowl stir together 225 g (*8 oz*) sugar and 5 ml (*1 tsp*) cinnamon; sprinkle over rolls. Sprinkle pecans over rolls. Cover with waxed paper; roll flat. Remove waxed paper. Bake for 8 to 12 min. or until golden brown. Remove from pan immediately.

Orange Krispies: Omit cinnamon in filling. Add 15 ml (*1 tbsp*) grated orange rind to filling. *Omit cinnamon and pecans in topping.* Add 75 g (*3 oz*) sliced almonds and 5 ml (*1 tsp*) grated orange rind to topping.

To Prepare Krispies:

1. Place on greased baking sheets 7 to 10 cm (*3 to 4 in*) apart (about 6 rolls per baking sheet). Cover with waxed paper. With rolling pin flatten each roll to about 7 cm (*3 in*) in diameter.

2. Sprinkle pecans over rolls. Cover with waxed paper; roll flat. Remove waxed paper.

How to: Prepare Yeast Bread

To Prepare Dough:

1. Use a thermometer to assure the correct water temperature for the yeast. Water should be 40 ° to 46 °C (*105 ° to 115 °F*).

2. Add just enough flour to make dough easy to handle. Dough should leave the side of the bowl almost clean when the correct amount has been mixed in.

3. Knead dough on a lightly floured surface. Add more flour as needed until dough no longer sticks.

4. To knead, fold dough toward you; with heels of hands push dough away, using a rocking motion. Turn dough a quarter turn and repeat. Continue repeating until dough is smooth and elastic.

5. Let dough rise in a warm (25 ° to 30 °C) (*80 ° to 85 °F*) place until double in size. Dough is ready if indentation remains when poked.

6. To release large air bubbles, punch down dough with fist. Shape dough as directed.

To Shape a Loaf:

1. Roll into an 45 x 23-cm (*18 x 9-in*) rectangle. Fold 23-cm (*9-in*) sides crosswise into thirds, overlapping ends.

2. Roll up tightly, beginning at one of the open ends. Pinch end of dough into roll to seal well.

3. Press each end with the side of your hand to seal, then fold the end underneath. Place loaves, seam sides down, in greased loaf tins. Let rise until double in size.

To Bake and Store Bread:

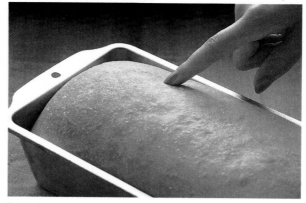

1. Bake as directed. Bread is done when loaf sounds hollow when tapped.

2. Remove from tins immediately. If desired, brush tops of loaves with butter.

3. Cool bread thoroughly. Store at room temperature in tightly sealed plastic bags for up to 1 week or freeze for up to 3 months.

SOUPS & STEWS

No special invitation is necessary when you share the hospitality of homemade soup. The savory aroma of a long-simmering soup or stew is invitation enough. Neither dainty nor elegant, your own made-from-scratch soups and stews will bring back memories of those marvelous kettles of goodness that bubbled on the back of Grandma's stove.

She always seemed to know how to add a pinch of this or that to create steaming mixtures that were unbelievably delicious. Like a spicy, tomato-rich stew, thick with beans and beef and pork sausage, just right for those cool fall days. Creamy chowder made with new red potatoes. Chicken noodle soup with those long flat noodles that were so much fun to slurp, even if it did bring a gentle scolding.

Soups, stews and chowders — so simple and nourishing — are among the classics of country cooking. Served for lunch or supper any time of the year, they satisfy the soul and the appetite in wonderfully familiar ways.

Hearty Bacon Potato Chowder

**6 servings
40 minutes**

A rich, hearty and simple soup welcome at almost any occasion.

8	rashers of bacon, cut into 2.5-cm (*1-in*) pieces	300 ml	(*½ pt*) milk
6	med. new red potatoes, cut into 1-cm (*½-in*) cubes	295-g	(*10.4-oz*) can condensed cream of chicken soup
2	med. onions, chopped	225 g	(*8 oz*) canned sweetcorn, drained
250 ml	(*8 fl oz*) sour cream	1 ml	(*¼ tsp*) pepper
		1 ml	(*¼ tsp*) thyme leaves

In 3-litre (*5-pt*) saucepan cook bacon over med. heat for 5 min.; add potatoes and onions. Continue cooking, stirring occasionally, until potatoes are tender (15 to 20 min.). Add remaining ingredients. Continue cooking, stirring occasionally, until heated through (10 to 12 min.).

Microwave Directions: In 3-litre (*5-pt*) casserole combine bacon, potatoes and onions. Cover; microwave on HIGH, stirring after half the time, until potatoes are tender (12 to 18 min.). Stir in remaining ingredients. Cover; microwave on HIGH until heated through (2 to 4 min.).

Seashore Chowder

**4 servings
50 minutes**

Feel free to use all oysters or all clams in this chowder from the sea.

6	rashers of bacon, cut into 2.5-cm (*1-in*) pieces	45 ml	(*3 tbsp*) plain flour
6	med. new red potatoes, cut into 1-cm (*½-in*) cubes	750 ml	(*1¼ pt*) milk
1	med. onion, chopped	225 g	(*8 oz*) canned oysters, drained, rinsed
1	celery stick, chopped	185 g	(*6½ oz*) canned clams, drained, rinsed
45 g	(*1½ oz*) butter or margarine	10 ml	(*2 tsp*) basil leaves
			Pinch of cayenne pepper
		50 ml	(*4 tbsp*) chopped fresh parsley

In 3-litre (*5-pt*) saucepan cook bacon over med. heat for 5 min.; add potatoes, onion and celery. Continue cooking, stirring occasionally, until potatoes are tender (15 to 20 min.). Remove from pan; set aside. In same pan melt butter; stir in flour until smooth and bubbly (1 min.). Add potato mixture and remaining ingredients *except* parsley. Cook over med. heat, stirring occasionally, until heated through (10 to 15 min.). Stir in parsley.

Microwave Directions: In 4-litre (*7-pt*) casserole combine bacon, potatoes, onion and celery. Cover; microwave on HIGH, stirring after half the time, until potatoes are tender (12 to 18 min.). Cut up butter; stir into vegetable mixture. Stir in flour until smooth. Stir in remaining ingredients *except* oysters, clams and parsley. Cover; microwave on HIGH, stirring after half the time, until slightly thickened (6 to 10 min.). Stir in remaining ingredients. Cover; microwave on HIGH until heated through (1 to 2 min.).

Hearty Bacon Potato Chowder

Creamy Spinach & Carrot Soup

4 servings
30 minutes

Subtly spiced with nutmeg and orange, this soup is colourful and delicious.

45 g	(*1¹/₂ oz*) butter or margarine
2	med. onions, chopped
30 ml	(*2 tbsp*) plain flour
250 ml	(*8 fl oz*) single cream
295-g	(*10.4-oz*) can chicken broth
2	med. carrots, shredded

275 g	(*10 oz*) frozen chopped spinach, thawed, drained
1 ml	(*¹/₄ tsp*) salt
1 ml	(*¹/₄ tsp*) pepper
	Pinch of nutmeg
	Zest or strip of orange rind

In 2-litre (*3¹/₂-pt*) saucepan melt butter; add onions. Cook over med. heat, stirring occasionally, until onions are tender (5 to 6 min.). Stir in flour until smooth and bubbly (1 min.). Stir in single cream and chicken broth. Add remaining ingredients *except* orange rind. Continue cooking over low heat, stirring occasionally, until soup is heated through (12 to 15 min.). Garnish with zest or strip of orange rind.

Microwave Directions: In 2.5-litre (*4¹/₄-pt*) casserole combine butter and onions. Microwave on HIGH, stirring after half the time, until onions are tender (2¹/₂ to 3 min.). Stir in flour until smooth. Microwave on HIGH until bubbly (30 to 45 sec.). Stir in single cream and chicken broth. Add remaining ingredients *except* orange rind. Cover; microwave on HIGH, stirring after half the time, until soup is heated through (8 to 10 min.). Garnish with zest or strip of orange rind.

To Make Strip of Orange Rind:

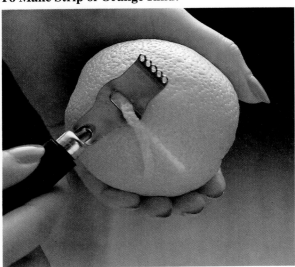

1. Using a canapé cutter, cut strips of rind from orange.

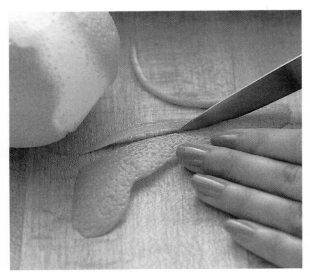

2. Or, cut a piece of rind from orange using a vegetable peeler. Scrape away any of the white pith on back of rind. Cut rind into fine strips with a sharp knife.

Creamy Spinach & Carrot Soup

Northwoods Wild Rice Soup

8 servings
60 minutes

The nutty flavour of wild rice rounds out this popular midwestern cream soup.

525 g	(*18 oz*) cooked wild rice		250 ml	(*8 fl oz*) chicken broth
300 g	(*11 oz*) cubed 2.5 cm (*1 in*) cooked chicken or turkey		50 ml	(*2 fl oz*) sherry or chicken broth
150 g	(*5 oz*) cubed 1 cm (*1/2 in*) cooked ham		1	med. onion, chopped
2	med. carrots, shredded		2 ml	(*1/2 tsp*) salt
2	celery sticks, cut into 1-cm (*1/2-in*) slices		1 ml	(*1/4 tsp*) pepper
1 litre	(*13/4 pt*) single cream		50 ml	(*4 tbsp*) plain flour
			45 g	(*11/2 oz*) butter or margarine, melted

In flameproof casserole, combine all ingredients *except* flour and butter. Cook over med. heat, stirring occasionally, until heated through (15 to 20 min.). In small bowl stir together flour and butter; stir into hot soup. Continue cooking, stirring occasionally, until thickened (5 to 8 min.).

Microwave Directions: In 4-litre (*7-pt*) casserole combine all ingredients *except* flour and butter. Cover; microwave on HIGH, stirring after half the time, until heated through (13 to 15 min.). In small bowl stir together flour and butter; stir into hot soup. Microwave on HIGH, stirring after half the time, until thickened (5 to 8 min.). Let stand 5 min.

Open Hearth Split Pea Soup

6 servings
2 hours 30 minutes

Homemade split pea soup, made with smoked ham, warms the heart and body.

450 g	(*1 lb*) dried green split peas		450 to 675 g	(*1 to 11/2 lb*) smoked ham hocks
3	celery sticks, chopped		5	sprigs fresh parsley
2	med. onions, chopped			Salt and pepper
2.3 litres	(*41/4 pt*) water			

In flameproof casserole combine all ingredients *except* salt and pepper. Cook over med. heat until mixture comes to a full boil. Cover; reduce heat to low. Continue cooking, stirring occasionally, 1½ hr. Remove cover; continue cooking until soup is thickened (30 to 60 min.). Remove ham hocks; when cool enough to handle, cut off meat. Discard bones; return meat to soup. Season to taste.

Microwave Directions: In 4-litre (*7-pt*) casserole combine all ingredients *except* salt and pepper. Cover; microwave on HIGH, stirring after half the time, until soup is thickened (40 to 60 min.). Remove ham hocks; when cool enough to handle, cut off meat. Discard bones; return meat to soup. Season to taste.

Northwoods Wild Rice Soup

Garden Courgette Bisque

4 servings
30 minutes

Rich and creamy with the delicate flavours of garden courgettes and mushrooms.

30 g	(*1 oz*) butter or margarine
2	med. courgettes, cut into 3-mm (*1/8-in*) slices
75 g	(*3 oz*) sliced 5 mm (*1/4 in*) fresh mushrooms
1	med. onion, chopped

50 ml	(*4 tbsp*) chopped fresh parsley
45 g	(*1 1/2 oz*) butter or margarine
45 ml	(*3 tbsp*) plain flour
295-g	(*10.4-oz*) can chicken broth
200 ml	(*7 fl oz*) double cream
	Pinch of pepper

In 3-litre (*5-pt*) saucepan melt 30 g (*1 oz*) butter; add courgettes, mushrooms, onion and parsley. Cook over med. heat, stirring occasionally, until vegetables are crisply tender (6 to 8 min.). Meanwhile, in 2-litre (*3 1/2-pt*) saucepan melt 45 g (*1 1/2 oz*) butter over med. heat; stir in flour until smooth and bubbly (1 min.). Add chicken broth; continue cooking, stirring occasionally, until soup is thickened (5 to 7 min.). Stir in cream, pepper and courgette mixture. Continue cooking until heated through (5 to 6 min.).

Microwave Directions: In 3-litre (*5-pt*) casserole melt 30 g (*1 oz*) butter on HIGH (30 to 40 sec.). Stir in courgettes, mushrooms, onion and parsley. Cover; microwave on HIGH until vegetables are crisply tender (2 1/2 to 3 1/2 min.). Cut up 45 g (*1 1/2 oz*) butter; stir into vegetable mixture until melted. Stir in flour until smooth; microwave on HIGH until bubbly (1 to 1 1/2 min.). Stir in remaining ingredients. Cover; microwave on HIGH, stirring after half the time, until slightly thickened and heated through (6 to 9 min.).

Tomato Barley Soup

6 servings
60 minutes

Fill your kitchen with the aroma of garlic, onions and vegetables.

2	med. onions, chopped
2	med. carrots, cut into 5-mm (*1/4-in*) slices
2	celery sticks, cut into 5-mm (*1/4-in*) slices
30 ml	(*2 tbsp*) vegetable oil
10 ml	(*2 tsp*) crushed fresh garlic
30 g	(*1 oz*) pearl barley

625 ml	(*1 pt*) water
2	med. ripe tomatoes, cut into 2.5-cm (*1-in*) cubes
400 g	(*14 oz*) canned whole tomatoes
295-g	(*10.4-oz*) can chicken broth
1 ml	(*1/4 tsp*) pepper

In 2-litre (*3 1/2-pt*) saucepan combine onions, carrots, celery, oil and garlic. Cook over med. heat, stirring occasionally, until vegetables are crisply tender (8 to 10 min.). Meanwhile, in 3-litre (*5-pt*) saucepan combine remaining ingredients. Cook until mixture comes to a full boil. Add vegetable mixture. Return to boil; reduce heat to low. Cover; cook until barley is tender (35 to 40 min.).

Microwave Directions: In 3-litre (*5-pt*) casserole combine onions, carrots, celery, oil and garlic. Cover; microwave on HIGH, stirring after half the time, until vegetables are crisply tender (3 to 4 min.). Add remaining ingredients. Cover; microwave on HIGH, stirring after half the time, until barley is tender (18 to 25 min.). Let stand 5 min.

Garden Courgette Bisque

Hearty Minestrone Soup

Homemade Chicken Broth

1.3 litres (*2¼ pt*)
4 hours

*Save the backs, wings and necks from chickens until you have 1.4 to 1.8 kg (3 to 4 lb);
then, prepare your own flavourful, economical chicken broth.*

1.3 to 1.8 kg	(*3 to 4 lb*) chicken backs, wings, necks
2 litres	(*3½ pt*) water
2	med. onions, cut into eighths
2	celery sticks with leaves, cut into thirds

2	carrots, cut into thirds
1	bay leaf
2 ml	(*½ tsp*) salt
1 ml	(*¼ tsp*) pepper

In large kettle or stockpot combine all ingredients. Cover; cook over high heat until mixture comes to a full boil (15 to 20 min.). Reduce heat to med. low; continue cooking 3 to 4 hr. Strain; skim fat. Stock can be refrigerated 2 to 3 days or frozen 3 to 4 months.

Microwave Directions: In 5-litre (*9-pt*) casserole combine all ingredients. Cover; microwave on HIGH until mixture comes to a full boil (25 to 30 min.). Stir. Cover; reduce power to MEDIUM (50% power). Microwave until carrots are crisply tender (30 to 40 min.). Let stand 5 min. Strain; skim fat. Store as directed left.

Hearty Minestrone Soup

14 (250 ml) (*8 fl oz*) servings
2 hours

Vegetables, fresh from the garden, make this soup extra special.

675 g	(*1½ lb*) cubed 2.5 cm (*1 in*) beef stew meat
2 litres	(*3½ pt*) water
10 ml	(*2 tsp*) salt
3	med. onions, chopped
2	med. carrots, cut into 5-mm (*¼-in*) slices
2	celery sticks, chopped
125 g	(*4 oz*) butter or margarine
15 ml	(*1 tbsp*) chopped fresh parsley

5 ml	(*1 tsp*) crushed fresh garlic
2	med. ripe tomatoes, chopped
2	med. potatoes, cut into 1-cm (*½-in*) cubes
1	med. courgette, unpeeled, cut into 5-mm (*¼-in*) slices
100 g	(*4 oz*) uncooked long grain rice
400 g	(*14 oz*) canned kidney beans, drained
	Salt and pepper

In flameproof casserole combine beef, water and salt. Cover; cook over med. heat until mixture comes to a full boil (10 to 12 min.). Reduce heat to low; continue cooking until beef is fork tender (about 1 hr.). Meanwhile, in 25-cm (*10-in*) frying pan combine onions, carrots, celery, butter, parsley and garlic. Cook over med. heat, stirring occasionally, until vegetables are crisply tender (5 to 6 min.). Add vegetable mixture to beef along with remaining ingredients *except* kidney beans. Cook over med. heat until mixture comes to a full boil (10 to 12 min.); reduce heat to low. Cover; continue cooking until vegetables are crisply tender (20 to 30 min.). Stir in kidney beans. Continue cooking until heated through (2 to 3 min.). Season to taste.

Microwave Directions: In 5-litre (*9-pt*) casserole combine beef, water and salt. Cover; microwave on HIGH until beef is fork tender (30 to 40 min.). Add rice. Cover; microwave on HIGH until rice is tender (12 to 15 min.). Let stand covered. Meanwhile, in 3-litre (*5-pt*) casserole melt butter on HIGH (70 to 80 sec.). Stir in remaining ingredients *except* tomatoes and kidney beans. Cover; microwave on HIGH until vegetables are crisply tender (5 to 8 min.). Add vegetable mixture to beef mixture. Cover; microwave on HIGH until vegetables are fork tender (10 to 12 min.). Add kidney beans. Cover; microwave on HIGH until heated through (8 to 10 min.). Stir in tomatoes. Let stand covered 5 min. Season to taste.

Crock of Savoury Vegetable Stew

Crock of Savoury Vegetable Stew

**6 servings
60 minutes**

Full of hearty ingredients and sweet savoury spices.

4	med. carrots, cut into 5-mm (*¼-in*) slices	400 ml	(*14 fl oz*) canned tomato sauce
2	med. onions, chopped	400 g	(*14 oz*) canned whole tomatoes
2	celery sticks, cut into 1-cm (*½-in*) slices	295-g	(*11.4-oz*) can tomato soup
450 g	(*1 lb*) pork sausage links, cut into 5-cm (*2-in*) pieces	1	bay leaf
300 g	(*11 oz*) shredded cabbage	2 ml	(*½ tsp*) salt
30 g	(*1 oz*) chopped fresh parsley	2 ml	(*½ tsp*) thyme leaves
250 ml	(*8 fl oz*) apple juice	1 ml	(*¼ tsp*) pepper

In 2-litre (*3½-pt*) saucepan combine carrots, onions, celery and sausage. Cook over med. heat, stirring occasionally, until sausage is browned and vegetables are crisply tender (8 to 12 min.). Pour off fat. Meanwhile, in 3-litre (*5-pt*) saucepan combine remaining ingredients. Cook over low heat, stirring occasionally, until heated through (12 to 15 min.). Stir in cooked sausage and vegetables. Continue cooking, stirring occasionally, until stew is thickened (20 to 30 min.).

Microwave Directions: In 3-litre (*5-pt*) casserole combine carrots, onions, celery and sausage. Cover; microwave on HIGH, stirring after half the time, until sausage is done and vegetables are crisply tender (4 to 8 min.). Stir in remaining ingredients. Cover; microwave on HIGH, stirring after half the time, until slightly thickened and heated through (10 to 15 min.).

Farmhouse Chicken Noodle Stew

**6 servings
60 minutes**

A marvelous heart-warming stew.

1.3 to 1.6 kg	(*3 to 3½ lb*) frying chicken, cut into 8 pieces	2	bay leaves
1.5 litres	(*2¾ pt*) hot water	15 ml	(*1 tbsp*) basil leaves
4	celery sticks, cut into 5-mm (*¼-in*) slices	5 ml	(*1 tsp*) thyme leaves
2	med. onions, chopped	5 ml	(*1 tsp*) marjoram leaves
30 g	(*1 oz*) chopped fresh parsley	5 ml	(*1 tsp*) salt
3	med. carrots, cut into 2.5-cm (*1-in*) pieces	2 ml	(*½ tsp*) pepper
		350 g	(*12 oz*) frozen egg noodles*

In flameproof casserole cover chicken with water. Cover; cook over med. high heat for 10 min. Meanwhile, prepare vegetables. Add vegetables and remaining ingredients *except* noodles. Cover; cook over med. high heat for 20 min. or until chicken is fork tender. Remove chicken pieces; add noodles. Return to a full boil, skimming off fat during cooking. (Some herbs will be removed.) Meanwhile, remove chicken from bones. Reduce heat to low. Add chicken. Cook until noodles are tender (20 to 25 min.).

*225 g (*8 oz*) uncooked med. egg noodles can be substituted for frozen egg noodles.

Microwave Directions: In 6-litre (*10½-pt*) casserole combine 1 litre (*1¾ pt*) water and remaining ingredients *except* noodles. Cover; microwave on HIGH, stirring after half the time, until chicken is fork tender (25 to 35 min.). Remove chicken from broth; skim off fat. Add noodles and 500 ml (*17 fl oz*) water; continue microwaving on HIGH (8 to 10 min.). Meanwhile, remove chicken from bones. Add chicken to noodle mixture. Cover; microwave on HIGH, stirring after half the time, until noodles are tender (18 to 20 min.).

Chicken Stew with Dumplings

8 servings
2 hours

A great Saturday night supper with tender homemade dumplings.

Stew

1.1 to 1.3 kg	(*2¹/₂ to 3 lb*) chicken thighs
1.3 litre	(*2¹/₄ pt*) water
4	new red potatoes, cut into sixths
3	carrots, cut into quarters
2	celery sticks, cut into 5-mm (*¹/₄-in*) slices
1	med. onion, cut into eighths
275 g	(*10 oz*) frozen peas
2 ml	(*¹/₂ tsp*) salt
	Pinch of pepper

Dumplings

225 g	(*8 oz*) plain flour
10 ml	(*2 tsp*) baking powder
3 ml	(*³/₄ tsp*) salt
45 g	(*1¹/₂ oz*) butter or margarine, softened
200 ml	(*7 fl oz*) milk
50 ml	(*4 tbsp*) chopped fresh parsley

In flameproof casserole place chicken; cover with water. Cover; cook over med. heat until fork tender (50 to 60 min.). Remove chicken from broth; skim fat. Remove chicken from bones; return to broth. Add remaining stew ingredients. Cover; cook over med. heat until vegetables are fork tender (15 to 20 min.). In large bowl stir together flour, baking powder and salt. Cut in butter until mixture is crumbly. Stir in milk and parsley. Drop dumplings by rounded tablespoonfuls into hot stew. Cook, uncovered, 10 min. Cover; continue cooking until dumplings are tender (8 to 10 min.).

Microwave Directions: *Cut carrots into 5-mm (¹/₄-in) slices. Reduce baking powder to 7 ml (1³/₄ tsp), butter to 25 ml (1¹/₂ tbsp) and milk to 125 ml (4 fl oz)*

plus 15 ml (1 tbsp). In 5-litre (*9-pt*) casserole place chicken; cover with water. Cover; microwave on HIGH until water comes to a full boil (16 to 18 min.). Rearrange chicken. Reduce power to MEDIUM (50% power); microwave 10 min. Remove chicken from broth; skim fat. Remove chicken from bones; return to broth. Add remaining stew ingredients *except* peas. Cover; microwave on HIGH 8 min. Reduce power to MEDIUM (50% power); microwave until vegetables are crisply tender (7 to 9 min.). Meanwhile, prepare dumplings as directed left. Add peas to stew. Microwave on HIGH until mixture comes to a full boil (3 to 4 min.). Drop dumplings by tablespoonfuls into hot stew. Cover; microwave on HIGH, turning dish ¹/₄ turn after half the time, until dumplings are tender (4 to 5 min.).

To Prepare Dumplings:

1. Drop dumplings by rounded tablespoonfuls into hot stew.

2. Cook, uncovered, 10 min. Cover; continue cooking until dumplings are tender (8 to 10 min.).

Chicken Stew with Dumplings

Country-Style French Onion Soup

6 servings
60 minutes

The light chicken broth and Dijon mustard bring out the mellow, rich flavour of onions.

Soup

30 g	*(1 oz)* butter or margarine
4	med. onions, cut into 3-mm *(1/8-in)* slices
2 ml	*(1/2 tsp)* crushed fresh garlic
50 ml	*(4 tbsp)* chopped fresh parsley
500 ml	*(17 fl oz)* water
295-g	*(10.4-oz)* can chicken broth
30 ml	*(2 tbsp)* country-style Dijon mustard
5 ml	*(1 tsp)* basil leaves
1 ml	*(1/4 tsp)* thyme leaves
1 ml	*(1/4 tsp)* pepper

Croutons

50 g	*(2 oz)* butter or margarine
5 ml	*(1 tsp)* basil leaves
2 ml	*(1/2 tsp)* crushed fresh garlic
125 g	*(4 oz)* cubed 2.5 cm *(1 in)* rye bread
6	*(30 g)* *(1 oz)* slices Mozzarella cheese

Heat oven to 200 °C *(400 °F)* mark 6. In 3-litre *(5-pt)* saucepan melt 30 g *(1 oz)* butter; add onions and 2 ml *(1/2 tsp)* garlic. Cook over med. heat, stirring occasionally, until onions are tender (7 to 10 min.). Add remaining soup ingredients; continue cooking until heated through (12 to 15 min.). Meanwhile, in 33 x 23-cm *(13 x 9-in)* baking dish melt 50 g *(2 oz)* butter in oven (4 to 6 min.). Stir in basil and 2 ml *(1/2 tsp)* garlic. Add bread cubes; toss to coat. Bake for 10 to 15 min., stirring occasionally, until toasted. Pour soup in ovenproof bowls; place 1 cheese slice in each bowl. Bake for 7 to 10 min. or until cheese is lightly browned. Serve with rye croutons.

Microwave Directions: In 4-litre *(7-pt)* casserole combine 30 g *(1 oz)* butter, onions and 2 ml *(1/2 tsp)* garlic. Cover; microwave on HIGH, stirring after half the time, until onions are tender (5 to 6 min.). Add remaining soup ingredients. Cover; microwave on HIGH, stirring after half the time, until heated through (8 to 10 min.). Let stand 5 min. In 25-cm *(10-in)* flan dish melt 50 g *(2 oz)* butter on HIGH (50 to 60 sec.). Stir in basil and 2 ml *(1/2 tsp)* garlic. Add bread cubes; toss to coat. Microwave on HIGH, stirring every 2 min., until dry to the touch (4 to 5 min.). Pour soup in bowls; place 1 cheese slice in each bowl. Microwave on HIGH until cheese is melted (30 to 45 sec.). Serve with rye croutons.

Country-Style French Onion Soup

Savoury Turkey Tomato Stew

Savoury Turkey Tomato Stew

4 to 6 servings
60 minutes

Italian sausage adds extra flavour to this garden fresh stew.

15 ml	(*1 tbsp*) vegetable oil	5 ml	(*1 tsp*) basil leaves
10 ml	(*2 tsp*) crushed fresh garlic	5 ml	(*1 tsp*) oregano leaves
450 g	(*1 lb*) Italian sausage links, casing removed, cut into 2.5-cm (*1-in*) pieces	2 ml	(*1/2 tsp*) salt
		1 ml	(*1/4 tsp*) cracked pepper
300 g	(*11 oz*) cooked, cubed 2.5 cm (*1 in*) turkey	2	med. ripe tomatoes, cut into 5-cm (*2-in*) pieces
625 ml	(*1 pt*) chicken broth	2	med. green peppers, cut into 2.5-cm (*1-in*) pieces
2	med. onions, cut into eighths		
150 g	(*5 oz*) canned tomato purée		

In flameproof casserole heat oil; add garlic. Cook over med. high heat 2 min. Add sausage pieces. Continue cooking, stirring occasionally, until lightly browned (4 to 7 min.). Drain fat. Reduce heat to med.; stir in remaining ingredients *except* tomatoes and green peppers. Cover; cook, stirring occasionally, until heated through (15 to 20 min.). Remove from heat; stir in tomatoes and green peppers. Cover; let stand 5 min. or until heated through.

Microwave Directions: Omit oil. In 2.5-litre (*4 1/4-pt*) casserole stir together garlic and sausage pieces. Cover; microwave on HIGH, stirring after half the time, until sausage is no longer pink (5 to 8 min.). Drain fat. Add remaining ingredients *except* tomatoes and green peppers. Cover; microwave on HIGH, stirring twice during last half of time, until heated through (12 to 13 min.). Stir in tomatoes and green peppers. Cover; microwave on HIGH until heated through (1 min.). Let stand 5 min.

Chilli Spiced Beef & Bean Stew

6 servings
60 minutes

It's not chilli or spaghetti but a spicy rich stew
with ground beef and pork sausage.

2	med. onions, chopped	30 ml	(*2 tbsp*) chilli powder
450 g	(*1 lb*) minced beef	15 ml	(*1 tbsp*) basil leaves
450 g	(*1 lb*) pork sausage	5 ml	(*1 tsp*) oregano leaves
250 ml	(*8 fl oz*) water	5 ml	(*1 tsp*) pepper
800 g	(*1 3/4 lb*) canned whole tomatoes	2 ml	(*1/2 tsp*) salt
450 g	(*1 lb*) canned kidney beans	45 ml	(*3 tbsp*) country-style Dijon mustard
450 ml	(*3/4 pt*) canned tomato sauce	225 g	(*8 oz*) uncooked spaghetti
350 g	(*12 oz*) canned tomato purée		

In 25-cm (*10-in*) frying pan cook onions, beef and sausage over med. heat until meat is browned (10 to 12 min.); pour off fat. Meanwhile, in flameproof casserole combine remaining ingredients *except* spaghetti. Cook over med. heat, stirring occasionally, for 15 min. Reduce heat to low; add browned meat. Cook, stirring occasionally, until stew is thickened (20 to 30 min.). Meanwhile, cook spaghetti according to pkg. directions. Serve stew over spaghetti.

Microwave Directions: In 4-litre (*7-pt*) casserole combine onions, crumbled minced beef and sausage. Cover; microwave on HIGH, stirring after half the time, until no longer pink (5 to 8 min.). Pour off fat. In same casserole combine meat and remaining ingredients *except* spaghetti. Cover; microwave on HIGH, stirring after half the time, until heated through (15 to 20 min.). Meanwhile, cook spaghetti according to pkg. directions. Serve stew over spaghetti.

How To: Prepare Soups & Stews

Tomato Barley Soup, p. 84; Seashore Chowder, p. 78

To Identify Clear Soups:

Stock: The liquid in which meat, fish or vegetables are slowly cooked together; often used as a base for other soups.

Broth: Stock that is ladled and served.

Bouillon: Clarified, strained and seasoned broth. A plain, clear soup. Also available in dried cubes or granules that are dissolved in hot water.

Consommé: Stock or broth reduced to half by boiling, thus intensifying flavour.

To Identify Hearty Soups:

Cream: Thickened with flour, egg yolk, rice or vegetables. Milk, cream or broth are used for the liquid.

Bisque: Cream soup with shellfish, vegetable puree or bits of solid food added.

Pureed: Similar to bisque or cream soup. Pureed vegetables are used as the thickening agent.

Chowder: Contains pieces of ingredients and is typically seafood or vegetable-based.

Stew: A combination of meat and vegetables cooked by simmering in a liquid.

To Make Better Soups & Stews:

To extract the most flavour from meats and vegetables in soups and stews, start with cold water.

Raw, uncooked bones with meat and marrow provide the most intense meat flavour.

Fresh aromatic vegetables such as onion, garlic, celery and carrot enrich the broth flavour.

Herbs such as parsley, bay leaf, thyme, basil and peppercorns add flavour and distinction to soups and stews.

Stewing is a good method for tenderizing inexpensive or tougher cuts of meat while producing good flavour.

To Store Soups & Stews:

Cool soups and stews quickly; store in airtight containers.

Bean soups and broth-type soups with meat and vegetables can be frozen for up to three months.

When planning to freeze stews, do not thicken with flour or starch when preparing; thicken when reheating.

Cream-based soups such as chowders and creamed vegetable soups or those containing cheese or eggs do not freeze well.

To Skim Fat:

It is common to remove fat using a large (metal) spoon. Here are other methods:

1. Chill soup or stew for several hours until fat has solidified on top. Remove solid fat layer and discard.

2. Cool soup or stew to lukewarm and add ice cubes. The fat will solidify around the ice cubes; remove ice cubes and fat with slotted spoon and discard.

3. Several paper towels can be used to absorb the fat from the top of the soup or stew.

4. A meat baster can be used to suction off the fat.

POULTRY

A special holiday or a family celebration. It's a time to put aside the demands of daily life, to gather loved ones who share in the joys of the occasion. And one of the time-honored traditions of a special event at home is the bounty of foods that welcomes family and friends to the dining room table.

When the guest list is a long one, holiday hospitality often begins with a turkey — plump, golden brown and trimmed with dishes that have become an expected part of the feast. Bread stuffing studded with apples and raisins. Baked sweet potatoes. Cranberry sauce with just a hint of orange. A basket of homemade dinner rolls. A big bowl of green vegetables, steaming hot and glistening with butter. And so much more!

A smaller gathering might call for chicken, rubbed with herbs and roasted, or chicken breasts simmered in a savory sauce or perhaps chicken fried crispy in the cast-iron skillet.

With special occasion cooking, there's the satisfaction of preparing a truly delectable feast of foods that are spectacular to see and a pleasure to eat. But even more rewarding is the chance to share this time with those most dear to you.

Roasted Chicken With Garden Vegetables

6 servings
3 hours

Reminiscent of Sunday pot roast and vegetables,
but oh-so-good with chicken and herbs.

1.8 to 2.3 kg	*(4 to 5 lb)* whole roasting chicken	10 ml	*(2 tsp)* crushed fresh garlic
125 g	*(4 oz)* butter or margarine, softened	6	new red potatoes, cut in half
10 ml	*(2 tsp)* rosemary leaves, crushed	6	carrots, cut in half crosswise
2 ml	*(1/2 tsp)* salt	2	med. onions, cut into quarters
1 ml	*(1/4 tsp)* pepper	30 ml	*(2 tbsp)* chopped fresh parsley

Heat oven to 180 °C (*350 °F*) mark 4. Secure wings to body of chicken. In small bowl stir together butter, rosemary, salt, pepper and garlic. Rub chicken with half of butter mixture. Place chicken on rack in roasting tin. Place potatoes, carrots and onions on bottom of tin around chicken. Dollop remaining butter mixture evenly over vegetables. Bake, basting chicken and vegetables occasionally, for 2 to 2½ hr. or until chicken is fork tender. Sprinkle with parsley.

Microwave Directions: Cut carrots into 5-cm (*2-in*) pieces. In small bowl stir together butter, rosemary, salt, pepper and garlic. In 5-litre (*9-pt*) casserole place chicken, breast side down. Rub chicken with small amount of butter mixture. Cover; microwave on HIGH 5 min. Reduce power to MEDIUM (50% power); microwave 20 min. Drain off fat and juice. Turn chicken, breast side up. Place carrots around chicken. Spread chicken and carrots with half of butter mixture. Cover; microwave on MEDIUM (50% power), turning dish ¼ turn after half the time, 10 min. Rearrange carrots. Place potatoes and onions on top of carrots. Spread vegetables with remaining butter mixture. Cover; microwave on HIGH, turning dish ¼ turn every 5 min., or until chicken is fork tender (15 to 17 min.). Tent with aluminum foil; let stand 5 min. Sprinkle with parsley.

Herb Butter Roasted Chicken

4 servings
2 hours 30 minutes

Rosemary, fresh parsley and garlic create a savoury roasted chicken.

1.8 to 2.3 kg	*(4 to 5 lb)* whole roasting chicken	1 ml	*(1/4 tsp)* pepper
50 g	*(2 oz)* butter or margarine, softened	30 ml	*(2 tbsp)* chopped fresh parsley
5 ml	*(1 tsp)* rosemary leaves, crushed	5 ml	*(1 tsp)* crushed fresh garlic
5 ml	*(1 tsp)* salt		

Heat oven to 180 °C (*350 °F*) mark 4. Secure wings to body of chicken. In small bowl stir together remaining ingredients. Rub chicken with butter mixture. Place on rack in roasting tin. Bake for 2 to 2½ hr. or until fork tender.

Microwave Directions: Secure wings to body of chicken. In small bowl stir together remaining ingredients and 2 ml (*1/2 tsp*) paprika. Rub chicken with half of butter mixture. Place chicken, breast side down, on microwave-safe roasting rack. Cover; microwave on HIGH 5 min. Reduce power to MEDIUM (50% power); microwave, turning rack ¼ turn after half the time, 30 min. Turn chicken, breast side up. Spread chicken with remaining butter mixture. Cover; microwave on MEDIUM (50% power), turning rack ¼ turn after half the time, until fork tender (25 to 35 min.). Tent with aluminum foil; let stand 5 to 10 min.

Roasted Chicken With Garden Vegetables

Red Apple Glazed Chicken

Spiced apples create a unique spiced chicken.

6 servings
3 hours

Stuffing

450 g	(*1 lb*) canned spiced apple rings, *reserve juice*
50 g	(*2 oz*) dried bread cubes
2	celery sticks, cut into 1-cm (*1/2-in*) slices
50 ml	(*4 tbsp*) chopped onion
50 g	(*2 oz*) butter or margarine, melted
30 ml	(*2 tbsp*) *reserved* spiced apple juice or water
2 ml	(*1/2 tsp*) salt
	Pinch of pepper
	Pinch of allspice
1.8 to 2.3 kg	(*4 to 5 lb*) whole roasting chicken

Glaze

50 ml	(*4 tbsp*) *reserved* spiced apple juice
30 ml	(*2 tbsp*) light corn syrup
30 ml	(*2 tbsp*) water

Heat oven to 180 °C (*350 °F*) mark 4. Cut 5 spiced apple rings into eighths; reserve remaining apple rings. In medium bowl stir together cut-up apples and remaining stuffing ingredients. Stuff chicken; secure wings to body of chicken. Place chicken on rack in roasting tin. In 1-litre (*1³/4-pt*) saucepan stir together all glaze ingredients. Cook over med. high heat, stirring occasionally, until heated through (5 to 6 min.). Spoon glaze over chicken. Bake, basting occasionally, for 1 hr. If needed, add 50 ml (*2 fl oz*) water to basting juices. Loosely cover chicken with aluminum foil. Continue baking, basting occasionally, for 1 to 1¹/2 hr. or until chicken is fork tender. Garnish with reserved apple rings.

Microwave Directions: Cut 5 spiced apple rings into eighths; reserve remaining apple rings. In medium bowl stir together cut-up apples and remaining stuffing ingredients. Stuff chicken; secure wings to body of chicken. In small bowl combine all glaze ingredients. Microwave on HIGH until heated through (45 to 60 sec.). Place chicken, breast side down, on microwave-safe roasting rack. Spoon half of glaze over chicken. Cover; microwave on HIGH 5 min. Reduce power to MEDIUM (50% power); microwave, turning rack ¹/4 turn after half the time, 25 min. Turn chicken, breast side up. Spoon remaining glaze over chicken. Cover; microwave on MEDIUM (50% power), turning rack ¹/4 turn after half the time, until chicken is fork tender (22 to 24 min.). Tent with aluminum foil; let stand 5 to 10 min. Garnish with reserved apple rings.

Red Apple Glazed Chicken

Country-Style Chicken Kiev

4 servings
2 hours

Preparation takes a little more time for this old favourite, but the taste is well worth the effort!

Filling

50 g	(*2 oz*) butter or margarine, softened
30 ml	(*2 tbsp*) chopped spring onion
15 ml	(*1 tbsp*) crushed fresh garlic
1 ml	(*1/4 tsp*) salt
	Pinch of cracked pepper

Chicken

4	whole boneless chicken breasts, skinned
50 g	(*2 oz*) butter or margarine
65 g	(*2 1/2 oz*) crushed buttery crackers
50 ml	(*4 tbsp*) chopped fresh parsley
1 ml	(*1/4 tsp*) salt
1 ml	(*1/4 tsp*) thyme leaves
	Pinch of cracked pepper

In medium bowl stir together all filling ingredients. Divide into 4 equal portions. Freeze portions at least 30 min. Heat oven to 180 °C (*350 °F*) mark 4. Flatten each chicken breast to about 5-mm (*1/4-in*) thickness by pounding between sheets of waxed paper. Place 1 portion of frozen filling onto each flattened breast. Roll and tuck in edges of chicken; secure with wooden picks. In 23-cm (*9-in*) sq. baking dish melt 50 g (*2 oz*) butter in oven (4 to 6 min.). Combine remaining chicken ingredients. Dip rolled chicken in melted butter, then coat with crumb mixture. Place chicken in same dish; sprinkle with remaining crumb mixture. Bake for 55 to 65 min. or until fork tender. Remove wooden picks before serving.

To Roll Chicken Breasts:

1. Flatten each chicken breast to about 5-mm (*1/4-in*) thickness by pounding between sheets of waxed paper.

2. Place 1 portion of frozen filling onto each flattened breast. Roll and tuck in edges of chicken; secure with wooden picks.

Country-Style Chicken Kiev

Cheesy Tomato Basil Chicken Breasts

6 servings
1 hour 15 minutes

Cheesy Tomato Basil Chicken Breasts

Fresh tomatoes, basil and Mozzarella cheese make chicken extra special.

Sauce

45 g	(*1½ oz*) butter or margarine
2	med. ripe tomatoes, cut into 2.5-cm (*1-in*) cubes
75 ml	(*5 tbsp*) chopped onion
150 g	(*5 oz*) canned tomato purée
15 ml	(*1 tbsp*) basil leaves
2 ml	(*½ tsp*) salt
1 ml	(*¼ tsp*) pepper
10 ml	(*2 tsp*) crushed fresh garlic
3	whole boneless chicken breasts, skinned, cut in half

Topping

130 g	(*4½ oz*) fresh breadcrumbs
50 ml	(*4 tbsp*) chopped fresh parsley
30 g	(*1 oz*) butter or margarine, melted
175 g	(*6 oz*) Mozzarella cheese, cut into strips

Heat oven to 180 °C (*350 °F*) mark 4. In 33 x 23-cm (*13 x 9-in*) baking dish melt 45 g (*1½ oz*) butter in oven (4 to 6 min.). Meanwhile, in medium bowl stir together remaining sauce ingredients *except* chicken; set aside. Place chicken in baking dish, turning to coat with butter. Spoon sauce mixture over chicken. Bake for 30 to 40 min. or until chicken is no longer pink. Meanwhile, in small bowl stir together all topping ingredients *except* cheese. Place cheese strips over chicken; sprinkle with topping mixture. Continue baking 5 to 10 min. or until chicken is fork tender and breadcrumbs are browned.

Microwave Directions: Topping: In small bowl melt 30 g (*1 oz*) butter on HIGH (40 to 50 sec.). Stir in breadcrumbs. Microwave on HIGH, stirring every 30 sec., until crumbs are toasted (3 to 4 min.). Stir in parsley; set aside. In 23-cm (*9-in*) sq. baking dish melt 45 g (*1½ oz*) butter on HIGH (40 to 50 sec.). Arrange chicken pieces in dish, turning to coat with butter. In medium bowl stir together remaining sauce ingredients. Spread over chicken. Cover with waxed paper; microwave on HIGH, turning dish ¼ turn twice during last half of time, until chicken is fork tender (16 to 20 min.). Place cheese strips over chicken. Cover; microwave on HIGH until cheese melts (2 to 2½ min.). Sprinkle toasted breadcrumbs over cheese. Microwave on HIGH to heat crumbs (1 min.).

4 to 6 servings (325 ml /*11 fl oz* dip)
1 hour 15 minutes

Picnic Drumsticks

Onion crispy drumsticks are served hot or cold with a fresh sour cream-cucumber dip.

Chicken

75 g	(*3 oz*) butter or margarine
75 ml	(*5 tbsp*) crushed saltine crackers
30 ml	(*2 tbsp*) onion soup mix
8	chicken legs

Dip

1	med. cucumber, peeled and chopped
250 ml	(*8 fl oz*) sour cream
7 ml	(*1½ tsp*) chopped fresh chives
2 ml	(*½ tsp*) salt
2 ml	(*½ tsp*) dill weed

Heat oven to 180 °C (*350 °F*) mark 4. In 33 x 23-cm (*13x9-in*) baking dish melt butter in oven (5 to 7 min.). Stir together crushed crackers and onion soup mix. Dip chicken legs into melted butter, then coat with crumb mixture. In same dish place chicken legs; sprinkle with remaining crumb mixture. Bake for 45 to 55 min. or until fork tender. Meanwhile, in medium bowl stir together all dip ingredients. Cover; refrigerate at least 1 hr. Serve chicken hot or cold with dip.

Sour Cream Onion-Chive Chicken

6 servings
1 hour 45 minutes

Succulent onion-flavoured chicken is topped with a creamy, flavourful sauce.

Coating

250 g	*(9 oz)* fresh breadcrumbs
2 ml	*(1/2 tsp)* salt
1 ml	*(1/4 tsp)* cracked pepper
1 ml	*(1/4 tsp)* onion powder
1 ml	*(1/4 tsp)* paprika
125 g	*(4 oz)* butter or margarine, melted
1.2 to 1.6 kg	*(2 1/2 to 3 1/2 lb)* frying chicken, cut into 8 pieces
3	med. onions, cut in half

Sauce

15 ml	*(1 tbsp)* plain flour
250 ml	*(8 fl oz)* sour cream
1 ml	*(1/4 tsp)* cracked pepper
	Milk
30 ml	*(2 tbsp)* chopped fresh chives

Heat oven to 180 °C (*350 °F*) mark 4. Combine all coating ingredients *except* butter. Dip chicken in melted butter; coat with crumb mixture. *Reserve remaining crumbs and butter.* In 33 x 23-cm (*13 x 9-in*) baking dish place chicken; add onions. Sprinkle remaining crumbs over onions; drizzle with remaining butter. Bake, basting occasionally, for 60 to 70 min. or until fork tender. Remove chicken to platter; keep warm. To make sauce, scrape baking dish; pour dish drippings into 2-litre (*3 1/2-pt*) saucepan. Stir in flour. Cook over med. high heat, stirring occasionally, until bubbly (1 min.). Reduce heat to med. Stir in sour cream and pepper. Continue cooking, stirring occasionally, until heated through (1 to 2 min.). If needed, add milk until desired consistency is reached. Serve sauce over chicken and onions. Sprinkle with chives.

Microwave Directions: Divide butter. In 1-litre (*1 3/4-pt*) casserole melt 50 g (*2 oz*) butter on HIGH (50 to 60 sec.). Stir in coating ingredients. Microwave on HIGH, stirring twice, until crumbs are toasted (4 to 5 min.). Set aside. In 30 x 20-cm (*12 x 8-in*) baking dish melt remaining butter on HIGH (50 to 60 sec.). Arrange chicken in dish, placing thickest part to outside edge, turning to coat with butter. Place onions over chicken. Cover; microwave on HIGH, turning dish 1/4 turn twice during time, until fork tender (21 to 23 min.). Remove chicken to platter; keep warm. Scrape drippings into small bowl. Stir in flour. Microwave on HIGH until bubbly (1 to 1 1/4 min.). Stir in sour cream and pepper. Reduce power to MEDIUM (50% power); microwave until sauce is heated through (3 to 4 min.). If needed, add milk until desired consistency is reached. Return chicken and onions to baking dish. Pour sauce over chicken and onions. Sprinkle toasted breadcrumbs on top. Microwave on HIGH to heat crumbs (2 1/2 to 3 min.). Sprinkle with chives.

Sour Cream Onion-Chive Chicken

Chicken Vegetable Bundles

6 servings
1 hour 15 minutes

Cut into these tasty chicken breasts for a colourful show of carrot and courgette,
seasoned just right with rosemary.

3	whole boneless chicken breasts, skinned, cut in half
45 g	(*1½ oz*) butter or margarine, melted
2	med. carrots, cut into (10 x 0.2 x 0.2-cm) (*4 x ⅛ x ⅛-in*) strips
1	med. courgette, cut into (10 x 0.2 x 0.2-cm) (*4 x ⅛ x ⅛-in*) strips
2 ml	(*½ tsp*) salt
1 ml	(*¼ tsp*) rosemary leaves, crushed
1 ml	(*¼ tsp*) pepper

6	rashers of bacon
50 ml	(*2 fl oz*) brandy or chicken broth
50 ml	(*2 fl oz*) chicken broth

Sauce

50 ml	(*4 tbsp*) *reserved* dish drippings or chicken broth
125 ml	(*4 fl oz*) sour cream
15 ml	(*1 tbsp*) plain flour

Heat oven to 180 °C (*350 °F*) mark 4. Flatten each chicken breast half to about 5-mm (*¼-in*) thickness by pounding between sheets of waxed paper; set aside. In medium bowl combine butter, carrots, courgette, salt, rosemary and pepper. Divide mixture evenly between each flattened chicken breast. Roll up chicken breasts. Wrap 1 bacon rasher around each chicken bundle; secure with wooden picks. In 33 x 23-cm (*13 x 9-in*) baking dish place chicken bundles. In small bowl stir together brandy and chicken broth. Pour over chicken. Bake, basting occasionally, for 35 to 40 min. or until chicken is fork tender. Place chicken bundles on platter; keep warm. *Reserve dish juices.* In 1-litre (*1¾-pt*) saucepan combine reserved dish juices plus enough chicken broth to equal 50 ml (*2 fl oz*). In small bowl stir together sour cream and flour. Stir into dish juice mixture. Cook over med. heat, stirring occasionally, until thickened (2 to 4 min.). DO NOT BOIL. Serve over chicken bundles.

To Prepare Chicken Breasts:

1. Flatten each chicken breast half to about 5-mm (*¼-in*) thickness by pounding between sheets of waxed paper; set aside.

2. Divide mixture evenly between each flattened chicken breast. Roll up chicken breasts. Wrap 1 bacon rasher around each chicken bundle; secure with wooden picks.

Chicken Vegetable Bundles

Pineapple-Tarragon Chicken Breasts

6 servings
60 minutes

Pineapple-Tarragon Chicken Breasts

Tarragon and the sweet tang of pineapple
complement each other in this delicious chicken.

Sauce

178-ml	(*6¼-oz*) carton frozen pineapple juice concentrate, thawed
50 ml	(*4 tbsp*) honey
5 ml	(*1 tsp*) tarragon leaves

2 ml	(*½ tsp*) salt
	Pinch of pepper
6	split chicken breasts

Prepare grill placing coals to one side; heat until coals are ash white. Make aluminum foil drip pan; place opposite coals. In 1-litre (*1¾-pt*) saucepan stir together all sauce ingredients. Cook over med. heat, stirring occasionally, until heated through (3 to 5 min.). Place chicken breasts on barbecue grid over drip pan. Baste with sauce. Grill, turning and basting occasionally with sauce, for 25 to 35 min. or until fork tender. To serve, cook remaining sauce over med. heat, stirring occasionally, until heated through (3 to 5 min.). Serve sauce over chicken.

Tip: 178-ml (*6¼-oz*) carton frozen orange juice concentrate, thawed, can be substituted for pineapple juice concentrate.

Microwave Directions: In small bowl stir together all sauce ingredients. Microwave on HIGH, stirring after 1 min., until heated through (1½ to 1¾ min.). In 30 x 20-cm (*12 x 8-in*) baking dish place chicken breasts. Sprinkle chicken with paprika. Spoon half of sauce over chicken. Cover; microwave on HIGH, rearranging pieces and spooning remaining sauce over chicken after half the time, until fork tender (19 to 21 min.). Serve sauce over chicken.

4 servings
1 hour 20 minutes

Chicken Breasts Southwestern

Green chillies and salsa add south-of-theborder flavour
to grilled chicken breasts.

Marinade

175 ml	(*6 fl oz*) vegetable oil
75 ml	(*5 tbsp*) lime juice
30 ml	(*2 tbsp*) chopped green chillies
5 ml	(*1 tsp*) crushed fresh garlic

2	whole boneless chicken breasts, skinned, halved
8	slices 5 x 2.5 x 0.5 cm (*2 x 1 x ¼ in*) Cheddar cheese
	Salsa (mexican sauce)

In 23-cm (*9-in*) sq. baking dish stir together all marinade ingredients. Add chicken breasts; marinate, turning once, in refrigerator at least 45 min. Meanwhile, prepare grill placing coals to one side; heat until coals are ash white. Make aluminum foil drip pan; place opposite coals. Remove chicken from marinade; drain. Grill chicken 7 min.; turn. Continue grilling until fork tender (6 to 8 min.). Top each chicken breast with 2 slices cheese. Continue grilling until cheese begins to melt (1 to 2 min.). Serve with salsa.

Garlic Grilled Chicken

6 servings
60 minutes

Company's Coming Kabobs

These kabobs can be assembled ahead of time, covered and refrigerated until the party starts!

4	whole boneless chicken breasts, skinned, cut into 2.5-cm (*1-in*) pieces

Sauce

175 ml	(*6 fl oz*) *reserved* pineapple juice
50 ml	(*4 tbsp*) honey
2 ml	(*1/2 tsp*) salt
1 ml	(*1/4 tsp*) pepper
1 ml	(*1/4 tsp*) ginger

Kabobs

2	med. green peppers, cut into 5-cm (*2-in*) pieces
12	cherry tomatoes
2	med. onions, cut into eighths
425 g	(*15 oz*) canned pineapple chunks, drained, *reserve juice*
6	(30-cm) (*12-in*) metal skewers

In medium bowl place chicken pieces. In 2-litre (*3 1/2-pt*) saucepan stir together all sauce ingredients. Cook over med. heat, stirring occasionally, until honey is melted (2 to 3 min.). Pour over chicken pieces; marinate, stirring occasionally, 20 min. Drain; *reserve marinade.* Prepare grill placing coals to one side; heat until coals are ash white. Make aluminum foil drip pan; place opposite coals. To assemble kabobs on metal skewers, alternate chicken pieces, green peppers, cherry tomatoes, onions and pineapple chunks. Place kabobs on barbecue grid over drip pan. Grill, turning and basting occasionally, until chicken is fork tender (8 to 12 min.). In 1-litre (*1 3/4-pt*) saucepan cook remaining marinade over med. heat, stirring occasionally, until mixture comes to a full boil (2 to 3 min.). Just before serving, spoon marinade over kabobs.

Microwave Directions: *Use 6 (30-cm) (12-in) wooden skewers. Use large cherry tomatoes.* In medium bowl place chicken pieces. In small bowl stir together all sauce ingredients. Microwave on HIGH, stirring after half the time, until honey is melted (1 1/2 to 2 min.). Pour over chicken pieces; marinate, stirring occasionally, 20 min. Drain; *reserve marinade.* To assemble kabobs on wooden skewers, alternate chicken pieces, green peppers, large cherry tomatoes, onions and pineapple chunks. Place kabobs on microwave-safe roasting rack. Microwave on HIGH, turning rack 1/4 turn after half the time, 7 min. Rearrange and turn kabobs over; baste. Microwave on HIGH, turning rack 1/4 turn after half the time, until chicken is fork tender (3 to 5 min.). Microwave reserved marinade on HIGH, stirring after half the time, until mixture comes to a full boil (2 to 2 1/2 min.). Just before serving, spoon marinade over kabobs.

4 to 6 servings
60 minutes

Garlic Grilled Chicken

The garlic in this recipe mellows during grilling, creating a rich aroma and flavour.

50 g	(*2 oz*) butter or margarine, melted
1 ml	(*1/4 tsp*) pepper
45 ml	(*3 tbsp*) crushed fresh garlic
30 ml	(*2 tbsp*) soy sauce
1.2 to 1.6 kg	(*2 1/2 to 3 1/2 lb*) whole frying chicken, cut in half

50 ml	(*4 tbsp*) chopped fresh parsley
	Cooked rice

In small bowl stir together butter, pepper, garlic and soy sauce. Heat grill. Place chicken on greased grill pan. Grill chicken 15 to 20 cm (*6 to 8 in*) from heat, turning every 10 min. and brushing with butter mixture during last 10 min., for 30 to 35 min. or until fork tender. Just before serving, brush with butter mixture and sprinkle with parsley. Serve with cooked rice.

Hot Chicken Salad Casserole

8 servings
1 hour 15 minutes

A popular casserole that uses your leftover chicken or turkey.

600 g	(*1 1/3 lb*) cooked, cubed 5 cm (*2 in*) chicken or turkey
400 g	(*14 oz*) cooked rice
2	celery sticks, chopped
75 g	(*3 oz*) slivered almonds
200 ml	(*7 fl oz*) mayonnaise
295-g	(*10.4-oz*) can condensed cream of chicken soup
50 g	(*2 oz*) canned chopped pimento, drained
3	hard cooked eggs, chopped
30 ml	(*2 tbsp*) chopped green pepper
30 ml	(*2 tbsp*) chopped onion
1 ml	(*1/4 tsp*) salt
15 ml	(*1 tbsp*) lemon juice
30 g	(*1 oz*) crushed potato chips

Heat oven to 180 °C (*350 °F*) mark 4. In large bowl stir together all ingredients *except* potato chips. Spread into greased 33 x 23-cm (*13 x 9-in*) baking dish. Sprinkle with chips. Bake for 40 to 50 min. or until heated through.

Microwave Directions: Prepare as directed left *except* spread into 30 x 20-cm (*12 x 8-in*) baking dish. Microwave on HIGH, stirring every 4 min., until heated through (14 to 15 min.). Sprinkle with chips. Microwave on HIGH to heat chips (1 to 1 1/2 min.).

Biscuit-Topped Spinach Chicken Pie

6 servings
60 minutes

Tender buttermilk biscuits top this savoury spinach and chicken pie.

Filling

300 g	(*11 oz*) cooked, shredded chicken
1	med. onion, chopped
300 g	(*11 oz*) frozen chopped spinach, thawed, drained
50 g	(*2 oz*) canned chopped pimento, drained
250 ml	(*8 fl oz*) sour cream
1	egg, slightly beaten
2 ml	(*1/2 tsp*) salt
1 ml	(*1/4 tsp*) pepper
	Pinch of nutmeg
5 ml	(*1 tsp*) crushed fresh garlic

Biscuits

225 g	(*8 oz*) plain flour
50 g	(*2 oz*) butter or margarine, melted
200 ml	(*7 fl oz*) buttermilk*
10 ml	(*2 tsp*) baking powder
2 ml	(*1/2 tsp*) salt

Heat oven to 190 °C (*375 °F*) mark 5. In large bowl stir together all filling ingredients. Spread in greased 23-cm (*9-in*) pie dish; set aside. In medium bowl stir together all biscuit ingredients. Drop dough by tablespoonfuls onto spinach mixture. Bake for 30 to 40 min. or until biscuits are golden brown and pie is heated through.

*15 ml (*1 tbsp*) vinegar plus enough milk to equal 250 ml (*8 fl oz*) can be substituted for 250 ml (*8 fl oz*) buttermilk.

Biscuit-Topped Spinach Chicken Pie

Deep Dish Chicken Pot Pie

4 to 6 servings
1 hour 30 minutes

This special pot pie crust — butter flaky and mouth-watering good — will make memories.

Crust

300 g	(*11 oz*) plain flour
1 ml	(*¼ tsp*) salt
175 g	(*6 oz*) butter or margarine
50 ml	(*2 fl oz*) cold water

Filling

350 g	(*12 oz*) cooked, cubed 2.5 cm (*1 in*) chicken
300 g	(*11 oz*) fresh or frozen peas
50 ml	(*4 tbsp*) finely chopped onion
3	med. sliced 2.5 cm (*1 in*) carrots
2	med. potatoes, peeled, cubed 2.5 cm (*1 in*)

Sauce

45 g	(*1½ oz*) butter or margarine
45 ml	(*3 tbsp*) plain flour
250 ml	(*8 fl oz*) single cream
125 ml	(*4 fl oz*) chicken broth
2 ml	(*½ tsp*) salt
1 ml	(*¼ tsp*) pepper
	Milk

Heat oven to 190 °C (*375 °F*) mark 5. In large bowl stir together 300 g (*11 oz*) flour and 1 ml (*¼ tsp*) salt. Cut in 175 g (*6 oz*) butter until crumbly; with fork mix in water. Divide dough into ⅔ and ⅓ portions. Set aside ⅓ dough. Roll ⅔ dough into 35-cm (*14-in*) circle 3 mm (*⅛ in*) thick. Gently fit into 3-litre (*5-pt*) deep dish casserole; set aside. In large bowl combine all filling ingredients; set aside. In 2-litre (*3½-pt*) saucepan melt 45 g (*1½ oz*) butter; stir in 45 ml (*3 tbsp*) flour. Cook over med. high heat, stirring occasionally, until hot and bubbly (3 to 4 min.). Whisk in single cream, chicken broth, 2 ml (*½ tsp*) salt and pepper.

Continue cooking, stirring occasionally, until sauce thickens (3 to 5 min.). Stir hot sauce into filling; spoon into prepared pie crust. Roll reserved ⅓ dough into 25-cm (*10-in*) circle 3 mm (*⅛ in*) thick. Place on top of pie. Flute edges to seal. Make 3 small slits in top crust; lightly brush top crust with milk. Bake for 50 to 60 min. or until golden brown.

Tip: 30 x 20-cm (*12 x 8-in*) baking dish can be used for 3-litre (*5-pt*) casserole. Roll ⅔ dough into 45 x 35-cm (*18 x 14-in*) rectangle. Roll reserved ⅓ dough into 33 x 23-cm (*13 x 9-in*) rectangle.

To Prepare Crust:

1. Cut in 175 g (*6 oz*) butter until crumbly.

2. Flute edges to seal.

Deep Dish Chicken Pot Pie

Beer Batter Fried Chicken

4 to 6 servings
60 minutes

Beer Batter Fried Chicken

*Chilli powder is the secret ingredient in this special deep-fried chicken;
the sour cream-spring onion sauce adds cool refreshment.*

1.2 to 1.6 kg	(*2¹/2 to 3¹/2 lb*) chicken, cut into 8 pieces
1 litre	(*1³/4 pt*) water
	Vegetable oil

Batter
150 g	(*5 oz*) plain flour
7 ml	(*1¹/2 tsp*) baking powder
5 ml	(*1 tsp*) salt
30 ml	(*2 tbsp*) chilli powder

5 ml	(*1 tsp*) cumin
2 ml	(*¹/2 tsp*) cayenne pepper
2 ml	(*¹/2 tsp*) pepper
1	egg white
200 ml	(*7 fl oz*) beer

Sauce
50 ml	(*4 tbsp*) chopped spring onions
250 ml	(*8 fl oz*) sour cream

In flameproof casserole combine chicken and water. Cover; cook over med. high heat, stirring occasionally, until water comes to a full boil (20 to 25 min.). Reduce heat to med. Cook for 20 min. Drain; pat dry. In deep-fryer or 3-litre (*5-pt*) saucepan heat 5 cm (*2 in*) of oil to 190 °C (*375 °F*). In medium bowl combine all batter ingredients *except* egg white and beer. In small mixer bowl beat egg white at med. speed until stiff (2 to 3 min.); set aside. Stir beer into flour mixture; fold in egg white. Dip chicken into batter; place in hot oil. Fry until golden brown (2 to 3 min. on each side). Remove from oil; drain on paper towels. Repeat with remaining chicken. In small bowl stir together spring onions and sour cream. Serve sauce with chicken.

4 to 6 servings
1 hour 30 minutes

Country Oven-Fried Chicken

Thyme and rosemary add extra flavour to this easy oven-fried chicken.

75 g	(*3 oz*) butter or margarine, melted
75 ml	(*5 tbsp*) plain flour
3 ml	(*3/4 tsp*) salt
2 ml	(*1/2 tsp*) pepper
1 ml	(*1/4 tsp*) thyme leaves

1 ml	(*1/4 tsp*) rosemary leaves, crushed
1 ml	(*1/4 tsp*) paprika
1.2 to 1.6 kg	(*2 1/2 to 3 1/2 lb*) chicken, cut into 8 pieces

Heat oven to 190 °C (*375 °F*) mark 5. In roasting tin melt butter in oven (4 to 6 min.). Meanwhile, combine remaining ingredients *except* chicken. Dip chicken in melted butter, then coat with flour mixture. In same tin place chicken, skin side down. Bake for 25 to 30 min.; turn chicken over. Continue baking for 30 to 35 min. or until fork tender.

Microwave Directions: Reduce butter to 50 g (*2 oz*). *Eliminate flour.* Increase paprika to 3 ml (*3/4 tsp*). In 30 x 20-cm (*12 x 8-in*) baking dish melt butter on HIGH (50 to 60 sec.). Arrange chicken in dish, placing thickest part to outside edge, turning to coat with butter. In small bowl stir together salt, pepper, thyme, rosemary and paprika. Sprinkle over chicken. Cover; microwave on HIGH, turning dish 1/4 turn twice during last half of time, until fork tender (18 to 25 min.).

---

4 servings
30 minutes

Country Chicken Piccata

Lemons and spring onions give a delicate taste to this elegant chicken dish.

50 ml	(*2 fl oz*) milk
1	egg, slightly beaten
75 ml	(*5 tbsp*) plain flour
75 ml	(*5 tbsp*) crushed cornflakes
1 ml	(*1/4 tsp*) salt
	Pinch of pepper
2	whole boneless chicken breasts, skinned, halved
90 g	(*3 1/2 oz*) butter or margarine

5 ml	(*1 tsp*) crushed fresh garlic
30 ml	(*2 tbsp*) lemon juice
100 g	(*4 oz*) sliced 2.5 cm (*1 in*) spring onions
75 g	(*3 oz*) fresh mushrooms, halved
	Lemon slices
	Fresh parsley

In small bowl combine milk and egg. Combine flour, crushed cornflakes, salt and pepper. Flatten each chicken breast half to about 5-mm (*1/4-in*) thickness by pounding between sheets of waxed paper. Dip chicken into milk mixture, then into flour mixture, turning to coat. In 25-cm (*10-in*) frying pan melt 50 g (*2 oz*) butter. Add garlic and chicken. Cook over med. heat, turning occasionally, until golden brown (5 to 6 min.). Place chicken on serving platter; keep warm. Add remaining butter to drippings in pan. Stir until butter melts; stir in lemon juice. Add spring onions and mushrooms. Continue cooking, stirring occasionally, until heated through (2 to 4 min.). Spoon over chicken. Garnish with lemon slices and parsley.

Country Chicken Piccata

Apple 'n Cabbage Chicken

6 servings
60 minutes

Cabbage, apples and caraway seed blend with chicken for a succulent harvest time meal.

8	rashers of bacon, cut into 2.5-cm (*1-in*) pieces
2	med. onions, chopped
1	celery stick, sliced 1 cm (*1/2 in*)
30 g	(*1 oz*) butter or margarine
8	chicken thighs
75 ml	(*5 tbsp*) apple juice
7 ml	(*1 1/2 tsp*) caraway seed
5 ml	(*1 tsp*) salt
1 ml	(*1/4 tsp*) pepper
1	small head cabbage, cut into eight wedges
2	med. tart red apples, cut into sixths

In flameproof casserole cook bacon over med. high heat until softened (5 to 7 min.). Add onion and celery; continue cooking until vegetables are tender (2 to 3 min.). With slotted spoon remove bacon mixture from casserole; set aside. Add butter to same casserole; heat until sizzling. Place half of chicken in casserole. Continue cooking, stirring occasionally, until chicken is lightly browned (5 to 8 min.). Remove from casserole; set aside. Repeat with remaining chicken. Reduce heat to med.; return chicken and bacon mixture to casserole. Add remaining ingredients *except* cabbage and apples. Place cabbage on top of chicken to steam. Cover; continue cooking, basting occasionally, until chicken is fork tender and cabbage is crisply tender (15 to 20 min.). Top with apples. Cover; continue cooking until apples are crisply tender (10 to 15 min.).

Microwave Directions: In 30 x 20-cm (*12 x 8-in*) baking dish place bacon pieces. Cover; microwave on HIGH until softened (8 to 9 min.). Stir in onions and celery. Cover; microwave on HIGH, stirring after half the time, until vegetables are tender (2 to 3 min.). With slotted spoon remove bacon mixture from dish; set aside. Add butter to same dish; melt butter on HIGH (40 to 50 sec.). Arrange chicken thighs in dish, turning to coat with butter; spoon bacon mixture over chicken. Cover; microwave on HIGH, rearranging chicken pieces after half the time, until chicken is fork tender (8 to 10 min.). Place cabbage on top of chicken. Add remaining ingredients *except* apples. Cover with vented plastic wrap; microwave on HIGH until cabbage is partially cooked (4 min.). Baste cabbage. Place apple pieces over cabbage. Cover; microwave on HIGH, turning dish 1/4 turn after half the time, until cabbage and apples are crisply tender (5 to 6 min.).

Apple 'n Cabbage Chicken

Chicken Breasts & Courgettes With Garlic Cream

Chicken Breasts & Courgettes With Garlic Cream

*The subtle flavour of chicken partners perfectly with courgettes
and a rich cream cheese garlic sauce.*

50 g	(*2 oz*) butter or margarine
3	whole boneless chicken breasts, skinned, halved
3	med. courgettes, sliced 3 mm (*⅛ in*)
75 ml	(*5 tbsp*) sliced 5 mm (*¼ in*) spring onions

Garlic Cream

30 g	(*1 oz*) butter or margarine
2 ml	(*½ tsp*) crushed fresh garlic
45 ml	(*3 tbsp*) plain flour
90 g	(*3 oz*) cream cheese
295 g	(*10.4 oz*) can chicken broth
2 ml	(*½ tsp*) pepper

Cooked rice

In 25-cm (*10-in*) frying pan melt 50 g (*2 oz*) butter until sizzling; add chicken breasts. Cook over med. high heat, turning once, until chicken is browned and fork tender (12 to 15 min.). Add courgettes and onions. Continue cooking, stirring occasionally, until courgettes are crisply tender (5 to 7 min.). Meanwhile, in 2-litre (*3½-pt*) saucepan melt 30 g (*1 oz*) butter until sizzling; add garlic. Cook over med. heat, stirring occasionally, for 1 min. Add flour; continue cooking until smooth and bubbly (1 min.). Add remaining garlic cream ingredients *except* rice. Continue cooking, stirring occasionally, until sauce is thickened (5 to 7 min.). Serve courgettes and chicken over rice; pour sauce over chicken.

Microwave Directions: Increase flour to 50 ml (*4 tbsp*). In 30 x 20-cm (*12 x 8-in*) baking dish melt butter on HIGH (30 to 45 sec.). Place chicken in dish; turn chicken to coat. Cover; microwave on HIGH, rearranging after half the time, until chicken is no longer pink (5 to 8 min.). Add courgettes and onions. Cover; microwave on HIGH until courgettes are crisply tender (5 to 6 min.). With slotted spoon remove chicken and vegetables to serving plate; keep warm. Stir 30 g (*1 oz*) butter, garlic, 50 ml (*4 tbsp*) flour, cream cheese, chicken broth and pepper into dish juices. Microwave on HIGH, stirring every 2 min., until sauce is thickened (4 to 6 min.). Serve courgettes and chicken over rice; pour sauce over chicken.

Corn on the Cob n' Chicken Dinner

Chosen for the cover photo, this colourful one-dish meal is finger-licking good.

45 g	(*1½ oz*) butter or margarine
1.4 kg	(*3 lb*) chicken legs
10 ml	(*2 tsp*) crushed fresh garlic
50 ml	(*2 fl oz*) water
3	ears fresh or frozen corn on the cob, husked, cut into thirds

5 ml	(*1 tsp*) tarragon leaves
2 ml	(*½ tsp*) salt
1 ml	(*¼ tsp*) pepper
2	med. courgettes, cut into 5-cm (*2-in*) pieces
2	med. ripe tomatoes, cut into 2.5-cm (*1-in*) pieces

In flameproof casserole melt butter; add chicken and garlic. Cook over high heat, stirring occasionally, until chicken is golden brown (10 to 15 min.). Reduce heat to med. Add remaining ingredients *except* cour- gettes and tomatoes. Cover; cook until chicken is fork tender (20 to 25 min.). Place courgettes on top of chicken and corn mixture. Cover; steam 3 to 6 min. Add tomatoes. Cover; let stand 5 min.

Cornish Hens With Herb-Buttered Vegetables

4 servings
2 hours

Garden vegetables make these oven-baked Cornish hens extra special.

4	Cornish game hens	5 ml	(*1 tsp*) salt
8	small carrots	2 ml	(*1/2 tsp*) sage leaves, crushed
8	small patty pan squash*	1 ml	(*1/4 tsp*) pepper
8	small new red potatoes	10 ml	(*2 tsp*) crushed fresh garlic
75 g	(*3 oz*) butter or margarine, melted		

Heat oven to 190 °C (*375 °F*) mark 5. Place hens, breast side up, on rack in large roasting tin. Arrange carrots, squash and potatoes around hens. In small bowl stir together remaining ingredients. Spoon over hens and vegetables. Cover; bake, basting occasionally, for 1 hr. Remove cover; continue baking for 30 to 45 min. or until hens are fork tender.

*Yellow summer squash or courgettes can be substituted for patty pan squash; add during last half hour of baking time.

Apricot-Glazed Cornish Hens

4 servings
2 hours 15 minutes

Apricots and marjoram add spark to these stuffed Cornish hens.

Stuffing

50 g	(*2 oz*) dried bread cubes
1	celery stick, sliced 5 mm (*1/4 in*)
50 ml	(*4 tbsp*) chopped onion
2 ml	(*1/2 tsp*) salt
1 ml	(*1/4 tsp*) pepper
1 ml	(*1/4 tsp*) marjoram leaves
175 g	(*6 oz*) apricot preserves
50 g	(*2 oz*) butter or margarine
30 to 45 ml	(*2 to 3 tbsp*) white wine or chicken broth

4	Cornish game hens

Sauce

175 g	(*6 oz*) apricot preserves
125 g	(*4 oz*) butter or margarine
2 ml	(*1/2 tsp*) marjoram leaves

Heat oven to 190 °C (*375 °F*) mark 5. In medium bowl stir together all stuffing ingredients *except* preserves, butter and wine. In 1-litre (*1¾-pt*) saucepan melt 175 g (*6 oz*) apricot preserves and 50 g (*2 oz*) butter. Stir into stuffing; add 30 to 45 ml (*2 to 3 tbsp*) wine to moisten stuffing. Stuff hens with stuffing; secure opening with wooden picks. Tuck under wings of hens. Place hens, breast side up, in roasting tin.

Bake for 1 hr. Meanwhile, in same saucepan combine all sauce ingredients. Cook over med. heat, stirring occasionally, until melted (2 to 3 min.). Brush hens with half of sauce. Continue baking, uncovered, for 40 to 50 min. or until hens are fork tender. Loosely cover with aluminum foil if browning too quickly. Serve with remaining sauce.

Apricot-Glazed Cornish Hens

6 to 8 servings
3 hours

Turkey Breast With Sausage-Raisin Stuffing

Sausage, combined with raisins and pecans, delights the senses when roasted with turkey.

350 g	(*12 oz*) pork sausage		1	med. onion, chopped
50 g	(*2 oz*) dried bread cubes		2 ml	(*1/2 tsp*) salt
2	celery sticks, sliced 1 cm (*1/2 in*)		1 ml	(*1/4 tsp*) sage leaves, crushed
120 g	(*4 oz*) pecan halves			Pinch of pepper
90 g	(*3 oz*) raisins			
50 g	(*2 oz*) butter or margarine, melted		2.3 to 3.2 kg	(*5 to 7 lb*) bone-in turkey breast
75 ml	(*5 tbsp*) chicken broth		45 g	(*1 1/2 oz*) butter or margarine, melted

Heat oven to 180 °C (*350 °F*) mark 4. In 25-cm (*10-in*) frying pan brown sausage over med. heat; drain off fat. In large bowl stir together browned sausage and remaining ingredients *except* turkey breast and 50 g (*2 oz*) butter. Gently loosen skin from turkey in neck area to make a large area to stuff. Stuff with sausage mixture; secure skin flap with wooden picks. Place remaining sausage mixture in 1-litre (*1 3/4-pt*) covered casserole; refrigerate. During last 30 min. of turkey breast baking time, bake remaining stuffing for 25 to 30 min. or until heated through. Place stuffed turkey breast, breast side up, on rack in roasting tin. Brush with melted 45 g (*1 1/2 oz*) butter. Bake, basting occasionally, for 2 to 2 1/2 hr. or until meat thermometer reaches 77 ° to 80 °C (*170 ° to 175 °F*) and turkey breast is fork tender. Let stand 10 min.

Microwave Directions: *Reduce 50 g (2 oz) butter to 45 g (1 1/2 oz).* In 2-litre (*3 1/2-pt*) casserole microwave sausage on HIGH, stirring twice during last half of time, until sausage is cooked through (4 1/2 to 5 min.). Stir in remaining ingredients *except* turkey breast and 45 g (*1 1/2 oz*) butter. Stuff as directed left. Place remaining sausage mixture in same 2-litre (*3 1/2-pt*) covered casserole; refrigerate. Place turkey breast, breast side down, in 30 x 20-cm (*12 x 8-in*) baking dish. Brush with melted 45 g (*1 1/2 oz*) butter. *Sprinkle with paprika.* Cover with vented plastic wrap; microwave on HIGH 10 min. Reduce power to MEDIUM (50% power); microwave, turning dish 1/4 turn after half the time, 25 min. Turn turkey breast, breast side up. Baste. *Sprinkle with paprika.* Cover; microwave on MEDIUM (50% power), turning dish 1/4 turn after half the time, until meat thermometer reaches 77 ° to 80 °C (*170 ° to 175 °F*) and turkey breast is fork tender (22 to 25 min.). Place turkey breast on serving platter. Tent with aluminum foil; let stand 5 to 10 min. Meanwhile, microwave remaining stuffing on HIGH, stirring after half the time, until heated through (5 1/2 to 6 1/2 min.).

To Stuff Turkey Breast:

1. Gently loosen skin from turkey in neck area to make a large area to stuff.

2. Stuff with sausage mixture; secure skin flap with wooden picks.

Turkey Breast With Sausage-Raisin Stuffing

Hearty Cheese, Turkey & Courgettes Supper

4 servings
30 minutes

Hearty Cheese, Turkey & Courgettes Supper

Rich Cheddar cheese sauce smothers turkey and courgettes served over English muffins.

Cheese Sauce

30 g	(*1 oz*) butter or margarine
15 ml	(*1 tbsp*) plain flour
1 ml	(*1/4 tsp*) salt
1 ml	(*1/4 tsp*) dry mustard
1 ml	(*1/4 tsp*) pepper
250 ml	(*8 fl oz*) milk
100 g	(*4 oz*) shredded Cheddar cheese

15 ml	(*1 tbsp*) chopped fresh chives
30 g	(*1 oz*) butter or margarine
1	med. courgette, sliced 5 mm (*1/4 in*)
5 ml	(*1 tsp*) basil leaves
4	English muffins, split, toasted
8	(30-g) (*1-oz*) slices cooked turkey

In 2-litre (*3 1/2-pt*) saucepan melt 30 g (*1 oz*) butter; stir in flour, salt, mustard and pepper. Cook over low heat, stirring constantly, until smooth and bubbly (1 min.). Add milk. Continue cooking over low heat, stirring constantly, until mixture thickens and comes to a full boil (4 to 5 min.). Boil 1 min. Remove from heat. Stir in cheese and chives until cheese is melted; keep warm. In 25-cm (*10-in*) frying pan melt 30 g (*1 oz*) butter; stir in courgette and basil. Cook over med. high heat, stirring occasionally, until crisply tender (3 to 5 min.). Place toasted English muffin halves on serving plate; top each half with 1 slice turkey, 1/8 courgette mixture and cheese sauce.

4 servings
30 minutes

Baked Broccoli & Turkey With Cheddar Sauce

Cheese sauce with a splash of lemon brings out extra flavour in this easy-to-prepare casserole.

8	(30-g) (*1-oz*) slices cooked turkey breast
225 g	(*8 oz*) individually frozen broccoli spears
1/2	med. red onion, sliced 3 mm (*1/8 in*)
45 g	(*1 1/2 oz*) butter or margarine
30 ml	(*2 tbsp*) plain flour

250 ml	(*8 fl oz*) single cream or milk
2 ml	(*1/2 tsp*) salt
1 ml	(*1/4 tsp*) pepper
5 ml	(*1 tsp*) lemon juice
100 g	(*4 oz*) shredded Cheddar cheese

Heat oven to 180 °C (*350 °F*) mark 4. Place turkey on bottom of greased 23-cm (*9-in*) sq. baking dish; top with broccoli and onion. Set aside. In 2-litre (*3 1/2-pt*) saucepan melt butter over med. heat; stir in flour until smooth and bubbly (1 min.). Stir in remaining ingredients *except* cheese. Continue cooking, stirring occasionally, until thickened (2 to 3 min.). Remove from heat; stir in cheese until melted. Pour over broccoli and onion. Bake for 15 to 20 min. or until heated through.

Microwave Directions: Place turkey on bottom of greased 23-cm (*9-in*) round baking dish; top with broccoli and onion. Cover with plastic wrap; microwave on HIGH until heated through (4 to 6 min.). Drain off excess moisture; set aside. In medium bowl melt butter on HIGH (50 to 60 sec.). Stir in flour. Microwave on HIGH until bubbly (45 to 60 sec.). Stir in remaining ingredients *except* cheese. Microwave on HIGH, stirring after half the time, until thickened (2 to 3 min.). Stir in cheese until melted. Pour over broccoli and onion. Cover with plastic wrap; microwave on HIGH until heated through (2 to 3 min.).

Spinach-Stuffed Turkey Breast

6 servings
2 hours 30 minutes

Spinach and bacon stuffing flavour this delightful grilled turkey.

Stuffing

30 g	(*1 oz*) dried bread cubes
2	celery sticks, sliced 1 cm (*1/2 in*)
75 g	(*3 oz*) butter or margarine, melted
50 ml	(*2 fl oz*) white wine or chicken broth
275 g	(*10 oz*) frozen chopped spinach, thawed, drained

6	rashers of crisply cooked bacon, cut into 2.5-cm (*1-in*) pieces
1	med. onion, chopped
2 ml	(*1/2 tsp*) salt
1 ml	(*1/4 tsp*) cracked pepper
2.3 to 3.2 kg	(*5 to 7 lb*) bone-in turkey breast
30 ml	(*2 tbsp*) butter or margarine, softened

Prepare grill placing coals to one side; heat until coals are ash white. Make aluminum foil drip pan; place opposite coals. In large bowl stir together all stuffing ingredients. Turn turkey, breast side down. To make a large area to stuff, gently loosen skin from meat in neck cavity. Stuff with stuffing. (Extra stuffing may be placed in aluminum foil pan, covered and heated during last 30 min. of grilling.) Secure skin over stuffing with wooden picks. Lightly rub turkey breast with butter. Place on barbecue grid over drip pan. Grill 1 1/2 to 2 hr. or until meat thermometer reaches 82 ° to 85 °C (*180 ° to 185 °F*) and turkey is fork tender.

Turkey Legs With Barbecue Sauce

6 servings
2 hours 30 minutes

*A spicy, chunky tomato sauce adds special flavour
to these hearty turkey legs.*

6	(335 to 450-g) (*3/4 to 1-lb*) turkey legs
1 to 1.5 litres	(*1 3/4 to 2 1/4 pt*) water

Sauce

50 ml	(*4 tbsp*) firmly packed brown sugar
1	med. ripe tomato, cubed 1 cm (*1/2 in*)
1	med. chopped onion

50 ml	(*4 tbsp*) country-style Dijon mustard
50 ml	(*2 fl oz*) red wine vinegar or cider vinegar
50 ml	(*2 fl oz*) tomato juice
150 g	(*5 oz*) canned tomato purée
2 ml	(*1/2 tsp*) salt
1 ml	(*1/4 tsp*) cracked pepper
15 ml	(*1 tbsp*) crushed fresh garlic

In flameproof casserole combine turkey legs and water. Cover; cook over med. heat, stirring occasionally, until turkey legs are just fork tender (40 to 60 min.). Drain; pat dry. Prepare grill placing coals to one side; heat until coals are ash white. Make aluminum foil drip pan; place opposite coals. Place turkey legs on barbecue grid over drip pan. Grill, turning occasionally, until fork tender and heated through (40 to 50 min.). Meanwhile, in 2-litre (*3 1/2-pt*) saucepan stir together all sauce ingredients. Cook over low heat, stirring occasionally, until heated through (10 to 15 min.). Baste turkey legs with sauce during last 15 min. Serve with remaining warm sauce.

Spinach-Stuffed Turkey Breast

Grilled Turkey & Vegetable Kabobs

6 servings
3 hours 45 minutes

Grilled Turkey & Vegetable Kabobs

A homemade teriyaki sauce adds flavour to these 'grilled to perfection' kabobs.

Marinade

75 ml	*(5 tbsp)*	lemon juice
50 ml	*(2 fl oz)*	soy sauce
50 ml	*(2 fl oz)*	vegetable oil
30 ml	*(2 tbsp)*	firmly packed brown sugar
2 ml	*(1/2 tsp)*	ginger
1 ml	*(1/4 tsp)*	pepper
45 ml	*(3 tbsp)*	catsup
5 ml	*(1 tsp)*	crushed fresh garlic

Kabobs

675 g	*(1 1/2 lb)*	fresh turkey breast, skinned, boned, cut into 3.5 x 2.5-cm *(1 1/2 x 1-in)* pieces
12		med. fresh mushrooms
2		med. red onions, each cut into 6 wedges
1		green pepper, cut into 12 pieces
12		cherry tomatoes
6		*(30-cm) (12-in)* metal skewers

In medium bowl combine all marinade ingredients. Stir in turkey pieces. Cover; refrigerate, stirring occasionally, 3 to 4 hr. Drain; *reserve marinade.* Prepare grill placing coals to one side; heat until coals are ash white. Make aluminum foil drip pan; place opposite coals. To assemble kabobs on metal skewers, alternate turkey pieces, mushrooms, onions, green pepper and cherry tomatoes. Brush kabobs with marinade. Place kabobs on barbecue grid over drip pan. Grill, turning and basting occasionally, until turkey is fork tender (15 to 20 min.).

3 hours

Turkey on the Grill

Juicy, tender turkey, cooked outdoors, is the center of a perfect summer meal.

Kettle or Covered Grill

Thaw and prepare 4.5 to 5.4 kg *(10 to 12 lb)* turkey for roasting as directed on pkg.; do not stuff. Season cavity with salt and brush skin with melted butter or margarine. Prepare grill placing coals to one side; heat until coals are ash white. Make aluminum foil drip pan; place opposite coals. Place top grilling rack over coals and drip pan. Place prepared turkey on grill over drip pan. Open bottom vents directly under coals. Cover grill, positioning top vent directly over side of grill with turkey. Adjust vent as necessary to keep a consistently hot fire. Add coals to fire as necessary. Grill turkey 11 to 20 min. per 450 g *(lb)*, turning half way through the time. Turkey is done when thermometer inserted in thigh muscle reaches 82 ° to 85 °C *(180 ° to 185 °F)*.

Gas Grill

Thaw and prepare 4.5 to 5.4 kg *(10 to 12 lb)* turkey for roasting as directed on pkg.; do not stuff. Season cavity with salt and brush skin with melted butter or margarine. If dual control gas grill is used, make aluminum foil drip pan; place over coals on one side of grill, then heat other side 10 to 15 min. on high. If single control gas grill is used, make aluminum foil drip pan and remove top rack; place over one half of coals to block out direct heat, then heat grill 10 to 15 min. on high. Reduce heat to med. Replace top rack; place turkey on rack directly above drip pan. Grill turkey on med. heat 11 to 20 min. per 450 g *(lb)*, turning half way through the time. Turkey is done when thermometer inserted in thigh muscle reaches 82 ° to 85 °C *(180 ° to 185 °F)*.

Roasted Turkey

The perfect oven-roasted turkey!

To Prepare:

1. Thaw turkey in original plastic wrapper according to chart below.

2. Remove turkey from plastic bag. Remove neck and giblets from cavities.

3. Rinse turkey thoroughly in cold water and drain well.

4. Stuff neck and body cavities lightly (about 100 g / *4 oz* of stuffing per 450 g /*lb* of turkey).

5. Fold neck skin to back of bird and secure. Fold wing tips under back or tie to body. Tuck tail into body cavity. Tie legs together.

6. If using a standard meat thermometer, insert into thigh muscle next to body, not touching bone. Turkey is done when meat thermometer reaches 82 ° to 85 °C (*180 ° to 185 °F*).

Approximate Thawing Times

Weight	In Cold Water*	In Refrigerator
4.5 to 6.5 kg (*10 - 14 lb*)	5 - 6 hours	2 - 3 days
6.5 to 8 kg (*14 - 18 lb*)	6 - 7 hours	2 - 3 days
8 to 10 kg (*18 - 22 lb*)	7 - 8 hours	3 - 4 days

*Change water frequently to keep cold.

Keep thawed turkey refrigerated. Do not stuff until ready to roast. Roast within 24 hours after thawing. Refreezing is not recommended.

To Roast:

1. Place turkey, breast up, in shallow tin and brush with melted butter.

2. Roast turkey in 160 °C (*325 °F*) mark 3 oven according to chart below. If roasting turkey unstuffed, subtract 3 minutes per 450 g (*lb*).

3. Giblets, *except* liver, may be simmered in salted water for 2 to 2½ hours; add liver for last half hour. Use cooked, chopped giblets in gravy or dressing.

Approximate Roasting Times

Weight	160 °C (*325 °F*) mark 3 Oven In Shallow Open Pan	160 °C (*325 °F*) mark 3 Oven In Loose Foil Tent
4.5 to 6.5 kg (*10 - 14 lb*)	3 - 4½ hours	3½ - 5 hours
6.5 to 8 kg (*14 - 18 lb*)	4 - 5 hours	4½ - 5½ hours
8 to 10 kg (*18 - 22 lb*)	4½ - 6 hours	5 - 6½ hours

Roasting time will be shorter or longer than indicated on the chart if the turkey is warmer or colder than refrigerator temperature.

Roasted Turkey

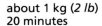

Spiced Fruit & Bread Stuffing

about 1 kg (*2 lb*)
20 minutes

Dried fruit adds new flavour to homemade stuffing.

125 g	(*4 oz*) dried bread cubes		2	med. onions, chopped
4	celery sticks, sliced 1 cm (*1/2 in*)		5 ml	(*1 tsp*) salt
125 g	(*4 oz*) butter or margarine, melted		1 ml	(*1/4 tsp*) pepper
125 ml	(*4 fl oz*) sherry or chicken broth		1 ml	(*1/4 tsp*) ground cloves
230 g	(*8 oz*) whole, mixed dried fruit, cut in half		1 ml	(*1/4 tsp*) ginger

In large bowl stir together all ingredients. Use to stuff 5.4 to 6.5 kg (*12 to 14 lb*) turkey.

Tip: Prepare half of recipe to stuff 1.8 to 2.3 kg (*4 to 5 lb*) roasting chicken, duck or goose.

Bread Sage Stuffing

about 1 kg (*2 lb*)
20 minutes

Traditional old-fashioned sage stuffing with ideas for new variations.

125 g	(*4 oz*) dried bread cubes		2	med. onions, chopped
4	celery sticks, sliced 1 cm (*1/2 in*)		15 ml	(*1 tbsp*) sage leaves, crushed
125 g	(*4 oz*) butter or margarine, melted		5 ml	(*1 tsp*) salt
125 ml	(*4 fl oz*) chicken broth			Pinch of pepper

In large bowl stir together all ingredients. Use to stuff 5.4 to 6.5 kg (*12 to 14 lb*) turkey.

Tip: Prepare half of recipe to stuff 1.8 to 2.3 kg (*4 to 5 lb*) roasting chicken, duck or goose.

Variations:

Oyster Stuffing — Add 525 g (*18 oz*) rinsed, drained oysters. Reduce salt to 2 ml (*1/2 tsp*).

Raisin-Nut Stuffing — Add 125 g (*4 oz*) whole pecans or walnuts and 175 g (*6 oz*) raisins.

Bread Sage Stuffing (top)
Spiced Fruit & Bread Stuffing (bottom)

Bacon Rice Stuffing

about 1 kg (*2 lb*)
30 minutes

Bacon Rice Stuffing

A moist rice stuffing with a smoky bacon flavour which makes your chicken,
duck or goose just a little more special.

800 g	(*1¾ lb*) cooked long grain rice*	1	med. onion, chopped
4	celery sticks, sliced 1 cm (*½ in*)	450 g	(*1 lb*) crisply cooked bacon, cut into
50 ml	(*4 tbsp*) chopped fresh parsley		2.5-cm (*1-in*) pieces
75 g	(*3 oz*) butter or margarine, melted	1 ml	(*¼ tsp*) salt
50 ml	(*2 fl oz*) white wine or chicken broth	1 ml	(*¼ tsp*) pepper

In large bowl stir together all ingredients. Use to stuff 5.4 to 6.5 kg (*12 to 14 lb*) turkey.

*Cooked wild rice can be substituted for all or part of long grain rice.

Tip: Prepare half of recipe to stuff 1.8 to 2.3 kg (*4 to 5 lb*) roasting chicken, duck or goose.

about 1 kg (*2 lb*)
30 minutes

Cornbread Stuffing

Cornbread and bacon are mixed for a one-of-a-kind country-style stuffing.

600 g	(*1½ lb*) crumbled cornbread*	1	med. onion, chopped
4	celery sticks, sliced 1 cm (*½ in*)	5 ml	(*1 tsp*) salt
50 g	(*2 oz*) butter or margarine, melted	1 ml	(*¼ tsp*) pepper
50 ml	(*2 fl oz*) chicken broth	45 ml	(*3 tbsp*) *reserved bacon drippings*
8	rashers of crisply cooked bacon, crumbled, *reserve drippings*		

In large bowl stir together all ingredients. Use to stuff 5.4 to 6.5 kg (*12 to 14 lb*) turkey.

*23-cm (*9-in*) sq. baking dish of cornbread will make 600 g (*1½ lb*) crumbled cornbread.

Tip: Prepare half of recipe to stuff 1.8 to 2.3 kg (*4 to 5 lb*) roasting chicken, duck or goose.

Creamy Mustard 'n Green Onion Sauce

500 ml (*17 fl oz*)
20 minutes

This creamy, smooth and tangy sauce livens up chicken.

45 g	(*1½ oz*) butter or margarine
30 ml	(*2 tbsp*) plain flour
75 ml	(*5 tbsp*) chopped spring onions
200 ml	(*7 fl oz*) chicken broth

1 ml	(*¼ tsp*) salt
	Pinch of pepper
15 ml	(*1 tbsp*) country-style Dijon mustard
250 ml	(*8 fl oz*) plain yogurt

In 2-litre (*1¾-pt*) saucepan melt butter over med. high heat. Stir in flour; continue cooking until bubbly (1 min.). Reduce heat to med. Stir in remaining ingredients *except* yogurt. Continue cooking, stirring occasionally, until sauce thickens (3 to 5 min.). Stir in yogurt. Continue cooking, stirring occasionally, until heated through (3 to 5 min.).

Microwave Directions: In small bowl melt butter on HIGH (40 to 50 sec.). Stir in remaining ingredients *except* yogurt. Microwave on HIGH, stirring twice during last half of time, until sauce thickens (2 to 2½ min.). Beat yogurt with wire whisk; stir into sauce mixture. Microwave on HIGH, stirring every 30 sec., until heated through (1¼ to 1½ min.).

Sour Cream White Wine Sauce

375 ml (*13 fl oz*)
15 minutes

An easy sauce to quickly dress up baked chicken breasts.

45 g	(*1½ oz*) butter or margarine
15 ml	(*1 tbsp*) crushed fresh garlic
30 ml	(*2 tbsp*) plain flour
50 ml	(*4 tbsp*) chopped fresh parsley
125 ml	(*4 fl oz*) chicken broth

50 ml	(*2 fl oz*) white wine
1 ml	(*¼ tsp*) salt
	Pinch of pepper
250 ml	(*8 fl oz*) sour cream

In 2-litre (*1¾-pt*) saucepan melt butter until sizzling; stir in garlic. Cook over med. high heat 1 min. Stir in flour; continue cooking until bubbly (1 min.). Reduce heat to med. Stir in remaining ingredients *except* sour cream. Cook, stirring occasionally, until sauce thickens (1 to 2 min.). Stir in sour cream. Continue cooking, stirring occasionally, until heated through (3 to 5 min.).

Microwave Directions: In small bowl melt butter on HIGH (40 to 50 sec.). Stir in garlic and flour. Microwave on HIGH 1 min. Stir in remaining ingredients *except* sour cream. Microwave on HIGH, stirring twice during last half of time, until sauce thickens (2 to 2½ min.). Stir in sour cream. Microwave on MEDIUM (50% power), stirring every min., until heated through (4 to 5 min.).

Creamy Mustard 'n Green Onion Sauce

Herb Wine Marinade

200 ml (*7 fl oz*)
60 minutes

Tarragon, rosemary and thyme are the flavourful herbs in this marinade.

175 ml	(*6 fl oz*) white wine
5 ml	(*1 tsp*) tarragon leaves
1 ml	(*1/4 tsp*) rosemary leaves, crushed
1 ml	(*1/4 tsp*) thyme leaves
30 ml	(*2 tbsp*) vegetable oil
15 ml	(*1 tbsp*) crushed fresh garlic

In medium bowl combine all marinade ingredients. Use to marinate 1 to 1.4 kg (2½ to 3 lb) of chicken pieces. Cook as desired, basting occasionally with marinade.

Tip: If desired, use to marinate 900 g to 1.4 kg (*2 to 3 lb*) of beef or pork.

Lemon Parsley Marinade

300 ml (*½ pt*)
60 minutes

This marinade brings a refreshing, light lemon flavour to chicken.

50 ml	(*4 tbsp*) chopped fresh parsley
125 ml	(*4 fl oz*) chicken broth
125 ml	(*4 fl oz*) lemon juice
4	slices lemon, halved
1 ml	(*1/4 tsp*) pepper
45 ml	(*3 tbsp*) vegetable oil

In medium bowl combine all marinade ingredients. Use to marinate 1 to 1.4 kg (2½ to 3 lb) of chicken pieces. Cook as desired, basting occasionally with marinade.

Lemon Parsley Marinade (top)
Herb Wine Marinade (bottom)

Brown Turkey Gravy

Brown Turkey Gravy

750 ml (*1¼ pt*)
15 minutes

This gravy method works for chicken, beef or pork gravy too.

	Chicken broth or water		Salt
125 ml	(*4 fl oz*) water		Cracked pepper
50 ml	(*4 tbsp*) plain flour		

Deglaze tin by stirring 50 ml (*2 fl oz*) water into tin with drippings. Heat, stirring and scraping tin, 2 to 3 min. Strain tin juices into 1-litre (*1¾-pt*) measure; remove excess fat, *reserving 45 ml* (3 tbsp) *fat*. Add enough chicken broth or water to equal 750 ml (*1¼ pt*) liquid. In 3-litre (*5-pt*) saucepan combine 750 ml (*1¼ pt*) tin juice mixture and 45 ml (*3 tbsp*) reserved fat; cook over med. heat until mixture comes to a full boil (3 to 5 min.). Meanwhile, in jar with lid combine 125 ml (*4 fl oz*) water and flour; shake well to mix. Slowly stir into hot tin juice mixture. Continue cooking, stirring constantly, until mixture comes to a full boil; boil 1 min. Season to taste.

Microwave Directions: Deglaze casserole as directed left. Strain casserole juices into 2-litre (*3½-pt*) measure; remove excess fat, *reserving 45 ml* (3 tbsp) *fat*. Add enough chicken broth or water to equal 750 ml (*1¼ pt*) liquid; add reserved 45 ml (*3 tbsp*) fat. Microwave on HIGH until mixture comes to a full boil (3 to 5 min.). Meanwhile, in jar with lid combine 125 ml (*4 fl oz*) water and flour; shake well to mix. Slowly stir into hot casserole juice mixture. Microwave on HIGH, stirring twice during time, until mixture comes to a full boil (3½ to 4½ min.). Season to taste.

Grandma's Cream Gravy

500 ml (*17 fl oz*)
15 minutes

Smooth creamy gravy, just like Grandma makes.

	Milk
45 ml	(*3 tbsp*) plain flour
	Salt
	Cracked pepper

Deglaze tin by stirring 50 ml (*2 fl oz*) water into tin with drippings. Heat, stirring and scraping tin, 2 to 3 min. Strain tin juices into 500-ml (*17-fl oz*) measure; remove excess fat, *reserving 30 ml* (2 tbsp) *fat*. Add enough milk to equal 500 ml (*17 fl oz*) liquid; set aside. In 2-litre (*3½-pt*) saucepan cook reserved 30 ml (*2 tbsp*) fat over med. heat until bubbly (1 to 1½ min.). Stir in flour. Continue cooking, stirring constantly, for 1 min. Stir in tin juice mixture. Continue cooking, stirring constantly, until thickened (3 to 5 min.). Season to taste.

Microwave Directions: Deglaze casserole as directed left. Strain casserole juices into 500-ml (*17-fl oz*) measure; remove excess fat, *reserving 30 ml* (2 tbsp) *fat*. Add enough milk to equal 500 ml (*17 fl oz*) liquid; set aside. In 1-litre (*1¾-pt*) glass measure combine reserved 30 ml (*2 tbsp*) fat and flour. Microwave on HIGH until bubbly (1 to 1½ min.). Stir in casserole juice mixture. Microwave on HIGH, stirring twice during last half of time, until thickened (3½ to 4½ min.). Season to taste.

How To:
Buy, Store & Thaw Poultry

TO BUY: Poultry is popular today, not only because it is nutritious and low in fat, but also because of its delicate flavour that blends well with herbs and spices. In addition, it is an economical buy at the super-market.

When purchasing poultry, look for a plump-bodied, blemish-free, smooth-skinned bird.

Chickens: Allow about 225 g (*1/2 lb*) chicken per serving. Whole chickens are usually the best buy — the bigger the bird, the more meat in proportion to bone. Chicken can also be purchased in a variety of cuts. Some of the different types and cuts of chicken you will find are:

Whole Roasting Chickens (A) are larger and older birds. They weigh between 1.5 to 2.3 kg (*3 1/2 to 5 lb*) and are excellent for stuffing and roasting.

Broilers — Fryers (B) are the most common type of chicken. The birds are young and weigh between 900 g to 1.5 kg (*2 to 3 1/2 lb*).

Cornish Game Hens (C) are the smallest and youngest of the chicken family, weighing about 450 to 675 g (*1 to 1 1/2 lb*). They are usually found in the grocer's freezer case.

Quartered Chickens (D) are cut into four pieces with wing attached to breast and leg attached to thigh.

Chicken Pieces consist of a whole chicken cut into eight pieces — two legs, two thighs, two wings and the breast split into two pieces. Sometimes the back and giblets are included.

Chicken Breasts (E) can be purchased whole, with or without ribs attached; split, with or without the ribs; or boneless.

Chicken Thighs, Legs and Wings (F) come in a variety of package sizes and should be purchased according to number of servings needed.

Turkeys: Allow about 225 to 350 g (*1/2 to 3/4 lb*) turkey per serving. The best buy in yield of meat per 450 g (*lb*) is in the 7 to 10-kg (*16 to 24-lb*) range. Turkey can also be purchased in a variety of cuts.

Whole Roasting Turkeys (A) weigh between 4.5 and 12 kg (*10 and 26 lb*) and are excellent for stuffing and roasting.

Turkey Breasts (B) can be whole or cut in half, with or without bones attached.

Turkey Legs and Wings (C) come in a variety of package sizes and should be purchased according to number of servings needed.

TO STORE: Proper storage of poultry is essential to maintain flavour and quality. Poultry may be kept safely in the refrigerator for up to two days and in the freezer for six months. Wash poultry in cold water, pat dry and wrap in plastic wrap or aluminum foil for refrigeration. If stored in freezer, wash in cold water, pat dry and wrap in freezer paper, aluminum foil or plastic freezer bags. The freezer temperature should be -18 °C (*0 °F*) or less.

TO THAW FROZEN POULTRY: The safest way to thaw poultry is in the refrigerator. Thawing a whole 1.8-kg (*4-lb*) bird takes 12 to 16 hours. Thawing a cut-up chicken takes 4 to 9 hours. If desired, poultry can be thawed in cold water. In large bowl, cover poultry with cold water; *change water frequently to keep water cold.*

Microwave Thawing Chart for Poultry

Poultry	Defrost or Low (30%) Power
Boneless Chicken Breasts	9 to 13 min./450 g (*lb*)
Chicken Pieces	4 to 8 min./450 g (*lb*)
Chicken Quarters	5 to 9 min./450 g (*lb*)
Cornish Game Hens	8 to 11 min./450 g (*lb*)
Duckling	7 to 10 min./450 g (*lb*)
Turkey Pieces	7 to 9 min./450 g (*lb*)
Turkey Halves	5 to 8 min./450 g (*lb*)
Whole Chickens	5 to 9 min./450 g (*lb*)

Rearrange poultry frequently during thawing time.

How To: Joint & Bone Chicken

To Joint a Whole Chicken:

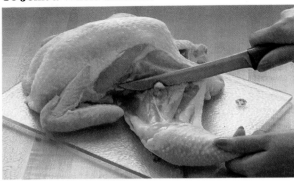

1. Pull leg away from body of chicken to find joint that connects thigh to backbone. With sharp knife, cut leg and thigh from body by cutting through joint.

2. To separate thigh and leg, bend to find joint. Cut through joint to separate.

3. Pull wing away from body of chicken to find joint that connects wing to body. Cut wing from body by cutting through joint, rolling knife to let blade follow through at the curve of the joint.

4. Stand bird upright on neck end. Cut along each side of the backbone through the rib joints to separate backbone.

5. Hold breast, skin side down and neck end at top. Cut through cartilage at V of neck. Bend back both sides to pull and pop out the bone and cartilage. Pull out bone and cartilage.

6. Cut breast into halves.

To Bone Chicken Breast:

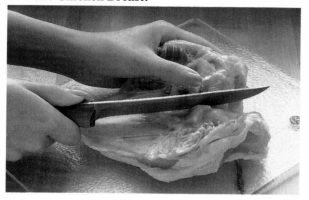

1. Place whole chicken breast, skin side down, on cutting surface. With sharp knife, cut through white gristle at the end of the bone at the center of the breast.

2. Bend breast halves back to pop out bone. Loosen and remove bone.

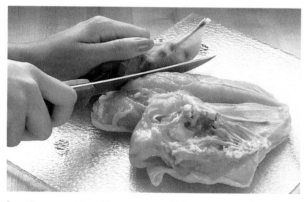

3. On one side of breast, cut rib bones away from breast. While cutting, gently pull the meat away from the rib bones. Cut through shoulder joint to remove entire rib cage. Repeat on other side.

4. Turn breast over and cut away wishbone. With knife, loosen and pull out white tendons.

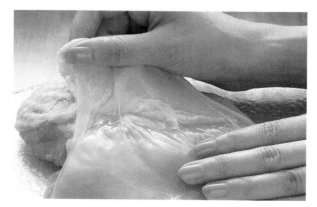

5. If desired, remove skin by pulling skin away from meat.

M

How To: Coat & Stuff Poultry

To Coat Chicken Pieces:

One method of coating chicken pieces is to combine all the dry coating ingredients in a plastic food bag and the wet ingredients in a pie plate. Dip the chicken into the wet ingredients and then place one to two pieces into the plastic food bag, shaking to coat.

Another method is to use two pie plates, one for dry ingredients and one for wet ingredients. Dip chicken pieces into wet ingredients and then roll in dry ingredients to coat.

To Stuff Poultry:

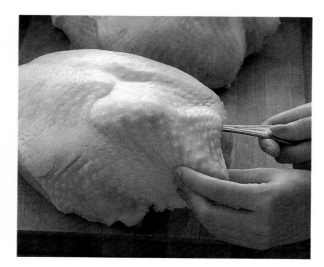

Neck and body cavities and the area underneath the breast skin can all be stuffed. Stuff cavities lightly, leaving space for stuffing to expand. Use about 100 g (*4 oz*) stuffing per 450 g (*lb*) of poultry. Spoon stuffing into cavities, filling about ¾ full.

Tip: When stuffing poultry, be sure stuffing mixture is cool. Always stuff the bird *just before baking*;

To stuff under breast skin, loosen skin with a spoon and fill out area between skin and breast with stuffing.

never stuff it the night before to avoid an increased chance of bacterial growth.

How To: Carve Poultry

1.   Separate Leg: To remove entire leg — drumstick and thigh — hold drumstick firmly with fingers and pull away from body. At the same time, cut through skin between leg and body. With skin cut, entire leg will pull freely from body.

2.   Remove Leg: Press leg away from body. The joint connecting leg to backbone will often snap free or may be severed easily with knife point. Cut dark meat completely from body by following body contour carefully with knife.

3.   Slicing Dark Meat: Place leg on separate plate and cut through connecting joint. Both pieces may be individually sliced. Hold drumstick with napkin and tilt to convenient angle, slice toward plate.

4.   Slicing Thigh: To slice thigh meat, hold firmly on plate with fork. Cut even slices parallel to the bone. Dark meat slices may be arranged neatly on a plate. Repeating this process with the other leg will provide ample meat.

5.   Preparing Breast: In preparing the breast for easy slicing, place knife parallel and as close to wing as possible. Make a deep cut into the breast, cutting right to the bone. This is your base cut. All breast slices will stop at this vertical cut.

6.   Carving Breast: After base cut, begin to slice breast. Start halfway up the side, carving down, ending at base cut. Start each new slice slightly higher up on breast. Keep slices thin and even.

MEATS

There's a closeness, a coziness that surrounds a table when friends and family gather for a meal. It might be a special occasion with a bowl of flowers centered on your best lace tablecloth and each place set with beautiful china and stemware. Maybe it's a casual evening around the picnic table or an informal supper at the kitchen table.

The setting you create is simply the stage for your warmth and hospitality. But don't be surprised if your friendly kitchen is the place to congregate before mealtime. One of your dear friends just may be tempted to peek into the oven to see how that delicious ham is coming along. Or sneak a taste of your beef stroganoff bubbling on the stovetop. And chances are, you'll get lots of offers to help with last-minute preparation — like stirring the barbecued pork or checking the roast in the oven.

There's something about a good home-cooked meal, served with love, that seems to bring out the best in all of us. Good conversation. Joy and laughter. And a feeling that all is well in the world.

Grandma's Sunday Roast

A special family recipe that makes any day of the week a Sunday.

6 servings
2 hours

1.4 to 1.8 kg	(*3 to 4 lb*) beef rump roast
3	med. onions, quartered
1	bay leaf
5 ml	(*1 tsp*) salt
5 ml	(*1 tsp*) pepper

5 ml	(*1 tsp*) crushed fresh garlic
250 ml	(*8 fl oz*) water
6	carrots, cut in half crosswise
6	med. potatoes, quartered

Heat oven to 180 °C (*350 °F*) mark 4. Place roast on rack in roasting tin. Add remaining ingredients *except* water, carrots and potatoes. Pour water over roast. Cover; bake for 45 min. Uncover; arrange carrots and potatoes around meat. Baste with tin juices. Cover; bake, basting occasionally, for 60 to 70 min. or until vegetables are fork tender and meat thermometer reaches 71 °C (*160 °F*) (Medium). Serve with pan juices.

Beef	**Internal Cooking Temperature**
Rare	60 °C (*140 °F*)
Medium	71 °C (*160 °F*)
Well	76 °C (*170 °F*)

Peppery Beef Roast

The aroma of garlic and pepper will fill the kitchen when you prepare this succulent roast.

6 servings
1 hour 30 minutes

| 1.4 to 1.8 kg | (*3 to 4 lb*) rolled beef rump roast |
| 50 ml | (*4 tbsp*) vegetable oil |

| 15 ml | (*1 tbsp*) crushed fresh garlic |
| 15 ml | (*1 tbsp*) fresh cracked pepper |

Heat oven to 160 °C (*325 °F*) mark 3. Place roast on rack in roasting tin. In small bowl stir together remaining ingredients. Spoon oil mixture over roast. Bake for 70 to 90 min. or until meat thermometer reaches 71 °C (*160 °F*) (Medium).

Beef	**Internal Cooking Temperature**
Rare	60 °C (*140 °F*)
Medium	71 °C (*160 °F*)
Well	76 °C (*170 °F*)

Grandma's Sunday Roast

Brisket With Stone-Ground Mustard

6 to 8 servings
3 hours 30 minutes

A tantalizing sauce of sweet, sour and spice is served over tender, boiled brisket.

Brisket

1.4 to 1.8 kg	(*3 to 4 lb*) beef brisket
1.5 litre	(*2¾ pt*) water
50 ml	(*4 tbsp*) chopped fresh parsley
4	celery sticks, cut into 2.5-cm (*1-in*) pieces
4	med. carrots, cut into 2.5-cm (*1-in*) pieces
2	med. onions, cut into 3.5-cm (*1½-in*) pieces
5 ml	(*1 tsp*) salt
5 ml	(*1 tsp*) coarsely ground pepper
5 ml	(*1 tsp*) thyme leaves
2	bay leaves

Sauce

45 ml	(*3 tbsp*) plain flour
140 g	(*4½ oz*) country-style Dijon mustard
150 g	(*5 oz*) currant jelly
125 ml	(*4 fl oz*) double cream
5 ml	(*1 tsp*) Worcestershire sauce

In flameproof casserole place brisket; cover with water. Add remaining brisket ingredients; bring to a full boil. Cover; cook over med. low heat for 2½ to 3 hr. or until brisket is fork tender. Remove bay leaves. Place brisket and vegetables on serving platter; *reserve broth*. In same casserole or 2-litre (*3½-pt*) saucepan place 375 ml (*13 fl oz*) reserved broth; whisk in flour. Cook over med. heat, stirring occasionally, until smooth and bubbly (2 to 3 min.). Stir in remaining sauce ingredients. Continue cooking, stirring occasionally, until sauce is thickened (4 to 5 min.). Serve over carved brisket and vegetables.

Winter Warm-Up Beef Simmer

8 servings
4 hours 30 minutes

While this rich, hearty supper simmers, enjoy the brisk autumn air or the first snowflakes of the season.

2	med. onions, chopped
6	rashers of bacon, cut into 1-cm (*½-in*) pieces
1.4 kg	(*3 lb*) beef chuck roast, trimmed, cut into 6-cm (*2½-in*) pieces
8	med. red potatoes, halved
3	med. carrots, cut into 2.5-cm (*1-in*) pieces
3	med. onions, halved
225 g	(*8 oz*) fresh mushrooms, halved
30 g	(*1 oz*) chopped fresh parsley

250 ml	(*8 fl oz*) apple juice
295-g	(*10.4-oz*) can beef broth
150 g	(*5 oz*) canned tomato purée
2 ml	(*½ tsp*) salt
2 ml	(*½ tsp*) pepper
2 ml	(*½ tsp*) thyme leaves
5 ml	(*1 tsp*) crushed fresh garlic
2	bay leaves

Heat oven to 160 °C (*325 °F*) mark 3. In flameproof casserole place onions, bacon and roast. Cook over med. high heat, stirring occasionally, until bacon and roast are browned (8 to 10 min.). Stir in vegetables. Stir in remaining ingredients. Cover; bake for 1½ hr. Uncover; continue baking, stirring occasionally, for 2 to 2½ hr. or until roast is fork tender.

Winter Warm-Up Beef Simmer

Spinach-Stuffed Steaks or Burgers

Home cooking like this brings out the best of steaks or burgers.

Stuffing

275 g	(*10 oz*) frozen spinach, thawed, drained
1 ml	(*¼ tsp*) salt
1 ml	(*¼ tsp*) pepper
2 ml	(*½ tsp*) crushed fresh garlic
2	(340-g) (*¾-lb*) steaks (rib, porterhouse, wing) OR 675 g (*1½ lb*) minced beef
6	rashers of bacon, cut into 1-cm (*½-in*) pieces
30 g	(*1 oz*) butter or margarine

Sauce

15 ml	(*1 tbsp*) plain flour
250 ml	(*8 fl oz*) water
1 ml	(*¼ tsp*) salt
30 ml	(*2 tbsp*) tomato purée
2 ml	(*½ tsp*) crushed fresh garlic

In small bowl stir together all stuffing ingredients; set aside. To prepare steaks, trim excess fat from steaks. Split each steak from outer edges toward bone, making a pocket. Divide spinach mixture; fill each pocket. To prepare burgers, divide minced beef into 4 equal portions. Form into oblong 10 x 8-cm (*4 x 3-in*) patties. Make indentation in middle of each pattie. Divide spinach mixture; fill each indentation. In 25-cm (*10-in*) frying pan cook bacon and butter over med. high heat until browned (5 min.). Place steaks or burgers in same frying pan. Cook over med. high heat, turning once, until desired doneness (7 to 9 min. for medium steaks or 10 to 15 min. for medium burgers). Place meat on platter; keep warm while preparing sauce. Pour off fat, leaving bacon and brown particles in pan. Reduce heat to med.; stir in flour. Cook, stirring occasionally, until mixture is smooth and bubbly (1 min.). Stir in remaining sauce ingredients. Continue cooking, stirring occasionally, until thickened (4 to 5 min.). Serve over steaks or burgers.

To Stuff Steaks:

1. Split each steak from outer edges toward bone, making a pocket.

2. Divide spinach mixture; fill each pocket.

Spinach-Stuffed Burgers

Ranch Steak Platter

4 servings
35 minutes

Ranch Steak Platter

Feed your family this hearty steak platter.

Marinade

2 ml	(*1/2 tsp*) salt
2 ml	(*1/2 tsp*) oregano leaves
2 ml	(*1/2 tsp*) pepper
30 ml	(*2 tbsp*) cider vinegar
30 ml	(*2 tbsp*) vegetable oil
15 ml	(*1 tbsp*) country-style Dijon mustard
5 ml	(*1 tsp*) crushed fresh garlic

Steak

675 g	(*1 1/2 lb*) sirloin steak
2	med. carrots, cut into 2.5-cm (*1-in*) pieces
1	med. onion, sliced 5 mm (*1/4 in*)
2	med. tomatoes, cut into 5-cm (*2-in*) pieces
1	med. green pepper, cut into 2.5-cm (*1-in*) strips

In 25-cm (*10-in*) frying pan stir together all marinade ingredients. Coat both sides of steak with marinade; place in same frying pan. Place carrots and onion around steak in marinade mixture. Cover; cook over med. high heat, turning once, until browned (10 to 12 min.). Reduce heat to med. Add remaining ingredients. Cover; cook, stirring occasionally, until vegetables are crisply tender and meat reaches desired doneness (5 to 7 min. for medium).

Microwave Directions: Cut steak in half. In 2-litre (*3 1/2-pt*) casserole stir together all marinade ingredients. Coat both sides of steak with marinade; place in same casserole. Place carrots and onion around steak in marinade mixture. Cover; microwave on HIGH, turning steak over after half the time (8 to 10 min.). Add remaining ingredients. Cover; microwave on HIGH until vegetables are crisply tender and meat reaches desired doneness (5 to 7 min. for medium).

4 servings
35 minutes

Beef Stroganoff With Button Onions

Cream cheese makes this stroganoff extra creamy and rich.

45 g	(*1 1/2 oz*) butter or margarine
675 g	(*1 1/2 lb*) sirloin steak, cut into 3.5-cm (*1 1/2-in*) pieces
2 ml	(*1/2 tsp*) salt
2 ml	(*1/2 tsp*) pepper
30 ml	(*2 tbsp*) plain flour
500 ml	(*17 fl oz*) single cream
75 g	(*3 oz*) cream cheese, softened
30 ml	(*2 tbsp*) tomato purée

225 g	(*8 oz*) fresh mushrooms, halved
150 g	(*5 oz*) frozen button onions, thawed, drained
50 ml	(*4 tbsp*) chopped fresh parsley
5 ml	(*1 tsp*) marjoram leaves
	Cooked egg noodles

In 25-cm (*10-in*) frying pan melt butter until sizzling. Add steak, salt and pepper. Cook over med. high heat, stirring occasionally, until browned (5 min.). Stir in flour to coat steak; add single cream, cream cheese and tomato paste. Reduce heat to med. Cook, stirring occasionally, until sauce is thickened (7 to 9 min.). Stir in remaining ingredients *except* noodles. Continue cooking, stirring occasionally, until mushrooms are tender (3 to 4 min.). Serve over noodles.

Microwave Directions: In 3-litre (*5-pt*) casserole melt butter on HIGH (30 to 40 sec.). Stir in steak, salt and pepper. Cover; microwave on HIGH, stirring after half the time, just until steak is no longer pink (3 to 4 min.). Stir in flour, single cream, cream cheese and tomato purée. Microwave on HIGH, stirring after half the time, until sauce is thickened (4 to 6 min.). Stir in remaining ingredients *except* noodles. Microwave on HIGH until mushrooms are tender (2 1/2 to 3 1/2 min.). Serve over noodles.

Marinated Beef & Broccoli Supper

4 servings
30 minutes

Sirloin steak is tenderized in a light, lemon-ginger marinade.

50 g	(*2 oz*) butter or margarine
225 g	(*8 oz*) broccoli flowerets
1	med. onion, sliced 3 mm (*1/8 in*)
3 ml	(*3/4 tsp*) ginger
1 ml	(*1/4 tsp*) salt
1 ml	(*1/4 tsp*) pepper
15 ml	(*1 tbsp*) lemon juice
15 ml	(*1 tbsp*) Worcestershire sauce

5 ml	(*1 tsp*) crushed fresh garlic
450 g	(*1 lb*) beef sirloin steak, cut into 8 x 1-cm (*3 x 1/2-in*) strips
2	med. ripe tomatoes, cut into 2.5-cm (*1-in*) pieces
	Cooked rice

In 25-cm (*10-in*) frying pan melt butter until sizzling. Add broccoli and onion. Cook over med. heat, stirring occasionally, until crisply tender (5 to 6 min.). Meanwhile, in medium bowl stir together remaining ingredients *except* steak, tomatoes and rice. Add sirloin strips; let stand 5 min. Add sirloin and marinade to vegetable mixture. Continue cooking, stirring occasionally, until meat is browned (6 to 8 min.). Stir in tomatoes. Cover; let stand 2 min. or until heated through. Serve meat and vegetables with juices over rice.

Microwave Directions: In 2-litre (*3 1/2-pt*) casserole melt butter on HIGH (40 to 50 sec.). Stir in broccoli and onion. Cover; microwave on HIGH until crisply tender (2 min.). Meanwhile, in medium bowl stir together remaining ingredients *except* steak, tomatoes and rice. Add sirloin strips; let stand 5 min. Add sirloin and marinade to vegetable mixture. Cover; microwave on HIGH, stirring after half the time, until meat is no longer pink (3 to 5 min.). Stir in tomatoes. Cover; let stand 5 min. Serve meat and vegetables with juices over rice.

Sweet & Tangy Family Steak

6 servings
1 day

The marinade enhances both the subtle flavour and the tenderness of this popular cut of meat.

Marinade

125 ml	(*4 fl oz*) catsup
50 ml	(*4 tbsp*) country-style Dijon mustard
30 ml	(*2 tbsp*) firmly packed brown sugar
15 ml	(*1 tbsp*) cider vinegar
5 ml	(*1 tsp*) crushed fresh garlic

2 ml	(*1/2 tsp*) fresh cracked pepper
1 ml	(*1/4 tsp*) salt
675 g	(*1 1/2 lb*) beef top round steak, cut 2.5 cm (*1 in*) thick

In medium bowl stir together all marinade ingredients. Pierce steak with fork; place steak in plastic food bag. Pour in marinade; seal bag. Place in 23-cm (*9-in*) sq. dish. Refrigerate 24 hr. Heat grill. Drain steak; *reserve marinade.* Place steak on greased grill pan. Grill 10 to 12.5 cm (*4 to 5 in*) from heat for 5 to 6 min. Turn steak over, brush with marinade; continue grilling 4 to 5 min. or until desired doneness. In 1-litre (*1 3/4-pt*) saucepan cook remaining marinade over med. heat until heated through (2 to 4 min.). To serve, cut steak, on the diagonal, into thin slices. Serve with hot marinade.

Barbecuing Directions: Marinate steak as directed left. Prepare grill placing coals to one side; heat until coals are ash white. Make aluminum foil drip pan; place opposite coals. Place steak barbecue grid over drip pan. Grill 5 to 8 min. Turn steak over, brush with marinade; continue grilling 5 to 8 min. or until desired doneness. In 1-litre (*1 3/4-pt*) saucepan cook remaining marinade over med. heat until heated through (2 to 4 min.). To serve, cut steak, on the diagonal, into thin slices. Serve with hot marinade.

Marinated Beef & Broccoli Supper

Cheddar Cheese-Pecan Rolled Flank Steak

6 to 8 servings
1 day

Slice into this tender, marinated flank steak and discover a moist, flavourful stuffing.

Marinade
2	med. onions, chopped
500 ml	(*17 fl oz*) pineapple juice
5 ml	(*1 tsp*) salt
5 ml	(*1 tsp*) thyme leaves
2 ml	(*1/2 tsp*) pepper
2 ml	(*1/2 tsp*) rosemary leaves, crushed
30 ml	(*2 tbsp*) Worcestershire sauce
675 to 900 g	(*1 1/2 to 2 lb*) beef flank steak

Stuffing
200 g	(*7 oz*) fresh breadcrumbs
175 g	(*6 oz*) shredded Cheddar cheese
65 g	(*2 1/2 oz*) chopped pecans
50 ml	(*4 tbsp*) chopped onion
50 ml	(*4 tbsp*) chopped fresh parsley
2 ml	(*1/2 tsp*) crushed fresh garlic

In medium bowl stir together all marinade ingredients *except* steak. With mallet, pound steak to 5-mm (*1/4-in*) thickness. Place steak in plastic food bag. Pour marinade into bag; seal tightly. Place bag in 33 x 23-cm (*13 x 9-in*) baking dish. Refrigerate, turning twice, 24 hr. Heat oven to 200 °C (*400 °F*) mark 6. Remove steak from marinade; *reserve marinade*. In medium bowl combine all stuffing ingredients. Place stuffing mixture over entire surface of steak; pressing slightly. Tightly roll up steak, Swiss roll fashion. Tie with string to secure filling inside roll. Line 33 x 23-cm (*13 x 9-in*) baking dish with heavy-duty aluminum foil. Place steak in prepared dish; baste with reserved marinade. Bake, basting with marinade every 15 min., for 50 to 60 min. or until meat thermometer reaches 71 °C (*160 °F*) (Medium). Just before serving, baste with marinade.

Beef	Internal Cooking Temperature
Rare	60 °C (*140 °F*)
Medium	71 °C (*160 °F*)
Well	76 °C (*170 °F*)

To Prepare Steak:

1. Place stuffing mixture over entire surface of steak; pressing slightly.

2. Tightly roll up steak, Swiss roll fashion. Tie with string to secure filling inside roll.

Cheddar Cheese-Pecan Rolled Flank Steak

Fillet of Beef With Blue Cheese

Fillet of Beef With Blue Cheese

6 to 8 servings
1 hour 15 minutes

This rich, noble beef fillet is full of character.

Beef

50 g	(*2 oz*) butter or margarine
2 ml	(*½ tsp*) coarsely ground pepper
5 ml	(*1 tsp*) crushed fresh garlic
900 g to 1.4 kg	(*2 to 3 lb*) fillet of beef, trimmed, tied

Sauce

30 g	(*1 oz*) butter or margarine
100 g	(*4 oz*) crumbled blue cheese
250 ml	(*8 fl oz*) beef broth
50 ml	(*2 fl oz*) Madeira wine
225 g	(*8 oz*) sliced 5 mm (*¼ in*) fresh mushrooms
65 g	(*2½ oz*) chopped pecans, toasted
75 g	(*3 oz*) pine nuts or sliced almonds, toasted
75 ml	(*5 tbsp*) sliced 5 mm (*¼ in*) spring onions

Heat oven to 200 °C (*400 °F*) mark 6. In 25-cm (*10-in*) frying pan melt 50 g (*2 oz*) butter until sizzling; stir in pepper and garlic. Place fillet in same frying pan. Cook over med. high heat until browned on all sides (7 to 9 min.). Remove from pan; *reserve pan juices and browned particles in frying pan.* Line 33 x 23-cm (*13 x 9-in*) baking dish with aluminum foil; place fillet in dish. Bake for 35 to 50 min. or until meat thermometer reaches 71 °C (*160 °F*) (Medium). Meanwhile, melt 30 g (*1 oz*) butter in same frying pan with reserved pan juices and browned particles until

sizzling; stir in blue cheese. Cook over med. heat, stirring occasionally, until cheese is melted (4 to 5 min.). Stir in beef broth and wine; add mushrooms. Continue cooking, stirring occasionally, until mushrooms are tender (4 to 5 min.). Stir in remaining sauce ingredients. Serve over carved fillet.

Beef	Internal Cooking Temperature
Rare	60 °C (*140 °F*)
Medium	71 °C (*160 °F*)
Well	76 °C (*170 °F*)

Grilled Steak With Herb Peppercorn Butter

4 servings
2 hours

Grilled steak is elegantly served with a wonderful herb butter that melts over the steak to provide superb flavour.

50 ml	(*2 fl oz*) dry white wine
15 ml	(*1 tbsp*) minced fresh shallots
15 ml	(*1 tbsp*) chopped fresh chives
5 ml	(*1 tsp*) chopped fresh tarragon
2 ml	(*½ tsp*) coarsely ground pepper

1 ml	(*¼ tsp*) salt
125 g	(*4 oz*) butter, softened
4	beef porterhouse or wing steaks

In 1-litre (*1¾-pt*) saucepan stir together all ingredients except butter and steaks. Cook over med. heat, stirring occasionally, until all liquid has evaporated (5 to 6 min.). Set aside; cool completely. In small bowl stir together butter and cooled herbs. Place mixture on waxed paper; shape into 10-cm (*4-in*) log. Refrigerate

until serving time. Meanwhile, grill steaks to desired doneness. Place 1-cm (*½-in*) slice herb butter on each grilled steak. Serve as butter is melting over steaks.

Tip: Remaining herb butter can be used to season cooked vegetables or to serve with breads.

M

Prairie Pot Roast With Dill

6 to 8 servings
3 hours 30 minutes

Prairie Pot Roast With Dill

A Sunday evening family favourite, served with a dill sour cream gravy.

Roast

30 ml	*(2 tbsp)* vegetable oil
30 ml	*(2 tbsp)* cider vinegar
5 ml	*(1 tsp)* salt
5 ml	*(1 tsp)* dill seed
2 ml	*(1/2 tsp)* pepper
1.4 to 1.8 kg	*(3 to 4 lb)* beef chuck roast
6 to 8	med. new red potatoes, cut into 2.5-cm *(1-in)* pieces
4 to 6	med. carrots, cut into 3.5-cm *(1 1/2-in)* pieces
2	leeks, quartered, sliced lengthwise into 5-cm *(2-in)* pieces*
50 ml	*(2 fl oz)* water
1	bay leaf

Gravy

50 ml	*(4 tbsp)* plain flour
2 ml	*(1/2 tsp)* salt
2 ml	*(1/2 tsp)* dill weed
250 ml	*(8 fl oz)* sour cream

Heat oven to 180 °C *(350 °F)* mark 4. In 33 x 23-cm *(13 x 9-in)* baking dish combine oil, vinegar, 5 ml *(1 tsp)* salt, dill seed and pepper; add roast. Turn to coat all sides of roast with herbs and oil. Let stand 15 min. Meanwhile, in large roasting tin place potatoes, carrots and leeks. Place roast and herb and oil mixture in roasting tin with vegetables; add water and bay leaf. Cover; bake, basting occasionally, for 2 1/2 to 3 hr. or until roast is fork tender. Remove bay leaf. Place roast and vegetables on serving platter; *reserve*

tin juices. In 2-litre *(3 1/2-pt)* saucepan place 375 ml *(13 fl oz)* reserved tin juices. Whisk in flour, 2 ml *(1/2 tsp)* salt and dill weed. Cook over med. heat, stirring occasionally, until smooth and bubbly (1 min.). Stir in sour cream; continue cooking, stirring occasionally, until gravy is thickened (4 to 5 min.). Serve over carved roast and vegetables.

*2 large onions, cut into 5-cm *(2-in)* pieces can be substituted for 2 leeks.

6 to 8 servings
1 day

Roasted Beef With Horseradish Cream

Marinating and slow cooking make this pot roast tender and flavourful.

Marinade

50 ml	*(4 tbsp)* vegetable oil
30 ml	*(2 tbsp)* cider vinegar
5 ml	*(1 tsp)* salt
5 ml	*(1 tsp)* pepper
15 ml	*(1 tbsp)* prepared horseradish
5 ml	*(1 tsp)* crushed fresh garlic
50 ml	*(4 tbsp)* chopped fresh parsley
1.4 to 1.8 kg	*(3 to 4 lb)* beef chuck roast

Horseradish Cream

125 ml	*(4 fl oz)* dairy sour cream
125 ml	*(4 fl oz)* mayonnaise
1 ml	*(1/4 tsp)* salt
1 ml	*(1/4 tsp)* pepper
15 ml	*(1 tbsp)* prepared horseradish
5 ml	*(1 tsp)* lemon juice
5 ml	*(1 tsp)* country-style Dijon mustard
50 ml	*(4 tbsp)* chopped fresh parsley

In flameproof casserole stir together all marinade ingredients except parsley and roast; stir in parsley. Place roast in marinade; turn to coat all sides with marinade. Cover; refrigerate overnight. Heat oven to 180 °C *(350 °F)* mark 4. Bake roast in marinade for

1 1/2 to 2 hr. or until roast is fork tender. Meanwhile, in small bowl stir together all horseradish cream ingredients *except* parsley. Stir in parsley. Cover; refrigerate until ready to serve. Serve over carved roast.

Peppery Steak With Pan Fries & Gravy

Peppery Steak With Pan Fries & Gravy

Honest, wonderful home-cooked fare that is sure to become a family favourite.

4 servings
40 minutes

Potatoes

50 g	(*2 oz*) butter or margarine
6	med. new red potatoes, cut into wedges
1 ml	(*1/4 tsp*) salt
1 ml	(*1/4 tsp*) pepper

Steak

75 ml	(*5 tbsp*) plain flour
1 ml	(*1/4 tsp*) salt
	Pinch of pepper
4	beef cubed steaks

Gravy

15 g	(*1/2 oz*) butter or margarine
15 ml	(*1 tbsp*) plain flour
250 ml	(*8 fl oz*) milk
1 ml	(*1/4 tsp*) salt
	Pinch of pepper

In 25-cm (*10-in*) frying pan melt 50 g (*2 oz*) butter until sizzling. Add remaining potato ingredients. Cook over med. high heat, turning occasionally, until golden brown (10 to 15 min.). Place potatoes on platter; keep warm while preparing steaks and gravy. In 23-cm (*9-in*) pie dish stir together all steak ingredients *except* steaks. Coat both sides of steaks with flour mixture. Place 2 steaks in same frying pan. Cook over med. high heat until brown and crispy (3 min. on each side). Remove steaks to platter with potatoes. Cook remaining steaks. Reduce heat to med. In same frying pan with drippings and brown particles melt 15 g (*1/2 oz*) butter; stir in 15 ml (*1 tbsp*) flour. Cook, stirring occasionally, until smooth and bubbly (1 min.). Stir in remaining gravy ingredients. Continue cooking, stirring occasionally, until gravy thickens (4 to 5 min.). Serve over steaks and potatoes.

Microwave Directions: In 33 x 23-cm (*13 x 9-in*) baking dish melt 50 g (*2 oz*) butter on HIGH (50 to 60 sec.). Stir in remaining potato ingredients. Cover; microwave on HIGH, stirring after half the time, until potatoes are tender (8 to 11 min.). Place potatoes on platter; keep warm while preparing steaks and gravy. Omit 75 ml (*5 tbsp*) flour. Place steaks in same dish; sprinkle with salt and pepper. Cover; microwave on HIGH, turning steaks over after half the time, until meat is no longer pink. Remove steaks to platter with potatoes. Omit 15 g (*1/2 oz*) butter; increase flour to 45 ml (*3 tbsp*). Stir 45 ml (*3 tbsp*) flour into dish juices. Microwave on HIGH until bubbly (1 to 1 1/2 min.). Stir in remaining gravy ingredients. Cover; microwave on HIGH, stirring after half the time, until gravy thickens (3 to 5 min.). Serve over steaks and potatoes.

4 servings
60 minutes

Meatballs With Garden Tomato Sauce

This recipe is sure to bring back memories of childhood.

Meatballs

450 g	(*1 lb*) minced beef
100 g	(*4 oz*) uncooked long grain rice
125 ml	(*4 fl oz*) water
2 ml	(*1/2 tsp*) salt
2 ml	(*1/2 tsp*) basil leaves
2 ml	(*1/2 tsp*) pepper

Sauce

250 ml	(*8 fl oz*) water
3	med. tomatoes, cut into 2.5-cm (*1-in*) pieces
2	celery sticks, sliced 1 cm (*1/2 in*)
1	med. onion, cut into 1-cm (*1/2-in*) pieces
150 g	(*5 oz*) canned tomato purée
2 ml	(*1/2 tsp*) salt
1 ml	(*1/4 tsp*) pepper
5 ml	(*1 tsp*) crushed fresh garlic

Heat oven to 190 °C (*375 °F*) mark 5. In medium bowl stir together all meatball ingredients. Form mixture into 12 meatballs; place in 30 x 20-cm (*12 x 8-in*) baking dish. In medium bowl stir together all sauce ingredients; pour over meatballs. Cover; bake for 45 to 50 min. or until rice is tender.

Microwave Directions: Prepare meatballs as directed left. Place meatballs in 30 x 20-cm (*12 x 8-in*) baking dish. In medium bowl stir together all sauce ingredients; pour over meatballs. Cover with plastic wrap; microwave on HIGH, stirring and rearranging meatballs after half the time, until rice is tender (25 to 35 min.). Let stand 5 min.

6 to 8 servings
1 hour 30 minutes

Herb-Spiced Meat Loaf

This spicy meat loaf makes a hearty and very special, old-fashioned meal.

200 g	(*7 oz*) fresh breadcrumbs
90 g	(*3 1/2 oz*) finely chopped onion
1/2	finely chopped red or green pepper
125 ml	(*4 fl oz*) tomato sauce
450 g	(*1 lb*) regular minced beef*
450 g	(*1 lb*) ground pork
150 g	(*5 oz*) canned tomato purée
2	eggs, slightly beaten
30 ml	(*2 tbsp*) chopped fresh parsley

15 ml	(*1 tbsp*) sage leaves, rubbed
5 ml	(*1 tsp*) salt
2 ml	(*1/2 tsp*) pepper
2 ml	(*1/2 tsp*) thyme leaves
15 ml	(*1 tbsp*) lemon juice
5 ml	(*1 tsp*) crushed fresh garlic
125 ml	(*4 fl oz*) double cream
15 ml	(*1 tbsp*) plain flour
2 ml	(*1/2 tsp*) thyme leaves

Heat oven to 180 °C (*350 °F*) mark 4. In large bowl stir together all ingredients *except* double cream, flour and 2 ml (*1/2 tsp*) thyme leaves. Form into loaf; place in 33 x 23-cm (*13 x 9-in*) baking dish. Bake for 55 to 65 min. or until browned. *Reserve dish juices.* In 1-litre (*1 3/4-pt*) saucepan stir together double cream, flour, 2 ml (*1/2 tsp*) thyme leaves and reserved 200 ml

(*7 fl oz*) dish juices. Cook over med. heat, stirring occasionally, until slightly thickened (3 to 4 min.). Serve with meat loaf.

*Do not substitute lean minced beef for regular minced beef.

Herb-Spiced Meat Loaf

Bunkhouse Stroganoff Squares

A meat pie that is easily prepared and satisfies the heartiest appetite.

Stroganoff

225 g	(*8 oz*) sliced 5 mm (*¼ in*) fresh mushrooms
2	med. onions, chopped
900 g	(*2 lb*) minced beef
50 g	(*2 oz*) chopped fresh parsley
65 g	(*2½ oz*) fresh breadcrumbs
225 g	(*8 oz*) cream cheese, softened
5 ml	(*1 tsp*) salt
2 ml	(*½ tsp*) pepper
2 ml	(*½ tsp*) thyme leaves

Crust

450 g	(*1 lb*) plain flour
30 ml	(*2 tbsp*) instant minced onion
5 ml	(*1 tsp*) salt
5 ml	(*1 tsp*) sugar
1 ml	(*¼ tsp*) pepper
125 g	(*4 oz*) butter or margarine
100 g	(*4 oz*) shortening
1	egg, slightly beaten
90 to 120 ml	(*3 to 4 fl oz*) cold water
1	egg, slightly beaten
15 ml	(*1 tbsp*) milk

Heat oven to 190 °C (*375 °F*) mark 5. In 25-cm (*10-in*) frying pan cook mushrooms, onions and minced beef over med. high heat, stirring occasionally, until browned (12 to 15 min.). Drain off fat. Stir in remaining stroganoff ingredients; cook over med. heat until cream cheese is melted (3 to 4 min.). In large bowl stir together flour, minced onion, 5 ml (*1 tsp*) salt, sugar and 1 ml (*¼ tsp*) pepper. Cut in butter and shortening until crumbly. With fork mix in 1 egg and water until flour is moistened. Divide dough in half; shape into 2 balls and flatten. Wrap 1 ball in plastic wrap; refrigerate. On lightly floured surface roll out other ball into 35-cm (*14-in*) sq. Place in 23-cm (*9-in*) baking dish. Trim pastry to 1 cm (*½ in*) from rim of dish. Fill with stroganoff mixture. Roll remaining pastry ball into 35-cm (*14-in*) sq.; place over stroganoff mixture. Trim pastry to 1 cm (*½ in*) from rim of dish. Roll edges of dough under to form rim inside of dish; crimp or flute crust. With sharp knife, cut X in each 8 cm (*3 in*) sq. of pastry to decorate 9 squares. In small bowl stir together 1 egg and milk; brush over pastry. Bake for 35 to 45 min. or until crust is golden brown. Let stand 5 min.; cut into squares.

Bunkhouse Stroganoff Squares

Blue Cheese-Stuffed Burgers

4 hamburgers
45 minutes

Blue cheese, mushrooms and onions are the fixings for this juicy burger.

675 g	(*1 1/2 lb*) minced beef		150 g	(*5 oz*) sliced 5 mm (*1/4 in*) fresh mushrooms
1 ml	(*1/4 tsp*) salt		2	med. onions, sliced 3 mm (*1/8 in*)
1 ml	(*1/4 tsp*) pepper		1 ml	(*1/4 tsp*) salt
75 ml	(*5 tbsp*) crumbled blue cheese		1 ml	(*1/4 tsp*) pepper
90 g	(*3 oz*) cream cheese, softened		15 ml	(*1 tbsp*) Worcestershire sauce
15 ml	(*1 tbsp*) country-style Dijon mustard		4	slices ripe tomato
4	onion buns			

In medium bowl stir together minced beef, 1 ml (*1/4 tsp*) salt and 1 ml (*1/4 tsp*) pepper. Form into 8 large 5-mm (*1/4-in*) thick patties. In small bowl stir together blue cheese, cream cheese and mustard. Place about 30 ml (*2 tbsp*) cheese mixture on top of each of 4 patties. Top each with remaining meat patty. Press around edges to seal. Place burgers in 25-cm (*10-in*) frying pan. Cook over med. heat, turning once, until desired doneness (12 to 15 min. for medium). Place burgers on buns. In same frying pan with drippings place mushrooms and onions; add 1 ml (*1/4 tsp*) salt, 1 ml (*1/4 tsp*) pepper and Worcestershire sauce. Cook over med. high heat, stirring occasionally, until tender (4 to 5 min.). Meanwhile, place tomato slice on each burger; top with grilled mushrooms and onions.

Microwave Directions: Assemble as directed left. Place burgers on microwave-safe bacon/roasting rack or 30 x 20-cm (*12 x 8-in*) baking dish. Cover; microwave on HIGH, turning burgers over and rearranging after half the time, until desired doneness (5 to 8 min. for medium). In medium bowl combine remaining ingredients *except* buns and tomatoes. Cover; microwave on HIGH until crisply tender (2 to 3 min.). Assemble sandwiches as directed left.

To Stuff Burgers:

1. Form into 8 large 5-mm (*1/4-in*) thick patties.

2. Place about 30 ml (*2 tbsp*) cheese mixture on top of each of 4 patties. Top each with remaining meat patty. Press around edges to seal.

Blue Cheese-Stuffed Burgers

Cider-Glazed Baked Ham

Fruit-Stuffed Pork Loin

10 to 12 servings
3 hours

Slice into this succulent herb-roasted pork to reveal an exquisite display of fruit stuffing.

250 ml	(8 fl oz) water
1	med. tart cooking apple, chopped
150 g	(5 oz) dried apricots
150 g	(5 oz) dried stoned prunes
1.8 to 2.3 kg	(4 to 5 lb) boneless middle cut pork loin roast (2 loins tied)
5 ml	(1 tsp) thyme leaves
2 ml	(½ tsp) rosemary leaves, crushed

2 ml	(½ tsp) sage leaves, crushed
2 ml	(½ tsp) salt
2 ml	(½ tsp) coarsely ground pepper
30 g	(1 oz) butter or margarine, melted
15 ml	(1 tbsp) plain flour
1 ml	(¼ tsp) salt
500 ml	(17 fl oz) water

Heat oven to 160 °C (*325 °F*) mark 3. In 2-litre (*3½-pt*) saucepan bring 250 ml (*8 fl oz*) water to a full boil; remove from heat. Add apple, apricots and prunes; let stand 5 min. Drain off water; set fruit aside. Untie roast; lay roast open. With sharp knife, cut 1-cm (*½-in*) slit down center through thick muscle of pork loin lengthwise from one end to the other on both loins. With wooden spoon pack fruit into both slits. Place both loins back together; tie with string to secure. In small bowl stir together remaining ingredients *except* butter, flour, 1 ml (*¼ tsp*) salt and water. Brush roast with melted butter; sprinkle herbs over entire roast. Place roast, fat side up, in roasting tin. Bake, basting with tin juices occasionally, for 2 to 2½ hr. or

until meat thermometer reaches 74 °C (*165 °F*). Remove from oven; let stand about 10 min. or until meat thermometer reaches 76 °C (*170 °F*). Place roast on serving platter; *reserve tin juices*. In same roasting tin place 50 ml (*4 tbsp*) reserved tin juices; stir in flour and 1 ml (*¼ tsp*) salt. Cook over med. heat until smooth and bubbly (1 min.). Stir in 500 ml (*17 fl oz*) water; continue cooking, stirring occasionally, until mixture comes to a full boil (4 to 5 min.). Serve over carved roast.

Tip: Insert meat thermometer into center of loin. (Do not touch fruit stuffing.)

Cider-Glazed Baked Ham

8 to 10 servings
1 hour 30 minutes

As the ham bakes, basted with apple cider, its own wonderful honey-mustard sauce is made.

1.8 to 2.3 kg	(4 to 5 lb) fully cooked boneless cured ham
250 ml	(8 fl oz) apple cider
50 ml	(4 tbsp) firmly packed brown sugar
50 ml	(4 tbsp) country-style Dijon mustard

50 ml	(4 tbsp) honey
2 ml	(½ tsp) liquid smoke
	Red, green and yellow apple slices

Heat oven to 180 °C (*350 °F*) mark 4. Place ham in 33 x 23-cm (*13 x 9-in*) baking dish. Pour apple cider over ham. In medium bowl stir together remaining ingredients *except* apple slices. Spoon sauce over entire ham. Bake, basting every 15 min. with dish juices, for 60 to 70 min. or until heated through. Serve carved ham with dish juices; garnish with apple slices.

Microwave Directions: Place ham in 33 x 23-cm (*13 x 9-in*) baking dish. Pour apple cider over ham. In medium bowl stir together remaining ingredients *except* apple slices. Spoon sauce over entire ham. Cover with plastic wrap. Microwave on HIGH 5 min. Reduce power to MEDIUM (50% power); microwave, basting every 15 min. with dish juices and turning ham over after half the time, until heated through (60 to 90 min.). If cut edge begins to dry, shield with aluminum foil. Serve carved ham with dish juices; garnish with apple slices.

8 to 10 servings
3 hours 20 minutes

Savoury Pork Roast

A simply prepared roast, covered with sage and roasted to perfection.

1.8 to 2.3 kg	(*4 to 5 lb*) pork shoulder roast
30 to 45 ml	(*2 to 3 tbsp*) vegetable oil
45 ml	(*3 tbsp*) sage leaves, crushed

2 ml	(*1/2 tsp*) salt
1 ml	(*1/4 tsp*) pepper

Heat oven to 180 °C (*350 °F*) mark 4. Coat roast with oil; rub sage over entire roast. Place roast, fat side up, on rack in roasting tin. Sprinkle with salt and pepper. Bake for 2 to 3 hr. or until meat thermometer reaches 76 °C (*170 °F*).

6 servings
1 hour 30 minutes

Basil Tomato Pork Chops

Moist, tender pork chops cooked in a fresh vegetable sauce.

30 g	(*1 oz*) butter or margarine
5 ml	(*1 tsp*) crushed fresh garlic
8	pork chops, 1-cm (*1/2-in*) thick
800 g	(*1 3/4 lb*) canned whole tomatoes
5 ml	(*1 tsp*) basil leaves
5 ml	(*1 tsp*) salt

2 ml	(*1/2 tsp*) pepper
125 ml	(*4 fl oz*) water
45 ml	(*3 tbsp*) cornflour
1	med. onion, sliced into rings
1	med. green pepper, sliced into rings

In flameproof casserole melt butter until sizzling; stir in garlic. Add 4 pork chops; brown on both sides. Remove from casserole; repeat with remaining pork chops. Return all pork chops to pan. Stir in remaining ingredients *except* water, cornflour, onion and green pepper. Cover; cook over med. heat, stirring occasionally, until pork chops are fork tender (50 to 60 min.). Remove pork chops; keep warm. In small bowl stir together water and cornflour. Stir cornflour mixture into hot cooking liquid in casserole; add onion and green pepper. Cook over med. high heat, stirring occasionally, until thickened and vegetables are crisply tender (5 to 6 min.). Serve sauce over pork chops.

Microwave Directions: In 33 x 23-cm (*13 x 9-in*) baking dish melt butter on HIGH (40 to 50 sec.). Stir in garlic; add pork chops. In medium bowl stir together remaining ingredients *except* water, cornflour, onion and green pepper. Pour over pork chops. Cover; microwave on HIGH, rearranging pork chops after half the time, until pork chops are fork tender (25 to 35 min.). Remove pork chops; keep warm. In small bowl stir together water and cornflour. Stir cornflour mixture into hot cooking liquid in baking dish; add onion and green pepper. Microwave on HIGH, stirring twice during the time, until thickened and vegetables are crisply tender (4 to 5 min.). Serve sauce over pork chops.

Basil Tomato Pork Chops

Apple-Nut-Stuffed Pork Chops

6 servings
1 hour 30 minutes

Fresh apples add extra taste and colour to hearty stuffed pork chops.

125 g	(*4 oz*) butter or margarine
75 ml	(*5 tbsp*) chopped onion
75 ml	(*5 tbsp*) chopped walnuts
75 ml	(*5 tbsp*) chopped apple
250 ml	(*8 fl oz*) water
225 g	(*8 oz*) dried crumbly style herb seasoned stuffing

6	(5 to 5.5-cm thick) (*2 to 2¼-in*) double rib pork chops, with 3.5 to 5-cm (*1½ to 2-in*) pocket cut in rib side
30 g	(*1 oz*) butter or margarine

Heat oven to 180 °C (*350 °F*) mark 4. In 25-cm (*10-in*) frying pan melt 125 g (*4 oz*) butter until sizzling; add onion. Cook over med. heat until tender (4 to 5 min.). Remove from heat. Stir in walnuts, apple, water and stuffing. Fill pockets in pork chops with stuffing. In same frying pan melt 30 g (*1 oz*) butter. Brown pork chops on both sides; place in 33 x 23-cm (*13 x 9-in*) baking dish. Cover; bake for 60 to 70 min. or until no longer pink and thermometer reaches 76 °C (*170 °F*).

Microwave Directions: *Eliminate 30 g (1 oz) butter.* In 33 x 23-cm (*13 x 9-in*) baking dish melt 125 g (*4 oz*) butter on HIGH (50 to 60 sec.); add onion. Cover; microwave on HIGH, stirring after half the time, until tender (2 to 3 min.). Stir in remaining ingredients *except* pork chops. Fill pockets in pork chops with stuffing. In same dish arrange pork chops with thickest edge to outside; *sprinkle with paprika.* Cover; microwave on HIGH, turning dish ½ turn after half the time, until no longer pink and thermometer reaches 76 °C (*170 °F*) (20 to 30 min.). Let stand 5 min.

Oven-Baked Pork Chops

6 servings
1 hour 30 minutes

Dinner is easy when pork chops and rice bake together in one pan.

6	(2.5 to 3-cm thick) (*1 to 1¼-in*) pork loin or rib chops
2	celery sticks, sliced 1 cm (*½ in*)
300 g	(*11 oz*) uncooked long grain rice
1	med. sliced onion

750 ml	(*1¼ pt*) water
20 ml	(*4 tsp*) instant chicken bouillon
5 ml	(*1 tsp*) Italian herb seasoning*
2 ml	(*½ tsp*) salt
1	med. green pepper, cut into 6 rings

Heat oven to 180 °C (*350 °F*) mark 4. In 25-cm (*10-in*) frying pan brown pork chops over med. heat. In 33 x 23-cm (*13 x 9-in*) baking dish stir together celery and uncooked rice. Place onion slices over rice; top with pork chops. In 2-litre (*3½-pt*) saucepan bring water to a full boil. Add remaining ingredients *except* green pepper. Stir to dissolve; pour over pork chops. Cover with aluminum foil; bake for 60 to 70 min. or

until rice is cooked and pork chops are fork tender. Remove foil; top pork chops with green pepper rings. Continue baking for 10 to 15 min. or until green pepper is crisply tender.

*1 ml (*¼ tsp*) each oregano leaves, marjoram leaves and basil leaves and a pinch of rubbed sage can be substituted for 5 ml (*1 tsp*) Italian herb seasoning.

Apple-Nut-Stuffed Pork Chops

4 servings
45 minutes

Pork Chops With Mushroom Pan Gravy

Serve tender pork chops over rice, then top with lots of traditional pan gravy.

6	rashers of bacon, cut into 1-cm (*1/2-in*) pieces
2	med. onions, sliced 3 mm (*1/8 in*)
4	(2-cm thick) (*3/4-in*) middle cut pork chops
45 ml	(*3 tbsp*) plain flour
2 ml	(*1/2 tsp*) salt
2 ml	(*1/2 tsp*) thyme leaves

1 ml	(*1/4 tsp*) pepper
500 ml	(*17 fl oz*) single cream
225 g	(*8 oz*) sliced 5 mm (*1/4 in*) fresh mushrooms
	Cooked rice

In 25-cm (*10-in*) frying pan cook bacon and onions over med. high heat, stirring occasionally, until browned (8 to 10 min.). Add pork chops, arranging bacon and onions on top of pork chops. Cover; continue cooking for 10 min. or until browned. Turn pork chops. Reduce heat to med. Cover; cook until pork chops are tender (10 to 15 min.). Place pork chops on platter; keep warm while preparing gravy. In same frying pan with drippings, brown particles, bacon and onions add remaining ingredients *except* single cream, mushrooms and rice. Cook over med. heat, stirring occasionally, until smooth and bubbly (1 min.). Stir in single cream and mushrooms. Continue cooking, stirring occasionally, until mixture is thickened (8 to 10 min.). Serve gravy over rice and pork chops.

Microwave Directions: In 30 x 20-cm (*12 x 8-in*) baking dish microwave bacon and onion on HIGH, stirring after half the time, until tender (4 to 8 min.). Place pork chops in same dish, arranging bacon and onions on top of pork chops. Cover; microwave on HIGH, turning pork chops over and rearranging after half the time, until pork chops are tender (10 to 18 min.). Place pork chops on platter; keep warm while preparing gravy. Pour off fat. In same baking dish add remaining ingredients *except* single cream, mushrooms and rice. Microwave on HIGH, stirring after half the time, until bubbly (3 to 5 min.). Stir in single cream and mushrooms. Microwave on HIGH, stirring after half the time, until mixture is thickened (5 1/2 to 7 1/2 min.). Serve gravy over rice and pork chops.

Pork Chops With Mushroom Pan Gravy

Pan-Fried Pork Cutlets

6 servings
30 minutes

Tender pork, lightly coated and pan-fried.

900 g	(*2 lb*) pork fillet, cut into 12 slices	100 g	(*4 oz*) dry unseasoned breadcrumbs
75 ml	(*5 tbsp*) plain flour	5 ml	(*1 tsp*) paprika
5 ml	(*1 tsp*) salt	125 g	(*4 oz*) butter or margarine
1 ml	(*¼ tsp*) pepper		
1	egg, beaten		Lemon slices
30 ml	(*2 tbsp*) milk		Parsley

Flatten each slice of pork to about 8 mm (*⅓ in*) thickness by pounding between sheets of waxed paper; set aside. In pie dish combine flour, salt and pepper. In small bowl stir together egg and milk. In pie dish combine breadcrumbs and paprika. Coat each slice of pork with flour mixture. Dip floured slices into egg mixture, then coat with breadcrumb mixture. In 25-cm (*10-in*) frying pan melt 50 g (*2 oz*) butter over med. heat. Cook 6 slices at a time, turning once, until golden brown and done throughout (3 to 4 min. per side). Remove from pan to platter; keep warm in oven. Repeat with remaining slices. Garnish with lemon and parsley.

Honey-Smoked Pork Fillet

4 servings
30 minutes

Country smokehouse flavour and hearty goodness.

45 g	(*1½ oz*) butter or margarine	1 ml	(*¼ tsp*) salt
450 g	(*1 lb*) (5-cm / 2-in diameter) pork fillet, sliced 5 cm (*2 in*)	1 ml	(*¼ tsp*) pepper
		1 ml	(*¼ tsp*) sage
4	med. carrots, sliced 2.5 cm (*1 in*)	45 ml	(*3 tbsp*) honey
3	celery sticks, sliced 2.5 cm (*1 in*)	30 ml	(*2 tbsp*) lemon juice
1	small onion, sliced 3 mm (*⅛ in*)	5 ml	(*1 tsp*) liquid smoke
2 ml	(*½ tsp*) ginger	2 ml	(*½ tsp*) crushed fresh garlic

In 25-cm (*10-in*) frying pan melt butter until sizzling; add pork and carrots. Cook over med. high heat, stirring occasionally, until meat is browned (5 to 6 min.). Reduce heat to med. Stir in remaining ingredients. Cover; cook, stirring occasionally, until vegetables are crisply tender (10 to 12 min.).

Microwave Directions: In 2-litre (*3½-pt*) casserole melt butter on HIGH (30 to 45 sec.); add pork and carrots. Cover; microwave on HIGH, stirring after half the time, until pork is no longer pink (8 to 10 min.). Stir in remaining ingredients. Cover; microwave on HIGH, stirring after half the time, until vegetables are crisply tender (5 to 9 min.). Place pork and vegetables on platter; keep warm. *Combine 10 ml (2 tsp) corn-flour with 10 ml (2 tsp) water.* Stir into hot casserole juices. Microwave on HIGH, stirring after half the time, until thickened (2 to 4 min.). Pour sauce over meat.

Honey-Smoked Pork Fillet

Autumn Squash With Savoury Pork

4 servings
60 minutes

Autumn Squash With Savoury Pork

Tantalizing pork served in acorn squash.

2	med. acorn squash, cut in half
125 ml	*(4 fl oz)* water
125 g	*(4 oz)* butter or margarine
2	med. onions, chopped
2	celery sticks, sliced 5 mm *(1/4 in)*
350 g	*(3/4 lb)* pork fillet, cut into 5 x 1-cm *(2 x 1/2-in)* strips

2 ml	*(1/2 tsp)* salt
2 ml	*(1/2 tsp)* marjoram leaves
2 ml	*(1/2 tsp)* pepper
2 ml	*(1/2 tsp)* thyme leaves
75 g	*(3 oz)* cubed 2.5 cm *(1 in)* rye bread
15 ml	*(1 tbsp)* grated orange rind

Heat oven to 190 °C *(375 °F)* mark 5. Place squash in 33 x 23-cm *(13 x 9-in)* baking dish; pour water in bottom of dish. Cover; bake for 45 to 50 min. or until fork tender. Meanwhile, in 25-cm *(10-in)* frying pan melt butter until sizzling. Add remaining ingredients *except* rye bread and orange rind. Cook over med. high heat, stirring occasionally, until meat is fork tender (15 to 20 min.). Stir in rye bread and orange rind. Continue cooking, stirring occasionally, until heated through (3 to 4 min.). To serve, divide mixture evenly among baked squash.

Microwave Directions: Place squash in 33 x 23-cm *(13 x 9-in)* baking dish. Omit 125 ml *(4 fl oz)* water. Cover; microwave on HIGH, rearranging after half the time, until squash is tender. Let stand 5 min. Meanwhile, in medium bowl combine remaining ingredients *except* rye bread and orange rind. Cover; microwave on HIGH, stirring after half the time, until meat is no longer pink (8 to 10 min.). Stir in rye bread and orange rind. Cover; microwave until heated through (2 to 3 min.).

6 servings
40 minutes

Herb Roasted Pork Casserole

Pork roast dinner in a hearty casserole.

125 g	*(4 oz)* butter or margarine
4	med. new red potatoes, cut into 2.5-cm *(1-in)* pieces
450 g	*(1 lb)* pork roast, cut into 2.5-cm *(1-in)* pieces
2 ml	*(1/2 tsp)* salt
2 ml	*(1/2 tsp)* crushed rosemary leaves
2 ml	*(1/2 tsp)* pepper
2 ml	*(1/2 tsp)* sage
5 ml	*(1 tsp)* crushed fresh garlic

225 g	*(8 oz)* crumbly style herb seasoned stuffing
2	celery sticks, sliced 1 cm *(1/2 in)*
175 g	*(6 oz)* chopped red onion
125 ml	*(4 fl oz)* apple juice
50 ml	*(4 tbsp)* chopped fresh parsley
2	med. ripe tomatoes, cut into 2.5-cm *(1-in)* pieces

In deep 25-cm *(10-in)* frying pan melt 50 g *(2 oz)* butter until sizzling; add potatoes. Cook over med. high heat, stirring occasionally, until potatoes are lightly browned (10 to 15 min.). Add pork, salt, rosemary, pepper, sage and garlic. Continue cooking, stirring occasionally, until meat is browned (10 to 12 min.). Reduce heat to med. Add remaining butter and remaining ingredients *except* parsley and tomatoes. Cover; cook until heated through (7 to 9 min.). Stir in parsley and tomatoes. Cover; let stand 2 min. or until heated through.

Microwave Directions: In 3-litre *(5-pt)* casserole melt 50 g *(2 oz)* butter on HIGH (50 to 60 sec.). Stir in potatoes, pork, salt, rosemary, pepper, sage and garlic. Cover; microwave on HIGH, stirring after half the time, until pork is no longer pink (10 to 13 min.). Stir in remaining butter and remaining ingredients *except* parsley and tomatoes. Cover; microwave on HIGH, stirring after half the time, until heated through (3 to 5 min.). Stir in parsley and tomatoes. Cover; let stand 2 min. or until heated through.

Country Ham Steak With Glazed Apples

4 servings
20 minutes

Country Ham Steak With Glazed Apples

Brown sugar-glazed apples add heartwarming goodness to ham steak.

45 g	(*1 1/2 oz*) butter or margarine	2	med. tart apples, cored, sliced 3 mm (*1/8 in*)
50 ml	(*4 tbsp*) firmly packed brown sugar		
30 ml	(*2 tbsp*) country-style Dijon mustard	450 g	(*1 lb*) (1-cm / *1/2-in* thick) ham steak

In 25-cm (*10-in*) frying pan melt butter until sizzling; stir in brown sugar and mustard. Add apples. Cook over med. heat, stirring occasionally, until apples are crisply tender (5 to 7 min.). Place ham steak in same frying pan, arranging apples on ham steak. Cover; continue cooking until ham steak is heated through (5 to 7 min.).

Microwave Directions: In 33 x 23-cm (*13 x 9-in*) baking dish melt butter on HIGH (30 to 45 sec.). Stir in brown sugar and mustard. Add apples. Place ham steak in baking dish, arranging apples on ham steak. Cover; microwave on HIGH, stirring apples after half the time, until apples are crisply tender and ham steak is heated through (5 to 8 min.).

6 servings
1 hour 30 minutes

Ham 'n Cheese Scalloped Potatoes

This heartland favourite, scalloped potatoes, bakes in a rich Cheddar cheese sauce.

4	large potatoes, thinly sliced	5 ml	(*1 tsp*) dry mustard
600 g	(*1 1/4 lb*) cubed 2.5 cm (*1 in*) cooked ham	2 ml	(*1/2 tsp*) pepper
1	med. onion, thinly sliced and separated into rings	500 ml	(*17 fl oz*) milk
		350 g	(*12 oz*) shredded Cheddar cheese
50 g	(*2 oz*) butter or margarine	30 ml	(*2 tbsp*) chopped fresh chives
75 ml	(*5 tbsp*) plain flour		

Heat oven to 180 °C (*350 °F*) mark 4. In 33 x 23-cm (*13 x 9-in*) baking dish layer potatoes, ham and onion. In 2-litre (*3 1/2-pt*) saucepan melt butter until sizzling. Stir in flour, mustard and pepper. Cook over med. heat, stirring constantly, until smooth and bubbly (1 min.). Add milk. Continue cooking, stirring occasionally, until sauce is thickened (2 to 3 min.). Stir in cheese until melted (3 to 4 min.). Pour sauce over potatoes; sprinkle with chives. Bake for 60 to 75 min. or until bubbly and potatoes are fork tender.

Microwave Directions: In 33 x 23-m (*13 x 9-in*) baking dish layer potatoes, ham and onion. In 2-litre (*3 1/2-pt*) casserole melt butter on HIGH (60 to 70 sec.). Stir in flour, mustard and pepper. Microwave on HIGH until bubbly (30 to 45 sec.). Add milk. Microwave on HIGH, stirring after half the time, until sauce is thickened (4 1/2 to 6 min.). Stir in cheese until melted. Pour sauce over potatoes. Cover with plastic wrap. Microwave on HIGH, stirring every 10 min., until bubbly and potatoes are fork tender (20 to 26 min.). Let stand 5 min. Sprinkle with chives.

Spicy Sausage & Potatoes in a Frying Pan

6 servings
35 minutes

Spicy sausage and new red potatoes are pan-fried until crispy,
then cooked with green pepper and onion.

675 g	(*1½ lb*) (6 links) mild Italian sausage, cut into 2.5-cm (*1-in*) pieces		125 g	(*4 oz*) sliced 3 mm (*⅛ in*) red onion
10	small new red potatoes, quartered		50 ml	(*4 tbsp*) chopped fresh parsley
2 ml	(*½ tsp*) pepper		1	green pepper, cut into 2.5-cm (*1-in*) pieces
2 ml	(*½ tsp*) thyme leaves			

In 25-cm (*10-in*) frying pan combine sausage, potatoes, pepper and thyme. Cook over med. high heat, stirring occasionally, until potatoes are browned (10 to 12 min.). Reduce heat to med. low. Cover; cook until potatoes are tender (8 to 10 min.). Stir in remaining ingredients. Continue cooking, uncovered, until vegetables are crisply tender (4 to 5 min.).

Microwave Directions: In 3-litre (*5-pt*) casserole combine sausage, potatoes, pepper and thyme. Cover; microwave on HIGH, stirring after half the time, until potatoes are tender (9 to 11 min.). Stir in remaining ingredients. Cover; microwave on HIGH until vegetables are crisply tender (4 to 6 min.).

Bratwursts & Sauerkraut Frying Pan Supper

4 servings
30 minutes

Taste the unique flavour that apple juice gives
to bratwursts and sauerkraut in this frying pan supper.

6	bratwurst sausages		2	med. green peppers, sliced into 5-mm (*¼-in*) rings
250 ml	(*8 fl oz*) apple juice		10 ml	(*2 tsp*) caraway seed
500 g	(*17½ oz*) sauerkraut, drained			

In 25-cm (*10-in*) frying pan place bratwursts. Cook over med. high heat, turning occasionally, until browned (5 min.). Reduce heat to med.; add apple juice. Cover; cook until fork tender (10 to 12 min.). Stir in remaining ingredients. Continue cooking, uncovered, until heated through (4 to 5 min.).

Microwave Directions: In 33 x 23-cm (*13 x 9-in*) baking dish place bratwursts and apple juice. Cover; microwave on HIGH, turning bratwursts after half the time, until almost done (5 to 8 min.). Add remaining ingredients. Cover; microwave on HIGH until heated through and bratwursts are no longer pink (5 to 8 min.).

Spicy Sausage & Potatoes in a Frying Pan

Orange-Glazed Stuffed Crown Roast

6 servings
2 hours 50 minutes

Serve this elegant spinach-stuffed roast when company's coming.

	Crown roast of lamb 1.4 to 1.8 kg (*3 to 4 lb*)
	Salt and pepper
50 g	(*2 oz*) butter or margarine
178-ml	(*6¼-oz*) carton frozen orange juice concentrate, thawed
30 ml	(*2 tbsp*) Madeira wine, optional

Stuffing

225 g	(*8 oz*) dried crumbly style herb seasoned stuffing
125 g	(*4 oz*) butter or margarine, melted
600 g	(*1¼ lb*) frozen chopped spinach, thawed, drained
2	rashers of bacon, cut into 1-cm (*½-in*) pieces
2	eggs, slightly beaten
2 ml	(*½ tsp*) dry mustard
1 ml	(*¼ tsp*) salt
1 ml	(*¼ tsp*) pepper

Heat oven to 160 °C (*325 °F*) mark 3. Line shallow roasting tin with aluminum foil. Place roast, bone end up, on rack in roasting tin. Protect ends of bones with aluminum foil. Season with salt and pepper. Bake roast for 30 to 35 min. per 450 g (*lb*) or until meat thermometer reaches 71 °C (*160 °F*) (Medium). Meanwhile, in 1-litre (*1¾-pt*) saucepan combine 50 g (*2 oz*) butter, orange juice concentrate and wine. Cook over med. heat until butter is melted (4 to 5 min.). One hour before roast is done begin brushing orange juice mixture over roast every 15 min. and prepare stuffing. In large bowl combine all stuffing ingredients; place in 1.5-litre (*2¾-pt*) casserole. Bake in same oven for 35 to 40 min. or until heated through. Let roast stand 15 min. before carving. Stuff center of roast with stuffing and serve with warm orange juice mixture.

Tip: For crisp bacon, precook before adding to stuffing.

To Prepare Crown Roast:

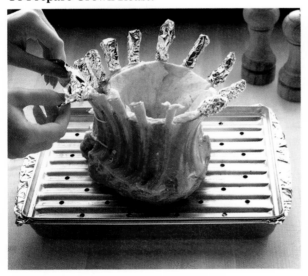

1. Line shallow roasting tin with aluminum foil. Place roast, bone end up, on rack in roasting tin. Protect ends of bones with aluminum foil.

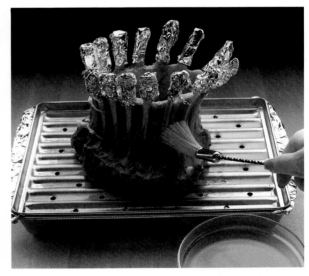

2. One hour before roast is done begin brushing orange juice mixture over roast every 15 min.

Orange-Glazed Stuffed Crown Roast

Sausage-Stuffed Lamb Chops

4 to 6 servings
1 hour 20 minutes

Sausage-Stuffed Lamb Chops

The pairing of lamb and Italian sausage provides the perfect balance of savoury flavours.

225 g	(*1/2 lb*) mild Italian sausage
1	med. onion, finely chopped
130 g	(*41/2 oz*) fresh breadcrumbs
50 ml	(*4 tbsp*) chopped fresh parsley
5 ml	(*1 tsp*) thyme leaves
2 ml	(*1/2 tsp*) marjoram leaves
2 ml	(*1/2 tsp*) coarsely ground pepper

2 ml	(*1/2 tsp*) grated orange rind
2 ml	(*1/2 tsp*) crushed fresh garlic
50 g	(*2 oz*) butter or margarine
2 ml	(*1/2 tsp*) thyme leaves
2 ml	(*1/2 tsp*) marjoram leaves
6	(5-cm)(*2-in*) double rib lamb chops, with 3.5-cm (*11/2-in*) pocket cut in loin side

Heat oven to 180 °C (*350 °F*) mark 4. In 25-cm (*10-in*) frying pan cook sausage and onion over med. high heat, stirring occasionally, until sausage is browned (7 to 9 min.). Drain off fat. Stir in remaining ingredients *except* butter, 2 ml (*1/2 tsp*) thyme, 2 ml (*1/2 tsp*) marjoram and lamb chops. Set aside. In same frying pan melt butter until sizzling; stir in remaining ingredients *except* lamb chops. Add lamb chops. Cook over med. high heat until browned (2 to 3 min. on each side). Stuff each lamb chop with about 50 ml (*4 tbsp*) filling. Place in 33 x 23-cm (*13 x 9-in*) baking dish. Bake for 30 to 40 min. or until meat thermometer reaches 71 °C (*160 °F*) (Medium).

Microwave Directions: In 2-litre (*31/2-pt*) casserole combine sausage and onion. Cover; microwave on HIGH, stirring after half the time, until sausage is cooked (4 to 51/2 min.). Drain off fat. Stir in remaining ingredients *except* butter, 2 ml (*1/2 tsp*) thyme, 2 ml (*1/2 tsp*) marjoram and lamb chops. Set aside. In 33 x 23-cm (*13 x 9-in*) baking dish melt butter on HIGH (50 to 60 sec.). Stir in remaining ingredients *except* lamb chops. Stuff each lamb chop with about 50 ml (*4 tbsp*) filling. Place in 33 x 23-cm (*13 x 9-in*) dish; turn lamb chops over to coat each side with butter. Cover; microwave on HIGH, turning pan 1/4 turn after half the time, 5 min. Reduce power to MEDIUM (50% power); microwave, turning lamb chops over and rearranging after half the time, until meat thermometer reaches 71 °C (*160 °F*) (10 to 15 min.).

Lamb	Internal Cooking Temperature
Rare	60 °C (*140 °F*)
Medium	71 °C (*160 °F*)
Well	76 °C (*170 °F*)

Country Vegetable & Lamb Kabobs

6 servings
1 hour 30 minutes

Leg of Lamb Roasted With Rosemary

Serve lamb with mint jelly, fresh peas and new potatoes for a traditional meal.

1.4 to 1.8 kg	*(3 to 4 lb)* leg of lamb	5 ml	*(1 tsp)* salt
30 ml	*(2 tbsp)* crushed fresh garlic	2 ml	*(1/2 tsp)* pepper
10 ml	*(2 tsp)* rosemary leaves, crushed		

Heat oven to 180 °C *(350 °F)* mark 4. Place lamb, fat side up, on rack in roasting tin. In small bowl stir together remaining ingredients. Spread over lamb. Bake for 60 to 90 min. or until meat thermometer reaches 71 °C *(160 °F)* (Medium).

Lamb	Internal Cooking Temperature
Rare	60 °C *(140 °F)*
Medium	71 °C *(160 °F)*
Well	76 °C *(170 °F)*

4 servings
60 minutes

Country Vegetable & Lamb Kabobs

A zesty marinade makes these colourful lamb kabobs irresistible.

Marinade

50 g	*(2 oz)* butter or margarine
75 ml	*(5 tbsp)* lemon juice
15 ml	*(1 tbsp)* sugar
5 ml	*(1 tsp)* thyme leaves
3 ml	*(3/4 tsp)* salt
1 ml	*(1/4 tsp)* oregano leaves
1 ml	*(1/4 tsp)* pepper
30 ml	*(2 tbsp)* finely chopped onion
5 ml	*(1 tsp)* hot pepper sauce
2 ml	*(1/2 tsp)* crushed fresh garlic

Kabobs

450 g	*(1 lb)* lamb, cut into about 32 (2.5-cm) *(1-in)* pieces
8	small mushrooms
8	cherry tomatoes
1	small green pepper, cut into 8 (2.5-cm) *(1-in)* pieces
1	small summer squash, cut into 8 (2.5-cm) *(1-in)* pieces
4	(30-cm) *(12-in)* metal skewers

Prepare grill placing coals to one side; heat until coals are ash white. Make aluminum foil drip pan; place opposite coals. In small saucepan combine all marinade ingredients. Cook over med. heat, stirring occasionally, until butter melts and mixture comes to a full boil (8 to 10 min.); remove from heat. Let cool 5 min. Stir in lamb pieces; set aside. Let marinate 15 min. To assemble kabobs on metal skewers, alternate lamb pieces with mushrooms, cherry tomatoes, green pepper and summer squash. Place kabobs on barbecue grid over drip pan. Grill, turning occasionally, until lamb is fork tender or desired doneness (10 to 15 min.). Heat remaining marinade; brush over kabobs before serving.

Grilling Directions: Prepare kabobs as directed left. Heat grill. Place kabobs on greased grill pan 10 to 12.5 cm *(4 to 5 in)* from heat. Grill until brown (5 to 7 min.). Turn, brush with marinade; continue grilling until lamb is fork tender or desired doneness (5 to 7 min.). Heat remaining marinade; brush over kabobs before serving.

Microwave Directions: *Use 4 (30-cm)* (12-in) *wooden skewers.* Prepare kabobs as directed left. Place kabobs in (30 x 20-cm) *(12 x 8-in)* baking dish. Microwave on HIGH 5 min. Turn kabobs over; brush with marinade. Microwave on HIGH until lamb is fork tender or desired doneness (4 to 5 min.). Heat remaining marinade; brush over kabobs before serving.

Marinated Herb Veal Roast

6 to 8 servings
1 day

A marinade with a blend of herbs imparts marvelous flavour to roasted veal.

Marinade

50 ml	(*4 tbsp*) olive or vegetable oil
15 ml	(*1 tbsp*) white wine vinegar
15 ml	(*1 tbsp*) sugar
5 ml	(*1 tsp*) basil leaves
5 ml	(*1 tsp*) thyme leaves
3 ml	(*3/4 tsp*) salt
1 ml	(*1/4 tsp*) pepper
30 ml	(*2 tbsp*) chopped fresh parsley
10 ml	(*2 tsp*) crushed fresh garlic

1 to 1.4 kg	(*2 to 3 lb*) boneless shoulder veal roast

Sauce

50 g	(*2 oz*) chopped fresh mushrooms
50 g	(*2 oz*) chopped red pepper
5 ml	(*1 tsp*) grated lemon rind
30 ml	(*2 tbsp*) chopped fresh chives

In flameproof casserole stir together oil and vinegar. Stir in remaining marinade ingredients *except* roast. Place roast in marinade; turn to coat all sides with herbs and oil. Cover; refrigerate 12 hr. or overnight. Heat oven to 180 °C (*350 °F*) mark 4. Cover; bake roast in marinade for 45 min. Uncover; continue baking, basting with casserole juices occasionally, for 1 to 1½ hr. or until meat thermometer reaches 71 °C (*160 °F*) (Medium). *Reserve casserole juices*; skim off fat. In 1-litre (*1¾-pt*) saucepan combine 75 ml (*5 tbsp*) reserved casserole juices and all sauce ingredients *except* chives. Cook over med. high heat until sauce comes to a full boil; boil 2 min. Stir in chives. Serve over carved roast.

Veal	Internal Cooking Temperature
Rare	60 °C (*140 °F*)
Medium	71 °C (*160 °F*)
Well	76 °C (*170 °F*)

Veal With Artichokes & Mushrooms

6 servings
20 minutes

A twist of fresh lemon flavours this quick, elegant entrée.

50 ml	(*4 tbsp*) plain flour
50 ml	(*4 tbsp*) freshly grated Parmesan cheese
1 ml	(*1/4 tsp*) salt
1 ml	(*1/4 tsp*) pepper
6	(5-mm) (*1/4-in*) boneless veal cutlets
2	eggs, slightly beaten
50 g	(*2 oz*) butter or margarine
30 ml	(*2 tbsp*) lemon juice
125 ml	(*4 fl oz*) double cream

75 g	(*3 oz*) sliced 5 mm (*1/4 in*) fresh mushrooms
250 g	(*9 oz*) frozen artichoke hearts, thawed, drained
30 ml	(*2 tbsp*) freshly grated Parmesan cheese
1 ml	(*1/4 tsp*) salt
	Dash cayenne pepper
30 ml	(*2 tbsp*) lemon juice
30 ml	(*2 tbsp*) chopped fresh parsley

In 23-cm (*9-in*) pie dish stir together flour, 50 ml (*4 tbsp*) Parmesan cheese, 1 ml (*1/4 tsp*) salt and pepper. Dip cutlets in eggs; lightly coat both sides of cutlets with flour mixture. In 25-cm (*10-in*) frying pan melt butter over med. heat until sizzling; stir in 30 ml (*2 tbsp*) lemon juice. Place 3 cutlets in melted butter and lemon juice; fry until browned (3 min. on each side). Remove cutlets to serving platter; keep warm. Repeat with remaining cutlets. In same frying pan with drippings and brown particles stir in double cream. Add remaining ingredients *except* parsley. Cook over med. heat, stirring occasionally, until sauce is slightly thickened and artichokes are heated through (4 to 6 min.). Stir in parsley. Serve over cutlets.

Veal With Artichokes & Mushrooms

How To: Barbecue or Grill

Many types of grills are available; the most common include:

- round covered kettle
- rectangular or square cooker with a hinged lid
- open brazier
- gas or electric grill

All work well and apply even heat to the food being cooked when properly used.

To Produce Best Results with a Grill:

Charcoal briquettes are most commonly used for barbecuing. All recipes in this cookbook were tested using charcoal briquettes and a gas grill. Other fuels available include mesquite, wood, hardwood charcoal and smoking or flavour chips. Each imparts a unique flavour to the cooked food.

To determine the number of charcoal briquettes needed, spread a single layer of charcoal briquettes 2.5 cm (*1 in*) beyond the edge of the food for small cuts of meat. For longer cooking foods, use additional charcoal briquettes. Stack the charcoal briquettes in a pyramid shape to provide proper ventilation.

Ignite briquettes 30 to 40 minutes before you intend to cook. Be sure to open any vents on the grill. Preheat gas grill according to manufacturer's directions. For indirect grilling on a dual control gas grill, use single control, opposite meat placement.

To Ignite Briquettes:

Use a fluid starter according to package directions. Ignite briquettes with matches or with an electric starter.

The coals are ready when they have burned to an ash white colour.

To Extinguish Coals:

Immediately after cooking, cover the grill and close all vents to extinguish the coals. Charcoal briquettes are reusable if thoroughly dried out. When relighting used charcoal briquettes, combine them with fresh charcoal briquettes and follow directions above.

There are two basic cooking methods used with the recipes in this cookbook: indirect and direct. The **indirect** method is a slower cooking method that minimizes flareups if dripping occurs. It is, therefore, the recommended method when sauces or marinades are applied. Indirect cooking is also used for large pieces of poultry, meat, fish or fatty foods to achieve more even cooking. Often the grill is covered to help distribute heat during cooking. The **direct** cooking method is faster since more intense heat is provided. Faster cooking meats or thin pieces of meat, poultry or fish are usually grilled over direct heat.

To Arrange Coals for Indirect Cooking:

1. Prepare grill placing coals to one side; heat until coals are ash white. Make aluminum foil drip pan; place opposite coals.

To Arrange Coals for Direct Cooking:

2. Prepare grill; heat until coals are ash white.

To Make Aluminum Foil Drip Pan: (Aluminum foil drip pans can be purchased ready-made.)

1. Tear off two sheets of heavy-duty aluminum foil that are 8 cm (*3 in*) longer than the food to be grilled. With the two sheets together, fold all sides inward about 5 cm (*2 in*).

2. Turn aluminum foil over. Score aluminum foil about 2.5 cm (*1 in*) from edge. At corners, score diagonally to edge.

3. Fold edges up and pinch corners.

4. Bring all sides up to form pan. Fold corners flat against sides.

FISH & SEAFOOD

Imagine a lazy summer day in the country. The sun is high and the fish are biting. So, you gather the fishing gear and head for the creek. But whether caught at the creek or selected at the market, nothing beats the lure of fresh fish and seafood cooked to perfection.

From virtually every part of this vast continent — the clear, inland lakes and streams, the icy-cold depths of the North Pacific, the rugged, rock-lined waters of the Atlantic — comes a bounty of fish and seafood. It's a rich and varied harvest, from sweet and tender scallops and shrimp to the distinctively robust taste of salmon.

Fish is delicious baked with seasoned stuffing or charcoal-grilled and dressed with a tangy herb sauce. To capture the delicate, mild flavor of fish, sauté it and serve with a simple lemon-butter mixture. Or perhaps you're hungry for the heartiness of old-fashioned country cooking. Invite a few friends in for a casual fish supper featuring light, flaky fillets coated in a special batter and fried to a crispy golden brown. No matter how it's prepared, fish is a delightfully versatile main course for family and company meals.

Seaside Harbour Dinner

A hearty and flavourful fish and vegetable dinner in a frying pan.

50 g	(*2 oz*) butter or margarine
6	small new red potatoes, quartered
3	celery sticks, sliced 2.5 cm (*1 in*)
3	carrots, sliced 2.5 cm (*1 in*)
2 ml	(*1/2 tsp*) salt
2 ml	(*1/2 tsp*) dry mustard

1 ml	(*1/4 tsp*) pepper
450 g	(*1 lb*) fresh or frozen perch fillets, thawed, drained
1	med. ripe tomato, cut into 2.5-cm (*1-in*) pieces

4 servings
35 minutes

In 25-cm (*10-in*) frying pan melt butter until sizzling; add remaining ingredients *except* fish and tomato. Cover; cook over med. high heat, stirring occasionally, until vegetables are browned and crisply tender (12 to 15 min.). Reduce heat to med. Place fish in same frying pan, arranging vegetables on top of fish. Sprinkle with tomato. Cover; cook until fish flakes with a fork (5 to 7 min.).

Microwave Directions: In 33 x 23-cm (*13 x 9-in*) baking dish melt butter on HIGH (50 to 60 sec.). Stir in remaining ingredients *except* fish and tomato. Cover; microwave on HIGH, stirring after half the time, until vegetables are crisply tender (9 to 11 min.). Place fish in same baking dish, arranging vegetables on top of fish. Sprinkle with tomato. Cover; microwave on HIGH, turning after half the time, until fish flakes with a fork (5 to 7 min.).

Fishermen's Supper

Garlic butter complements the simple combination of sole, courgette and red onion.

450 g	(*1 lb*) fresh or frozen sole fillets, thawed, drained
1	med. courgette, sliced 3 mm (*1/8 in*)
125 g	(*4 oz*) sliced 3 mm (*1/8 in*) red onion, separated into rings

50 g	(*2 oz*) butter or margarine, melted
1 ml	(*1/4 tsp*) salt
1 ml	(*1/4 tsp*) pepper
5 ml	(*1 tsp*) crushed fresh garlic
30 ml	(*2 tbsp*) chopped fresh parsley

4 servings
30 minutes

Heat oven to 190 °C (*375 °F*) mark 5. Place fish in 23-cm (*9-in*) sq. baking dish. Layer courgette and red onion evenly over fish. In small bowl stir together remaining ingredients *except* parsley; pour over vegetables. Cover; bake for 20 to 25 min. or until vegetables are crisply tender and fish flakes with a fork. Sprinkle with parsley.

Microwave Directions: Place fish in 23-cm (*9-in*) sq. baking dish. Place courgette and red onion evenly over fish. In small bowl stir together remaining ingredients *except* parsley; pour over vegetables. Cover; microwave on HIGH, turning dish 1/4 turn after half the time, until fish flakes with a fork (8 to 10 min.). Sprinkle with parsley.

Seaside Harbour Dinner

Crunchy Fish & Potatoes

Pan-Fried Cornmeal Batter Fish

6 servings
20 minutes

The catch of the day is dipped in a crispy cornmeal batter and pan-fried.

75 g	(*3 oz*) plain flour	1 ml	(*¼ tsp*) cayenne pepper
125 ml	(*4 fl oz*) milk	1 ml	(*¼ tsp*) oregano leaves
1	egg	75 g	(*3 oz*) yellow cornmeal
15 ml	(*1 tbsp*) sugar	900 g	(*2 lb*) fish fillets, steaks or pan-dressed
2 ml	(*½ tsp*) salt		fish, thawed, drained
2 ml	(*½ tsp*) paprika	125 ml	(*4 fl oz*) vegetable oil

In 23-cm (*9-in*) pie dish stir together all ingredients *except* cornmeal, fish and oil. On waxed paper place cornmeal. Coat both sides of fish with cornmeal, then dip into batter. In 25-cm (*10-in*) frying pan heat oil until hot. Place 3 to 4 fish in hot oil. Cook over med. heat until golden brown (3 to 4 min.). Turn; continue cooking until golden brown and fish flakes with a fork (2 to 3 min.). Repeat with remaining fish.

Crunchy Fish & Potatoes

4 servings
60 minutes

Perch fillets and potatoes team up in the same pan for a tasty dinner.

75 g	(*3 oz*) butter or margarine	2 ml	(*½ tsp*) garlic powder
2	med. potatoes, sliced 5 mm (*¼ in*)	1 ml	(*¼ tsp*) salt
75 g	(*3 oz*) crushed buttery crackers	30 ml	(*2 tbsp*) chopped fresh parsley
5 ml	(*1 tsp*) paprika	450 g	(*1 lb*) fresh or frozen perch fillets, thawed, drained

Heat oven to 180 °C (*350 °F*) mark 4. In 33 x 23-cm (*13 x 9-in*) baking dish melt butter in oven (5 to 7 min.). Add potato slices; stir to coat. Cover with aluminum foil; bake for 20 to 25 min. or until potato slices are fork tender. Meanwhile, in 23-cm (*9-in*) pie dish stir together remaining ingredients *except* perch fillets. Spoon potatoes to one side of baking dish. Dip perch fillets into melted butter that potatoes were baked in, then coat with crumb mixture. Place fillets, to one side, in same baking dish with potatoes. Sprinkle fish and potatoes with remaining crumb mixture. Bake for 20 to 30 min. or until fish flakes with a fork.

Microwave Directions: In 33 x 23-cm (*13 x 9-in*) baking dish melt butter on HIGH (60 to 70 sec.). Add potato slices; stir to coat. Cover; microwave on HIGH, stirring after half the time, until potato slices are fork tender (5 to 6 min.). Meanwhile, in 23-cm (*9-in*) pie dish stir together remaining ingredients *except* perch fillets. Spoon potatoes to one side of baking dish. Dip perch fillets into melted butter that potatoes were baked in, then coat with crumb mixture. Place fillets, to one side, in same baking dish with potatoes. Sprinkle fish and potatoes with remaining crumb mixture. Microwave on HIGH until fish flakes with a fork (7 to 9 min.).

Codfish Cakes With Spring Onions & Dill

6 cod cakes
20 minutes

Codfish cakes are fried until crispy and golden brown.

450 g	(*1 lb*) fresh or frozen cod fillets, thawed, drained	2 ml	(*1/2 tsp*) salt
250 g	(*9 oz*) coarse fresh breadcrumbs	1 ml	(*1/4 tsp*) dill weed
50 ml	(*4 tbsp*) chopped spring onions	1 ml	(*1/4 tsp*) pepper
2	eggs, slightly beaten	15 ml	(*1 tbsp*) lemon juice
		50 g	(*2 oz*) butter or margarine

Flake cod fillets apart with fork or mallet. In medium bowl stir together flaked cod and remaining ingredients *except* butter. Form into 6 (8-cm) (*3-in*) patties. In 25-cm (*10-in*) frying pan melt butter until sizzling. Place 3 patties in same frying pan. Cook over med. high heat until golden brown (4 to 5 min.). Turn; continue cooking until browned and fish flakes with a fork (3 to 4 min.). Repeat with remaining patties.

Microwave Directions: In medium bowl melt butter on HIGH (50 to 60 sec.). Flake cod fillets with fork or mallet. In same bowl stir together remaining ingredients and flaked cod. Form into 6 (8-cm) (*3-in*) patties; *sprinkle with paprika*. Place in 33 x 23-cm (*13 x 9-in*) baking dish. Cover; microwave on HIGH, turning dish 1/2 turn after half the time, until fish flakes with a fork (5 to 7 min.).

Vegetable Garden Fish Kabobs

6 kabobs
45 minutes

*Serve with a fresh spinach salad, sourdough bread
and tall glasses of iced tea for a quick, relaxing summer meal.*

450 g	(*1 lb*) fish fillets (cod or haddock), cut into 2.5-cm (*1-in*) cubes	6	(30-cm) (*12-in*) metal skewers
1	med. courgette, cut into 1-cm (*1/2-in*) pieces	**Sauce**	
12	cherry tomatoes	125 g	(*4 oz*) butter or margarine, melted
12	med. fresh mushrooms	50 ml	(*4 tbsp*) teriyaki sauce or soy sauce
1	med. green pepper, cored, cut into 2.5-cm (*1-in*) pieces	30 ml	(*2 tbsp*) lemon juice

Prepare grill, placing coals to one side; heat until coals are ash white. Make aluminum foil drip pan; place opposite coals. Alternate cubes of fish and vegetables on skewers. In small bowl stir together all sauce ingredients; brush over kabobs. Place kabobs on barbecue grid over drip pan. Grill, turning occasionally and basting with sauce, 10 to 20 min. or until fish flakes with a fork. Serve with remaining sauce.

Microwave Directions: *Use 6 (30-cm)* (12-in) *wooden skewers.* Assemble kabobs and prepare sauce as directed left. Place kabobs in 33 x 23-cm (*13 x 9-in*) baking dish or large microwave-safe baking sheet. Cover; microwave on HIGH, turning and basting with sauce after half the time, until fish flakes with a fork (8 to 10 min.). Serve with remaining sauce.

Vegetable Garden Fish Kabobs

Lemon Sole & Carrot Bundles

4 servings
40 minutes

*Fish fillets are rolled and stuffed with sweet, tender carrots
and topped with the country goodness of herb stuffing.*

4	med. carrots, cut into 12.5 x 0.5-cm (5 x ¼-in) strips
200 g	(7 oz) crumbly style herb seasoned stuffing
75 g	(3 oz) butter or margarine, melted

2 ml	(½ tsp) salt
1 ml	(¼ tsp) pepper
30 ml	(2 tbsp) lemon juice
450 g	(1 lb) fresh or frozen sole fillets, thawed, drained

Heat oven to 190 °C (375 °F) mark 5. In 2-litre (3½-pt) saucepan place carrots; add enough water to cover. Bring to a full boil. Cook over med. heat until carrots are crisply tender (6 to 8 min.). Meanwhile, in small bowl stir together remaining ingredients *except* fish; set aside. Separate fillets and divide carrots equally among fillets. Wrap each fillet around each portion of carrots. Place fillets, seam side down, in 23-cm (9-in) sq. baking dish. Sprinkle with stuffing mixture. Cover; bake for 10 min. Uncover; continue baking for 8 to 10 min. or until fish flakes with a fork.

Microwave Directions: In 2-litre (3½-pt) bowl combine 50 ml (2 fl oz) water and carrots. Cover; microwave on HIGH, stirring after half the time, until crisply tender (5 to 6 min.). Meanwhile, in small bowl stir together remaining ingredients *except* fish; set aside. Separate fillets and divide carrots equally among fillets. Wrap each fillet around each portion of carrots. Place fillets, seam side down, in 1.5-litre (2¾-pt) casserole. Sprinkle with stuffing mixture. Microwave on HIGH until fish flakes with a fork (7 to 9 min.).

To Wrap Fillets:

1. Separate fillets and divide carrots equally among fillets.

2. Wrap each fillet around each portion of carrots. Place fillets, seam side down, in 23-cm (9-in) sq. baking dish.

Lemon Sole & Carrot Bundles

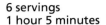

Sole Fillets Stuffed With Cheese

6 servings
1 hour 5 minutes

Fresh sole fillets are stuffed with cheese and tomato, and baked until the cheese is creamy and melted.

75 g	(*3 oz*) butter or margarine		1	large ripe tomato, cut into 6 slices
7 ml	(*1½ tsp*) garlic powder		12	(8 x 3.5 x 0.5-cm) (*3 x 1½ x ¼-in*)
7 ml	(*1½ tsp*) basil leaves			slices cheddar cheese
30 ml	(*2 tbsp*) chopped spring onions		30 ml	(*2 tbsp*) grated Parmesan cheese
6	(150 g) (*5 oz*) fresh sole fillets, each cut in half			

Heat oven to 180 °C (*350 °F*) mark 4. In 33 x 23-cm (*13 x 9-in*) baking dish melt butter. Stir in garlic powder, basil and spring onions. Dip both sides of sole fillet halves into melted seasoned butter. Set 6 sole fillet halves aside. Place remaining 6 sole fillet halves in same baking dish; layer *each* with 1 tomato slice and 2 cheese slices. Top each with a remaining sole fillet half. Sprinkle with Parmesan cheese. Bake for 25 to 35 min. or until fish flakes with a fork. To serve, spoon remaining butter in bottom of dish over sole fillets.

Rainbow Trout With Crunchy Gazpacho

6 servings
30 minutes

This chunky cold tomato and vegetable sauce, ladled over rainbow trout, presents glorious colour and flavour.

Gazpacho

2	med. ripe tomatoes, cut into 1-cm (*½-in*) pieces
1	med. peeled cucumber, cut into 1-cm (*½-in*) pieces
1	med. red or green pepper, cut into 1-cm (*½-in*) pieces
100 g	(*4 oz*) red onion, cut into 5-mm (*¼-in*) pieces
50 ml	(*4 tbsp*) chopped fresh parsley
50 ml	(*4 tbsp*) olive or vegetable oil
2 ml	(*½ tsp*) salt
2 ml	(*½ tsp*) pepper
45 ml	(*3 tbsp*) red wine vinegar
15 ml	(*1 tbsp*) Worcestershire sauce
1 ml	(*¼ tsp*) hot pepper sauce

Trout

50 g	(*2 oz*) butter or margarine
2 ml	(*½ tsp*) crushed fresh garlic
75 g	(*3 oz*) chopped red onion
50 ml	(*4 tbsp*) chopped fresh parsley
2 ml	(*½ tsp*) salt
1 ml	(*¼ tsp*) pepper
6	(225 to 350 g) (*½ to ¾ lb*) pan-dressed rainbow trout

In medium bowl stir together all gazpacho ingredients. In 1.25-litre (*2¼-pt*) blender container place about ⅓ mixture. Blend on high speed until saucy (30 to 45 sec.). Stir back into remaining gazpacho mixture; set aside. In 25-cm (*10-in*) frying pan melt butter and garlic until sizzling. Meanwhile, in small bowl stir together remaining trout ingredients *except* trout. Place about 30 ml (*2 tbsp*) mixture in cavity of each trout. Place 3 trout in same frying pan; cook over med. high heat, turning once, until fish flakes with a fork (4 to 5 min. on each side). Remove to serving platter; keep warm. Repeat with remaining trout. Spoon 250 ml (*8 fl oz*) sauce over trout; serve remaining sauce with trout.

Grill Directions: *Omit butter and garlic.* Prepare gazpacho as directed left. Prepare grill; heat until coals are ash white. Prepare trout as directed left. Brush trout with vegetable oil. Grill trout over medium hot coals until fish flakes with a fork (7 to 10 min. on each side). Remove to serving platter. Spoon 250 ml (*8 fl oz*) sauce over trout; serve remaining sauce with trout.

Rainbow Trout With Crunchy Gazpacho

Hearty Salmon Pie

6 servings
1 hour 30 minutes

A chunky, fresh tomato sauce is served over a rich seafood pie.

Crust

50 g	(*2 oz*) butter or margarine
100 g	(*4 oz*) finely crushed dried crumbly style herb seasoned stuffing

Filling

250 g	(*9 oz*) crushed dried crumbly style herb seasoned stuffing
100 g	(*4 oz*) shredded Cheddar cheese
250 ml	(*8 fl oz*) water
125 ml	(*4 fl oz*) milk
450 g	(*16 oz*) canned red salmon, drained, bones removed, flaked*
2	eggs
5 ml	(*1 tsp*) instant chicken bouillon
2 ml	(*1/2 tsp*) dry mustard
30 ml	(*2 tbsp*) chopped fresh parsley
15 ml	(*1 tbsp*) finely chopped onion

Sauce

75 g	(*3 oz*) butter or margarine
30 ml	(*2 tbsp*) cornflour
325 ml	(*11 fl oz*) water
5 ml	(*1 tsp*) dill weed
2 ml	(*1/2 tsp*) salt
2	med. ripe tomatoes, cubed 1 cm (*1/2 in*)

Heat oven to 180 °C (*350 °F*) mark 4. In 3-litre (*5-pt*) saucepan melt 50 g (*2 oz*) butter. Stir in 100 g (*4 oz*) finely crushed stuffing. Press stuffing mixture on bottom and up sides of greased 23-cm (*9-in*) pie dish; set aside. In same saucepan stir together all filling ingredients; spoon into crust. Bake for 50 to 55 min. or until heated through; let stand 10 min. Meanwhile, in 2-litre (*3 1/2-pt*) saucepan melt 75 g

(*3 oz*) butter. Stir in cornflour. Stir in remaining sauce ingredients *except* tomatoes. Cook over med. heat, stirring occasionally, until mixture comes to a full boil (5 to 7 min.). Add tomatoes; boil 1 min. To serve, cut pie into 6 wedges; serve sauce over wedges.

*550 g (*19 oz*) canned tuna, drained, flaked, can be substituted for 450 g (*16 oz*) canned salmon.

Hearty Salmon Pie

Garden Courgette & Shrimp (top)
Jambalaya-in-the-Pan (bottom)

Jambalaya-in-the-Pan

Spicy rice simmers in a frying pan with shrimp and garden vegetables.

250 ml	(*8 fl oz*) water
295-g	(*10.4-oz*) can chicken broth
15 ml	(*1 tbsp*) chilli powder
3 ml	(*3/4 tsp*) salt
2 ml	(*1/2 tsp*) paprika
2 ml	(*1/2 tsp*) pepper
30 ml	(*2 tbsp*) vegetable oil
5 ml	(*1 tsp*) crushed fresh garlic
200 g	(*7 oz*) uncooked long grain rice
275 g	(*10 oz*) frozen deveined large shrimp, thawed, drained
225 g	(*8 oz*) fresh or frozen fish fillets, thawed, drained
2	med. ripe tomatoes, cut into 2.5-cm (*1-in*) pieces
1	med. green pepper, cut into 2.5-cm (*1-in*) pieces
100 g	(*4 oz*) sliced 1 cm (*1/2 in*) spring onions
50 ml	(*4 tbsp*) chopped fresh parsley
275 g	(*10 oz*) frozen peas, thawed, drained

In 25-cm (*10-in*) frying pan stir together water, chicken broth, chilli powder, salt, paprika, pepper, oil and garlic. Bring to a full boil. Stir in rice. Cover; cook over med. low heat for 15 min. Stir in remaining ingredients *except* onions, parsley and peas. Continue cooking, uncovered, until liquid is absorbed and rice is tender (10 to 15 min.). Stir in remaining ingredients. Continue cooking until heated through (4 to 5 min.).

Microwave Directions: In 3-litre (*5-pt*) casserole stir together water, chicken broth, chilli powder, salt, paprika, pepper, oil, garlic and rice. Cover; microwave on HIGH, stirring after half the time, until rice is just tender (15 to 20 min.). Stir in remaining ingredients *except* onions, parsley and peas. Cover; microwave on HIGH, stirring after half the time, until fish flakes with fork (7 to 9 min.). Add remaining ingredients. Cover; microwave on HIGH until heated through (2 to 3 min.). Let stand 5 min.

Garden Courgette & Shrimp

Dill and garlic add a light flavour to this shrimp frying pan meal.

75 g	(*3 oz*) butter or margarine
2	med. courgettes, sliced 5 mm (*1/4 in*)
50 ml	(*4 tbsp*) chopped fresh parsley
20	med. fresh or frozen raw shrimp, shelled, deveined, rinsed
2 ml	(*1/2 tsp*) dill weed
1 ml	(*1/4 tsp*) salt
30 ml	(*2 tbsp*) chopped onion
15 ml	(*1 tbsp*) lemon juice
2 ml	(*1/2 tsp*) crushed fresh garlic
	Hot cooked rice

In 25-cm (*10-in*) frying pan melt butter over med. heat (3 to 6 min.). Stir in remaining ingredients *except* rice. Cook over med. heat, stirring occasionally, until shrimp turn pink and courgettes are crisply tender (5 to 8 min.). To serve, spoon shrimp with courgettes and butter sauce over hot cooked rice.

Microwave Directions: In 30 x 20-cm (*12 x 8-in*) baking dish melt butter on HIGH (60 to 70 sec.). Stir in remaining ingredients *except* rice. Cover; microwave on HIGH, stirring after half the time, until shrimp turn pink and courgettes are crisply tender (3 1/2 to 5 min.). To serve, spoon shrimp with courgettes and butter sauce over hot cooked rice.

Marmalade-Glazed Shrimp

4 servings
30 minutes

Orange marmalade and toasted coconut beautifully complement the flavour of sautéed shrimp.

450 g	(*1 lb*) (about 24 med.) fresh or frozen raw shrimp
50 g	(*2 oz*) butter or margarine
2 ml	(*1/2 tsp*) ground ginger
1 ml	(*1/4 tsp*) salt
1 ml	(*1/4 tsp*) pepper

5 ml	(*1 tsp*) crushed fresh garlic
175 g	(*6 oz*) orange marmalade
10 ml	(*2 tsp*) prepared horseradish
50 ml	(*4 tbsp*) desiccated coconut, toasted

Peel and devein shrimp, leaving tail intact. (If shrimp is frozen, do not thaw; peel under running cold water.) In 25-cm (*10-in*) frying pan melt butter until sizzling. Stir in ginger, salt, pepper and garlic; add shrimp. Cook over med. heat, stirring occasionally, until shrimp turn pink (5 to 7 min.). In small bowl stir together marmalade and horseradish; stir into shrimp. Continue cooking, stirring occasionally, until heated through (3 to 4 min.). If desired, sprinkle with toasted coconut.

Microwave Directions: Peel and devein shrimp, leaving tail intact. (If shrimp is frozen, do not thaw; peel under running cold water.) In 2-litre (*3 1/2-pt*) casserole melt butter on HIGH (50 to 60 sec.). Stir in ginger, salt, pepper and garlic; add shrimp. Cover; microwave on HIGH, stirring every 2 min., until shrimp turn pink (4 to 6 min.)*. In small bowl stir together marmalade and horseradish; stir into shrimp. Microwave on HIGH, stirring after half the time, until heated through (1 to 1 1/2 min.). If desired, sprinkle with toasted coconut.

*If using frozen shrimp, microwave on HIGH, stirring every 2 min., until shrimp turn pink (6 1/2 to 8 1/2 min.).

Roasted Crab & Clam Bake

8 servings
1 hour 30 minutes

An informal and fun way to serve seafood, dazzling with flavour and colour.

1.4 kg	(*3 lb*) crab claws*
16	clams
8	new red potatoes, quartered
8	fresh ears of corn on the cob, husked, *each* cut into thirds
2	med. onions, cut into 5-cm (*2-in*) pieces
50 g	(*2 oz*) chopped fresh parsley
50 ml	(*4 tbsp*) torn fresh basil leaves

250 ml	(*8 fl oz*) dry white wine or chicken broth
125 ml	(*4 fl oz*) olive or vegetable oil
5 ml	(*1 tsp*) coarsely ground pepper
2 ml	(*1/2 tsp*) salt
10 ml	(*2 tsp*) crushed fresh garlic
5 ml	(*1 tsp*) hot pepper sauce
3	bay leaves
50 g	(*2 oz*) butter or margarine

Heat oven to 200 °C (*400 °F*) mark 6. In large roasting tin layer crab, clams, potatoes, corn and onions. In medium bowl stir together remaining ingredients *except* bay leaves and butter; pour over ingredients in roasting tin. Add bay leaves. Cover; bake for 30 min. Then, stir ingredients to baste with tin juices. Continue baking covered, stirring after 15 min., for 30 to 35 min. or until seafood is steamed and vegetables are fork tender. Remove bay leaves. Dot butter over top of seafood and vegetables; serve with tin juices.

*1.4 kg (*3 lb*) crab legs and crab clusters (the knuckle of the crab leg) can be substituted for 1.4 kg (*3 lb*) crab claws.

Roasted Crab & Clam Bake

Scallops & Tomatoes Over Crusty Bread

Creamed Oysters with Spinach

6 servings
60 minutes

Ladle this rich creamed oyster and spinach medley over fresh-baked cornbread or biscuits for delicious country-style fare.

30 g	(*1 oz*) butter or margarine
1	med. onion, chopped
2 ml	(*½ tsp*) crushed fresh garlic
30 ml	(*2 tbsp*) plain flour
2 ml	(*½ tsp*) salt
2 ml	(*½ tsp*) coarsely ground pepper
2 ml	(*½ tsp*) thyme leaves
125 ml	(*4 fl oz*) reserved oyster liquor or clam juice

125 ml	(*4 fl oz*) double cream
250 g	(*9 oz*) torn spinach leaves*
2 doz.	fresh shucked oysters, drained, *reserve liquor*
	Cornbread, biscuits or toast**

In 25-cm (*10-in*) frying pan melt butter until sizzling. Stir in onion and garlic. Cook over med. heat, stirring occasionally, until onion is tender (3 to 4 min.). Stir in flour, salt, pepper and thyme. Continue cooking, stirring constantly, until smooth and bubbly (30 sec.). Stir in reserved oyster liquor and whipping cream. Continue cooking, stirring occasionally, until mixture is thickened (3 to 5 min.). Stir in spinach and oysters; continue cooking until oysters are tender (5 to 6 min.). Serve over cornbread, biscuits or toast.

*600 g (*1¼ lb*) frozen chopped spinach, thawed, welldrained, can be substituted for 250 g (*9 oz*) torn spinach leaves.

Microwave Directions: In 3-litre (*5-pt*) casserole melt butter on HIGH (30 to 60 sec.). Add onion and garlic. Microwave on HIGH until onion is tender (2 to 3 min.). Stir in flour, salt, pepper and thyme. Microwave on HIGH until bubbly (30 to 60 sec.). Add reserved oyster liquor and double cream. Microwave on HIGH until mixture is thickened (1½ to 2 min.). Stir in spinach and oysters. Cover; microwave on HIGH, stirring after half the time, until oysters are tender (4 to 5½ min.). Serve over cornbread, biscuits or toast.

**See Breads page 44 for Honey-Moist Cornbread or Flaky Buttermilk Biscuits.

Scallops & Tomatoes Over Crusty Bread

6 servings
30 minutes

Scallops simmer in a rich burgundy sauce and are served over crusty slices of toasted bread.

8	rashers of bacon, cut into 1-cm (*½-in*) pieces
15 ml	(*1 tbsp*) plain flour
2 ml	(*½ tsp*) thyme leaves
2 ml	(*½ tsp*) coarsely ground pepper
5 ml	(*1 tsp*) crushed fresh garlic
45 ml	(*3 tbsp*) tomato purée
450 g	(*1 lb*) bay scallops, rinsed, drained

3	med. ripe tomatoes, cut into 2.5-cm (*1-in*) pieces
75 g	(*3 oz*) stoned ripe olives, halved
30 ml	(*2 tbsp*) dry red wine
50 ml	(*4 tbsp*) chopped fresh parsley
6	diagonally cut slices crusty French bread

In 25-cm (*10-in*) frying pan cook bacon over med. high heat, stirring occasionally, until bacon is browned (6 to 8 min.). Stir in flour, thyme, pepper and garlic. Reduce heat to med. Cook, stirring constantly, until smooth and bubbly (30 sec.). Stir in tomato purée and remaining ingredients *except* wine, parsley and bread. Continue cooking, stirring occasionally, until scallops are white (4 to 5 min.). If desired, stir in wine. Stir in parsley. Toast bread in toaster or oven. Serve scallop mixture over toasted bread.

To Fillet Fish: # How To: Fillet Fish & Identify Forms of Fish

1. Lift pectoral fin. Using a thin, flexible sharp knife, angle the knife toward the back of the head and cut to the backbone.

2. Turn the blade parallel to the backbone. Cut toward tail with a sawing motion. Cut fillet off.

3. Remove rib bones by sliding the blade along the ribs. Turn fish over and remove second fillet.

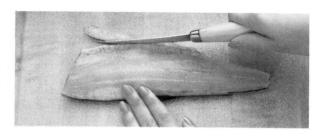

4. Cut off the strip of fatty belly flesh. Discard guts, belly, bones and head.

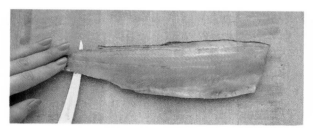

5. If desired, skin the fillet by cutting into the tail flesh to the skin. Turn the blade parallel to the skin.

6. Pull the skin firmly while moving the knife in a sawing action between the skin and the flesh.

To Identify Forms of Fish:

Form	Definition
A. Whole	The entire fish.
B. Drawn or Pan-Dressed	The whole fish that has been eviscerated and scaled.
C. Fillets	Boneless pieces cut from the side of the fish.
D. Steaks	Pieces cut crosswise through the backbone.

EGGS & CHEESE

Farm-fresh eggs, gathered when the sun is just coming up in the east. Big rounds of richly robust sharp Cheddar. Creamy white bricks of mellow Monterey Jack. And wheels of sweet, nutty Swiss. These are the makings of country-style dishes that add a warm, comforting touch to any meal.

Eggs scrambled with bacon, new potatoes, onions and green pepper, then topped with shredded cheese. What a bright and cheerful way to wake up the family on a busy Saturday morning. If it's a cozy lunch or supper for two, enjoy your private time and good conversation over a puffy cheese omelet, dressed with a homemade herb sauce. Or if you're having a weekend brunch, an egg and cheese pie makes entertaining easy. As you greet your guests and welcome them into your home, the pie can be baking to its rich golden, delectable finish.

Whatever the time of day, whatever the occasion, dishes that start with eggs and cheese provide the kind of hearty nourishment and good eating that only country fare can.

Garden Grill Omelette

1 omelette (2 servings)
30 minutes

*A homemade herb sauce made with garden-ripened tomatoes
makes this courgette, mushroom omelette absolutely delightful.*

Omelette

30 g	(*1 oz*) butter or margarine
125 g	(*4 oz*) sliced 5 mm (*¼ in*) fresh mushrooms
1	med. courgette, sliced 5 mm (*¼ in*)
4	eggs, slightly beaten
1 ml	(*¼ tsp*) salt
1 ml	(*¼ tsp*) pepper
45 ml	(*3 tbsp*) water
15 g	(*½ oz*) butter or margarine
50 g	(*2 oz*) shredded Mozzarella cheese

Tomato Sauce

15 g	(*½ oz*) butter or margarine
1	med. ripe tomato, cut into 1-cm (*½-in*) pieces
30 ml	(*2 tbsp*) chopped fresh parsley
2 ml	(*½ tsp*) basil leaves
	Pinch of salt
2 ml	(*½ tsp*) crushed fresh garlic

In 20-cm (*8-in*) omelette pan or 25-cm (*10-in*) frying pan melt 30 g (*1 oz*) butter until sizzling. Add mushrooms and courgette. Cook over med. heat, stirring occasionally, until vegetables are crisply tender (4 to 5 min.). Remove from frying pan; set aside. In small bowl stir together remaining omelette ingredients *except* butter and cheese. In same frying pan melt 15 g (*½ oz*) butter until sizzling. Pour egg mixture into frying pan. Cook over med. heat, lifting slightly with a spatula to allow uncooked portion to flow underneath, until omelette is set (3 to 4 min.). Place sautéed vegetables and cheese on half of omelette. Gently fold other half of omelette over filling. Meanwhile, in 1-litre (*1¾-pt*) saucepan melt 15 g (*½ oz*) butter; add remaining sauce ingredients. Cook over med. heat, stirring occasionally, until heated through (4 to 5 min.). Serve sauce over omelette.

Microwave Directions: In 25-cm (*10-in*) flan dish place 30 g (*1 oz*) butter, mushrooms and courgette. Cover; microwave on HIGH, stirring after half the time, until vegetables are crisply tender (3 to 4 min.). Remove from flan dish; set aside. Meanwhile, in small bowl combine remaining omelette ingredients *except* butter and cheese. In same flan dish melt 15 g (*½ oz*) butter on HIGH (20 to 35 sec.). Pour egg mixture into dish. Cover; microwave on HIGH, stirring after half the time, until just set (2 to 4 min.). Place sautéed vegetables and cheese on half of omelette. Gently fold other half of omelette over filling. In small bowl combine sauce ingredients. Cover; microwave on HIGH, stirring after half the time, until heated through (2 to 3 min.). Serve sauce over omelette.

Garden Grill Omelette

Country-Style Potato & Onion Pie

4 servings
50 minutes

*This egg and Swiss cheese quiche-like pie is a satisfying food
that brings warmth to family gatherings at meal time.*

30 g	(*1 oz*) butter or margarine
3	small new red potatoes, sliced 3 mm (*1/8 in*)
1	med. onion, sliced 3 mm (*1/8 in*), separated into rings
100 g	(*4 oz*) shredded Swiss cheese
75 ml	(*5 tbsp*) chopped fresh parsley
75 ml	(*5 tbsp*) milk
8	eggs, slightly beaten
2 ml	(*1/2 tsp*) salt
1 ml	(*1/4 tsp*) pepper
1	med. ripe tomato, sliced 5 mm (*1/2 in*)

Heat oven to 200 °C (*400 °F*) mark 6. In 25-cm (*10-in*) ovenproof frying pan melt butter in oven (3 to 4 min.). Add potatoes and onion. Bake, stirring once, for 15 to 20 min. or until vegetables are crisply tender. Meanwhile, in small bowl stir together remaining ingredients *except* tomato slices. Pour over baked potatoes and onion; arrange tomato slices over eggs. Return to oven; continue baking for 17 to 22 min. or until eggs are set and lightly browned.

Microwave Directions: In 25-cm (*10-in*) flan dish melt butter on HIGH (30 to 45 sec.). Add potatoes and onion. Cover; microwave on HIGH, stirring after half the time, until vegetables are crisply tender (3 to 5 min.). Let stand 5 min. Meanwhile, in medium bowl stir together remaining ingredients *except* tomato slices. Cover; microwave on HIGH, stirring every 2 min., until mixture is warm and starts to thicken (5 to 7 min.). Pour warmed egg mixture over potatoes and onion. Cover; microwave on HIGH, turning 1/2 turn after half the time, until eggs are set in center (5 to 7 min.). Top with tomatoes during last 2 min. of time.

Springtime Quiche

6 servings
1 hour 30 minutes

*Fresh chives in the crust and fresh asparagus in the quiche
create a savoury springtime delight.*

Crust

150 g	(*5 oz*) plain flour
1 ml	(*1/4 tsp*) salt
75 g	(*3 oz*) butter or margarine
30 ml	(*2 tbsp*) chopped fresh chives
30 ml	(*2 tbsp*) cold water

Filling

225 g	(*8 oz*) shredded Cheddar cheese
150 g	(*5 oz*) cooked, shredded chicken
6	rashers of crisply cooked bacon, cut into 2.5-cm (*1-in*) pieces
125 g	(*8 oz*) fresh asparagus
375 ml	(*13 fl oz*) single cream or milk
4	eggs, slightly beaten
1 ml	(*1/4 tsp*) salt
	Pinch of pepper

Heat oven to 200 °C (*400 °F*) mark 6. In medium bowl combine flour and salt; cut in butter until crumbly. Stir in chives and water (mixture will be crumbly). Shape into ball. On lightly floured surface, roll dough into 30-cm (*12-in*) circle 3-mm (*1/8-in*) thick. Fold into quarters; unfold and ease into 25-cm (*10-in*) flan tin, pressing firmly against bottom and sides.

Flute edges. Spread cheese over bottom of crust; top with chicken. Sprinkle bacon over chicken. Place asparagus spears in spoke pattern on top of bacon. In small bowl stir together remaining filling ingredients. Pour over chicken mixture. Bake for 40 to 45 min. or until golden and set in center. Let stand 10 min.

Country-Style Potato & Onion Pie

Country Scrambled Eggs

Farm fresh eggs are scrambled with lots of healthy, hearty ingredients.

4 servings
35 minutes

8	rashers of bacon, cut in 1-cm (*1/2-in*) pieces
275 g	(*10 oz*) cubed 2.5 cm (*1 in*) new red potatoes
2	med. onions, chopped
1/2	green pepper, chopped
50 ml	(*2 fl oz*) milk
8	eggs, slightly beaten
2 ml	(*1/2 tsp*) salt
1 ml	(*1/4 tsp*) pepper
100 g	(*4 oz*) shredded Cheddar cheese

In 25-cm (*10-in*) frying pan cook bacon over med. heat for 5 min. Add potatoes; continue cooking, stirring occasionally, until potatoes are browned and crisply tender (12 to 15 min.). Add onions and green pepper. Continue cooking until crisply tender (3 to 4 min.). Pour off fat. Meanwhile, in small bowl stir together remaining ingredients *except* cheese. Pour egg mixture over vegetables; stir to blend. Cook over med. heat, gently lifting portions with spatula so uncooked portion flows to bottom of pan, until eggs are set (4 to 5 min.). Sprinkle cheese over eggs; let stand until cheese is melted (2 to 4 min.).

Microwave Directions: In 3-litre (*5-pt*) casserole microwave bacon on HIGH until softened (2½ to 3 min.). Add potatoes. Cover; microwave on HIGH, stirring after half the time, until potatoes are crisply tender (5 to 8 min.). Stir in onions and green pepper. Cover; microwave on HIGH, stirring after half the time, until crisply tender (2 to 2½ min.). Pour off fat. Meanwhile, in small bowl stir together remaining ingredients *except* cheese. Pour egg mixture over vegetables; stir to blend. Cover; microwave on HIGH, stirring after half the time, until eggs are just dry and set (4 to 5 min.). Sprinkle cheese over eggs; let stand until cheese is melted (2 to 4 min.).

Country Scrambled Eggs

Cheddar Spinach Strata (top)
Sundown Oven Pancake (bottom)

240

Sundown Oven Pancake

*An oven pancake that puffs up in the pan to form a shell
for crispy vegetables and Cheddar cheese.*

15 g	(*½ oz*) butter or margarine	1	med. green pepper, cut into 2.5-cm (*1-in*) pieces
75 g	(*3 oz*) plain flour	1	med. ripe tomato, cut into 2.5-cm (*1-in*) pieces
125 ml	(*4 fl oz*) milk		
2	eggs, slightly beaten	1 ml	(*¼ tsp*) salt
1 ml	(*¼ tsp*) salt	1 ml	(*¼ tsp*) pepper
30 g	(*1 oz*) butter or margarine	175 g	(*6 oz*) shredded Cheddar cheese
150 g	(*5 oz*) broccoli flowerets		
1	med. onion, cut into 2.5-cm (*1-in*) pieces		

Heat oven to 220 °C (*425 °F*) mark 7. In 23-cm (*9-in*) pie dish melt 15 g (*½ oz*) butter in oven (2 to 3 min.). Meanwhile, in small bowl stir together flour, milk, eggs and 1 ml (*¼ tsp*) salt. Pour into pie dish with melted butter. Bake for 12 to 15 min. or until golden brown. Meanwhile, in 25-cm (*10-in*) frying pan melt 30 g (*1 oz*) butter. Add remaining ingredients *except* cheese. Cook over med. heat, stirring occasionally, until vegetables are crisply tender (12 to 15 min.). Sprinkle 50 g (*2 oz*) cheese in bottom of pancake; top with vegetable mixture. Sprinkle with remaining cheese. Return to oven; continue baking for 5 to 7 min. or until cheese is melted.

Cheddar Spinach Strata

Make this strata the night before and bake it the next day for an easy brunch.

8	slices wholewheat bread, cubed 1 cm (*½ in*)	50 g	(*2 oz*) canned diced pimento, drained
350 g	(*12 oz*) shredded Cheddar cheese	6	eggs, beaten
600 g	(*1¼ lb*) frozen chopped spinach, thawed, drained	750 ml	(*1¼ pt*) milk
		7 ml	(*1½ tsp*) onion salt
		2 ml	(*½ tsp*) pepper

In 33 x 23-cm (*13 x 9-in*) baking dish layer: ½ of bread cubes, cheese, spinach, pimento and remaining bread cubes. In medium bowl stir together remaining ingredients; pour over layered ingredients. Cover; refrigerate at least 1 hr. or overnight. Heat oven to 160 °C (*325 °F*) mark 3. Bake for 60 to 75 min. or until knife inserted near center comes out clean. Let stand 5 min. before serving.

Microwave Directions: In 33 x 23-cm (*13 x 9-in*) baking dish assemble strata as directed left. Cover; refrigerate at least 1 hr. or overnight. Cover; microwave on HIGH, turning dish ½ turn twice during time, until knife inserted near center comes out clean (27 to 32 min.). Let stand 5 min. before serving.

Shrimp Dilled Deviled Eggs

1 dozen
2 hours

*Place these shrimp and dill-seasoned deviled eggs in an egg carton
for easy carrying to a picnic or barbecue.*

6	eggs
50 ml	(*4 tbsp*) mayonnaise
100 g	(*4 oz*) canned deveined medium shrimp, rinsed, drained
30 ml	(*2 tbsp*) chopped spring onions
15 ml	(*1 tbsp*) chopped fresh dill weed*

	Pinch of pepper
15 ml	(*1 tbsp*) lime juice
10 ml	(*2 tsp*) country-style Dijon mustard
1 ml	(*¼ tsp*) hot pepper sauce
	Fresh dill weed

In 2-litre (*3½-pt*) saucepan place eggs; add enough cold water to come 2.5 cm (*1 in*) above eggs. Cook over high heat until water comes to a full boil. Remove from heat. Cover; let stand 20 to 25 min. Immediately cool eggs in cold water to prevent further cooking; peel. Cut eggs crosswise in half. Remove yolks from egg whites; set egg whites aside. Place cooked egg yolks in medium bowl; mash with fork. Add mayonnaise, shrimp, onions, 15 ml (*1 tbsp*) dill,

pepper, lime juice, mustard and hot pepper sauce to egg yolks; stir to blend. Spoon about 15 ml (*1 tbsp*) egg yolk mixture into each egg white; garnish with sprig of dill weed. Place in egg carton to transport; refrigerate until served.

*5 ml (*1 tsp*) dried dill weed can be substituted for 15 ml (*1 tbsp*) fresh dill weed.

Fresh Herb-Baked Eggs

6 servings
60 minutes

Eggs, soft-cooked in pastry shells, give an entirely new style to shirred eggs.

6	frozen ready-to-bake puff pastry shells
30 g	(*1 oz*) butter or margarine, melted
15 ml	(*1 tbsp*) sherry or vinegar
5 ml	(*1 tsp*) Worcestershire sauce

6	eggs
1 ml	(*¼ tsp*) salt
1 ml	(*¼ tsp*) pepper
1 ml	(*¼ tsp*) dill weed
15 ml	(*1 tbsp*) thinly sliced spring onion

Prepare pastry shells according to pkg. directions *except* bake only 20 min. Heat oven to 180 °C (*350 °F*) mark 4. Place 6 baked pastry shells in greased 33 x 23-cm (*13 x 9-in*) baking dish. In each pastry shell place 5 ml (*1 tsp*) melted butter; sprinkle each

pastry shell with 2 ml (*½ tsp*) sherry and a few drops of Worcestershire sauce. Crack 1 egg into each pastry shell; season with dash of salt, pepper and dill weed. Sprinkle with 2 ml (*½ tsp*) spring onion. Bake for 20 to 25 min. or until egg white is set.

Shrimp Dilled Deviled Eggs

Crispy Mexican Supper

4 servings
45 minutes

*A crispy fried tortilla is layered with pork sausage,
courgette slices and lots of shredded cheese.*

125 ml	*(4 fl oz)* vegetable oil	100 g	*(4 oz)* shredded Cheddar cheese
4	*(18-cm)* *(7-in)* flour tortillas	1	med. chopped ripe tomato
175 g	*(6 oz)* pork sausage		
3	med. courgettes, sliced 3 mm *(1/8 in)*		Salsa *(mexican sauce)*
	Pinch of salt		Sour cream
	Pinch of cayenne pepper		
100 g	*(4 oz)* shredded Cheshire cheese		

Heat oven to 200 °C (*400 °F*) mark 6. In 25-cm (*10-in*) frying pan heat oil over med. high heat. Fry each tortilla in hot oil for 1 min.; turn. Continue frying until crispy and lightly browned (1 min.). Set aside. In 2-litre (*3 1/2-pt*) saucepan cook sausage over med. heat, stirring occasionally, until browned (4 to 5 min.). Stir in courgettes, salt and cayenne pepper. Continue cooking, stirring occasionally, until courgettes are crisply tender (4 to 5 min.). Pour off fat. Place tortillas on baking sheet. Top each tortilla with courgette and sausage mixture, 50 ml (*4 tbsp*) Cheshire cheese and 50 ml (*4 tbsp*) Cheddar cheese. Sprinkle with 50 ml (*4 tbsp*) chopped tomato. Bake for 8 to 12 min. or until heated through and cheese is melted. Serve with salsa and sour cream.

Microwave Directions: Fry tortillas as directed left. In 2-litre (*3 1/2-pt*) casserole crumble sausage. Cover; microwave on HIGH, stirring after half the time, until sausage is no longer pink (3 to 5 min.). Pour off fat. Stir in courgettes, salt and cayenne pepper. Cover; microwave on HIGH, stirring after half the time, until courgettes are crisply tender (3 to 4 min.). Assemble as directed left. Microwave one tortilla on HIGH until cheese is melted (1 to 1 1/2 min.). Repeat with remaining tortillas.

To Fry Tortillas:

1. In 25-cm (*10-in*) frying pan heat oil over med. high heat. Fry each tortilla in hot oil for 1 min.; turn.

2. Continue frying until crispy and lightly browned (1 min.).

Crispy Mexican Supper

Pan Pizza

*A homemade deep-dish pizza with a
buttery, tender crust that's baked in a frying pan.*

4 servings
50 minutes

Crust

30 g	(*1 oz*) butter or margarine
225 g	(*8 oz*) plain flour
10 ml	(*2 tsp*) sugar
10 ml	(*2 tsp*) baking powder
2 ml	(*½ tsp*) salt
175 ml	(*6 fl oz*) milk

Sauce

250 ml	(*8 fl oz*) canned tomato sauce
150 g	(*5 oz*) canned tomato purée
5 ml	(*1 tsp*) basil leaves
2 ml	(*½ tsp*) oregano leaves
1 ml	(*¼ tsp*) pepper
2 ml	(*½ tsp*) crushed fresh garlic

Topping

175 g	(*6 oz*) shredded Mozzarella cheese
125 g	(*4 oz*) sliced 5 mm (*¼ in*) fresh mushrooms
50 g	(*2 oz*) sliced pepperoni
1	med. green pepper, sliced 3 mm (*⅛ in*)
1	med. ripe tomato, sliced 3 mm (*⅛ in*)
75 g	(*3 oz*) stoned ripe olives, sliced 5 mm (*¼ in*)

Heat oven to 220 °C (*425 °F*) mark 7. In 25-cm (*10-in*) ovenproof frying pan melt butter in oven (3 to 4 min.). Meanwhile, in medium bowl stir together all crust ingredients *except* milk. Stir in milk just until moistened. On lightly floured surface knead dough until smooth (1 min.). Press dough on bottom and half-way up sides of frying pan with melted butter. Bake for 10 min. Meanwhile, in small bowl stir together all sauce ingredients. Spread tomato sauce over partially baked crust. Sprinkle with ⅔ cheese and mushrooms. Arrange pepperoni, green pepper and tomato on pizza; sprinkle with olives and remaining cheese. Return to oven; continue baking for 15 to 20 min. or until heated through and cheese is melted.

Pan Pizza

Brunch Omelette Torte

Brunch Omelette Torte

This do-ahead recipe requires some time to prepare, but is sensational for a special breakfast or brunch.

2	sheets of frozen puff pastry, thawed

Potatoes

50 g	(*2 oz*) butter or margarine
6	med. new red potatoes sliced 3 mm (*1/8 in*)
1	med. onion, sliced 3 mm (*1/8 in*), separated into rings
1 ml	(*1/4 tsp*) salt
1 ml	(*1/4 tsp*) pepper

Omelette

30 g	(*1 oz*) butter or margarine
6	eggs
50 ml	(*4 tbsp*) chopped fresh parsley
	Pinch of salt
	Pinch of pepper
30 ml	(*2 tbsp*) water

Filling

225 g	(*8 oz*) thinly sliced cooked ham
225 g	(*8 oz*) shredded Cheddar cheese
1	egg, slightly beaten
15 ml	(*1 tbsp*) water

On lightly floured surface roll each sheet of puff pastry into a 30-cm (*12-in*) sq. Lay 1 sheet puff pastry into 25-cm (*10-in*) pie dish; set aside. In 25-cm (*10-in*) frying pan melt 50 g (*2 oz*) butter until sizzling. Add potatoes, onion, 1 ml (*1/4 tsp*) salt and 1 ml (*1/4 tsp*) pepper. Cover; cook over med. high heat, turning occasionally, until potatoes are lightly browned and crisply tender (12 to 15 min.). Set aside. In cleaned frying pan melt 15 g (*1/2 oz*) butter until sizzling. Meanwhile, in small bowl stir together all omelette ingredients *except* remaining butter. Pour half of omelette mixture into frying pan with sizzling 15 g (*1/2 oz*) butter. Cook over med. heat. As omelette mixture sets, lift slightly with spatula to allow uncooked portion to flow underneath. Continue cooking until set (2 to 3 min.). Slide omelette onto baking sheet. Repeat with remaining butter and omelette mixture. Layer ingredients into pie dish

with puff pastry in the following order: 1 omelette, 100 g (*4 oz*) ham, half of fried potatoes, 100 g (*4 oz*) shredded cheese, remaining potatoes, ham, cheese and omelette. Top with remaining sheet of puff pastry. Press together edges of both sheets of puff pastry to form a rim; trim off excess puff pastry. Crimp or flute edges of puff pastry. Cover; refrigerate overnight or heat oven to 190 °C (*375 °F*) mark 5. In small bowl stir together 1 egg and 15 ml (*1 tbsp*) water; brush over puff pastry. Bake for 30 to 35 min. or until golden brown. Let stand 5 min.; cut into wedges. If torte is refrigerated overnight, let stand at room temperature 30 min. before baking. Bake as directed above.

Tip: Your favourite deli meats can be substituted for ham.

Cheddar-Vegetable Stuffed Shells

Cheddar cheese and dill enhance vegetables nestled in pasta shells.

4 servings
45 minutes

12	jumbo macaroni shells
350 g	*(12 oz)* frozen vegetable medley
175 g	*(6 oz)* cubed 1 cm *(1/2 in)* Cheddar cheese
30 g	*(1 oz)* butter or margarine, melted
2 ml	*(1/2 tsp)* dill weed

Heat oven to 180 °C *(350 °F)* mark 4. Cook shells according to pkg. directions. Drain; rinse in cold water. Dry on paper towel. Place shells in 23-cm *(9-in)* sq. baking dish. In small bowl stir together vegetables and cheese. Stuff each shell with about 50 ml *(4 tbsp)* mixture. In small bowl stir together melted butter and dill weed; brush over shells. Cover; bake for 20 to 25 min. or until heated through.

Microwave Directions: Prepare and stuff pasta shells as directed left. Place shells in 23-cm *(9-in)* sq. baking dish. In small bowl stir together melted butter and dill weed; brush over shells. Cover; microwave on HIGH until heated through (4 1/2 to 5 1/2 min.).

Country Vegetable Fondue

Vegetables create crunch and colour in this quick-to-fix fondue.

1 litre *(1 3/4 pt)*
30 minutes

125 ml	*(4 fl oz)* white wine or milk
450 g	*(16 oz)* pasteurized process cheese spread, cut into cubes
225 g	*(8 oz)* cream cheese, cut into cubes
50 ml	*(4 tbsp)* chopped spring onions
75 ml	*(5 tbsp)* chopped celery
275 g	*(10 oz)* frozen chopped spinach, thawed, drained
125 g	*(4 oz)* canned chopped pimento, drained
	Pinch of dry mustard
	Pinch of cayenne pepper
	Bread cubes
	Tortilla chips
	Vegetable sticks

In 2-litre *(3 1/2-pt)* saucepan or fondue pot stir together wine, cheese spread and cream cheese. Cook over med. heat, stirring occasionally, until cheeses are melted (8 to 10 min.). Stir in remaining ingredients *except* bread cubes, tortilla chips and vegetable sticks. Continue cooking, stirring occasionally, until heated through (8 to 10 min.). Serve with bread cubes, tortilla chips or vegetable sticks.

Microwave Directions: In 2-litre *(3 1/2-pt)* casserole stir together wine, cheese spread and cream cheese. Microwave on HIGH, stirring after half the time, until cheeses are melted (5 to 6 min.). Stir in remaining ingredients *except* bread cubes, tortilla chips and vegetable sticks. Microwave on HIGH, stirring after half the time, until heated through (3 to 4 min.). Serve with bread cubes, tortilla chips or vegetable sticks.

Country Vegetable Fondue

Lasagna Roll-Ups With Cream Sauce

Lasagna Roll-Ups With Cream Sauce

8 servings
1 hour 15 minutes

These lasagna roll-ups are filled with the fresh tastes of garden vegetables and herbs.

Lasagna

8	uncooked lasagna noodles
30 g	(*1 oz*) butter or margarine
5 ml	(*1 tsp*) crushed fresh garlic
1	med. courgette, sliced 3 mm (*1/8 in*)
1	med. yellow, red or green pepper, cut into 2.5-cm (*1-in*) pieces
1/2	med. red onion, coarsely chopped
2 ml	(*1/2 tsp*) salt
1 ml	(*1/4 tsp*) pepper
30 ml	(*2 tbsp*) torn fresh basil*
5 ml	(*1 tsp*) chopped fresh oregano*
1	egg, slightly beaten
100 g	(*4 oz*) shredded Mozzarella cheese
50 g	(*2 oz*) freshly grated Parmesan cheese
425 g	(*15 oz*) Ricotta cheese**
2	med. ripe tomatoes, cut into 1-cm (*1/2-in*) pieces

Herb Sauce

30 g	(*1 oz*) butter or margarine
30 ml	(*2 tbsp*) plain flour
1 ml	(*1/4 tsp*) salt
1 ml	(*1/4 tsp*) pepper
250 ml	(*8 fl oz*) milk
100 g	(*4 oz*) shredded Mozzarella cheese
50 ml	(*4 tbsp*) chopped fresh parsley
15 ml	(*1 tbsp*) torn fresh basil*
30 ml	(*2 tbsp*) freshly grated Parmesan cheese

Heat oven to 180 °C (*350 °F*) mark 4. Cook lasagna noodles according to pkg. directions; rinse. In 25-cm (*10-in*) frying pan melt 30 g (*1 oz*) butter until sizzling; stir in garlic. Add courgette, pepper, onion, salt, pepper, basil and oregano. Cook over med. heat, stirring occasionally, until vegetables are crisply tender (5 to 6 min.). Meanwhile, in large bowl stir together egg and cheeses. Stir in tomatoes and cooked vegetables. Place about 120 ml (*8 tbsp*) filling on one end of each lasagna noodle. Roll up lasagna noodle, Swiss roll fashion. (Some filling will spill out each end.) Place, seam side down, in 30 x 20-cm (*12 x 8-in*) baking dish. Fill in around rollups with excess filling. Set aside. In 2-litre (*3 1/2-pt*) saucepan melt prepare sauce by melting butter over med. heat.; stir in flour, salt and pepper. Cook, stirring occasionally, until smooth and bubbly (30 sec.). Add milk; continue cooking until sauce begins to thicken (1 to 2 min.). Stir in Mozzarella cheese, parsley and basil. Continue cooking, stirring occasionally, until cheese is melted (2 to 4 min.). Pour over lasagna rollups; sprinkle with 30 ml (*2 tbsp*) Parmesan cheese. Bake for 25 to 30 min. or until heated through.

*10 ml (*2 tsp*) dried basil leaves can be substituted for 30 ml (*2 tbsp*) torn fresh basil.

*1 ml (*1/4 tsp*) dried oregano leaves can be substituted for 5 ml (*1 tsp*) chopped fresh oregano.

*5 ml (*1 tsp*) dried basil leaves can be substituted for 15 ml (*1 tbsp*) torn fresh basil.

**350 g (*12 oz*) cottage cheese can be substituted for 425 g (*15 oz*) Ricotta cheese.

SALADS & SANDWICHES

What a great day to be outdoors. Fresh breezes are blowing, and puffy white clouds float lazily by as you bask in the warm sunshine of a perfect spring day. The first wild flowers of the season are in bloom, and the quiet is punctuated only by the sweet sound of birds singing in the trees.

It's not time for lunch yet, but somehow being outdoors seems to awaken your appetite. Perhaps it's knowing that the wicker basket is so close by. A peek inside reveals a banquet of picnic goodies. French loaves generously filled with slices of smoked meat and three kinds of cheese. Crunchy chicken salad on golden-brown rolls. Fresh vegetables and pasta tossed with a tangy mustard dressing. For dessert, there are sweet, fresh fruits and homemade cookies.

The fare is simple and delicious. Foods that are equally at home at a family supper or a backyard party. Sandwiches and salads re-create the pleasures of picnicking anytime, anywhere.

Lemon Dill Chicken Loaves

4 servings
25 minutes

*Delicious, delightful and delectable describes sautéed chicken
served in French rolls and seasoned with cream cheese and dill.*

30 g	(*1 oz*) butter or margarine	100 g	(*4 oz*) cream cheese, softened
1 ml	(*¹/₄ tsp*) salt	2 ml	(*¹/₂ tsp*) dill weed
1 ml	(*¹/₄ tsp*) dill weed	1 ml	(*¹/₄ tsp*) salt
	Pinch of pepper	15 ml	(*1 tbsp*) lemon juice
1 ml	(*¹/₄ tsp*) crushed fresh garlic	4	French rolls or hoagie buns, split
2	whole, boneless chicken breasts, skinned, halved	4	lettuce leaves
150 ml	(*¹/₄ pt*) sour cream	8	slices ripe tomato

In 25-cm (*10-in*) frying pan melt butter until sizzling; stir in salt, dill weed, pepper and garlic. Add chicken breasts. Cook over med. high heat, turning occasionally, until chicken is browned and fork tender (10 to 15 min.). Meanwhile, in small bowl stir together remaining ingredients *except* rolls, lettuce and tomato slices. To assemble each sandwich spread about 15 ml (*1 tbsp*) cream cheese mixture over bottom half of roll. Top with 1 lettuce leaf, 2 slices tomato and sautéed chicken breast. Spoon about 15 ml (*1 tbsp*) cream cheese mixture over chicken; top with remaining bun.

Microwave Directions: In 30 x 20-cm (*12 x 8-in*) baking dish melt butter on HIGH (20 to 35 sec.). Stir in salt, dill weed, pepper and garlic. Place chicken in baking dish, turning to coat. Cover; microwave on HIGH, turning chicken over and rearranging after half the time, until chicken is no longer pink (5 to 7 min.). Assemble sandwiches as directed left.

Crunchy Chicken Salad Sandwich

12 sandwiches (6 servings)
1 hour 30 minutes

*Fresh radish, celery and cucumber
add a crunchy new taste to a chicken sandwich.*

300 g	(*11 oz*) cooked, cubed 2.5 cm (*1 in*) chicken	125 ml	(*4 fl oz*) mayonnaise
1	celery stick, sliced 5 mm (*¹/₄ in*)	5 ml	(*1 tsp*) dill weed
¹/₂	cucumber, sliced 5 mm (*¹/₄ in*), cut in half	1 ml	(*¹/₄ tsp*) salt
75 ml	(*5 tbsp*) sliced 5 mm (*¹/₄ in*) radish, cut in half	12	small sandwich rolls Lettuce

In large bowl stir together all ingredients *except* rolls and lettuce. Cover; refrigerate at least 1 hr. to blend flavours. Spread on rolls; garnish with lettuce.

Crunchy Chicken Salad Sandwich (top)
Lemon Dill Chicken Loaves (bottom)

Avocado Chicken Clubhouse

4 sandwiches
20 minutes

Country-style mustard adds hearty flavour to this sandwich.

12	slices wholewheat bread	1	med. avocado, peeled, sliced
50 ml	(*4 tbsp*) chopped spring onions	8	slices ripe tomato
150 ml	(*¼ pt*) mayonnaise	8	rashers crisply cooked bacon, cut in half
45 ml	(*3 tbsp*) country-style Dijon mustard		Lettuce
8	(30-g) (*1-oz*) slices cooked chicken or turkey		

Toast bread. In small bowl stir together onions, mayonnaise and mustard. Spread mayonnaise mixture on 1 side of each slice of toast. To assemble each sandwich place 2 slices turkey on 1 slice toast, top with avocado slices. Top with 1 slice toast, mayonnaise side down; spread mayonnaise on toast. Place 2 tomato slices on toast; top with 4 pieces bacon and lettuce. Place toast on top. Repeat for remaining sandwiches. Secure with long wooden picks.

To Prepare Avocados:

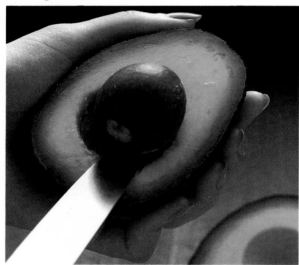

1. Cut avocado in half lengthwise, remove stone.

2. Peel off skin and slice.

Avocado Chicken Clubhouse

Ranch-Hand Sandwich

6 servings
20 minutes

After a hard day's work, enjoy this wholesome and hearty sandwich with a blue cheese spread.

50 g	(*2 oz*) butter or margarine, softened	1	med. ripe tomato, cut into 6 slices
50 ml	(*4 tbsp*) crumbled blue cheese	12	(15-g) (*1/2-oz*) thin slices cooked turkey
450 g	(*1 lb*) loaf Italian bread or French bread, sliced in half lengthwise	12	(7-g) (*1/4-oz*) thin slices hard salami
8	lettuce leaves	4	(30-g) (*1-oz*) slices Mozzarella cheese, cut in half

In small bowl stir together butter and blue cheese. Spread butter mixture on each half of bread. Place both halves of bread on baking sheet. Grill 12 to 15 cm (*5 to 6 in*) from heat for 2 to 4 min. or until butter is melted and bread is toasted. To assemble sandwich arrange lettuce leaves on bottom half of bun. Layer tomato, turkey, hard salami and cheese. Top with remaining bun. With serrated knife cut into individual servings.

Turkey 'n Chive Sandwich

4 sandwiches
20 minutes

For that perfect picnic meal-on-a-bun.

225 g	(*8 oz*) cream cheese, softened	1	med. ripe tomato, sliced 5 mm (*1/4 in*)
30 ml	(*2 tbsp*) chopped fresh chives	1	med. green pepper, sliced into 5-mm (*1/4-in*) rings
4	individual French bread rolls, split		
4	lettuce leaves	4	(30-g) (*1-oz*) slices Swiss cheese
8	(30-g) (*1-oz*) slices cooked turkey		

In small bowl stir together cream cheese and chives. Spread on roll halves. To assemble each sandwich layer bottom half of roll with lettuce leaf, 2 slices turkey, tomato, green pepper and 1 slice cheese. Top with remaining roll. Repeat for remaining sandwiches.

Turkey 'n Chive Sandwich

Horseradish Roast Beef Special

4 sandwiches
20 minutes

*The special of the day is this bountiful sandwich with sourdough bread,
a horseradish spread and roast beef.*

Horseradish Spread

125 ml	(*4 fl oz*) sour cream
1 ml	(*¼ tsp*) salt
	Pinch of pepper
15 ml	(*1 tbsp*) country-style Dijon mustard
5 ml	(*1 tsp*) prepared horseradish

Sandwich

50 g	(*2 oz*) butter or margarine, softened
2 ml	(*½ tsp*) crushed fresh garlic
8	slices sourdough bread
12	slices roast beef
8	slices ripe tomato
12	slices cucumber

In small bowl stir together all spread ingredients. In small bowl stir together butter and garlic. Spread 1 side of each slice bread with garlic butter. Place on baking sheet. Grill 12 to 15 cm (*5 to 6 in*) from heat for 3 to 4 min. or until bread is toasted. To assemble each sandwich layer 1 slice bread with 3 slices roast beef, 2 slices tomato and 3 slices cucumber. Spoon about 30 ml (*2 tbsp*) spread over cucumbers. Top with 1 slice bread.

Best Ever Hoagie Sandwich

4 sandwiches
20 minutes

*Butter crisp fried buns enhance the tasty,
satisfying layers of meat and cheese in this hearty sandwich.*

50 g	(*2 oz*) butter or margarine, softened
4	individual hoagie buns or individual French rolls
50 ml	(*4 tbsp*) chopped spring onions
125 ml	(*4 fl oz*) sour cream
50 ml	(*4 tbsp*) country-style Dijon mustard
225 g	(*8 oz*) sliced ham, roast beef or smoked turkey

100 g	(*4 oz*) sliced Mozzarella cheese
100 g	(*4 oz*) sliced Cheddar cheese
100 g	(*4 oz*) sliced Swiss cheese
1	med. ripe tomato, cut into 8 slices
	Leaf lettuce
4	(15-cm) (*6-in*) wooden picks

Spread butter inside top and bottom of buns. Heat 25-cm (*10-in*) frying pan or griddle. Fry bread, buttered side down, until golden brown (4 to 5 min.). Meanwhile, in small bowl stir together spring onions, sour cream and mustard. Spread on fried buns. Divide meat and cheese evenly on bottom of buns. Top each with 2 tomato slices, leaf lettuce and top of bun. Secure with wooden picks.

Best Ever Hoagie Sandwich (top)
Horseradish Roast Beef Special (bottom)

Open-Faced Egg Salad Sandwich

4 sandwiches
40 minutes

Open-Faced Egg Salad Sandwich

Toasted wholewheat bread is topped with crispy cucumbers,
juicy tomatoes, creamy egg salad and crisscrossed with bacon.

Egg Salad

6	eggs
2	celery sticks, sliced 5 mm (*¼ in*)
175 ml	(*6 fl oz*) mayonnaise
30 ml	(*2 tbsp*) chopped spring onion
1 ml	(*¼ tsp*) salt
1 ml	(*¼ tsp*) pepper
5 ml	(*1 tsp*) prepared horseradish

Sandwich

8	rashers bacon
4	slices wholewheat bread
4	lettuce leaves
8	slices ripe tomato
12	slices cucumber

In 2-litre (*3½-pt*) saucepan place eggs; add enough cold water to come 2.5 cm (*1 in*) above eggs. Cook over high heat until water comes to a full boil. Remove from heat. Cover; let stand 20 to 25 min. Immediately cool eggs in cold water to prevent further cooking; peel. Chop hard cooked eggs; place in medium bowl. Stir in remaining egg salad ingredients. Fry or microwave bacon until crispy (4 to 5 min.). Meanwhile, toast bread. Top each slice toast with 1 lettuce leaf, 2 slices tomato, 3 slices cucumber and ¼ of egg salad. Crisscross cooked bacon strips over sandwich.

8 sandwiches
20 minutes

Garden Tuna Melt

A family favourite — tuna — livened up with fresh vegetables.

50 ml	(*4 tbsp*) chopped celery
50 ml	(*4 tbsp*) mayonnaise
175 g	(*6 oz*) canned tuna, drained
4	English muffins, split, toasted
8	green pepper rings

8	slices ripe tomato
8	(8 x 8-cm) (*3 x 3-in*) slices Cheddar cheese
30 ml	(*2 tbsp*) sliced spring onion

Heat oven to 180 °C (*350 °F*) mark 4. In medium bowl stir together celery, mayonnaise and tuna. Place English muffins on baking sheet. Spread tuna mixture on muffins. Layer each with 1 green pepper ring and 1 tomato slice. Bake for 10 to 12 min. or until heated through. Remove from oven; top each with 1 slice cheese. Garnish with spring onion. Continue baking for 1 to 2 min. or until cheese melts.

Microwave Directions: Prepare muffins as directed left. Top each with 1 slice cheese. Garnish with green onion. For each serving: place 2 muffins on a plate lined with paper towel. Microwave on HIGH until heated through (1½ to 2 min.).

8 sandwiches
30 minutes

Open-Face Turkey & Broccoli Sandwich

*Broccoli, red onion and cheese top this grilled open-face turkey sandwich
flavoured with a touch of tarragon.*

125 g	(*4 oz*) butter or margarine, softened
2 ml	(*1/2 tsp*) tarragon leaves
450 g	(*1 lb*) loaf French bread, cut into fourths, sliced horizontally
450 g	(*1 lb*) cooked, sliced turkey
175 ml	(*6 fl oz*) mayonnaise
3 ml	(*3/4 tsp*) tarragon leaves
225 g	(*8 oz*) broccoli flowerets
1	med. red onion, sliced 5 mm (*1/4 in*), separated into rings
8	(30-g) (*1-oz*) slices Cheddar cheese

Heat grill. In small bowl stir together butter and 2 ml (*1/2 tsp*) tarragon; spread on cut bread. Divide turkey among bread. In small bowl stir together mayonnaise and 3 ml (*3/4 tsp*) tarragon; spread over turkey, top with broccoli and onion rings. Place sandwiches on baking sheet. Grill 7 to 10 cm (*3 to 4 in*) from heat for 3 to 5 min. or until sandwiches are heated through. Top with cheese; grill 2 to 3 min. or until cheese is melted.

6 sandwiches
20 minutes

Horseradish Turkey 'n Ham Melt

A hearty hot sandwich with the tang of horseradish and the crunch of green pepper.

6	slices rye bread
75 g	(*3 oz*) butter or margarine, softened
30 ml	(*2 tbsp*) prepared horseradish
6	(30-g) (*1-oz*) slices cooked turkey
6	(30-g) (*1-oz*) slices cooked ham
6	slices ripe tomato
1	med. green pepper, sliced into 6 rings
6	(30-g) (*1-oz*) slices Cheddar cheese

Heat grill. Toast bread. In small bowl stir together butter and horseradish; spread butter mixture on toast. Layer each slice toast with 1 slice turkey, 1 slice ham, 1 slice tomato and 1 slice green pepper. Place sandwiches on baking sheet. Grill 7 to 10 cm (*3 to 4 in*) from heat for 3 to 4 min. or until sandwiches are heated through. Top with cheese; grill 2 to 3 min. or until cheese is melted.

Microwave Directions: Prepare as directed left. Place 3 sandwiches on large plate. Microwave on MEDIUM (50% power), turning plate 1/4 turn after half the time, until cheese is melted (3 to 3 1/2 min.). Repeated with remaining sandwiches.

Open-Face Turkey & Broccoli Sandwich

Ham & Maple Apple Stack

4 servings
30 minutes

Create this waffle stack with smoked ham and tart, crisp apples
that have been simmered in maple syrup.

30 g	(*1 oz*) butter or margarine	8	(30-g) (*1-oz*) slices cooked ham
2	med. tart apples, cored, sliced 5 mm (*¼ in*)	8	frozen waffles
50 ml	(*4 tbsp*) maple syrup		Maple syrup
1 ml	(*¼ tsp*) nutmeg		

In 25-cm (*10-in*) frying pan melt butter until sizzling; add apples, syrup and nutmeg. Cook over med. heat, stirring occasionally, until apples are crisply tender (3 to 4 min.). Place ham in same frying pan, placing apples on ham slices. Continue cooking until heated through (5 to 6 min.). Meanwhile, toast or bake waffles according to pkg. directions. Divide ham and apple mixture between 4 toasted waffles. Top with remaining toasted waffles. Serve with maple syrup.

Microwave Directions: In 33 x 23-cm (*13 x 9-in*) baking dish melt butter on HIGH (20 to 30 sec.). Stir in apples, syrup and nutmeg. Place ham in baking dish; arrange apples over ham. Cover; microwave on HIGH until apples are crisply tender and ham is heated through (3 to 5 min.). Assemble sandwiches as directed left.

Smokehouse Barbecued Pork

6 servings
45 minutes

This rich, zesty barbecue sauce tastes like it has been simmering all day.

Sauce

50 ml	(*4 tbsp*) firmly packed brown sugar
75 ml	(*5 tbsp*) country-style Dijon mustard
400 ml	(*14 fl oz*) catsup
1 ml	(*¼ tsp*) oregano leaves
1 ml	(*¼ tsp*) chilli powder
30 ml	(*2 tbsp*) cider vinegar
30 ml	(*2 tbsp*) Worcestershire sauce
2 ml	(*½ tsp*) liquid smoke
3	slices lemon

Pork

30 g	(*1 oz*) butter or margarine
1	celery stick, sliced 1 cm (*½ in*)
450 g	(*1 lb*) pork fillet, cut into 2.5-cm (*1-in*) pieces*
2	med. onions, sliced 3 mm (*⅛ in*)
1 ml	(*¼ tsp*) salt
1 ml	(*¼ tsp*) pepper
8	wholewheat buns

In 3-litre (*5-pt*) saucepan stir together all sauce ingredients. Cook over low heat, stirring occasionally, until heated through (5 to 10 min.). Meanwhile, in 25-cm (*10-in*) frying pan melt butter until sizzling. Add remaining pork ingredients *except* buns. Cook over med. high heat until meat is browned (13 to 18 min.). Add pork mixture to barbecue sauce. Serve barbecued pork in buns.

*450 g (*1 lb*) shredded baked pork roast can be substituted for pork fillet.

Microwave Directions: In 3-litre (*5-pt*) casserole combine all sauce ingredients. Cover; microwave on HIGH, stirring after half the time, until heated through (3 to 5 min.). Stir in remaining pork ingredients *except* buns. Cover; microwave on HIGH, stirring after half the time, until meat is fork tender (10 to 13 min.). Assemble sandwiches as directed left.

Ham & Maple Apple Stack

Crusty Bread Stuffed With Sausage (top)
Grilled Sausage Patties on Rye (bottom)

Grilled Sausage Patties on Rye

4 servings
30 minutes

*Lots of Mozzarella cheese melts between sausage patties,
onions and grilled caraway rye bread.*

450 g	(*1 lb*) pork sausage
1	med. onion, sliced 3 mm (*⅛ in*)
8	green pepper rings

8	(30-g) (*1-oz*) slices Mozzarella cheese
8	slices caraway rye bread
90 g	(*3½ oz*) butter or margarine

Form sausage into 8 patties. Place in 25-cm (*10-in*) frying pan. Cook over med. heat, turning once, until browned and cooked through (6 to 8 min.). Add onion and green pepper. Continue cooking, stirring occasionally, until vegetables are crisply tender (4 to 5 min.). Remove sausage patties and vegetables from frying pan; pour off fat. To assemble each sandwich place 1 slice cheese on slice of bread. Top with 2 sausage patties, ¼ of onion slices, 2 green pepper rings, 1 slice cheese and slice of bread. In same frying pan melt 45 g (*1½ oz*) butter until sizzling. Place 2 sandwiches in frying pan. Cover; cook over med. heat until browned (3 min.). Turn. Cover; continue cooking until cheese is melted (2 to 3 min.). Remove sandwiches

to platter; keep warm while grilling remaining sandwiches in remaining butter.

Microwave Directions: Form sausage into 8 patties. Place in 33 x 23-cm (*13 x 9-in*) baking dish. Cover; microwave on HIGH until partially cooked (3 to 4 min.). Turn patties over; add onion and green pepper. Cover; microwave on HIGH until vegetables are crisply tender and sausage is cooked through (3 to 4 min.). Pour off fat. Assemble sandwiches as directed left. Place in same baking dish. Cover; microwave on HIGH until cheese is melted (1½ to 2 min.).

Crusty Bread Stuffed With Sausage

6 servings
45 minutes

*Sourdough bread is filled with the savoury and robust flavours of
sausage, onions, mushrooms, tomatoes and green pepper.*

675 g	(*1½ lb*) (6 links) mild Italian sausage, cut into 2.5-cm (*1-in*) pieces
2	med. onions, sliced 3 mm (*⅛ in*)
225 g	(*8 oz*) fresh mushrooms, halved
2	med. ripe tomatoes, cut into 2.5-cm (*1-in*) pieces
1	med. green pepper, cut into 1-cm (*½-in*) strips

50 ml	(*4 tbsp*) chopped fresh parsley
150 g	(*5 oz*) canned tomato purée
5 ml	(*1 tsp*) basil leaves
1 ml	(*¼ tsp*) salt
1 ml	(*¼ tsp*) pepper
450 g	(*1 lb*) round loaf sourdough bread

Heat oven to 190 °C (*375 °F*) mark 5. In 25-cm (*10-in*) frying pan cook sausage and onions over med. high heat, stirring occasionally, until browned (8 to 10 min.). Pour off fat. Reduce heat to med. Add mushrooms, tomatoes and green pepper. Cook, stirring occasionally, until vegetables are crisply tender (5 to 7 min.). Stir in remaining ingredients *except* bread. Continue cooking, stirring occasionally, until heated

through (5 to 7 min.). Meanwhile, cut thin lengthwise slice off top of bread; reserve. Hollow out center of bread leaving 2.5-cm (*1-in*) shell. (Save inside bread and use for fresh bread crumbs.) Place bread on baking sheet; bake bread shell for 12 to 15 min. or until crusty. Fill hot bread with sausage mixture. With serrated knife cut into wedges.

Farmers' Market Sandwich (top)
Bacon Tomato Sandwich With Cheddar (bottom)

272

4 servings
20 minutes

Bacon Tomato Sandwich With Cheddar

The familiar bacon tomato sandwich is made special
with zesty mayonnaise and melted Cheddar cheese.

8	rashers bacon
4	onion buns, split
75 ml	*(5 tbsp)* mayonnaise
15 ml	*(1 tbsp)* country-style Dijon mustard
4	slices ripe tomato

12	red onion rings
12	slices cucumber
8	*(11 x 2.5 x 0.2-cm) (2¼ x 1 x ⅛-in)* strips Cheddar cheese

Heat oven to 190 °C *(375 °F)* mark 5. Fry or microwave bacon until crispy (4 to 5 min.). Place split onion buns on baking sheet. In small bowl stir together mayonnaise and mustard. To assemble each sandwich spread about 15 ml *(1 tbsp)* mayonnaise mixture on each bun half. Top bottom half of bun with 1 tomato slice, 3 onion rings and 3 cucumber slices. Crisscross 2 bacon strips over cucumber slices. Crisscross 2 slices cheese over bacon. Bake for 3 to 5 min. or until cheese is melted. Top with remaining bun.

Microwave Directions: Place bacon on microwave-safe bacon/roasting rack. Cover; microwave on HIGH until crisp (5 to 8 min.). Assemble sandwiches as directed left; place on large platter. Microwave on HIGH until cheese is melted (2 to 3 min.). Top with remaining bun.

4 servings
30 minutes

Farmers' Market Sandwich

Gather the produce at the market to make these bagels
topped with sautéed fresh vegetables and Cheddar cheese.

45 g	*(1½ oz)* butter or margarine
2	med. courgettes, sliced 3 mm *(⅛ in)*
150 g	*(5 oz)* sliced 5 mm *(¼ in)* fresh mushrooms
½	med. red onion, sliced 3 mm *(⅛ in)*, separated into rings
5 ml	*(1 tsp)* basil leaves

1 ml	*(¼ tsp)* salt
1 ml	*(¼ tsp)* pepper
2 ml	*(½ tsp)* crushed fresh garlic
4	plain bagels, split
225 g	*(8 oz)* shredded Cheddar cheese
8	slices ripe tomato

Heat oven to 190 °C *(375 °F)* mark 5. In 25-cm *(10-in)* frying pan melt butter until sizzling. Stir in remaining ingredients *except* bagels, cheese and tomato. Cook over med. heat, stirring occasionally, until vegetables are crisply tender (4 to 5 min.). Meanwhile, place bagels on baking sheet; place 30 ml *(2 tbsp)* cheese on each bagel half. Bake for 5 min. or until cheese is melted. Remove from oven; top each with 1 slice tomato. Divide courgette mixture between bagels. Top with remaining cheese. Return to oven; continue baking 4 to 5 min. or until cheese is melted.

Microwave Directions: In 2-litre *(3½-pt)* casserole melt butter on HIGH (30 to 45 sec.). Stir in remaining ingredients *except* bagels, cheese and tomato. Cover; microwave on HIGH, stirring after half the time, until vegetables are crisply tender (3 to 4 min.). Place bagels on large platter; place 30 ml *(2 tbsp)* cheese on each bagel half. Microwave on HIGH until cheese is melted (1 to 1½ min.). Remove from microwave; top each with 1 slice tomato. Divide courgette mixture between bagels. Top with remaining cheese. Microwave on HIGH until cheese is melted (2½ to 3½ min.).

Chicken Salad-in-the-Pan

4 servings
15 minutes

Unique preparation and combinations in a creamy chicken salad.

45 g	(*1 1/2 oz*) butter or margarine	75 ml	(*5 tbsp*) sour cream
3	whole boneless chicken breasts, skinned, halved, cut into 8 x 1-cm (*3 x 1/2-in*) strips	75 ml	(*5 tbsp*) mayonnaise
		2 ml	(*1/2 tsp*) mustard seed
1 ml	(*1/4 tsp*) salt	15 ml	(*1 tbsp*) country-style Dijon mustard
1 ml	(*1/4 tsp*) pepper	15 ml	(*1 tbsp*) lemon juice
50 ml	(*4 tbsp*) sliced 5 mm (*1/4 in*) celery	8	lettuce leaves
50 ml	(*4 tbsp*) chopped spring onions	150 g	(*5 oz*) cherry tomato halves
50 ml	(*4 tbsp*) chopped fresh parsley		

In 25-cm (*10-in*) frying pan melt butter until sizzling. Stir in chicken, salt and pepper. Cook over med. high heat, stirring occasionally, until chicken is browned and fork tender (10 to 15 min.). Stir in remaining ingredients *except* lettuce leaves and cherry tomatoes. On platter or individual salad plates place lettuce leaves. Place chicken salad on lettuce; arrange cherry tomatoes around salad.

Chicken Taco Salad

6 servings
1 hour 30 minutes

Hot salsa will add extra spice to this chicken salad.

Dressing

250 ml	(*8 fl oz*) sour cream
2 ml	(*1/2 tsp*) chilli powder
2 ml	(*1/2 tsp*) cumin
2 ml	(*1/2 tsp*) salt

Salad

375 g	(*13 oz*) cooked, cubed 2.5 cm (*1 in*) chicken
75 ml	(*5 tbsp*) chopped onion
2	med. ripe tomatoes, cut into 1-cm (*1/2-in*) pieces; *reserve 30 ml (2 tbsp)*
100 g	(*4 oz*) sliced ripe olives
1	large lettuce, shredded
250 ml	(*8 fl oz*) salsa (mexican sauce)
125 g	(*4 oz*) shredded Cheddar cheese Tortilla chips

In large bowl stir together all dressing ingredients. Stir in chicken, onion, tomatoes *except* reserved 30 ml (*2 tbsp*) and ripe olives. Cover; refrigerate at least 1 hr. To serve, line large serving platter with shredded lettuce. Top with chicken mixture. Spoon salsa over chicken mixture; sprinkle with cheese and reserved 30 ml (*2 tbsp*) tomatoes. Garnish with tortilla chips.

Chicken Salad-in-the-Pan

Summer Light Chicken Salad

4 servings
30 minutes

Hot Chicken & Lettuce Salad

A tangy, warm salad dressing complements mandarin oranges and bacon in this delicious salad.

1	med. lettuce, torn into pieces
100 g	*(4 oz)* torn spinach leaves
300 g	*(11 oz)* canned mandarin orange segments, drained
1	celery stick, sliced 5 mm *(1/4 in)*
50 ml	*(4 tbsp)* chopped onion
8	rashers bacon, cut into 2.5-cm *(1-in)* pieces

375 g	*(13 oz)* cooked, shredded chicken
75 ml	*(5 tbsp)* cider vinegar
50 ml	*(4 tbsp)* vegetable oil
2 ml	*(1/2 tsp)* cracked pepper
15 ml	*(1 tbsp)* Worcestershire sauce

In large bowl combine lettuce, spinach and mandarin oranges; set aside. In 25-cm *(10-in)* frying pan cook celery, onion and bacon over med. heat, stirring occasionally, until bacon is browned and vegetables are crisply tender (8 to 10 min.). Stir in remaining ingredients. Cook over med. high heat, stirring occasionally, just until chicken is heated through (5 to 7 min.). Toss with lettuce. Serve immediately.

Microwave Directions: In large bowl combine lettuce, spinach and mandarin oranges; set aside. In 2-litre *(3 1/2-pt)* casserole microwave bacon on HIGH for 4 min. Stir in celery and onion. Microwave until bacon is cooked and vegetables are crisply tender (6 to 8 min.). With slotted spoon remove bacon-vegetable mixture. Drain fat *except* for 45 ml *(3 tbsp)*. Stir remaining ingredients and bacon-vegetable mixture into reserved 45 ml *(3 tbsp)* fat. Microwave on HIGH just until chicken is heated through (4 to 5 min.). Toss with lettuce. Serve immediately.

4 to 6 servings
1 hour 30 minutes

Summer Light Chicken Salad

A light dressing of lemon juice, oil and nutmeg makes this refreshing salad perfect for a hot summer day.

Dressing

75 ml	*(5 tbsp)* vegetable oil
75 ml	*(5 tbsp)* lemon juice
2 ml	*(1/2 tsp)* salt
1 ml	*(1/4 tsp)* nutmeg
2 ml	*(1/2 tsp)* crushed fresh garlic

Salad

375 g	*(13 oz)* cooked, cubed 2.5 cm *(1 in)* chicken
150 g	*(5 oz)* halved, seedless red grapes
2	celery sticks, sliced 5 mm *(1/4 in)*
50 ml	*(4 tbsp)* sliced spring onions
1	large lettuce, shredded

In jar with lid combine all dressing ingredients. Shake to mix. In large bowl combine all salad ingredients *except* lettuce. Toss salad with half of dressing.

Cover; refrigerate at least 1 hr. Place lettuce on serving platter; top with salad. Drizzle remaining dressing over salad and lettuce.

6 servings
1 hour 15 minutes

Apple Harvest Salad

*Sour cream and cinnamon are combined to make a smooth,
sparkling dressing for this harvest time salad.*

375 g	(*13 oz*) cooked, cubed 2.5 cm (*1 in*) chicken	30 ml	(*2 tbsp*) finely chopped onion
100 g	(*4 oz*) walnut halves	2 ml	(*1/2 tsp*) salt
1	celery stick, sliced 5 mm (*1/4 in*)	250 ml	(*8 fl oz*) sour cream
2	med. tart apples, cubed 1 cm (*1/2 in*)	2 ml	(*1/2 tsp*) cinnamon
		6	lettuce cups

In large bowl stir together all ingredients *except* sour cream, cinnamon and lettuce. In small bowl stir together sour cream and cinnamon; fold into chicken mixture. Cover; refrigerate at least 1 hr. To serve, line six bowls with lettuce cups; fill each with salad.

6 servings
2 hours 30 minutes

Turkey in a Melon

*Cream cheese and nutmeg make a refreshing dressing
to serve with this turkey and melon salad.*

2	cantaloupe melons, cut into quarters, seeded, *reserve 2 quarters*

Salad

300 g	(*11 oz*) cooked, cubed 2.5 cm (*1 in*) turkey
1	celery stick, sliced 5 mm (*1/4 in*)
65 g	(*2 1/2 oz*) chopped pecans
30 ml	(*2 tbsp*) chopped spring onion
	Leaf lettuce

Dressing

75 g	(*3 oz*) cream cheese, softened
15 ml	(*1 tbsp*) milk
1 ml	(*1/4 tsp*) nutmeg

Skin and cube reserved cantaloupe quarters. In large bowl stir together cubed cantaloupe and all salad ingredients *except* lettuce; set aside. In 1.25-litre (2 1/4-pt) blender container combine dressing ingredients. Blend on high speed until smooth (1 to 2 min.). Fold dressing into turkey mixture. Cover; refrigerate at least 2 hr. To serve, place cantaloupe quarters on lettuce-lined plates; spoon salad into cantaloupe.

Turkey in a Melon

Country Turkey & Grape Salad

6 servings
15 minutes

The best made Parmesan-basil mayonnaise complements this and other salads.

Salad

600 g	(*1¼ lb*) cooked turkey, cut into 3.5-cm (*1½-in*) pieces
150 g	(*5 oz*) seedless green grapes
150 g	(*5 oz*) seedless red grapes

Dressing

2	egg yolks
5 ml	(*1 tsp*) basil leaves
1 ml	(*¼ tsp*) salt
1 ml	(*¼ tsp*) pepper

15 ml	(*1 tbsp*) country-style Dijon mustard
250 ml	(*8 fl oz*) vegetable oil
50 ml	(*4 tbsp*) lemon juice
75 ml	(*5 tbsp*) grated Parmesan cheese
8	lettuce leaves
	Clusters of seedless green and red grapes

In large bowl stir together all salad ingredients. In blender or food processor combine all dressing ingredients *except* oil, lemon juice and Parmesan cheese. Cover; blend on high until thoroughly combined. With blender still running, take off cover and slowly add 125 ml (*4 fl oz*) oil, lemon juice and remaining oil.

Blend until thickened (1 to 2 min.). By hand, stir in Parmesan cheese. Stir 125 ml (*4 fl oz*) dressing into salad. On platter or individual salad plates place lettuce leaves. Spoon turkey salad on lettuce; arrange clusters of grapes around salad. Serve with remaining dressing.

To Prepare Homemade Mayonnaise:

1. With blender still running, take off cover and slowly add 125 ml (*4 fl oz*) oil, lemon juice and remaining oil.

2. Blend until thickened. By hand, stir in Parmesan cheese. Stir 125 ml (*4 fl oz*) dressing into salad.

Country Turkey & Grape Salad

6 servings
40 minutes

Springtime Ham & Asparagus Salad

Enjoy spring's bounty with a lemon cream dressing.

Salad

16	asparagus spears
1	large lettuce, torn into pieces
300 g	(*11 oz*) cubed 1 cm (*½ in*) cooked ham
2	hard cooked eggs, quartered

Dressing

125 ml	(*4 fl oz*) sour cream
30 ml	(*2 tbsp*) chopped fresh parsley
15 ml	(*1 tbsp*) chopped fresh chives
	Pinch of salt
	Pinch of pepper
30 ml	(*2 tbsp*) lemon juice
15 ml	(*1 tbsp*) mayonnaise

In 25-cm (*10-in*) frying pan place asparagus; add enough water to cover. Cook over med. high heat until water comes to a full boil. Boil 1 to 2 min.; drain. Rinse with cold water. On platter or individual salad plates place lettuce. Arrange ham, eggs and asparagus spears on lettuce. In small bowl stir together all dressing ingredients. Pour dressing over salad.

6 servings
15 minutes

Orange Citrus Tuna Salad

Tuna salad with the freshness of orange and the spark of ginger.

Dressing

150 ml	(*¼ pt*) mayonnaise
2 ml	(*½ tsp*) ginger
1 ml	(*¼ tsp*) pepper
30 ml	(*2 tbsp*) orange juice
30 ml	(*2 tbsp*) country-style Dijon mustard
2 ml	(*½ tsp*) crushed fresh garlic

Salad

2	celery sticks, coarsely chopped
350 g	(*12 oz*) canned tuna, drained
30 ml	(*2 tbsp*) chopped fresh parsley
1	large lettuce, torn into pieces
2	oranges, pared, sliced 5 mm (*¼ in*)

In large bowl stir together all dressing ingredients. Stir in all salad ingredients *except* lettuce and oranges. On platter or individual salad plates place lettuce.

Spoon tuna salad on lettuce; arrange orange slices around tuna salad.

Orange Citrus Tuna Salad (top)
Springtime Ham & Asparagus Salad (bottom)

Tarragon Beef & Pasta Salad

4 servings
30 minutes

Layered Pepperoni Pizza Salad

Deliver the savoury taste of pizza in this fresh salad.

450 g	(*1 lb*) minced beef	225 g	(*8 oz*) shredded Mozzarella cheese
375 ml	(*13 fl oz*) pizza sauce	100 g	(*4 oz*) sliced ripe olives
50 g	(*2 oz*) thinly sliced pepperoni, cut in half	20 g	(*3/4 oz*) cheese-flavoured croutons
1	large lettuce, chopped		
1	med. ripe tomato, chopped		

In 25-cm (*10-in*) frying pan brown minced beef (5 to 8 min.); drain. In same frying pan stir in pizza sauce and pepperoni; continue cooking over med. heat, stirring occasionally, until meat mixture is heated through (2 to 3 min.). In large bowl layer half of lettuce, tomato, 100 g (*4 oz*) cheese, meat mixture, remaining lettuce, remaining cheese, olives and croutons. Serve immediately.

6 servings
1 hour 30 minutes

Tarragon Beef & Pasta Salad

Yogurt and fresh herbs dress this unique pasta salad.

Salad

100 g	(*4 oz*) uncooked med. shell macaroni
225 g	(*8 oz*) sliced, cooked roast beef, cut into 5 x 1-cm (*2 x 1/2-in*) strips
2	celery sticks, sliced 1 cm (*1/2 in*)
150 g	(*5 oz*) halved cherry tomatoes
1/2	red onion, sliced 5 mm (*1/4 in*), separated into rings

Dressing

250 ml	(*8 fl oz*) plain yogurt
125 ml	(*4 fl oz*) mayonnaise
50 ml	(*4 tbsp*) chopped fresh parsley
50 ml	(*4 tbsp*) chopped fresh chives
3 ml	(*3/4 tsp*) chopped fresh tarragon*
1 ml	(*1/4 tsp*) salt
1 ml	(*1/4 tsp*) pepper

Cook macaroni according to pkg. directions. Rinse with cold water. Drain; set aside. In large bowl stir together all remaining salad ingredients; stir in macaroni. Cover; refrigerate at least 1 hr. In small bowl stir together all dressing ingredients. Cover; refrigerate at least 1 hr. Pour dressing over salad; toss gently to coat.

*1 ml (*1/4 tsp*) dried tarragon leaves can be substituted for 3 ml (*3/4 tsp*) fresh tarragon.

6 servings
40 minutes

Market Pasta Salad

*Popular with the summer crowd, especially when made with fresh vegetables
right from the farmers' market.*

Salad

225 g	(*8 oz*) uncooked, medium shell macaroni
150 g	(*5 oz*) broccoli flowerets
1	med. chopped onion
2	med. yellow squash, sliced 5 mm (*1/4 in*) or courgettes
1	med. red pepper, cut into strips
100 g	(*4 oz*) cubed 1 cm (*1/2 in*) Cheddar cheese

Dressing

125 ml	(*4 fl oz*) vegetable oil
2 ml	(*1/2 tsp*) salt
1 ml	(*1/4 tsp*) pepper
45 ml	(*3 tbsp*) lemon juice
30 ml	(*2 tbsp*) country-style Dijon mustard
5 ml	(*1 tsp*) Worcestershire sauce
2 ml	(*1/2 tsp*) crushed fresh garlic
30 ml	(*2 tbsp*) grated Parmesan cheese

Cook macaroni according to pkg. directions; drain. In large bowl stir together all salad ingredients *except* cheese; stir in hot macaroni. Refrigerate 10 min. Stir in cheese. Meanwhile, in medium bowl stir together all dressing ingredients *except* Parmesan cheese. Pour dressing over salad; toss to coat. Sprinkle with Parmesan cheese.

6 servings
45 minutes

Fettuccine Chicken Salad

*A colourful mix of fresh vegetables, chicken and fettuccine
make this a hearty main dish salad.*

Dressing

150 ml	(*1/4 pt*) vegetable oil
125 ml	(*4 fl oz*) white wine vinegar
5 ml	(*1 tsp*) basil leaves
5 ml	(*1 tsp*) oregano leaves
5 ml	(*1 tsp*) crushed fresh garlic
5 ml	(*1 tsp*) salt
2 ml	(*1/2 tsp*) pepper

Salad

175 g	(*6 oz*) uncooked fettuccine, broken into thirds
375 g	(*13 oz*) cooked, cubed 2.5 cm (*1 in*) chicken or turkey
150 g	(*5 oz*) broccoli flowerets
2	med. carrots, sliced 5 mm (*1/4 in*)
1/2	med. red onion, sliced into 3-mm (*1/8-in*) rings
150 g	(*5 oz*) halved cherry tomatoes

In jar with tight-fitting lid combine all dressing ingredients. Shake to mix; set aside. Cook fettuccine according to pkg. directions; drain. Rinse with cold water. In large bowl combine remaining salad ingredients and drained fettuccine. Gently stir in dressing.

Market Pasta Salad (top)
Fettuccine Chicken Salad (bottom)

Sunshine Pasta Salad

4 servings
30 minutes

Sunshine Pasta Salad

Prepare this lemon pasta salad when tomatoes are garden-ripe and bursting with flavour.

100 g	(*4 oz*) your favourite uncooked pasta	2 ml	(*¹/₂ tsp*) salt
1	med. cucumber, sliced 3 mm (*¹/₈ in*)	2 ml	(*¹/₂ tsp*) dill weed
30 g	(*1 oz*) chopped fresh parsley	1 ml	(*¹/₄ tsp*) pepper
175 g	(*6 oz*) marinated artichoke hearts,	15 ml	(*1 tbsp*) grated lemon rind
	quartered, *reserve marinade*	30 ml	(*2 tbsp*) lemon juice
		4	med. ripe tomatoes

Cook pasta according to pkg. directions; drain. Rinse with cold water. In large bowl combine pasta and remaining ingredients *except* tomatoes. Toss to coat with reserved artichoke marinade. Remove stems from tomatoes; cut *each* tomato into 4 wedges, leaving 1-cm (*¹/₂-in*) base to keep tomato intact. Serve 1 portion of pasta over each tomato.

6 servings
1 hour 30 minutes

Dill 'n Salmon Pasta Salad

A light refreshing summertime supper: serve with multi-grain bread and fresh fruit.

200 g	(*7 oz*) uncooked corkscrew or twist pasta	30 ml	(*2 tbsp*) sliced spring onion
225 g	(*8 oz*) salmon fillet, cooked, chunked	75 ml	(*5 tbsp*) vegetable oil
225 g	(*8 oz*) cubed 1 cm (*¹/₂ in*) Cheddar	50 ml	(*4 tbsp*) lemon juice
	cheese	5 ml	(*1 tsp*) dill weed
75 ml	(*5 tbsp*) cubed 1 cm (*¹/₂ in*) red pepper	2 ml	(*¹/₂ tsp*) garlic salt
			Salt and pepper

Cook pasta according to pkg. directions; drain. Rinse with cold water. In large bowl stir together all ingredients; season with salt and pepper to taste. Cover; refrigerate at least 1 hr.

Tip: To cook salmon, place in 25-cm (*10-in*) frying pan; cover with water. Cook over med. heat until salmon flakes with a fork (12 to 15 min.).

Herb Garden Salad

8 servings
1 hour

Layered Rainbow Pasta Salad

*Sun-kissed tomato and artichoke hearts combine with an array
of colourful ingredients in this main dish salad.*

100 g	(*4 oz*) uncooked corkscrew or twist pasta	400 g	(*14 oz*) canned artichoke hearts, drained, cut into 2.5-cm (*1-in*) pieces
1	large lettuce, torn into pieces		
350 g	(*12 oz*) shredded Cheddar cheese	12	rashers crisply cooked, crumbled bacon
1	large ripe tomato, sliced 5 mm (*¼ in*), slices halved	2	rashers crisply cooked bacon Italian dressing*

Cook pasta according to pkg. directions. Rinse with cold water; drain. To assemble salad, in large clear salad bowl layer half of torn lettuce, half of cheese, tomato, pasta, remaining lettuce, artichoke hearts, crumbled bacon and remaining cheese. Garnish top with bacon rashers; serve with Italian dressing.

*Or serve with Basil Vinaigrette; see Sandwiches & Salads page 320.

6 servings
30 minutes

Herb Garden Salad

Cool and crisp, this garden-fresh salad is enhanced with herbs fresh from the garden.

Salad

1	large lettuce, torn in pieces
100 g	(*4 oz*) sliced 5 mm (*¼ in*) fresh mushrooms
1	med. red onion, sliced 3 mm (*⅛ in*), separated into rings
30 g	(*1 oz*) torn fresh basil, parsley, mint or lemon balm
2	med. ripe tomatoes, each cut into 12 wedges
350 g	(*12 oz*) fresh French beans, blanched

Dressing

75 ml	(*5 tbsp*) olive or vegetable oil
2 ml	(*½ tsp*) coarsely ground pepper
1 ml	(*¼ tsp*) salt
30 ml	(*2 tbsp*) red wine vinegar
5 ml	(*1 tsp*) crushed fresh garlic
5 ml	(*1 tsp*) country-style Dijon mustard

In large bowl toss together all salad ingredients. In small bowl stir together all dressing ingredients. Pour dressing over salad; toss to coat.

Tip: To blanch green beans, place in boiling water for 7 to 9 min. Rinse in cold water.

Blue Cheese BLT Salad

Backwoods Spinach Salad

6 servings
60 minutes

A slightly sweet, warm bacon dressing tossed with spinach, wild rice and crispy radishes.

75 g	(*3 oz*) uncooked wild rice	30 ml	(*2 tbsp*) honey
8	rashers bacon, cut into 1-cm (*1/2-in*) pieces	200 g	(*7 oz*) torn spinach leaves
50 ml	(*4 tbsp*) cider vinegar	100 g	(*4 oz*) sliced 5 mm (*1/4 in*) fresh mushrooms
1 ml	(*1/4 tsp*) salt	125 g	(*4 oz*) sliced 5 mm (*1/4 in*) radishes
1 ml	(*1/4 tsp*) pepper		

Cook wild rice according to pkg. directions. Meanwhile, in 25-cm (*10-in*) frying pan cook bacon over med. high heat, stirring occasionally, until browned (6 to 8 min.). Drain bacon fat, *reserving 30 ml* (2 tbsp). In same skillet stir together vinegar, salt, pepper, honey and reserved bacon fat. Cook over med. heat, stirring occasionally, until heated through (3 to 4 min.). In large bowl combine remaining ingredients. Pour warm dressing over salad; toss to coat.

Blue Cheese BLT Salad

6 servings
20 minutes

Flavourful, colourful and delicious.

Dressing

50 ml	(*4 tbsp*) cider vinegar
15 ml	(*1 tbsp*) sugar
2 ml	(*1/2 tsp*) pepper
1 ml	(*1/4 tsp*) salt
30 ml	(*2 tbsp*) vegetable oil
15 ml	(*1 tbsp*) lemon juice
2 ml	(*1/2 tsp*) crushed fresh garlic

Salad

1	large lettuce, torn into pieces
1	med. ripe avocado, peeled, cut into wedges
1	med. ripe tomato, cut into wedges
1	onion, sliced 3 mm (*1/8 in*), separated into rings
300 g	(*11 oz*) canned mandarin orange segments, drained
50 g	(*2 oz*) crumbled blue cheese
8	rashers crisply cooked, crumbled bacon

In small bowl stir together all dressing ingredients. On platter or individual salad plates place lettuce. Arrange avocado, tomato, onion and mandarin orange segments on lettuce; sprinkle with blue cheese and bacon. Pour dressing over salad.

8 servings
2 hours 30 minutes

Spinach Salad With Yogurt Dressing

A homemade yogurt-based salad dressing is served with this fresh spinach salad.

Dressing
250 ml	(*8 fl oz*) plain yogurt
125 ml	(*4 fl oz*) mayonnaise
30 ml	(*2 tbsp*) sliced spring onions
1 ml	(*¼ tsp*) garlic salt
	Milk

Salad
300 g	(*11 oz*) fresh spinach, torn in bite-size pieces
225 g	(*8 oz*) shredded Cheddar cheese
3	hard cooked eggs, quartered
75 ml	(*5 tbsp*) salted peanuts

In small bowl stir together all dressing ingredients *except* milk. Stir in milk until desired consistency is reached. Cover; refrigerate at least 2 hr. In large bowl toss together all salad ingredients; serve with dressing.

6 servings
30 minutes

Garden Tomato & French Bean Salad

Summer salads — so flavourful with fresh tomatoes and French beans right from the garden.

450 g	(*16 oz*) fresh French beans, trimmed
125 ml	(*4 fl oz*) mayonnaise
125 ml	(*4 fl oz*) sour cream
5 ml	(*1 tsp*) basil leaves
2 ml	(*½ tsp*) pepper
1 ml	(*¼ tsp*) salt

30 ml	(*2 tbsp*) chopped fresh parsley
30 ml	(*2 tbsp*) milk
15 ml	(*1 tbsp*) country-style Dijon mustard
2	med. ripe tomatoes, sliced 5 mm (*¼ in*)
½	med. red onion, sliced 3 mm (*⅛ in*), separated into rings

Place beans in 3-litre (*5-pt*) saucepan; add enough water to cover. Bring to a full boil. Cook over med. heat until beans are crisply tender (12 to 15 min.). Meanwhile, in small bowl stir together remaining ingredients *except* tomatoes and onion. Rinse cooked French beans with cold water. On platter or individual salad plates arrange French beans, tomatoes and onion rings. Pour dressing over salad.

Spinach Salad With Yogurt Dressing (top)
Garden Tomato & French Bean Salad (bottom)

Midsummer Artichoke Salad (top)
Picnic Potato Salad (bottom)

4 servings
40 minutes

Picnic Potato Salad

A comforting and familiar salad made even better with a hint of dill.

1 litre	(*1¾ pt*) water	1 ml	(*¼ tsp*) pepper
5 ml	(*1 tsp*) salt	30 ml	(*2 tbsp*) chopped fresh parsley
12	quartered small new red potatoes	15 ml	(*1 tbsp*) country-style Dijon mustard
75 ml	(*5 tbsp*) sour cream	2 ml	(*½ tsp*) crushed fresh garlic
75 ml	(*5 tbsp*) mayonnaise	4	rashers crisply cooked, crumbled bacon
2 ml	(*½ tsp*) dill weed	30 ml	(*2 tbsp*) sliced 3 mm (*⅛ in*) spring onion
1 ml	(*¼ tsp*) salt		

In 3-litre (*5-pt*) saucepan bring water and salt to a full boil; add potatoes. Cook over high heat until potatoes are tender (12 to 15 min.). Rinse under cold water. In large bowl stir together remaining ingredients *except* bacon and spring onion. Add potatoes; toss to coat. Sprinkle with bacon and spring onion.

6 servings
15 minutes

Midsummer Artichoke Salad

Taste the sun in lush, ripe tomatoes tossed with artichokes, mushrooms and Mozzarella cheese.

1	med. lettuce, torn in pieces	350 g	(*12 oz*) marinated artichoke hearts, *reserve marinade*
225 g	(*8 oz*) fresh mushrooms, halved	2	med. ripe tomatoes, cut into wedges
100 g	(*4 oz*) cubed 1 cm (*½ in*) Mozzarella cheese	30 ml	(*2 tbsp*) grated Parmesan cheese
		1 ml	(*¼ tsp*) coarsely ground pepper

In large bowl stir together all ingredients; toss to coat with reserved artichoke marinade.

Summer Squash Salad

6 servings
20 minutes

*A hearty fresh courgette, yellow squash and ripe tomato salad
with a splash of Parmesan dressing.*

2	med. courgettes, sliced 3 mm (*1/8 in*)	1 ml	(*1/4 tsp*) pepper
2	med. yellow squashes, halved lengthwise, sliced 3 mm (*1/8 in*)	1 ml	(*1/4 tsp*) basil leaves
		30 ml	(*2 tbsp*) vegetable oil
50 ml	(*4 tbsp*) grated Parmesan cheese	2 ml	(*1/2 tsp*) crushed fresh garlic
50 ml	(*4 tbsp*) cider vinegar	1/2	med. red onion, sliced 3 mm (*1/8 in*), separated into rings
1 ml	(*1/4 tsp*) salt	2	med. ripe tomatoes, cut into wedges

In 2-litre (*3 1/2-pt*) saucepan place courgettes and yellow squashes; add enough water to cover. Cook over med. high heat until water comes to a full boil. Boil 1 to 2 min.; drain. Rinse with cold water. In large bowl stir together remaining ingredients *except* onion and tomatoes. Add courgettes, yellow squashes, onion and tomatoes; toss to coat.

Crispy Cucumbers in Dill Dressing

6 servings
15 minutes

Cucumbers, tomatoes and onion add spark to simple summer fare.

50 ml	(*4 tbsp*) cider vinegar	2	med. cucumbers, sliced 3 mm (*1/8 in*)
5 ml	(*1 tsp*) sugar	1	med. red onion, sliced 3 mm (*1/8 in*), separated into rings
2 ml	(*1/2 tsp*) salt		
2 ml	(*1/2 tsp*) dill weed	2	med. ripe tomatoes, cut into wedges
1 ml	(*1/4 tsp*) pepper		
30 ml	(*2 tbsp*) vegetable oil		

In large bowl stir together all ingredients *except* cucumbers, onion and tomatoes. Add remaining ingredients; toss to coat. Let stand 15 min. before serving.

Crispy Cucumbers in Dill Dressing

Crisp Vegetable Salad

6 servings
15 minutes

Crisp Vegetable Salad

Crisp and crunchy salad with an enticing cucumber dressing.

Dressing

75 ml	(*5 tbsp*) sour cream
75 ml	(*5 tbsp*) mayonnaise
2 ml	(*1/2 tsp*) dill weed
1 ml	(*1/4 tsp*) salt
1 ml	(*1/4 tsp*) dry mustard
	Pinch of pepper
15 ml	(*1 tbsp*) lemon juice
1/2	cucumber, chopped

Salad

150 g	(*5 oz*) broccoli flowerets
150 g	(*5 oz*) cauliflower flowerets
2	med. carrots, sliced 5 mm (*1/4 in*)
1	med. cucumber, sliced 3 mm (*1/8 in*)

In large bowl stir together all dressing ingredients *except* cucumber. Stir in cucumber. Add all salad ingredients; toss to coat.

6 servings
20 minutes

Backporch Cabbage Slaw

A colourful layered cabbage salad that's perfect for barbecues and picnics.

Dressing

125 ml	(*4 fl oz*) sour cream
75 g	(*3 oz*) cream cheese, softened
30 ml	(*2 tbsp*) chopped fresh parsley
5 ml	(*1 tsp*) salt
1 ml	(*1/4 tsp*) pepper
45 ml	(*3 tbsp*) milk
15 ml	(*1 tbsp*) lemon juice

Salad

300 g	(*11 oz*) shredded red cabbage
275 g	(*10 oz*) frozen peas, thawed, drained
2	med. carrots, shredded carrots
1	med. cucumber, sliced 3 mm (*1/8 in*)
30 ml	(*2 tbsp*) chopped fresh parsley

In small bowl stir together all dressing ingredients. In large bowl layer half of: cabbage, peas, carrots and cucumber. Pour 125 ml (*4 fl oz*) dressing over salad.

Repeat with remaining ingredients. Pour remaining dressing over salad. Sprinkle with 30 ml (*2 tbsp*) parsley.

Blue Cheese Coleslaw

12 servings
2 hours 30 minutes

Adding crumbled blue cheese to homemade coleslaw provides a burst of flavour.

Dressing

50 ml	(*4 tbsp*) sugar
50 g	(*2 oz*) blue cheese, crumbled
250 ml	(*8 fl oz*) mayonnaise
50 ml	(*4 tbsp*) vinegar
2 ml	(*1/2 tsp*) celery seed
2 ml	(*1/2 tsp*) garlic salt
15 ml	(*1 tbsp*) prepared mustard

Salad

600 g	(*1 1/4 lb*) finely shredded cabbage
2	med. carrots, shredded
50 ml	(*4 tbsp*) sliced spring onions
50 g	(*2 oz*) blue cheese, crumbled
150 g	(*5 oz*) cherry tomato halves

In medium bowl stir together all dressing ingredients. Cover; refrigerate at least 2 hr. In large bowl combine cabbage, carrots and spring onions. Just before serving, stir together dressing and cabbage mixture. Sprinkle with blue cheese. Garnish with cherry tomatoes. Serve immediately.

Bountiful Garden Salad With Pepper Salsa

10 servings
30 minutes

This festive salad is perfect summer fare; it's casual, but dramatic, with colourful garden vegetables.

6	fresh ears of corn on the cob, blanched*
3	med. courgettes or yellow squashes, sliced 5 mm (*1/4 in*)
1	med. cucumber, sliced 3 mm (*1/8 in*)
2	med. ripe tomatoes, *each* cut into 12 wedges

Salsa (mexican sauce)

2 ml	(*1/2 tsp*) salt
2 ml	(*1/2 tsp*) cumin
1 ml	(*1/4 tsp*) pepper
30 ml	(*2 tbsp*) chopped fresh cilantro or parsley
30 ml	(*2 tbsp*) lime juice
15 ml	(*1 tbsp*) vegetable oil
7 ml	(*1 1/2 tsp*) minced jalapeño chillies
75 g	(*3 oz*) chopped green pepper
50 g	(*2 oz*) chopped spring onions

With sharp knife cut corn off cobs. In large bowl place cut corn, courgettes, cucumber and tomatoes. In medium bowl stir together all salsa ingredients *except* green pepper and onions. Stir in green pepper and onions. Stir salsa into salad ingredients; toss to coat.

*600 g (*1 1/4 lb*) frozen whole kernel corn, thawed, can be substituted for 6 fresh ears of corn.

Tip: To blanch corn, place in boiling water for 2 min. Remove from heat; let stand 10 min. Rinse in cold water.

Bountiful Garden Salad With Pepper Salsa

Frosted Cranberry Squares

12 servings
7 hours 30 minutes

Frosted Cranberry Squares

This white-capped cranberry salad is the perfect accompaniment to your holiday meal.

Gelatin

175 g	(*6 oz*) raspberry flavour gelatin
500 ml	(*17 fl oz*) boiling water
350 g	(*12 oz*) fresh or frozen cranberries, thawed
450 g	(*16 oz*) sugar
150 ml	(*¼ pt*) orange juice
575 g	(*1¼ lb*) canned crushed pineapple in pineapple juice
5 ml	(*1 tsp*) grated orange rind

Topping

75 g	(*3 oz*) cream cheese, softened
250 ml	(*8 fl oz*) double cream
50 g	(*2 oz*) miniature marshmallows

Orange slices or zest of orange rind
Sugared cranberries

In large bowl dissolve gelatin in boiling water; set aside. In 1.25-litre (*2¼-pt*) blender container blend cranberries, half at a time, on high speed, stopping blender frequently to scrape sides, until well chopped (1 to 2 min.). Stir cranberries and remaining gelatin ingredients into dissolved gelatin mixture. Pour into 33 x 23-cm (*13 x 9-in*) dish. Cover; refrigerate until firm (6 hr. or overnight). In small mixer bowl beat cream cheese at med. speed, scraping bowl often, until light and fluffy (1 to 2 min.). Scrape cheese off beaters; add double cream. Beat at low speed until mixed. Increase speed to high. Continue beating, scraping bowl often, until stiff peaks form (1 to 2 min.). By hand, fold in marshmallows. Spread over firm cranberry gelatin. Refrigerate at least 1 hr. Cut into squares. If desired, garnish with orange slices or zest of orange rind and sugared cranberries.

8 to 10 servings
7 hours

Chilled Peaches 'n Cream Salad

Scoops of ice cream blend with chunky peaches in a chilled, refreshing gelatin salad.

175 g	(*6 oz*) peach flavour gelatin
250 ml	(*8 fl oz*) boiling water
250 ml	(*8 fl oz*) cold water
500 ml	(*17 fl oz*) vanilla ice cream, softened
	Pinch of nutmeg

450 g	(*1 lb*) sliced fresh or frozen peaches, cut into 1-cm (*½-in*) pieces, *reserve ½ fresh peach or 6 peach slices*

Lettuce leaves

In large bowl dissolve gelatin in boiling water; stir in cold water, ice cream and nutmeg. Whisk until ice cream is melted. Refrigerate until slightly thickened (about 30 min.). Whisk mixture until smooth (1 to 2 min.); fold in peaches. Pour into greased 1.5-litre (*2¾-pt*) mould. Refrigerate until firm (6 hr. or overnight). Unmould onto lettuce leaves; garnish with reserved peach slices.

Sparkling Fruit Moulded Salad

8 to 10 servings
7 hours

*Ginger ale adds sparkle to this cool, refreshing salad layered
with red grapes, cantaloupe and green grapes.*

15 g	(*1/2 oz*) unflavoured gelatin	75 g	(*3 oz*) seedless red grapes
125 ml	(*4 fl oz*) water	150 g	(*5 oz*) cubed 2.5 cm (*1-in*) cantaloupe
100 g	(*4 oz*) sugar		melon
500 ml	(*17 fl oz*) ginger ale	150 g	(*5 oz*) seedless green grapes
10 ml	(*2 tsp*) grated lime rind		
30 ml	(*2 tbsp*) lime juice		Lime slices

In 1-litre (*1¾-pt*) saucepan soften gelatin in water. Cook over low heat, stirring occasionally, until gelatin is dissolved (3 to 5 min.). In large bowl stir together sugar and dissolved gelatin. Stir in ginger ale, lime rind and lime juice. Refrigerate until slightly thickened (about 45 min.). Pour ⅓ of gelatin mixture into greased 1.5-litre (*2¾-pt*) mould; refrigerate remaining slightly thickened gelatin. Add red grapes to gelatin in mould; refrigerate 15 min. Arrange cantaloupe on top of red grape gelatin mixture; spoon over just enough thickened gelatin to cover cantaloupe. Arrange green grapes on top of cantaloupe gelatin mixture. Spoon remaining thickened gelatin over green grapes. Refrigerate 6 hr. or overnight until firm. Unmould onto serving plate; garnish with lime slices.

Iced Banana Berry Salad

8 servings
7 hours

A mosaic of summer berries and bananas makes this simple frozen salad beautiful.

175 g	(*6 oz*) sugar	150 g	(*5 oz*) blueberries*
250 ml	(*8 fl oz*) sour cream	125 g	(*4 oz*) raspberries**
15 ml	(*1 tbsp*) grated lemon rind		
30 ml	(*2 tbsp*) lemon juice		Mint leaves
250 ml	(*8 fl oz*) double cream		Raspberries
5 ml	(*1 tsp*) vanilla		Blueberries
2	med. bananas, sliced 5 mm (*1/4 in*)		

In large bowl stir together sugar, sour cream, lemon rind and lemon juice. In chilled small mixer bowl, beat chilled double cream at high speed, scraping bowl often, until stiff peaks form (1 to 2 min.). By hand, fold whipped cream, vanilla, bananas and berries into sour cream mixture. Spoon into individual 125-ml (*4-fl oz*) moulds. Freeze 6 hr. or overnight. Unmould on small salad plates. If desired, garnish with mint leaves, raspberries and blueberries.

*175 g (*6 oz*) frozen blueberries can be substituted for 150 g (*5 oz*) blueberries.

**150 g (*5 oz*) frozen raspberries can be substituted for 125 g (*4 oz*) raspberries.

Tip: 20 x 10-cm (*8 x 4-in*) loaf tin, lined with aluminum foil, can be substituted for individual moulds. Freeze 6 hr. or overnight. Lift salad from tin, using aluminum foil as handles. Remove aluminum foil. To serve, cut into 8 (2.5-cm) (*1-in*) slices.

Iced Banana Berry Salad (top)
Sparkling Fruit Moulded Salad (bottom)

1 basket (250 ml / *8 fl oz* dressing)
45 minutes

Star-Studded Fruit Basket

Become the 'star' at your next picnic with this fruit-filled, watermelon showpiece.

Dressing

50 ml	(*4 tbsp*) honey
50 ml	(*4 tbsp*) frozen orange juice concentrate, thawed
125 ml	(*4 fl oz*) double cream
5 ml	(*1 tsp*) poppy seed
1 ml	(*¼ tsp*) ginger

In small bowl stir together honey and orange juice concentrate. Stir in remaining dressing ingredients. Cover; refrigerate at least 1 hr. To make watermelon basket, measure and mark a horizontal line around the centre of melon. Measure and mark a 5-cm (*2-in*) wide centre strip crosswise over top of melon for handle. Place 3.5-cm (*1½-in*) starshaped cookie cutter or cardboard pattern on marked horizontal line; trace around with pencil. Repeat, with star tips touching, all around middle of melon. Next, place star shape in centre of 5-cm (*2-in*) handle strip; trace around with pencil. Repeat, with star tips touching, over handle. With

Basket

Large watermelon
Assorted fresh fruit pieces

small sharp knife cut out stars, leaving bottom points attached to watermelon. Remove rind and melon. Cut out stars on handle, leaving bottom and top tips attached to one another. Carefully cut pink melon from handle, leaving white rind on handle. Remove remaining watermelon from basket with melon baller or spoon. Fill basket with assorted fresh fruit pieces. Serve dressing with fresh fruit.

Tip: Melon can be prepared one day ahead. Wrap tightly in plastic wrap and refrigerate.

To Prepare Basket:

1. Place 3.5-cm (*1½-in*) starshaped cookie cutter or cardboard pattern on marked horizontal line; trace around with pencil. Repeat, with star tips touching, all around middle of melon.

2. Next, place star shape in centre of 5-cm (*2-in*) handle strip; trace around with pencil. Repeat, with star tips touching, over handle.

3. With small sharp knife cut out stars, leaving bottom points attached to watermelon.

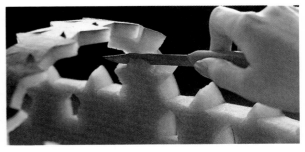

4. Carefully cut pink melon from handle, leaving white rind on handle.

Star-Studded Fruit Basket

Summer Fruits With Lime Cooler

6 servings
10 minutes

A squeeze of lime enhances fresh fruits and berries.

Dressing

125 ml	(*4 fl oz*) sour cream
30 ml	(*2 tbsp*) sugar
5 ml	(*1 tsp*) grated lime rind
15 ml	(*1 tbsp*) lime juice

Fruit

4	plums, sliced
2	peaches, sliced
300 g	(*11 oz*) strawberries, hulled, halved
150 g	(*5 oz*) raspberries

In small bowl stir together all dressing ingredients; set aside. In large bowl or individual fruit bowls toss together fruit. Serve dressing over fruit.

Nutmeg Cream Melon Salad

6 servings
20 minutes

So simple to make and refreshing to eat.

75 g	(*3 oz*) cream cheese, softened	300 g	(*11 oz*) seedless red or green grapes
15 ml	(*1 tbsp*) icing sugar	300 g	(*11 oz*) cubed 2.5 cm (*1 in*) cantaloupe melon
1 ml	(*¼ tsp*) nutmeg		
	Pinch of salt	300 g	(*11 oz*) cubed 2.5 cm (*1 in*) honeydew
15 ml	(*1 tbsp*) milk		

In large bowl stir together all ingredients *except* grapes, cantaloupe and honeydew. Add remaining ingredients; toss to coat.

Nutmeg Cream Melon Salad (top)
Summer Fruits With Lime Cooler (bottom)

4 to 6 servings
1 hour 30 minutes

Cinnamon Chicken Fruit Salad

For a special luncheon, serve this elegant chicken fruit salad in pineapple halves.

Salad

375 g	(*13 oz*) cooked, cubed 2.5 cm (*1 in*) chicken
300 g	(*11 oz*) seedless green grapes, cut in half
300 g	(*11 oz*) stoned sweet cherries
2	celery sticks, sliced 5 mm (*¼ in*)
30 ml	(*2 tbsp*) finely chopped onion
1	large fresh pineapple, cubed 2.5 cm (*1 in*); *reserve shell for serving*

Dressing

125 ml	(*4 fl oz*) mayonnaise
125 ml	(*4 fl oz*) vanilla yogurt
1 ml	(*¼ tsp*) ginger
1 ml	(*¼ tsp*) cinnamon
50 ml	(*4 tbsp*) toasted coconut

In large bowl combine all salad ingredients *except* pineapple; set aside. In small bowl stir together all dressing ingredients *except* coconut. Pour over salad; toss gently to coat. Cover; refrigerate at least 1 hr. Just before serving, place pineapple shells on large lettuce-lined platter. Stir cubed pineapple into salad. Spoon into pineapples; sprinkle with coconut.

Tip: Seedless red grapes can be substituted for the cherries.

To Prepare Pineapple Shells:

1. Leaving greens attached, cut pineapple into quarters or sixths lengthwise.

2. Holding pineapple securely, cut fruit from rind.

Cinnamon Chicken Fruit Salad

Orchard Salad With Almond Cream

6 servings
20 minutes

Orchard Salad With Almond Cream

Juicy ripe pears and crisp, tart apples blend with sweet apricots in a light almond whipped cream.

2	med. ripe pears, cut into 2.5-cm (*1-in*) pieces	250 ml	(*8 fl oz*) double cream
2	med. tart apples, cored, sliced 5 mm (*¼ in*)	30 ml	(*2 tbsp*) sugar
		50 ml	(*4 tbsp*) reserved apricot juice
450 g	(*16 oz*) canned apricot halves, drained, *reserve juice*	15 ml	(*1 tbsp*) grated orange rind
		2 ml	(*½ tsp*) almond extract

In large bowl place pears, apples and apricots. In chilled small mixer bowl beat chilled double cream at high speed, scraping bowl often, until soft peaks form.

Gradually add sugar; continue beating until stiff peaks form (1 to 2 min.). By hand, fold in remaining ingredients. Fold whipped cream into fruit mixture.

To Prepare Whipping Cream:

1. In chilled small mixer bowl beat chilled double cream at high speed, scraping bowl often, until soft peaks form. Gradually add sugar; continue beating until stiff peaks form (1 to 2 min.).

2. By hand, fold in remaining ingredients.

Honey-Glazed Citrus Salad

6 servings
30 minutes

A refreshing combination of flavours.

30 ml	(*2 tbsp*) vegetable oil
30 ml	(*2 tbsp*) cider vinegar
30 ml	(*2 tbsp*) honey
1	large lettuce, torn into pieces
½	med. red onion, chopped
50 ml	(*4 tbsp*) chopped fresh parsley
2	oranges, pared, sectioned, drained
2	grapefruit, pared, sectioned, drained

   In large bowl stir together oil, vinegar and honey.
Add remaining ingredients; toss to coat.

To Section Grapefruit or Oranges:

1.   Using sharp paring knife, remove the rind and
white membrane by cutting in a spiral pattern.

2.   For each section, cut toward the center of the fruit
between the section and the membrane.

3.   Turn knife, sliding knife down the other side of
the section next to the membrane. Remove any seeds.

Honey-Glazed Citrus Salad

Glazed Cranberry Citrus Compote

Grandma's Winter Fruit Medley

6 servings
40 minutes

A delicious fruit salad served with a thickened fruit juice dressing.

Fruit
300 g	(*11 oz*) seedless green grapes
300 g	(*11 oz*) seedless red grapes
575 g	(*1¼ lb*) canned pineapple chunks, drained, *reserve juice*
300 g	(*11 oz*) canned mandarin orange segments, drained, *reserve juice*
2	med. bananas, sliced 1 cm (*½ in*)

Dressing
100 g	(*4 oz*) sugar
175 ml	(*6 fl oz*) *reserved* fruit juices
1	egg
15 ml	(*1 tbsp*) plain flour
5 ml	(*1 tsp*) lemon juice

Place fruit in large bowl. In 1-litre (*1¾-pt*) saucepan stir together all dressing ingredients. Cook over med. heat, stirring occasionally, until dressing is thickened (3 to 5 min.). Let stand 5 min. Pour dressing over fruit; toss to coat. Chill 15 min.

Glazed Cranberry Citrus Compote

6 servings
2 hours

A refreshing, unique blend of chilled citrus fruits and sugar-glazed cranberries.

100 g	(*4 oz*) fresh or frozen whole cranberries, thawed
50 ml	(*4 tbsp*) sugar
15 ml	(*1 tbsp*) grated fresh gingerroot

3	oranges, pared, sectioned, *reserve juice*
2	grapefruit, pared, sectioned, *reserve juice*
15 ml	(*1 tbsp*) grated orange rind
1	kiwi, peeled, sliced 3 mm (*⅛ in*)

In 2-litre (*3½-pt*) saucepan place cranberries; sprinkle with sugar and gingerroot. Cover; cook over med. heat for 2 min. Stir cranberries. Continue cooking for 1 to 2 min. or until cranberries begin to soften but still hold their shape. Meanwhile, in large bowl stir together oranges, grapefruit and reserved juices; sprinkle with orange rind. Stir in glazed cranberries. Spoon into individual fruit dishes; top each with slice of kiwi. Refrigerate 1 hr. or until served.

Microwave Directions: In medium bowl combine cranberries, sugar and gingerroot. Cover with plastic wrap; microwave on HIGH until cranberries begin to soften but still hold their shape (1½ to 2 min.). Meanwhile, in large bowl stir together oranges, grapefruit and reserved juices; sprinkle with orange rind. Stir in glazed cranberries. Spoon into individual fruit dishes; top each with slice of kiwi. Refrigerate 1 hr. or until served.

250 ml (*8 fl oz*)
15 minutes

Basil Vinaigrette

This light basil dressing will make your garden-fresh lettuce and vegetables sparkle.

125 ml	(*4 fl oz*) vegetable or olive oil	5 ml	(*1 tsp*) crushed fresh garlic
75 ml	(*5 tbsp*) white vinegar	1 ml	(*1/4 tsp*) salt
15 ml	(*1 tbsp*) torn fresh basil	1 ml	(*1/4 tsp*) pepper

In jar with lid combine all ingredients. Shake well. Store refrigerated.

500 ml (*17 fl oz*)
1 hour 15 minutes

Creamy Herb Dressing

Herbs, fresh from the garden, are the secret to this flavourful dressing.

75 ml	(*5 tbsp*) chopped fresh parsley	125 ml	(*4 fl oz*) buttermilk*
50 ml	(*4 tbsp*) chopped spring onions	5 ml	(*1 tsp*) chopped fresh thyme leaves**
250 ml	(*8 fl oz*) sour cream	1 ml	(*1/4 tsp*) salt
50 ml	(*4 tbsp*) mayonnaise	1 ml	(*1/4 tsp*) pepper

In small bowl stir together all ingredients. Cover; refrigerate at least 1 hr.

*7 ml (*1 1/2 tsp*) vinegar plus enough milk to equal 125 ml (*4 fl oz*) can be substituted for 125 ml (*4 fl oz*) buttermilk.

**2 ml (*1/2 tsp*) dried thyme leaves, crushed, can be substituted for 5 ml (*1 tsp*) fresh thyme leaves.

Basil Vinaigrette

PASTA, RICE & BEANS

Do you recall your favorite meal as a child? For many, it was macaroni and cheese. There was something so comforting about that dish, especially after a rough day at school or exhausting play with friends. As you came in the back door, you could smell that familiar aroma and just knew that Mom had made your favorite.

Think of the best baked beans you ever ate. They were lightly sweetened with brown sugar, and across the top were thick strips of bacon. Baked in a brown crock, the beans came from the oven bubbling hot and so tempting that you could hardly wait for the first delicious bite.

Then there was Mom's spaghetti. She made the sauce herself — a spicy-rich sauce that was chunky with stewed tomatoes and pepperoni. Lots of people asked for the recipe, but Mom's was always a little bit better.

Hearty, full-of-flavor dishes that start with pasta, rice or beans. Foods that satisfy so completely. The kind of old-fashioned food that memories are made of.

Country Pasta With Mozzarella

6 servings
45 minutes

*A hearty home-style pasta filled with
bacon, broccoli and Mozzarella cheese.*

225 g	(*8 oz*) uncooked rigatoni
8	rashers bacon, cut into 2.5-cm (*1-in*) pieces
150 g	(*5 oz*) broccoli flowerets
2 ml	(*1/2 tsp*) crushed fresh garlic
225 g	(*8 oz*) shredded Mozzarella cheese

50 ml	(*4 tbsp*) grated Parmesan cheese
	Pinch of cayenne pepper
50 ml	(*4 tbsp*) chopped fresh parsley

Cook rigatoni according to pkg. directions; drain. Meanwhile, in 25-cm (*10-in*) frying pan cook bacon over med. high heat, stirring occasionally, until bacon is browned (6 to 8 min.). Reduce heat to med. Add broccoli and garlic. Cook, stirring occasionally, until broccoli is crisply tender (4 to 5 min.). Add rigatoni and remaining ingredients *except* parsley. Continue cooking, stirring occasionally, until cheese is melted (3 to 5 min.). Sprinkle with parsley.

Microwave Directions: Cook rigatoni according to pkg. directions; drain. In 3-litre (*5-pt*) casserole microwave bacon on HIGH until tender (4 to 5 min.). Add broccoli and garlic. Microwave on HIGH until broccoli is crisply tender (3 to 4 min.). Add rigatoni and remaining ingredients *except* parsley. Cover; microwave on HIGH, stirring after half the time, until heated through (2 to 3 min.). Let stand 2 min. Sprinkle with parsley.

Spicy Spaghetti Sauce With Pepperoni

6 servings
35 minutes

*A chunky spaghetti sauce that's ready when you are
and abundant in taste and aroma.*

225 g	(*8 oz*) uncooked spaghetti
100 g	(*4 oz*) sliced 1 cm (*1/2 in*) fresh mushrooms
2	med. onions, chopped
200 g	(*7 oz*) stoned ripe olives, sliced 1 cm (*1/2 in*)
30 g	(*1 oz*) chopped fresh parsley
250 ml	(*8 fl oz*) water

800 g	(*1 3/4 lb*) canned stewed tomatoes
150 g	(*5 oz*) canned tomato purée
10 ml	(*2 tsp*) basil leaves
2 ml	(*1/2 tsp*) oregano leaves
1 ml	(*1/4 tsp*) pepper
15 ml	(*1 tbsp*) country-style Dijon mustard
5 ml	(*1 tsp*) crushed fresh garlic
75 g	(*3 oz*) sliced pepperoni

Cook spaghetti according to pkg. directions; drain. Meanwhile, in 3-litre (*5-pt*) saucepan combine all ingredients *except* pepperoni. Cook over med. heat, stirring occasionally, until sauce is thickened (15 to 20 min.). Stir in pepperoni; continue cooking until heated through (4 to 5 min.). Serve over spaghetti.

Microwave Directions: Cook spaghetti according to pkg. directions; drain. In 3-litre (*5-pt*) casserole combine 175 ml (*6 fl oz*) water and remaining ingredients *except* pepperoni. Cover; microwave on HIGH, stirring after half the time, until heated through (8 to 10 min.). Stir in pepperoni. Microwave on HIGH until pepperoni is heated through (2 to 3 min.). Serve over spaghetti.

Country Pasta With Mozzarella

Home-Style Macaroni & Cheese

6 servings
40 minutes

Home-Style Macaroni & Cheese

Macaroni with chunks of Cheddar cheese is baked until bubbling
for a soothing and satisfying supper.

200 g	(*7 oz*) uncooked elbow macaroni
50 g	(*2 oz*) butter or margarine
45 ml	(*3 tbsp*) plain flour
500 ml	(*17 fl oz*) milk
225 g	(*8 oz*) cream cheese, softened
2 ml	(*¹/₂ tsp*) salt
2 ml	(*¹/₂ tsp*) pepper

10 ml	(*2 tsp*) country-style Dijon mustard
225 g	(*8 oz*) cubed 1 cm (*¹/₂ in*) Cheddar cheese
125 g	(*4 oz*) fresh breadcrumbs
30 g	(*1 oz*) butter or margarine, melted
30 ml	(*2 tbsp*) chopped fresh parsley

Heat oven to 200 °C (*400 °F*) mark 6. Cook macaroni according to pkg. directions; drain. Meanwhile, in 3-litre (*5-pt*) saucepan melt 50 g (*2 oz*) butter; stir in flour. Cook over med. heat, stirring occasionally, until smooth and bubbly (1 min.). Stir in milk, cream cheese, salt, pepper and mustard. Continue cooking, stirring occasionally, until sauce is thickened (3 to 4 min.). Stir in macaroni and cheese. Pour into 2-litre (*3¹/₂-pt*) casserole. In small bowl stir together remaining ingredients; sprinkle over macaroni and cheese. Bake for 15 to 20 min. or until golden brown and heated through.

Microwave Directions: Cook macaroni according to pkg. directions; drain. Meanwhile, in 3-litre (*5-pt*) casserole melt 50 g (*2 oz*) butter on HIGH (50 to 60 sec.). Stir in flour. Microwave on HIGH until bubbly (1 to 1¹/₂ min.). Stir in milk, cream cheese, salt, pepper and mustard. Microwave on HIGH, stirring after half the time, until thickened (4 to 5 min.). Stir in macaroni and cheese. In small bowl stir together remaining ingredients; sprinkle over macaroni and cheese. Microwave on HIGH until heated through (8 to 10 min.).

**6 servings
30 minutes**

Herb Garden & Lemon Pasta

*Toss fresh garden ingredients together with pasta
for an enjoyable light supper.*

225 g	(*8 oz*) uncooked corkscrew or twist pasta
75 ml	(*5 tbsp*) vegetable oil
3	med. courgettes, sliced 5 mm (*¼ in*)
1	red onion chopped
50 ml	(*4 tbsp*) freshly grated Parmesan cheese
50 ml	(*4 tbsp*) chopped fresh basil
50 ml	(*4 tbsp*) chopped fresh chives
50 ml	(*4 tbsp*) chopped fresh parsley
2	med. ripe tomatoes, cut into wedges
2 ml	(*½ tsp*) salt
2 ml	(*½ tsp*) pepper
30 ml	(*2 tbsp*) lemon juice

Cook pasta according to pkg. directions; drain. Meanwhile, in 25-cm (*10-in*) frying pan heat oil; add courgettes and onion. Cook over med. heat, stirring occasionally, until courgettes are crisply tender (5 to 7 min.). Add remaining ingredients and pasta. Cover; let stand 2 min. or until tomatoes are heated through.

Microwave Directions: Cook pasta according to pkg. directions; drain. In 3-litre (*5-pt*) casserole combine oil, courgettes and onion. Cover; microwave on HIGH, stirring after half the time, until courgettes are crisply tender (3 to 4 min.). Add remaining ingredients and pasta. Cover; microwave on HIGH, stirring after half the time, until tomatoes are heated through (1 to 2 min.).

**4 servings
25 minutes**

Fettuccine With Spinach Cream Sauce

Butter and cream make this delicate spinach sauce rich in flavour.

225 g	(*8 oz*) uncooked fettuccine
45 g	(*1½ oz*) butter or margarine
100 g	(*4 oz*) sliced 5 mm (*¼ in*) fresh mushrooms
15 ml	(*1 tbsp*) plain flour
50 ml	(*4 tbsp*) grated Parmesan cheese
375 ml	(*13 fl oz*) single cream
275 g	(*10 oz*) frozen chopped spinach, thawed, drained
15	cherry tomatoes, halved
5 ml	(*1 tsp*) basil leaves
2 ml	(*½ tsp*) salt
1 ml	(*¼ tsp*) pepper

Cook fettuccine according to pkg. directions; drain. Meanwhile, in 25-cm (*10-in*) frying pan melt butter; add mushrooms. Cook over med. heat, stirring occasionally, until mushrooms are tender (2 to 3 min.). Stir in flour until smooth and bubbly (1 min.). Stir in remaining ingredients. Continue cooking, stirring occasionally, until heated through (6 to 8 min.). Serve over fettuccine.

Microwave Directions: Cook fettuccine according to pkg. directions; drain. Meanwhile, in 2-litre (*3½-pt*) casserole melt butter on HIGH (30 to 40 sec.). Stir in mushrooms. Microwave on HIGH until mushrooms are tender (1 to 2 min.). Stir in flour. Microwave on HIGH until smooth and bubbly (1 to 1½ min.). Add remaining ingredients *except* spinach and tomatoes. Microwave on HIGH until thickened (2 to 3 min.). Stir in spinach and tomatoes. Microwave on HIGH until heated through (1 to 2 min.). Serve over fettuccine.

Herb Garden & Lemon Pasta

Creamy Vegetables & Fettuccine

A colourful pasta side dish; serve with roast beef and a green salad for a hearty meal.

4	med. carrots, diagonally sliced 1 cm (*1/2 in*)	30 ml	(*2 tbsp*) plain flour
175 g	(*6 oz*) uncooked fettuccine	2 ml	(*1/2 tsp*) salt
150 g	(*5 oz*) broccoli flowerets	2 ml	(*1/2 tsp*) nutmeg
75 g	(*3 oz*) butter or margarine	250 ml	(*8 fl oz*) milk
		50 ml	(*4 tbsp*) grated Parmesan cheese

In 3-litre (*5-pt*) saucepan bring 2 litres (*3 1/2 pt*) water to a full boil. Add carrots and fettuccine. Cook over med. heat 6 min. Add broccoli; continue cooking until carrots and broccoli are crisply tender (4 to 5 min.); drain. Rinse with hot water; set aside. In same saucepan melt butter. Stir in flour, salt and nutmeg until smooth and bubbly (1 min.). Add milk; cook over med. heat, stirring occasionally, until mixture comes to a full boil (4 to 6 min.). Boil 1 min. Stir in fettuccine mixture. Reduce heat to low; continue cooking until heated through (3 to 4 min.). To serve, sprinkle with Parmesan cheese.

Poppy Seed Noodles 'n Cream

Poppy seed and sour cream bring old world flavour to this quick side dish.

225 g	(*8 oz*) uncooked extra wide egg noodles	10 ml	(*2 tsp*) poppy seed
250 ml	(*8 fl oz*) dairy sour cream	1 ml	(*1/4 tsp*) salt
50 g	(*2 oz*) butter or margarine		

In 3-litre (*5-pt*) saucepan cook noodles according to pkg. directions; drain well. Return to pan; add remaining ingredients. Cook over med. heat, stirring constantly, until smooth and heated through (1 to 2 min.).

Creamy Vegetables & Fettuccine

Pasta & Vegetable Dish (top)
Fresh Herb Linguine (bottom)

4 servings
15 minutes

Fresh Herb Linguine

A buttery, fresh herb sauce makes this pasta a perfect accompaniment to most any meat.

225 g	(*8 oz*) uncooked linguine
75 g	(*3 oz*) butter or margarine
2 ml	(*1/2 tsp*) crushed fresh garlic
75 ml	(*5 tbsp*) chopped fresh parsley

7 ml	(*1 1/2 tsp*) chopped fresh oregano leaves*
15 ml	(*1 tbsp*) lemon juice
100 g	(*4 oz*) freshly grated Parmesan cheese

In 3-litre (*5-pt*) saucepan cook linguine according to pkg. directions; drain. In same saucepan place butter and garlic. Cook over med. heat until butter is melted (3 to 4 min.). Stir in linguine and remaining ingredients *except* Parmesan cheese. Cook over med. heat, stirring constantly, until heated through (2 to 3 min.). Sprinkle with Parmesan cheese.

*2 ml (*1/2 tsp*) dried oregano leaves can be substituted for 7 ml (*1 1/2 tsp*) fresh oregano leaves.

Microwave Directions: Cook linguine according to pkg. directions; drain. In 2-litre (*3 1/2-pt*) casserole place butter and garlic. Microwave on HIGH until butter is melted (60 to 70 sec.). Stir in linguine and remaining ingredients *except* Parmesan cheese. Microwave on HIGH until heated through (1 1/2 to 2 min.). Sprinkle with Parmesan cheese.

---

4 servings
30 minutes

Pasta & Vegetable Dish

A new way to use the plentiful courgettes from your garden.

100 g	(*4 oz*) uncooked bow tie pasta*
50 g	(*2 oz*) butter or margarine
5 ml	(*1 tsp*) crushed fresh garlic
1	med. courgette, cut into 1-cm (*1/2-in*) pieces
1	small aubergine, cut into 1-cm (*1/2-in*) pieces
1	med. red onion, cut into eighths

5 ml	(*1 tsp*) basil leaves
2 ml	(*1/2 tsp*) salt
2 ml	(*1/2 tsp*) pepper
175 g	(*6 oz*) shredded Mozzarella cheese

Cook pasta according to pkg. directions; drain. In 25-cm (*10-in*) frying pan melt butter until sizzling; stir in garlic. Stir in remaining ingredients *except* pasta and cheese. Cook over med. heat, stirring occasionally, until vegetables are crisply tender (4 to 6 min.). Stir in pasta. Continue cooking, stirring occasionally, until heated through (2 to 3 min.). Stir in cheese. Serve immediately.

*100 g (*4 oz*) of your favourite uncooked pasta can be substituted for 100 g (*4 oz*) uncooked bow tie pasta.

Microwave Directions: Cook pasta according to pkg. directions; drain. In 3-litre (*5-pt*) casserole melt butter on HIGH (40 to 50 sec.); stir in garlic. Microwave on HIGH 1 min. Stir in remaining ingredients *except* pasta and cheese. Cover; microwave on HIGH, stirring after half the time, until vegetables are crisply tender (5 to 6 min.). Stir in pasta. Microwave, stirring after half the time, until heated through (2 to 3 min.). Stir in cheese. Serve immediately.

Cheesy Confetti Rice (top)
Savoury Rice & Vegetables (bottom)

8 servings
40 minutes

Savoury Rice & Vegetables

There's no need for a dressing on this hearty salad.

Rice

200 g	(*7 oz*) uncooked long grain rice
50 ml	(*4 tbsp*) vegetable oil
175 ml	(*6 fl oz*) water
295 g	(*10.4 oz*) canned chicken broth
5 ml	(*1 tsp*) paprika
1 ml	(*1/4 tsp*) salt
1 ml	(*1/4 tsp*) pepper
	Pinch of cayenne pepper

Vegetables

150 g	(*5 oz*) broccoli flowerets
200 g	(*7 oz*) stoned ripe olives
50 ml	(*4 tbsp*) sliced 5 mm (*1/4 in*) spring onions
50 ml	(*4 tbsp*) chopped fresh parsley
1	med. ripe tomato, cut into wedges
1	med. green pepper, cut into strips
225 g	(*8 oz*) sliced 3 mm (*1/8 in*) summer sausage, halved

In 25-cm (*10-in*) frying pan combine rice and oil. Cook over med. low heat, stirring occasionally, until rice is browned (5 min.). Stir in remaining rice ingredients. Cover; continue cooking until liquid is absorbed (15 to 20 min.). Meanwhile, in large bowl stir together all vegetable ingredients. Pour hot rice over vegetables; toss to combine.

6 (150-ml) (*1/4-pt*) servings
50 minutes

Cheesy Confetti Rice

Cheese combines with rice and vegetables for a colourful and tasty side dish.

50 g	(*2 oz*) butter or margarine
200 g	(*7 oz*) uncooked long grain rice
50 ml	(*4 tbsp*) chopped onion
600 ml	(*1 pt*) water
100 g	(*4 oz*) canned diced mild green chillies, drained

15 ml	(*1 tbsp*) instant chicken bouillon
100 g	(*4 oz*) shredded Cheddar cheese
50 ml	(*4 tbsp*) sliced ripe olives
50 g	(*2 oz*) canned diced pimento, drained
30 ml	(*2 tbsp*) chopped fresh parsley

In 2-litre (*3 1/2-pt*) saucepan melt butter. Add rice and onion. Cook over med. heat, stirring constantly, until rice is a golden colour (8 to 10 min.). Slowly add water, green chillies and chicken bouillon. Continue cooking until mixture comes to a full boil (8 to 10 min.); reduce heat to low. Cover; simmer until rice is tender (25 to 30 min.). Stir in remaining ingredients. Serve immediately.

Microwave Directions: In 3-litre (*5-pt*) casserole melt butter on HIGH (50 to 60 sec.). Add rice and onion. Cover; microwave on HIGH until rice is a golden colour (5 to 6 min.). Slowly add water, green chillies and chicken bouillon. Cover; microwave on HIGH until mixture comes to a full boil (5 to 6 min.). Reduce power to MEDIUM (50% power); microwave until rice is tender (10 to 12 min.). Stir in remaining ingredients. Serve immediately.

Springtime Garden Pilaf

Crunchy almonds and colourful vegetables liven up rice.

8 (150-ml) (*¼-pt*) servings
35 minutes

650 ml	(*23 fl oz*) water	250 g	(*9 oz*) uncooked long grain rice
50 g	(*2 oz*) butter or margarine	1	finely chopped carrot
30 ml	(*2 tbsp*) instant chicken bouillon	75 g	(*3 oz*) slivered almonds, toasted
1 ml	(*¼ tsp*) salt	50 ml	(*4 tbsp*) chopped fresh parsley
	Pinch of pepper	30 ml	(*2 tbsp*) sliced spring onion
1 ml	(*¼ tsp*) crushed fresh garlic		

In 2-litre (*3½-pt*) saucepan bring water, butter, chicken bouillon, salt, pepper and garlic to a full boil (5 to 7 min.). Add rice and carrot; return to a full boil. Reduce heat to low; simmer until rice is tender (25 to 30 min.). Stir in remaining ingredients.

Microwave Directions: In 3-litre (*5-pt*) casserole combine water, butter, chicken bouillon, salt, pepper and garlic. Cover; microwave on HIGH until mixture comes to a full boil (4 to 5 min.). Add rice and carrots. Cover; microwave on HIGH 5 min. Reduce power to MEDIUM (50% power); microwave until rice is tender (10 to 15 min.). Stir in remaining ingredients. Cover; let stand 5 min.

Crunchy Rice Medley

Water chestnuts add crunch to this flavourful side dish.

6 (125-ml) (*4-fl oz*) servings
25 minutes

175 g	(*6 oz*) long grain & wild rice mix	100 g	(*4 oz*) canned sliced mushrooms, drained
50 g	(*2 oz*) butter or margarine	50 g	(*2 oz*) canned chopped pimento, drained
225 g	(*8 oz*) canned sliced water chestnuts, drained		

Cook rice according to pkg. directions. Stir in remaining ingredients. Continue cooking until butter is melted and vegetables are heated through (3 to 4 min.).

Springtime Garden Pilaf

Trappers' Wild Rice

6 servings
60 minutes

A sweet, full-flavoured wild rice that is a perfect accompaniment to game or roasted meat.

150 g	(*5 oz*) uncooked wild rice
1 litre	(*1³/4 pt*) water
2	med. carrots, sliced 3 mm (*¹/8 in*)
1	med. onion, sliced 3 mm (*¹/8 in*)
5 ml	(*1 tsp*) salt
5 ml	(*1 tsp*) sage leaves, rubbed

2 ml	(*¹/2 tsp*) pepper
10 ml	(*2 tsp*) crushed fresh garlic
5 ml	(*1 tsp*) grated fresh gingerroot
125 ml	(*4 fl oz*) apple juice
45 ml	(*3 tbsp*) honey
30 ml	(*2 tbsp*) chopped fresh parsley

Rinse wild rice. In 2-litre (*3¹/2-pt*) saucepan combine wild rice and remaining ingredients *except* apple juice, honey and parsley. Bring to a full boil (6 to 8 min.). Cover; cook over med. heat until wild rice is tender (45 to 50 min.). Drain off any excess liquid; stir in apple juice and honey. Continue cooking until heated through (4 to 5 min.). Stir in parsley.

Microwave Directions: Rinse wild rice. In 2-litre (*3¹/2-pt*) casserole combine wild rice and remaining ingredients *except* apple juice, honey and parsley. Cover; microwave on HIGH until mixture comes to full boil (9 to 12 min.). Reduce power to MEDIUM (50% power); microwave, stirring occasionally, until wild rice is tender (40 to 50 min.). Drain off any excess liquid; stir in apple juice and honey. Microwave on HIGH until heated through (2 to 3 min.). Stir in parsley.

Barn-Raising Beans

8 servings
3 hours 30 minutes

Serve these mildly spiced beans with accompaniments of rice, sour cream and spring onions.

450 g	(*1 lb*) dried red beans*
6	rashers of bacon, cut into 1-cm (*¹/2-in*) pieces
2	med. onions, chopped
50 ml	(*4 tbsp*) chopped fresh cilantro or parsley
50 g	(*2 oz*) butter or margarine
2	med. carrots, coarsely chopped
15 ml	(*1 tbsp*) chilli powder

7 ml	(*1¹/2 tsp*) salt
2 ml	(*¹/2 tsp*) cumin
2 ml	(*¹/2 tsp*) thyme leaves
2	bay leaves
2	whole cloves
10 ml	(*2 tsp*) crushed fresh garlic
1 litre	(*1³/4 pt*) water

In large bowl place beans; cover with water. Soak for 1 hr. Meanwhile, in 3-litre (*5-pt*) saucepan cook bacon over med. high heat, stirring occasionally, until bacon is browned (6 to 8 min.). Reduce heat to med. Add remaining ingredients *except* 1 litre (*1³/4 pt*) water and beans. Cook, stirring occasionally, until onions are crisply tender (2 to 3 min.). Drain beans; add to vegeta-ble mixture. Add water. Cook over high heat until mixture comes to a full boil. Reduce heat to med. Cover; cook, stirring occasionally, until beans are fork tender (1¹/2 to 2 hr.). Remove bay leaves and cloves.

*450 g (*1 lb*) dried kidney beans can be substituted for 450 g (*1 lb*) dried red beans. Cook for 60 to 70 min.

Trappers' Wild Rice (top)
Barn-Raising Beans (bottom)

2 litres (*3¹/₂ pt*)
1 day

Robust Country Baked Beans

Long, slow cooking brings out old-time flavour in these hearty baked beans.

400 g	(*14 oz*) dried Great Northern or white beans
200 g	(*7 oz*) dried kidney beans
100 g	(*4 oz*) firmly packed brown sugar
375 ml	(*13 fl oz*) boiling water
50 ml	(*4 tbsp*) country-style Dijon mustard

50 ml	(*4 fl oz*) dark molasses
225 g	(*8 oz*) thick-sliced bacon, cut into 2.5-cm (*1-in*) pieces
225 g	(*8 oz*) salt pork, cubed 2.5 cm (*1 in*)
2	med. onions, chopped

In flameproof casserole stir together white beans, kidney beans and enough cold water to cover beans; soak overnight. If needed, add more water to cover beans. Cook over high heat until water comes to a full boil. Reduce heat to med.; continue cooking 30 to 45 min. or until beans are tender. Heat oven to 160 °C (*325 °F*) mark 3. Drain beans. In large bean pot or flameproof casserole combine beans and remaining ingredients. Bake, stirring occasionally, for 6 to 9 hr. or until beans are a rich brown colour and sauce has thickened. If beans become dry during baking, add 250 to 500 ml (*8 to 17 fl oz*) water.

Same Day: For same day preparation do not soak overnight. Instead, cook over high heat until water comes to a full boil. Reduce heat to med.; boil 2 min. Remove from heat. Cover; let stand 1 hr. Continue as directed left, beginning at 'If needed, add more water to cover beans.'

4 servings
30 minutes

American Style Black-Eyed Peas & Rice

A variation on a southern specialty called Hopping John.

350 g	(*12 oz*) cooked black-eyed peas
200 g	(*7 oz*) cooked long grain rice
50 g	(*2 oz*) butter or margarine
200 g	(*7 oz*) torn fresh spinach*
4	rashers of bacon, cut into 2.5-cm (*1-in*) pieces

30 ml	(*2 tbsp*) grated Parmesan cheese
2 ml	(*¹/₂ tsp*) salt
1 ml	(*¹/₄ tsp*) hot pepper sauce
100 g	(*4 oz*) shredded Cheddar cheese

Have cooked black-eyed peas and rice ready. In 2-litre (*3¹/₂-pt*) saucepan melt butter. Stir in spinach and bacon. Cook over med. heat, stirring occasionally, until spinach is tender (4 to 6 min.). Stir in black-eyed peas, rice and remaining ingredients *except* Cheddar cheese. Continue cooking, stirring occasionally, until heated through (7 to 10 min.). Just before serving, stir in Cheddar cheese.

*275 g (*10 oz*) frozen chopped spinach, thawed and drained, can be substituted for torn fresh spinach.

Microwave Directions: Have cooked black-eyed peas and rice ready. In 2-litre (*3¹/₂-pt*) casserole melt butter on HIGH (50 to 60 sec.). Stir in spinach and bacon. Microwave on HIGH, stirring after half the time, until spinach is tender (3 to 4 min.). Stir in black-eyed peas, rice and remaining ingredients *except* Cheddar cheese. Microwave on HIGH, stirring after half the time, until heated through (4 to 5 min.). Just before serving, stir in Cheddar cheese.

Robust Country Baked Beans (top)
American Style Black-Eyed Peas & Rice (bottom)

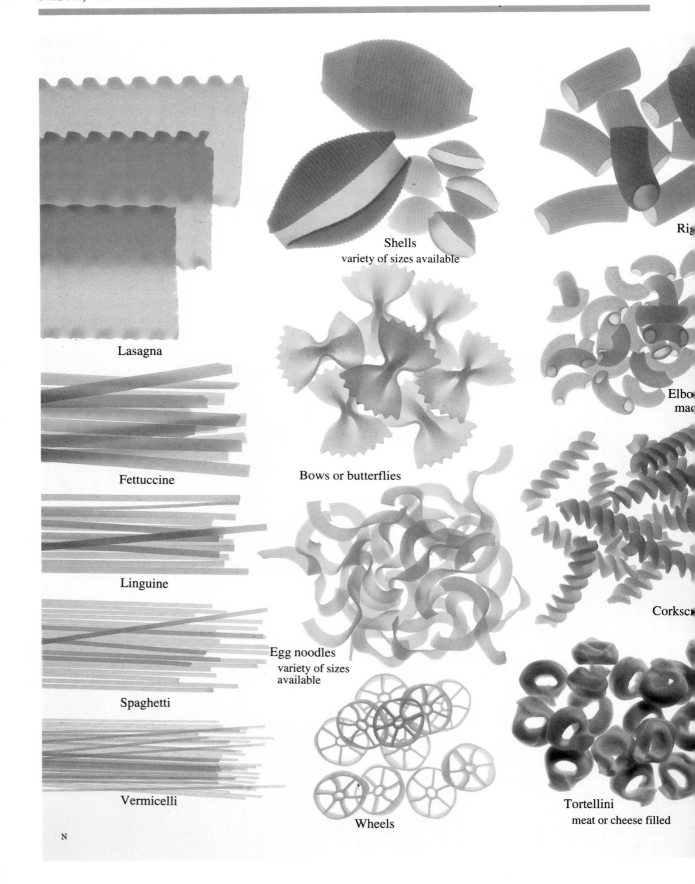

Lasagna

Fettuccine

Linguine

Spaghetti

Vermicelli

Shells
variety of sizes available

Bows or butterflies

Egg noodles
variety of sizes
available

Wheels

Ri

Elbo
mac

Corksc

Tortellini
meat or cheese filled

N

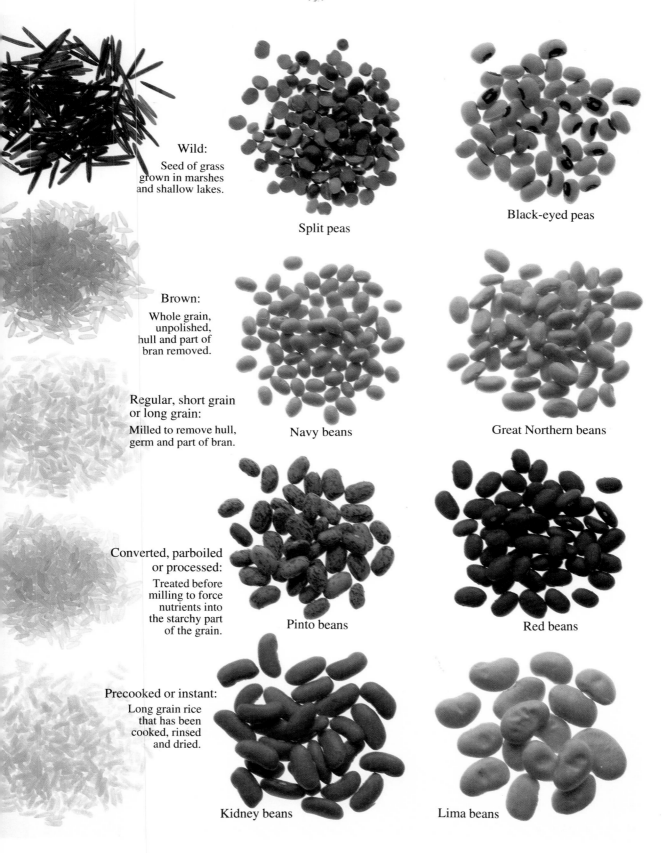

Wild:
Seed of grass grown in marshes and shallow lakes.

Split peas

Black-eyed peas

Brown:
Whole grain, unpolished, hull and part of bran removed.

Regular, short grain or long grain:
Milled to remove hull, germ and part of bran.

Navy beans

Great Northern beans

Converted, parboiled or processed:
Treated before milling to force nutrients into the starchy part of the grain.

Pinto beans

Red beans

Precooked or instant:
Long grain rice that has been cooked, rinsed and dried.

Kidney beans

Lima beans

VEGETABLES

Fresh from the farm or country roadside stand, vegetables present a kaleidoscope of shapes, sizes, colors and tastes. And no matter which way you turn, each variety looks more inviting than the last.

Fresh green beans, crisp enough to snap between your fingers. Imagine them cooked with bacon and rings of red onion. You can almost taste the flavor. And carrots with their lacy-leafed tops, so good whether creamed, glazed or as part of an old-fashioned pot roast dinner. Plump, vine-ripened tomatoes, bright red inside and out and sweeter than you ever imagined. Tender ears of corn, still in their fresh green husks with silky, golden topknots. The pleasures of sweet corn-on-the-cob, served piping hot with plenty of butter, are nothing less than legendary.

As beautiful as they are delicious, these are the fruits of the earth. And every vegetable dish you prepare brings a touch of the country into your home.

Tender Asparagus Spears With Garlic Mustard

4 servings
25 minutes

From the garden or market an abundance of asparagus is always a joy.

450 g	(*1 lb*) (24) asparagus spears, trimmed
50 g	(*2 oz*) butter or margarine
225 g	(*8 oz*) sliced 5 mm (*1/4 in*) fresh mushrooms

30 ml	(*2 tbsp*) country-style Dijon mustard
1 ml	(*1/4 tsp*) pepper
	Pinch of salt
2 ml	(*1/2 tsp*) crushed fresh garlic

In 25-cm (*10-in*) frying pan place asparagus spears; add enough water to cover. Bring to a full boil. Cook over med. heat until asparagus is crisply tender (5 to 7 min.). Drain; return to frying pan. Add remaining ingredients, pushing asparagus to side just until butter is melted. Cook over med. heat, stirring occasionally, until heated through (5 to 7 min.).

Microwave Directions: In 30 x 20-cm (*12 x 8-in*) baking dish melt butter on HIGH (50 to 60 sec.). Stir in all ingredients *except* asparagus and mushrooms; mix well. Place asparagus, heads toward centre of dish, and mushrooms in dish; turn to coat with butter mixture. Cover; microwave on HIGH, stirring after half the time, until vegetables are crisply tender (6 to 9 min.). Let stand 2 min.

Garden French Beans With Bacon

6 servings
60 minutes

Fresh, tender French beans cooked with flavourful bacon and onion provide old-fashioned goodness.

450 g	(*1 lb*) fresh French beans, trimmed
4	rashers bacon, cut into 1-cm (*1/2-in*) pieces
1	med. red onion, sliced 3 mm (*1/8 in*), separated into rings

45 g	(*1 1/2 oz*) butter or margarine
2 ml	(*1/2 tsp*) pepper
1 ml	(*1/4 tsp*) salt

In 3-litre (*5-pt*) saucepan place beans and bacon; add enough water to cover. Bring to a full boil. Cook over med. heat, stirring occasionally, until beans are crisply tender (20 to 25 min.); drain. Return to pan; add remaining ingredients. Cook over med. heat, stirring occasionally, until onion is crisply tender (5 to 7 min.).

Microwave Directions: In 3-litre (*5-pt*) casserole combine beans and 125 ml (*4 fl oz*) water. Cover; microwave on HIGH, stirring after half the time, until beans are crisply tender (8 to 10 min.). Drain; return to casserole. Add remaining ingredients. Cover; microwave on HIGH until heated through (3 to 5 min.).

Garden French Beans With Bacon (top)
Tender Asparagus Spears With Garlic Mustard (bottom)

Country Vegetable Simmer

Country Vegetable Simmer

**6 servings
45 minutes**

*Simmer fresh French beans, sweet new potatoes and juicy tomatoes
with just a hint of basil for a hearty vegetable dish.*

225 g	*(8 oz)* fresh French beans, trimmed	5 ml	*(1 tsp)* basil leaves
4	small new red potatoes, quartered	1 ml	*(¼ tsp)* salt
2	small onions, quartered	1 ml	*(¼ tsp)* pepper
45 g	*(1½ oz)* butter or margarine	1 ml	*(¼ tsp)* thyme leaves
8	fresh mushrooms, halved	30 ml	*(2 tbsp)* tomato purée
1	med. ripe tomato, cut into 1-cm *(½-in)* pieces	2 ml	*(½ tsp)* crushed fresh garlic
		50 ml	*(4 tbsp)* chopped fresh parsley

In 3-litre *(5-pt)* saucepan combine beans, potatoes and onions. Add enough water to cover; bring to a full boil. Cook over med. heat, stirring occasionally, until vegetables are crisply tender (15 to 20 min.); drain. Return to pan; add remaining ingredients *except* parsley. Cook over med. heat, stirring occasionally, until heated through (10 to 12 min.). Stir in parsley.

Microwave Directions: In 3-litre *(5-pt)* casserole combine beans, potatoes, onions and 125 ml *(4 fl oz)* water. Cover; microwave on HIGH, stirring after half the time, until vegetables are crisply tender (10 to 13 min.). Drain; return to casserole. Add remaining ingredients *except* parsley. Cover; microwave on HIGH until heated through (2 to 3 min.). Stir in parsley.

Family Favourite French Beans

**4 servings
15 minutes**

French beans special enough for a party, but perfect for a family meal.

45 g	*(1½ oz)* butter or margarine		Pinch of pepper
1	med. onion, cut into eighths	225 g	*(8 oz)* fresh mushrooms, cut into thirds
275 g	*(10 oz)* frozen French beans	50 g	*(2 oz)* shredded Cheddar Cheese
2 ml	*(½ tsp)* rosemary		
1 ml	*(¼ tsp)* salt		

In 2-litre *(3½-pt)* saucepan melt butter. Stir in onion; cook over med. heat until tender (2 to 3 min.). Add remaining ingredients *except* mushrooms and cheese. Cover; continue cooking, stirring occasionally, until beans are thawed and separated (3 to 5 min.). Remove cover. Stir in mushrooms; continue cooking, stirring occasionally, until beans are crisply tender (5 to 7 min.). Sprinkle with cheese. Cover; let stand 1 min.

Microwave Directions: In 1.5-litre *(2¾-pt)* casserole melt butter on HIGH (40 to 50 sec.). Stir in onion. Cover; microwave on HIGH 1 min. Stir in remaining ingredients *except* cheese. Cover; microwave on HIGH, stirring after half the time, until beans are crisply tender (4 to 5 min.). Sprinkle with cheese. Cover; let stand 1 min.

Southern Lima Beans & Bacon

4 to 6 servings
30 minutes

A hearty, stick-to-the-ribs country way to prepare lima beans.

30 ml	(*2 tbsp*) butter or margarine	400 g	(*14 oz*) canned stewed tomatoes
4	thick rashers of bacon, cut into 2.5-cm (*1-in*) pieces	275 g	(*10 oz*) frozen lima beans
1	med. onion, cut into eighths	1 ml	(*¼ tsp*) pepper
175 g	(*6 oz*) frozen sweet corn	1 ml	(*¼ tsp*) celery seed

In 25-cm (*10-in*) frying pan melt butter until sizzling; stir in bacon and onion. Cook over med. high heat, stirring occasionally, 5 min.; drain. Reduce heat to med.; stir in remaining ingredients. Continue cooking, stirring occasionally, until lima beans are tender (8 to 10 min.).

Microwave Directions: In 3-litre (*5-pt*) casserole melt butter on HIGH (30 to 40 sec.). Stir in bacon and onion. Microwave on HIGH, stirring after half the time, 3 min.; drain. Stir in remaining ingredients. Cover; microwave on HIGH, stirring after half the time, until lima beans are tender (5 to 8 min.).

Home-Style Beetroot With Sour Cream

4 servings
60 minutes

This duo of fresh beetroots and carrots, accented with chives, is a fall favourite.

5	med. fresh beetroots	2 ml	(*½ tsp*) salt
2	med. carrots, sliced 5 mm (*¼ in*)	2 ml	(*½ tsp*) dill weed
45 g	(*1½ oz*) butter or margarine		Pinch of pepper
15 ml	(*1 tbsp*) chopped fresh chives		Sour cream

In 2-litre (*3½-pt*) saucepan bring 750 ml (*1¼ pt*) water to a full boil. Add beetroots. Cover; cook over med. heat until beetroots are fork tender (35 to 45 min.). Drain. Run cold water over beetroots; slip off skins and remove root ends. Cut beetroots into 1-cm (*½-in*) cubes; set aside. In 1-litre (*1¾-pt*) saucepan bring 175 ml (*6 fl oz*) water to a full boil. Add carrots. Cover; cook over med. heat until carrots are crisply tender (8 to 10 min.). Drain; set aside. In same 2-litre (*3½-pt*) saucepan melt butter. Add beetroots, carrots and remaining ingredients *except* sour cream. Cover; cook over med. heat, stirring occasionally, until heated through (5 to 7 min.). Serve with a dollop of sour cream.

Microwave Directions: In 2-litre (*3½-pt*) casserole combine 50 ml (*2 fl oz*) water and beetroots. Cover; microwave on HIGH, stirring after half the time, until beetroots are fork tender (15 to 17 min.). Let stand 2 min. Drain. Run cold water over beets; slip off skins and remove root ends. Cut beetroots into 1-cm (*½-in*) cubes; set aside. In 1-litre (*1¾-pt*) casserole combine 125 ml (*4 fl oz*) water and carrots. Cover; microwave on HIGH, stirring after half the time, until carrots are crisply tender (4 to 5 min.). Let stand 1 min. Drain; set aside. In same 2-litre (*3½-pt*) casserole melt butter on HIGH (40 to 50 sec.). Add beetroots, carrots and remaining ingredients *except* sour cream. Cover; microwave on HIGH, stirring after half the time, until heated through (3 to 4 min.). Let stand 1 min. Serve with a dollop of sour cream.

Home-Style Beetroot With Sour Cream

Lemon Pepper Broccoli

4 servings
20 minutes

Fresh broccoli spears are simply seasoned with cayenne pepper and zest of lemon.

675 g	(*1½ lb*) bunch of broccoli, cut into 12 spears
45 g	(*1½ oz*) butter or margarine
50 g	(*2 oz*) canned diced pimento, drained

	Pinch of salt
	Pinch of cayenne pepper
10 ml	(*2 tsp*) grated lemon rind

In 25-cm (*10-in*) frying pan place broccoli spears; add enough water to cover. Bring to a full boil. Cook over med. heat until broccoli is crisply tender (5 to 7 min.). Drain; return to frying pan. Add remaining ingredients, pushing broccoli to side just until butter is melted. Cook over med. heat, stirring occasionally, until broccoli is heated through (5 to 7 min.).

Microwave Directions: In 30 x 20-cm (*12 x 8-in*) baking dish place broccoli spears with heads toward centre. Dot with butter; sprinkle with remaining ingredients. Cover; microwave on HIGH, turning dish ½ turn after half the time, until crisply tender (6 to 8 min.).

Broccoli & Onion Au Gratin

6 servings
60 minutes

Rosemary adds excitement to broccoli baked in a creamy Swiss cheese sauce.

Cheese Sauce

30 g	(*1 oz*) butter or margarine
30 ml	(*2 tbsp*) plain flour
2 ml	(*½ tsp*) salt
1 ml	(*¼ tsp*) rosemary leaves, crushed
1 ml	(*¼ tsp*) pepper
375 ml	(*13 fl oz*) milk
100 g	(*4 oz*) shredded Swiss cheese

150 g	(*5 oz*) broccoli flowerets
1	med. onion, cut into eighths

Topping

250 g	(*9 oz*) fresh breadcrumbs
75 g	(*3 oz*) butter or margarine, melted
50 ml	(*4 tbsp*) chopped fresh parsley

Heat oven to 180 °C (*350 °F*) mark 4. In 1-litre (*1¾-pt*) saucepan melt 30 g (*1 oz*) butter; stir in flour, salt, rosemary and pepper. Cook over med. heat, stirring constantly, until smooth and bubbly (30 sec.). Stir in milk. Continue cooking, stirring occasionally, until mixture thickens and comes to a full boil (4 to 5 min.). Boil 1 min. Remove from heat; stir in cheese until smooth. Set aside. In greased shallow 1-litre (*1¾-pt*) casserole or 23-cm (*9-in*) sq. baking dish place broccoli and onion. Stir in cheese sauce. In small bowl stir together all topping ingredients. Sprinkle over broccoli mixture. Bake for 25 to 35 min. or until top is golden brown and broccoli is crisply tender.

Microwave Directions: In small bowl melt 30 g (*1 oz*) butter on HIGH (40 to 50 sec.). Stir in flour, salt, rosemary and pepper. Microwave on HIGH until smooth and bubbly (20 to 30 sec.). Stir in milk. Microwave on HIGH, stirring every min., until mixture thickens (5 to 6 min.). Stir in cheese until smooth; set aside. In greased shallow 1-litre (*1¾-pt*) baking dish or 25-cm (*10-in*) flan dish place broccoli and onion. Stir in cheese sauce. In small bowl stir together all topping ingredients. Sprinkle over broccoli mixture. Microwave on HIGH, turning ½ turn after half the time, until broccoli is crisply tender (6 to 7 min.).

Lemon Pepper Broccoli (top)
Broccoli & Onion Au Gratin (bottom)

Broccoli With Three Cheeses

Broccoli With Three Cheeses

6 servings
20 minutes

*Cream cheese, Cheddar cheese and blue cheese blend together to make
a smooth, rich sauce for broccoli spears.*

675 g	(*1½ lb*) broccoli, cut into spears		250 ml	(*8 fl oz*) milk
250 ml	(*8 fl oz*) water		90 g	(*3 oz*) cream cheese, softened
30 g	(*1 oz*) butter or margarine		125 g	(*4 oz*) shredded Cheddar cheese
30 ml	(*2 tbsp*) plain flour		75 ml	(*5 tbsp*) crumbled blue cheese
1 ml	(*¼ tsp*) pepper		50 ml	(*4 tbsp*) chopped pecans

In flameproof casserole place broccoli spears; add water. Cover; bring to a full boil. Cook over med. heat until broccoli is crisply tender (5 to 7 min.); drain. Meanwhile, in 1-litre (*1¾-pt*) saucepan melt butter; stir in flour and pepper. Cook over med. heat, stirring constantly, until smooth and bubbly (30 sec.). Stir in milk and cream cheese. Continue cooking, stirring occasionally, until mixture thickens and comes to a full boil (4 to 5 min.). Stir in Cheddar cheese and blue cheese. Continue cooking, stirring occasionally, until cheeses are melted (1 to 2 min.). Serve cheese sauce over broccoli; sprinkle with pecans.

Microwave Directions: *Decrease water to 125 ml* (4 fl oz). In 20-cm (*8-in*) sq. baking dish place broccoli spears with heads toward centre. Add 125 ml (*4 fl oz*) water. Cover with plastic wrap; microwave on HIGH, turning dish ½ turn after half the time, until crisply tender (6 to 8 min.). Let stand covered while preparing sauce; drain. In small bowl melt butter on HIGH (30 to 60 sec.). Stir in flour and pepper. Microwave on HIGH until bubbly (30 to 60 sec.). Stir in milk and cream cheese. Microwave on HIGH, stirring after half the time, until mixture thickens and comes to a full boil (2 to 3 min.). Stir until smooth. Stir in Cheddar cheese and blue cheese. Microwave on HIGH until cheeses are melted (1 to 1½ min.). Serve cheese sauce over broccoli; sprinkle with pecans.

Broccoli With Garlic Butter & Cashews

4 servings
15 minutes

Tender broccoli spears served with melted butter, flavoured with garlic and soy sauce.

675 g	(*1½ lb*) broccoli, cut into spears		1 ml	(*¼ tsp*) pepper
250 ml	(*8 fl oz*) water		45 ml	(*3 tbsp*) soy sauce
75 g	(*3 oz*) butter or margarine		10 ml	(*2 tsp*) vinegar
15 ml	(*1 tbsp*) firmly packed brown sugar		1 ml	(*¼ tsp*) crushed fresh garlic
			75 ml	(*5 tbsp*) salted whole cashews

In flameproof casserole place broccoli spears; add water. Cover; bring to a full boil. Cook over med. heat until crisply tender (5 to 7 min.); drain. Remove to serving platter; keep warm. In same flameproof casserole melt butter. Add remaining ingredients *except* cashews. Cook over med. heat, stirring occasionally, until mixture comes to a full boil (3 to 4 min.). Stir in cashews. Serve broccoli with sauce.

Lemon Chive Brussels Sprouts

6 servings
30 minutes

Chives with their sweet oniony flavour and lemon add zest to Brussels sprouts.

450 g	(*1 lb*) (40) Brussels sprouts, trimmed		7 ml	(*1 1/2 tsp*) fresh dill weed*
50 g	(*2 oz*) butter or margarine		1 ml	(*1/4 tsp*) salt
30 ml	(*2 tbsp*) chopped fresh chives		1 ml	(*1/4 tsp*) pepper
10 ml	(*2 tsp*) grated lemon rind			

In 2-litre (*3 1/2-pt*) saucepan place Brussels sprouts; add enough water to cover. Bring to a full boil. Cook over med. heat until Brussels sprouts are crisply tender (12 to 15 min.); drain. Return to pan; add remaining ingredients. Cook over med. heat, stirring occasionally, until heated through (4 to 6 min.).

*2 ml (*1/2 tsp*) dried dill weed can be substituted for 7 ml (*1 1/2 tsp*) fresh dill weed.

Microwave Directions: In 2-litre (*3 1/2-pt*) casserole place Brussels sprouts and 50 ml (*2 fl oz*) water. Cover; microwave on HIGH until crisply tender (3 to 4 min.). Add remaining ingredients. Cover; microwave on HIGH, stirring after half the time, until heated through (2 1/2 to 4 min.).

To Trim Brussels Sprouts:

1. To trim Brussels sprouts: remove any loose or discoloured leaves.

2. Cut off stem ends, leaving enough stem to prevent outer leaves from falling off during cooking.

Lemon Chive Brussels Sprouts

Buttery Apples 'n Cabbage

**6 servings
20 minutes**

Buttery Apples 'n Cabbage

Crisp fall apples complement buttery cabbage; the perfect side dish to serve with pork.

250 ml	(*8 fl oz*) water
½	small head cabbage, cubed 2.5 cm (*1 in*)
50 g	(*2 oz*) butter or margarine

2 ml	(*½ tsp*) salt
1 ml	(*¼ tsp*) nutmeg
2	med. tart red apples, unpeeled, cubed 1 cm (*½ in*)
30 ml	(*2 tbsp*) chopped fresh parsley

In 2-litre (*3½-pt*) saucepan bring water to a full boil; add cabbage. Cover; cook over med. heat, stirring occasionally, until cabbage is crisply tender (5 to 6 min.). Drain; stir in remaining ingredients *except* apples and parsley. Cover; cook over med. heat, stirring occasionally, until butter is melted (1 to 2 min.). Stir in apples. Cover; continue cooking, stirring occasionally, until apples are crisply tender (3 to 4 min.). Sprinkle with parsley.

Microwave Directions: *Decrease water to 50 ml (2 fl oz).* In 2-litre (*3½-pt*) casserole combine water and cabbage. Cover; microwave on HIGH, stirring after half the time, until cabbage is crisply tender (6 to 7 min.). Let stand 1 min.; drain. Cut butter into pieces. In same casserole combine cabbage, butter and remaining ingredients *except* parsley. Cover; microwave on HIGH, stirring after half the time, until butter is melted and apples are crisply tender (2 to 3 min.). Let stand 1 min. Sprinkle with parsley.

**6 servings
30 minutes**

Garden Carrot Medley

Serve this colourful medley when the vegetables are ready to be picked fresh from the garden.

175 ml	(*6 fl oz*) water
4	med. carrots, cut into 5 x 0.5-cm (*2 x ¼-in*) strips
45 g	(*1½ oz*) butter or margarine
1	med. yellow summer squash or courgette, trim off ends, cut in half lengthwise and cut crosswise into 5-mm (*¼-in*) slices

50 ml	(*4 tbsp*) chopped green pepper
2 ml	(*½ tsp*) salt
2 ml	(*½ tsp*) basil leaves

In 2-litre (*3½-pt*) saucepan bring water to a full boil. Add carrots. Cover; cook over med. heat until carrots are crisply tender (8 to 10 min.). Drain; add butter, stirring until melted. Stir in remaining ingredients. Cover; cook over med. heat, stirring occasionally, until squash is crisply tender (6 to 8 min.).

Microwave Directions: *Decrease water to 125 ml (4 fl oz).* In 2-litre (*3½-pt*) casserole combine water and carrots. Cover; microwave on HIGH, stirring after half the time, until carrots are crisply tender (5 to 6 min.). Let stand 1 min. Drain; add butter, stirring until melted. Stir in remaining ingredients. Cover; microwave on HIGH, stirring after half the time, until squash is crisply tender (4 to 5 min.). Let stand 1 min.

Chuckwagon Carrots

Crisp bacon gives smoked flavour to hearty chunks of carrots.

4 servings
30 minutes

6	med. carrots, sliced 1 cm (*1/2 in*)
50 ml	(*4 tbsp*) cooked, crumbled bacon
45 g	(*1 1/2 oz*) butter or margarine
15 ml	(*1 tbsp*) firmly packed brown sugar
30 ml	(*2 tbsp*) sliced 3 mm (*1/8 in*) spring onions
1 ml	(*1/4 tsp*) salt
	Pinch of pepper

In 2-litre (*3 1/2-pt*) saucepan place carrots; add enough water to cover. Bring to a full boil. Cook over med. heat until carrots are crisply tender (8 to 12 min.). Drain; return to pan. Add remaining ingredients. Cover; cook over med. heat, stirring occasionally, until heated through (5 to 7 min.).

Microwave Directions: In 2-litre (*3 1/2-pt*) casserole combine 125 ml (*4 fl oz*) water and carrots. Cover; microwave on HIGH, stirring after half the time, until carrots are crisply tender (6 to 8 min.). Let stand 1 min. Drain; set aside. In same casserole melt butter on HIGH (40 to 50 sec.). Stir in carrots and remaining ingredients. Cover; microwave on HIGH, stirring after half the time, until heated through (3 to 4 min.). Let stand 1 min.

Glazed Orange Ginger Carrots

6 servings
30 minutes

The natural sweetness of carrots is intriguing when combined with a unique blend of ginger and caraway.

10	med. carrots, cut into 2.5-cm (*1-in*) pieces
45 g	(*1 1/2 oz*) butter or margarine
15 ml	(*1 tbsp*) firmly packed brown sugar
2 ml	(*1/2 tsp*) ginger
2 ml	(*1/2 tsp*) caraway seed
15 ml	(*1 tbsp*) grated orange rind
30 ml	(*2 tbsp*) orange juice

In 2-litre (*3 1/2-pt*) saucepan place carrots; add enough water to cover. Bring to a full boil. Cook over med. heat until carrots are crisply tender (10 to 12 min.); drain. Return to pan; add remaining ingredients. Cook over med. heat, stirring occasionally, until heated through (4 to 7 min.).

Microwave Directions: In 2-litre (*3 1/2-pt*) casserole combine carrots and 30 ml (*2 tbsp*) water. Cover; microwave on HIGH, stirring after half the time, until carrots are crisply tender. Drain; return to casserole. Add remaining ingredients. Cover; microwave on HIGH (1 to 1 1/2 min.). Let stand 2 min.

Chuckwagon Carrots

Pan-Roasted Vegetables

6 servings
30 minutes

Pick of the Season Minted Carrots

A sprinkling of mint brings out the sweetness of fresh-picked carrots.

10	med. carrots with tops, peeled*
30 g	(*1 oz*) butter or margarine
	Pinch of salt
	Pinch of pepper

15 ml	(*1 tbsp*) grated orange rind
30 ml	(*2 tbsp*) orange juice
30 ml	(*2 tbsp*) chopped fresh mint

Cut carrots into 5-cm (*2-in*) pieces, leaving 5 cm (*2 in*) greens on top of carrots. In 2-litre (*3½-pt*) saucepan place carrots; add enough water to cover. Bring to a full boil. Cook over med. heat until carrots are crisply tender (10 to 15 min.); drain. Return to pan; add remaining ingredients *except* mint. Cook over med. heat, stirring occasionally, until butter is melted (3 to 4 min.). Sprinkle with mint.

*Carrots without tops can be substituted for carrots with tops.

Microwave Directions: Cut carrots into 5-cm (*2-in*) pieces, leaving 5 cm (*2 in*) greens on top of carrots. In 2-litre (*3½-pt*) casserole combine carrots and 50 ml (*2 fl oz*) water. Cover; microwave on HIGH, stirring after half the time, until carrots are crisply tender (8 to 11 min.). Drain; return to casserole. Add remaining ingredients *except* mint. Cover; microwave on HIGH until butter is melted (1½ to 2 min.). Let stand 2 min. Sprinkle with mint.

6 servings
40 minutes

Pan-Roasted Vegetables

Pan-roasting vegetables with herbs brings out their natural flavours.

75 g	(*3 oz*) butter or margarine
2 ml	(*½ tsp*) thyme leaves
1 ml	(*¼ tsp*) salt
1 ml	(*¼ tsp*) pepper
225 g	(*8 oz*) cauliflower flowerets

225 g	(*8 oz*) broccoli flowerets
4	med. carrots, cut into julienne strips
2	small onions, quartered

Heat oven to 200 °C (*400 °F*) mark 5. In 33 x 23-cm (*13 x 9-in*) baking dish melt butter in oven (5 to 6 min.). Stir in thyme, salt and pepper. Add remaining ingredients; toss to coat. Cover with aluminum foil; bake for 22 to 27 min. or until vegetables are crisply tender.

Microwave Directions: In 33 x 23-cm (*13 x 9-in*) baking dish melt butter on HIGH (60 to 70 sec.). Stir in thyme, salt and pepper. Add remaining ingredients; toss to coat. Cover with plastic wrap; microwave on HIGH, stirring after half the time, until vegetables are crisply tender (7 to 9 min.).

Smokehouse Cauliflower Medley

6 servings
25 minutes

The smoky bacon flavour enhances fresh cauliflower and parsley.

50 g	(*2 oz*) butter or margarine		5 ml	(*1 tsp*) dry mustard
1	med. head cauliflower, cut into flowerets		2 ml	(*½ tsp*) salt
125 g	(*4 oz*) bacon, cooked, cut into 2.5-cm (*1-in*) pieces		30 ml	(*2 tbsp*) water
50 g	(*2 oz*) canned sliced pimento, drained		15 ml	(*1 tbsp*) chopped fresh parsley

In 3-litre (*5-pt*) saucepan melt butter. Stir in remaining ingredients *except* parsley. Cover; cook over med. heat, stirring occasionally, until cauliflower is crisply tender (10 to 12 min.). Sprinkle with parsley.

Microwave Directions: In 2-litre (*3½-pt*) casserole melt butter on HIGH (50 to 60 sec.). Stir in remaining ingredients *except* parsley. Cover; microwave on HIGH, stirring after half the time, until cauliflower is crisply tender (5 to 6 min.). Sprinkle with parsley; let stand 1 min.

Garden Patch Corn

4 servings
15 minutes

Basil and parsley spice up this vegetable trio.

75 g	(*3 oz*) butter or margarine		2 ml	(*½ tsp*) salt
275 g	(*10 oz*) frozen sweet whole kernel corn		1	med. ripe tomato, cubed 1 cm (*½ in*)
50 g	(*2 oz*) chopped green pepper		15 ml	(*1 tbsp*) fresh chopped parsley
5 ml	(*1 tsp*) basil leaves			

In 2-litre (*3½-pt*) saucepan melt butter. Stir in remaining ingredients *except* tomato and parsley. Cover; cook over med. heat, stirring occasionally, until vegetables are crisply tender (10 to 12 min.). Remove from heat. Stir in tomato and parsley. Cover; let stand 1 min. or until tomato is heated through.

Microwave Directions: In 1.5-litre (*2¾-pt*) casserole melt butter on HIGH (60 to 70 sec.). Stir in remaining ingredients *except* tomato and parsley. Cover; microwave on HIGH, stirring after half the time, until vegetables are crisply tender (5 to 8 min.). Stir in tomato and parsley. Cover; let stand 1 min. or until tomato is heated through.

Garden Patch Corn (top)
Smokehouse Cauliflower Medley (bottom)

Zesty Horseradish Corn on the Cob

4 servings
60 minutes

*Sweet yellow, tender ears of corn are enticing
with a horseradish mustard butter.*

125 g	(*4 oz*) butter or margarine, softened
2 ml	(*1/2 tsp*) salt
1 ml	(*1/4 tsp*) pepper
15 ml	(*1 tbsp*) chopped fresh parsley

30 ml	(*2 tbsp*) country-style Dijon mustard
10 ml	(*2 tsp*) prepared horseradish
8	fresh ears of corn on the cob, husked

Prepare grill or heat oven to 190 °C (*375 °F*) mark 5. In small bowl stir together all ingredients *except* corn. Spread about 15 g (*1/2 oz*) butter mixture evenly over each ear of corn. Wrap tightly in heavy-duty double thickness aluminum foil, sealing well. Place on grill rack directly over coals or low flame, turning every 5 min., for 20 to 25 min. or until tender.
If baking, place foil-wrapped corn on Swiss roll tin. Bake for 40 to 45 min. or until heated through.

Tip: Horseradish butter can be used as a spread for sandwiches or vegetables.

Microwave Directions: In 33 x 23-cm (*13 x 9-in*) baking dish stir together all ingredients *except* corn. Place corn in dish; turn to coat. Cover; microwave on HIGH, turning dish 1/2 turn after half the time, until corn is heated through (14 to 18 min.). Let stand 3 min.

Zesty Horseradish Corn on the Cob

Oven-Roasted Corn on the Cob

6 servings
60 minutes

Garlic, herbs and tomato add a special flavour to corn on the cob.

6	fresh ears of corn on the cob, husked
125 ml	(*4 fl oz*) olive or vegetable oil
7 ml	(*1¹/2 tsp*) salt
5 ml	(*1 tsp*) basil leaves

2 ml	(*¹/2 tsp*) thyme leaves
2 ml	(*¹/2 tsp*) pepper
10 ml	(*2 tsp*) crushed fresh garlic
1	med. ripe tomato, cut into 12 wedges

Heat oven to 180 °C (*350 °F*) mark 4. Cut each ear of corn into thirds; set aside. In small bowl combine all ingredients *except* corn and tomato. Place corn in 33 x 23-cm (*13 x 9-in*) baking dish; pour oil mixture over corn. Cover with aluminum foil. Bake, turning corn after 30 min., for 60 to 70 min. or until corn is tender. Add tomato wedges; return to oven for 5 min. or until tomato is heated through.

Microwave Directions: *Add 30 ml* (2 tbsp) *water and omit salt.* Cut each ear of corn into thirds; set aside. In small bowl combine oil, basil, thyme, pepper and garlic. Dip corn into oil mixture; place in 33 x 23-cm (*13 x 9-in*) baking dish. Add 30 ml (*2 tbsp*) water. Cover with plastic wrap. Microwave on HIGH, rearranging corn after half the time, until corn is tender (12 to 15 min.). Add tomato wedges. Cover with plastic wrap; let stand 3 min. or until tomato is heated through. If desired, season with salt.

Corn in Tomato Shells

8 servings
45 minutes

Sensational taste in this quick corn dish served in hollowed-out tomatoes.

4	med. ripe tomatoes
15 ml	(*1 tbsp*) butter or margarine
1	med. red onion, cut into 1-cm (*¹/2-in*) pieces
250 ml	(*8 fl oz*) chunky-style salsa (mexican sauce)
450 g	(*16 oz*) frozen sweet whole kernel corn, thawed, drained

5 ml	(*1 tsp*) cumin
15 ml	(*1 tbsp*) lime juice
100 g	(*4 oz*) sliced 5 mm (*¹/4 in*) ripe olives
30 g	(*1 oz*) chopped fresh parsley
	Sour cream

Heat oven to 180 °C (*350 °F*) mark 4. Cut tomatoes in half. Hollow out tomato pulp to form 1-cm (*¹/2-in*) shells; *reserve pulp*. Set aside. In 2-litre (*3¹/2-pt*) saucepan melt butter over med. heat. Stir in remaining ingredients *except* olives, parsley, sour cream and tomatoes. Stir in reserved tomato pulp. Continue cooking, stirring occasionally, until heated through (10 to 12 min.). Stir in olives and parsley. Place tomato halves on oven-proof serving platter or in 33 x 23-cm (*13 x 9 -in*) baking dish. Fill each tomato half with corn mixture; spoon remaining corn around tomatoes. Bake for 10 to 12 min. or until tomato halves are heated through. Serve with sour cream.

Tip: Tomato shells can be omitted; serve corn in serving dish.

Microwave Directions: Prepare tomatoes as directed left; *reserve pulp*. Set aside. In 3-litre (*5-pt*) bowl melt butter on high (15 to 30 sec.). Stir in remaining ingredients *except* olives, parsley, sour cream and tomatoes. Stir in reserved tomato pulp. Cover; microwave on HIGH, stirring after half the time, until heated through (6 to 8 min.). Stir in olives and parsley. Place tomato halves on microwave-safe serving platter. Fill each tomato half with corn mixture; spoon remaining corn around tomatoes. Cover; microwave on HIGH until tomato halves are heated through (5 to 7 min.). Serve with sour cream.

Corn in Tomato Shells

Bacon Crackle Corn Bake

8 servings
45 minutes

*This creamy corn casserole, topped with crispy bacon,
fresh snipped parsley and chives, is full of country goodness.*

6	rashers of bacon, cut into 1-cm (*1/2-in*) pieces	250 ml	(*8 fl oz*) sour cream
1	med. onion, chopped	900 g	(*1 lb*) frozen whole kernel corn, thawed, drained
30 ml	(*2 tbsp*) plain flour	15 ml	(*1 tbsp*) chopped fresh parsley
2 ml	(*1/2 tsp*) salt	15 ml	(*1 tbsp*) chopped fresh chives
2 ml	(*1/2 tsp*) pepper		
2 ml	(*1/2 tsp*) crushed fresh garlic		

Heat oven to 180 °C (*350 °F*) mark 4. In 25-cm (*10-in*) frying pan cook bacon over med. high heat, stirring occasionally, until partially cooked (4 min.). Add onion; continue cooking until bacon is browned (4 to 5 min.). Drain off fat *except* for 15 ml (*1 tbsp*); set bacon and onion aside. Stir flour, salt, pepper and garlic into reserved 15 ml (*1 tbsp*) fat. Cook over med. heat, stirring constantly, until smooth and bubbly (30 sec.). Stir in sour cream, corn and 1/3 of bacon and onion mixture. Pour into 1.5 litre (*2 3/4-pt*) casserole; sprinkle with remaining bacon and onion mixture. Bake for 25 to 30 min. or until heated through. Sprinkle with parsley and chives.

Microwave Directions: *Do not thaw corn.* Place bacon in 2-litre (*2-pt*) casserole. Cover with waxed paper. Microwave on HIGH, stirring after half the time, until partially cooked (4 to 5 1/2 min.). Add onion; microwave on HIGH until bacon is cooked (2 to 3 min.). Drain off fat *except* for 15 ml (*1 tbsp*); set bacon and onion aside. Stir flour, salt, pepper and garlic into reserved 15 ml (*1 tbsp*) fat. Microwave on HIGH until bubbly (30 to 60 sec.). Stir in sour cream, *frozen* corn and 1/3 of bacon and onion mixture; sprinkle with remaining bacon and onion mixture. Cover with plastic wrap; microwave on HIGH, stirring every 3 min., until heated through (10 to 13 min.). Sprinkle with parsley and chives.

Garlic Parmesan Aubergine Slices

4 servings
30 minutes

These crispy aubergines slices are pan-fried and topped with garden-fresh tomato.

450 g	(*1 lb*) sliced 5 mm (*1/4 in*) aubergine	75 ml	(*5 tbsp*) olive or vegetable oil
5 ml	(*1 tsp*) salt	2 ml	(*1/2 tsp*) pepper
75 g	(*3 oz*) plain flour	5 ml	(*1 tsp*) crushed fresh garlic
65 g	(*2 1/2 oz*) seasoned breadcrumbs	2	eggs, slightly beaten
50 ml	(*4 tbsp*) freshly grated Parmesan cheese	1	med. ripe tomato, chopped
15 ml	(*1 tbsp*) basil leaves		

Place aubergine slices on (38 x 25 x 2.5-cm) (*15 x 10 x 1-in*) Swiss roll tin; sprinkle with salt. In 23-cm (*9-in*) flan dish stir together flour, breadcrumbs, Parmesan cheese and basil. In 25-cm (*10-in*) frying pan cook olive oil, pepper and garlic over med. heat until sizzling. Meanwhile, dip aubergine slices into eggs; coat with flour mixture. Fry 1/2 of aubergine slices in olive oil until golden brown (2 to 3 min. on each side). Remove to serving platter; keep warm. Repeat with remaining aubergine slices. Remove to serving platter; sprinkle with tomato. Cover with aluminum foil; let stand 2 min. or until tomato is heated through.

Bacon Crackle Corn Bake (top)
Garlic Parmesan Aubergine Slices (bottom)

Burgundy Mushrooms

A delicious side dish for roasted or grilled meats.

50 g	(*2 oz*) butter or margarine
15 ml	(*1 tbsp*) plain flour
2 ml	(*1/2 tsp*) salt
2 ml	(*1/2 tsp*) coarsely ground pepper
1 ml	(*1/4 tsp*) dry mustard
5 ml	(*1 tsp*) crushed fresh garlic
75 ml	(*5 tbsp*) dry red wine or beef broth

1	med. green pepper, cut into 1-cm (*1/2-in*) pieces
1	med. red onion, thinly sliced, separated into rings
450 g	(*1 lb*) fresh mushrooms, halved

In 25-cm (*10-in*) frying pan melt butter over med. heat. Stir in flour, salt, pepper, mustard and garlic; continue cooking until smooth and bubbly (30 sec.). Stir in wine; add remaining ingredients. Continue cooking, stirring occasionally, until mushrooms are tender (10 to 12 min.).

Microwave Directions: *Increase flour to 30 ml (2 tbsp).* In 2-litre (*3 1/2-pt*) casserole melt butter on HIGH (50 to 60 sec.). Stir in 30 ml (*2 tbsp*) flour, salt, pepper, mustard and garlic. Microwave on HIGH until smooth and bubbly (15 to 30 sec.). Stir in wine; add remaining ingredients. Microwave on HIGH, stirring after half the time, until mushrooms are tender (5 to 7 min.). Let stand 2 min.

Savoury Mushroom Sauté

Fresh mushrooms with savoury herbs make a perfect accompaniment for grilled meat, chicken or fish.

75 g	(*3 oz*) butter or margarine
675 g	(*1 1/2 lb*) fresh mushrooms, halved
30 ml	(*2 tbsp*) chopped onion
2 ml	(*1/2 tsp*) tarragon leaves

2 ml	(*1/2 tsp*) nutmeg
1 ml	(*1/4 tsp*) salt
1 ml	(*1/4 tsp*) pepper
50 ml	(*4 tbsp*) chopped fresh parsley

In 25-cm (*10-in*) frying pan melt butter. Stir in remaining ingredients *except* parsley. Cook over med. heat, stirring occasionally, until mushrooms are tender (3 to 4 min.). Stir in parsley.

Savoury Mushroom Sauté

Sliced Onions 'n Blue Cheese Bake

6 servings
40 minutes

Sliced Onions 'n Blue Cheese Bake

Onions, blended with blue cheese and mushrooms,
add zest and richness when served with grilled meats.

4	med. onions, sliced 5 mm (*1/4 in*)	5 ml	(*1 tsp*) dill weed
50 g	(*2 oz*) crumbled blue cheese	1 ml	(*1/4 tsp*) pepper
225 g	(*8 oz*) sliced 5 mm (*1/4 in*) fresh mushrooms	15 ml	(*1 tbsp*) Worcestershire sauce
50 g	(*2 oz*) butter or margarine, softened	50 ml	(*4 tbsp*) chopped fresh parsley

Heat oven to 200 °C (*400 °F*) mark 6. In 23-cm (*9-in*) sq. baking tin layer half of onions. In small bowl combine 25 g (*1 oz*) blue cheese and remaining ingredients *except* parsley and remaining onions; stir to blend. Sprinkle cheese mixture over onions; top with remaining onions. Bake for 10 min.; stir. Crumble remaining blue cheese over onions; sprinkle with parsley. Continue baking for 10 to 15 min. or until onions are crisply tender.

Microwave Directions: *Add 30 ml* (2 tbsp) *plain flour.* In medium bowl mix onions with 30 ml (*2 tbsp*) flour. In 2-litre (*3 1/2-pt*) casserole layer half of onions. In small bowl combine 25 g (*1 oz*) blue cheese and remaining ingredients *except* parsley and remaining onions; stir to blend. Sprinkle cheese mixture over onions; top with remaining onions. Cover; microwave on HIGH until onions are crisply tender (2 1/2 to 3 1/2 min.). Stir; top with remaining blue cheese and parsley. Cover; microwave on HIGH until cheese starts to melt (1 to 1 1/2 min.). Let stand 2 min.

6 servings
30 minutes

Cream-Glazed Onion Halves With Peas

Choose onions with a sweet taste.

3	med. sweet onions	125 ml	(*4 fl oz*) double cream
50 g	(*2 oz*) butter or margarine	275 g	(*10 oz*) frozen tender tiny peas, thawed, drained
3 ml	(*3/4 tsp*) seasoned salt		
1 ml	(*1/4 tsp*) pepper	50 ml	(*4 tbsp*) chopped fresh parsley

Skin onions; cut each in half. Hollow out inner 2 to 3 rings of onions to form shells; chop removed onion. In 25-cm (*10-in*) frying pan melt butter until sizzling; stir in chopped onion, seasoned salt and pepper. Place onions, cut side down, in frying pan. Cook over med. heat for 10 min. Carefully turn onions over; stir in whipping cream. Continue cooking for 3 to 5 min. or until cream mixture is bubbly. Place some peas into each onion shell; sprinkle remaining peas and parsley into cream mixture. Continue cooking, stirring occasionally, until peas are crisply tender (8 to 10 min.).

Microwave Directions: *Do not thaw peas.* Skin onions; cut each in half. Hollow out inner 2 to 3 rings of onions to form shells; chop removed onion. In 20-cm (*8-in*) sq. baking dish melt butter on HIGH (50 to 60 sec.). Stir in chopped onion, seasoned salt and pepper. Place onions, cut side down, in dish. Cover with plastic wrap. Microwave on HIGH until onions just begin to soften (3 to 4 min.). Carefully turn onions over; stir in double cream. Cover; microwave on HIGH, stirring after half the time, until cream mixture is bubbly (2 to 3 min.). Place some frozen peas into each onion shell; sprinkle remaining peas and parsley into cream mixture. Cover; microwave on HIGH until peas are crisply tender (5 to 7 min.).

Butter-Fried Parsnips

4 to 6 servings
30 minutes

Parsnips with a new twist — seasoned and pan-fried in butter.

5 to 6	med. parsnips, peeled, cut lengthwise into quarters	125 g	(*4 oz*) butter or margarine, melted
1 litre	(*1¾ pt*) water	50 ml	(*4 tbsp*) plain flour
		2 ml	(*½ tsp*) seasoned salt

In covered 3-litre (*5-pt*) saucepan boil parsnips in water until tender (8 to 10 min.); drain. Dip parsnips in 50 g (*2 oz*) melted butter. In plastic bag combine flour and seasoned salt. Add parsnips; shake to coat with flour mixture. In 25-cm (*10-in*) frying pan melt remaining butter until sizzling. Add parsnips. Cook over med. high heat, turning occasionally, until all sides are golden brown (8 to 10 min.).

Indian Summer Medley

4 servings
15 minutes

Simply seasoned and prepared, a delightful pea, corn and tomato medley.

45 g	(*1½ oz*) butter or margarine	2 ml	(*½ tsp*) salt
50 ml	(*4 tbsp*) chopped fresh parsley		Pinch of pepper
275 g	(*10 oz*) frozen peas, thawed, drained	1	med. ripe tomato, cut into wedges
225 g	(*8 oz*) canned sweet corn, drained		

In 2-litre (*3½-pt*) saucepan melt butter over med. heat. Add remaining ingredients *except* tomato. Continue cooking until vegetables are crisply tender (5 to 7 min.). Add tomato wedges. Cover; let stand 2 min. or until tomatoes are heated through.

Microwave Directions: In 1-litre (*1¾-pt*) casserole combine all ingredients *except* tomatoes. Cover; microwave on HIGH, stirring after half the time, until vegetables are crisply tender (3½ to 5½ min.). Add tomato wedges. Cover; microwave on HIGH until tomatoes are heated through (1 min.). Let stand 3 min.

Butter-Fried Parsnips

Aunt Rebecca's Creamed Potatoes & Peas (top)
Honey-Glazed Mangetout & Carrots (bottom)

**6 servings
30 minutes**

Aunt Rebecca's Creamed Potatoes & Peas

Tender potatoes and tiny peas are served in a rich, bacon-flavoured cream sauce.

12	small new red potatoes, cut into 3.5-cm (1½-in) pieces	3 ml	(¾ tsp) thyme leaves
8	rashers of bacon, cut into 1-cm (½-in) pieces	2 ml	(½ tsp) salt
1	med. red onion, cut into 1-cm (½-in) pieces	2 ml ·	(½ tsp) pepper
30 ml	(2 tbsp) plain flour	250 ml	(8 fl oz) double cream
		350 g	(10 oz) frozen tender tiny peas, thawed, drained

In 2-litre (3½-pt) saucepan place potatoes. Add enough water to cover; bring to a full boil. Cook over med. heat, stirring occasionally, until potatoes are tender (10 to 15 min.). Meanwhile, in 25-cm (10-in) frying pan cook bacon over med. high heat, stirring occasionally, until partially cooked (4 min.). Add onion; continue cooking until browned (4 to 5 min.). Drain off fat *except* for 30 ml (2 tbsp); set bacon and onion aside. Stir flour, thyme leaves, salt and pepper into reserved 30 ml (2 tbsp) fat. Cook over med. heat, stirring constantly, until smooth and bubbly (30 sec.). Stir in double cream, peas, bacon, onion and potatoes. Continue cooking, stirring occasionally, until mixture thickens and is heated through (3 to 4 min.).

Microwave Directions: In 2-litre (3½-pt) casserole place potatoes. Add 50 ml (2 fl oz) water. Cover; microwave on HIGH, stirring after half the time, until potatoes are tender (8 to 10 min.). Let stand covered 3 min.; drain. Set aside. In same 2-litre (3½-pt) casserole place bacon. Cover with waxed paper. Microwave on HIGH until partially cooked (3 to 4 min.). Stir in onion. Cover; microwave on HIGH until onion is tender and bacon is cooked (2 to 3 min.). Drain off fat *except* for 30 ml (2 tbsp). Stir in flour, thyme leaves, salt and pepper. Microwave on HIGH until bubbly (30 to 60 sec.). Stir in double cream; microwave on HIGH until mixture just comes to a boil (1 to 2 min.). Add peas and potatoes. Cover; microwave on HIGH, stirring after half the time, until mixture thickens and is heated through (4 to 6 min.).

**6 servings
30 minutes**

Honey-Glazed Mangetout & Carrots

A touch of golden honey flavours these tender mangetout mixed with sweet carrots.

175 ml	(6 fl oz) water	45 g	(1½ oz) butter or margarine
4	med. carrots, diagonally sliced 5 mm (¼ in) carrots	2 ml	(½ tsp) cornflour
225 g	(8 oz) fresh mangetout, washed, remove tips and strings*	30 ml	(2 tbsp) honey

In 2-litre (3½-pt) saucepan bring water to a full boil. Add carrots. Cover; cook over med. heat until carrots are crisply tender (10 to 12 min.). Add mangetout. Continue cooking until pea pods are crisply tender (1 to 2 min.). Drain; set aside. In same pan melt butter; stir in cornflour. Add carrots, mangetout and honey. Cook over med. heat, stirring occasionally, until heated through (2 to 3 min.).

*350 g (12 oz) frozen mangetout can be substituted for 225 g (8 oz) fresh mangetout.

Microwave Directions: *Decrease water to 125 ml (4 fl oz).* In 2-litre (3½-pt) casserole combine water and carrots. Cover; microwave on HIGH, stirring after half the time, until carrots are crisply tender (8 to 10 min.). Add mangetout. Cover; microwave on HIGH until mangetout are crisply tender (1 to 2 min.). Drain; set aside. In same casserole melt butter on HIGH (50 to 60 sec.). Stir in cornflour. Microwave on HIGH 1 min. Stir in carrots, mangetout and honey. Cover; microwave on HIGH until heated through (1 to 2 min.).

Pan Green Peppers

5 servings
15 minutes

A unique and easy way to prepare garden-fresh green peppers.

50 g	(*2 oz*) butter or margarine
2	med. green peppers, cut into 5-mm (*1/4-in*) strips
5 ml	(*1 tsp*) Italian herb seasoning*

2 ml	(*1/2 tsp*) crushed fresh garlic
75 g	(*3 oz*) halved cherry tomatoes
25 g	(*1 oz*) croutons

In 25-cm (*10-in*) frying pan melt butter. Stir in remaining ingredients *except* tomatoes and croutons. Cook over med. heat, stirring occasionally, until peppers are crisply tender (6 to 8 min.). Add tomatoes. Continue cooking 1 min. Sprinkle with croutons; serve immediately.

*1 ml (*1/4 tsp*) each oregano leaves, marjoram leaves and basil leaves and a pinch of rubbed sage can be substituted for 5 ml (*1 tsp*) Italian herb seasoning.

Microwave Directions: In 1.5-litre (*2 3/4-pt*) casserole melt butter on HIGH (50 to 60 sec.). Stir in remaining ingredients *except* tomatoes and croutons. Cover; microwave on HIGH, stirring after half the time, until peppers are crisply tender (4 to 5 min.). Add tomatoes. Cover; microwave on HIGH 1 min. Let stand 1 min. Sprinkle with croutons; serve immediately.

Hot & Tangy German Potatoes

4 to 6 servings
30 minutes

Serve these tangy potatoes with hearty sausage and applesauce.

4	med. red potatoes, cooked, peeled, sliced 5 mm (*1/4 in*)
8	rashers of thick-sliced bacon, cut into 2.5-cm (*1-in*) pieces
2	celery sticks, sliced 1 cm (*1/2 in*)
2	med. onions, cut into eighths

50 ml	(*4 tbsp*) sugar
175 ml	(*6 fl oz*) cider vinegar
50 ml	(*2 fl oz*) water
2 ml	(*1/2 tsp*) salt
1 ml	(*1/4 tsp*) pepper
50 ml	(*4 tbsp*) chopped fresh parsley

Have potatoes ready. In 3-litre (*5-pt*) saucepan cook bacon, stirring constantly, over high heat 3 min. Stir in celery and onions. Reduce heat to med; continue cooking, stirring occasionally, until vegetables are crisply tender (5 to 8 min.). Stir in remaining ingredients *except* potatoes and parsley. Continue cooking, stirring occasionally, until mixture comes to a full boil (3 to 5 min.). Stir in potatoes; continue cooking until potatoes are heated through (5 to 10 min.). Sprinkle with parsley.

Microwave Directions: Have potatoes ready. In 3-litre (*5-pt*) casserole microwave bacon on HIGH 3 min. Stir in celery and onions. Cover; microwave on HIGH, stirring after half the time, until vegetables are crisply tender (3 to 4 min.). Stir in remaining ingredients *except* potatoes and parsley. Microwave on HIGH, stirring after half the time, until mixture comes to a full boil (3 to 4 min.). Stir in potatoes. Microwave on HIGH, stirring after half the time, until potatoes are heated through (6 to 7 min.). Sprinkle with parsley.

Hot & Tangy German Potatoes (top)
Pan Green Peppers (bottom)

Garlic Roasted Potato Wedges (top)
New Potatoes With Lemon Horseradish (bottom)

Garlic Roasted Potato Wedges

6 servings
40 minutes

Garlic and potato lovers' delight.

4	large red potatoes	5 ml	(*1 tsp*) crushed fresh garlic
50 g	(*2 oz*) butter or margarine	2 ml	(*1/2 tsp*) salt
50 ml	(*4 tbsp*) grated Parmesan cheese	1 ml	(*1/4 tsp*) pepper

Heat oven to 220 °C (*425 °F*) mark 7. Cut potatoes in half lengthwise; cut each half into 4 wedges. In 3-litre (*5-pt*) saucepan place potato wedges; add enough water to cover. Bring to a full boil. Cook over med. heat until potatoes are tender (8 to 12 min.); drain. In 33 x 23-cm (*13 x 9-in*) baking tin melt butter in oven (5 to 6 min.). Stir in remaining ingredients. Add potato wedges; coat both sides with butter mixture. Bake for 10 min.; turn potatoes. Continue baking for 10 to 15 min. or until lightly browned.

Microwave Directions: Prepare potatoes as directed left. In 25-cm (*10-in*) flan dish melt butter on HIGH (50 to 60 sec.). Stir in remaining ingredients. Add potato wedges; coat both sides with butter mixture. Cover; microwave on HIGH, stirring after half the time, until potatoes are tender (11 to 15 min.).

New Potatoes With Lemon Horseradish

4 to 6 servings
1 hour 20 minutes

New potatoes served with a zesty twist.

50 g	(*2 oz*) butter or margarine	675 g	(*1 1/2 lb*) tiny new potatoes, washed, unpeeled *except* for 1-cm (*1/2-in*) strip around centre of potato
2 ml	(*1/2 tsp*) salt		
	Pinch of pepper		
15 ml	(*1 tbsp*) prepared horseradish	6	slices 5 mm (*1/4 in*) lemon
10 ml	(*2 tsp*) lemon juice	30 ml	(*2 tbsp*) chopped fresh parsley

Heat oven to 180 °C (*350 °F*) mark 4. In 2-litre (*3 1/2-pt*) casserole melt butter in oven (6 to 8 min.). Stir in salt, pepper, horseradish and lemon juice. Stir in potatoes until well coated with butter. Cover; bake for 55 to 65 min. or until potatoes are fork tender. Garnish with lemon slices and sprinkle with parsley. To serve, spoon butter sauce over potatoes.

Microwave Directions: In 2-litre (*3 1/2-pt*) casserole melt butter on HIGH (50 to 60 sec.). Stir in salt, pepper, horseradish and lemon juice. Stir in potatoes until well coated with butter. Cover; microwave on HIGH, stirring after half the time, until potatoes are fork tender (10 to 12 min.). Let stand 5 min. Garnish with lemon slices and sprinkle with parsley. Serve as directed left.

Apple-Filled Sweet Potatoes

6 servings
1 hour 30 minutes

Twice-baked sweet potatoes, subtly flavoured with orange rind and nutmeg.

6	med. sweet potatoes or yams		1	med. apple, peeled, cored, coarsely chopped
50 ml	(*4 tbsp*) firmly packed brown sugar		50 ml	(*4 tbsp*) chopped pecans, toasted
125 g	(*4 oz*) butter or margarine			
	Pinch of nutmeg			Pecan halves
2 ml	(*1/2 tsp*) grated orange rind			

Heat oven to 190 °C (*375 °F*) mark 5. Prick sweet potatoes with fork to allow steam to escape. Bake for 35 to 45 min. or until fork tender. Cut thin lengthwise slice from top of each sweet potato; scoop out inside, leaving a thin shell. Set shells aside. In large mixer bowl place hot sweet potato and remaining ingredients *except* apple, chopped pecans and pecan halves. Beat at med. speed, scraping bowl often, until well mixed and no lumps remain (2 to 3 min.). By hand, stir in apple and chopped pecans. Place shells on (38 x 25 x 2.5-cm) (*15 x 10 x 1-in*) baking pan; fill shells with sweet potato mixture. If desired, garnish each sweet potato with pecan halves. Bake for 15 to 20 min. or until heated through.

Tip: If desired, do not stuff shells. Spoon hot sweet potato mixture into serving bowl. If desired, toast pecan halves and use to garnish sweet potato mixture.

Elegant Spinach Timbales

5 servings
45 minutes

Cheese sauce crowns these delightful individual servings of spinach.

Timbales

600 g	(*1 1/4 lb*) frozen chopped spinach
4	eggs
50 g	(*2 oz*) butter or margarine, softened
2 ml	(*1/2 tsp*) salt
15 ml	(*1 tbsp*) lemon juice

Cheese Sauce

30 g	(*1 oz*) butter or margarine
30 ml	(*2 tbsp*) plain flour
2 ml	(*1/2 tsp*) dry mustard
1 ml	(*1/4 tsp*) salt
1 ml	(*1/4 tsp*) pepper
250 ml	(*8 fl oz*) milk
175 g	(*6 oz*) shredded Cheddar cheese

Cook spinach according to pkg. directions; drain. In small mixer bowl beat eggs at med. speed until foamy (1 to 2 min.). By hand, stir in cooked spinach and remaining timbale ingredients. Divide mixture between 5 greased 175-ml (*6fl-oz*) ramekin dishes. Place custard cups on a rack in 25-cm (*10-in*) frying pan. Add hot (not boiling) water to just below rack. Cover; cook over med. heat for 18 to 22 min. or until knife inserted in centre comes out clean. If water begins to boil, reduce heat to low. Meanwhile, in 1-litre (*1 3/4-pt*) saucepan melt 30 g (*1 oz*) butter. Add flour, mustard, 1 ml (*1/4 tsp*) salt and pepper. Cook over med. heat until smooth and bubbly (30 sec.). Stir in milk. Continue cooking, stirring occasionally, until sauce comes to a full boil (4 to 5 min.); boil 1 min. Stir in cheese until melted. Loosen edges of timbales with knife; unmould. Serve cheese sauce over timbales.

Apple-Filled Sweet Potatoes

Courgettes & Onions With Mozzarella

6 servings
30 minutes

Midsummer vegetables are a delight sautéed with herbs and lots of Mozzarella cheese.

45 g	(*1½ oz*) butter or margarine	1 ml	(*¼ tsp*) oregano leaves
3	med. courgettes sliced 3 mm (*⅛ in*)		Pinch of salt
1	med. onion, sliced 3 mm (*⅛ in*)	2 ml	(*½ tsp*) crushed fresh garlic
2 ml	(*½ tsp*) basil leaves	1	med. ripe tomato, cut into wedges
		125 g	(*4 oz*) shredded Mozzarella cheese

In 25-cm (*10-in*) frying pan melt butter over med. heat. Add remaining ingredients *except* tomato and cheese. Continue cooking, stirring occasionally, until courgettes are crisply tender (7 to 10 min.). Add tomato wedges; sprinkle with cheese. Cover; let stand 2 min. or until cheese is melted.

Microwave Directions: In 2-litre (*3½-pt*) casserole melt butter on HIGH (30 to 45 sec.). Add remaining ingredients *except* tomato and cheese. Cover; microwave on HIGH, stirring after half the time, until courgettes are crisply tender (3 to 4½ min.). Add tomato wedges; sprinkle with cheese. Cover; let stand 2 min. or until cheese is melted.

Quick Squash Medley

6 servings
15 minutes

The entire family will enjoy this slightly sweet, colourful squash medley.

50 g	(*2 oz*) butter or margarine	15 ml	(*1 tbsp*) firmly packed brown sugar
500 g	(*1 lb*) peeled, cubed 2.5 cm (*1 in*) butternut squash		Pinch of nutmeg
200 g	(*7 oz*) unpeeled, quartered, sliced 1 cm (*½ in*) yellow squash	200 g	(*7 oz*) unpeeled, sliced 3 mm (*⅛ in*) courgette

In 25-cm (*10-in*) frying pan melt butter; stir in remaining ingredients *except* courgette. Cook over med. heat, stirring occasionally, 5 min. Stir in courgette; continue cooking until squash are crisply tender (4 to 5 min.).

Microwave Directions: In 2-litre (*3½-pt*) casserole melt butter on HIGH (50 to 60 sec.). Stir in butternut squash. Cover; microwave on HIGH 1½ min. Stir in remaining ingredients. Cover; microwave on HIGH, stirring after half the time, until squash are crisply tender (6 to 7 min.).

Courgettes & Onions With Mozzarella

Savoury Herb Tomato Halves (top)
Harvest Acorn Squash (bottom)

Harvest Acorn Squash

4 servings
60 minutes

The tartness of apples and sweetness of acorn squash blend with honey
to make a mouth-watering delight.

2	med. acorn squash, halved, remove seeds
125 ml	(*4 fl oz*) apple juice or water
50 g	(*2 oz*) butter or margarine, melted
1 ml	(*¼ tsp*) nutmeg

30 ml	(*2 tbsp*) honey
5 ml	(*1 tsp*) grated orange rind
2	med. tart apples, cored, sliced 3 mm (*⅛ in*)

Heat oven to 190 °C (*375 °F*) mark 5. In 33 x 23-cm (*13 x 9-in*) baking dish place squash cut side up. Pour apple juice in dish; set aside. In small bowl combine remaining ingredients *except* apples. Divide apple slices evenly among squash halves. Pour about 25 g (*1 oz*) butter mixture over apple slices. Cover with aluminum foil; bake for 45 to 50 min. or until squash is fork tender.

Microwave Directions: In 30 x 20-cm (*12 x 8-in*) baking dish place squash cut side up. Pour apple juice in dish; set aside. In small bowl combine remaining ingredients *except* apples. Divide apple slices evenly among squash halves. Pour about 25 g (*1 oz*) butter mixture over apple slices. Cover with plastic wrap; microwave on HIGH, turning ¼ turn after half the time, until squash is fork tender (12 to 15 min.). Let stand 5 min.

Savoury Herb Tomato Halves

8 servings
40 minutes

Fresh breadcrumbs and herbs top tomato halves to make an easy and delicious side dish.

150 g	(*5 oz*) fresh breadcrumbs
75 g	(*3 oz*) butter or margarine, melted
15 ml	(*1 tbsp*) chopped fresh parsley
5 ml	(*1 tsp*) basil leaves
1 ml	(*¼ tsp*) garlic powder
1 ml	(*¼ tsp*) salt

1 ml	(*¼ tsp*) oregano leaves
1 ml	(*¼ tsp*) cracked pepper
4	med. ripe tomatoes, stems removed, halved crosswise

Heat oven to 180 °C (*350 °F*) mark 4. In small bowl stir together all ingredients *except* tomatoes. Place tomatoes, cut side up, on 38 x 25 x 2.5-cm (*15 x 10 x 1-in*) Swiss roll tin. Spoon a heaping tablespoonful of crumb mixture on each tomato half. Bake for 15 to 18 min. or until tomatoes are heated through, yet firm.

Microwave Directions: In small bowl stir together all ingredients *except* tomatoes. Place four tomato halves, cut side up, in flan dish. Spoon a heaping tablespoonful of crumb mixture on each tomato half. Cover with plastic wrap. Microwave on HIGH, turning plate ½ turn after half the time, until tomatoes are heated through, yet firm (2½ to 3½ min.). Repeat with remaining tomato halves.

Buttery Crunch-Topped Tomatoes

4 servings
15 minutes

Frying pan tomatoes with the oh-so-good taste of stuffed tomatoes.

30 g	(*1 oz*) butter or margarine, melted
75 ml	(*5 tbsp*) coarsely crushed buttery crackers
50 g	(*2 oz*) shredded Cheddar cheese
15 ml	(*1 tbsp*) chopped fresh parsley
30 g	(*1 oz*) butter or margarine

2 ml	(*1/2 tsp*) caraway seed
1 ml	(*1/4 tsp*) salt
	Pinch of pepper
15 ml	(*1 tbsp*) chopped onion
2	large ripe tomatoes, each cut into 10 wedges

In small bowl stir together 30 g (*1 oz*) melted butter, crushed crackers, cheese and parsley; set aside. In 25-cm (*10-in*) frying pan melt 30 g (*1 oz*) butter. Stir in caraway seed, salt, pepper and onion. Add tomatoes. Cover; cook over med. heat, stirring occasionally, until tomatoes are heated through (2 to 3 min.). Sprinkle with cheese mixture. Cover; let stand 1 min. Serve immediately.

Microwave Directions: In small bowl stir together 30 g (*1 oz*) melted butter, crushed crackers, cheese and parsley; set aside. In 2-litre (*3 1/2-pt*) casserole melt 30 g (*1 oz*) butter on HIGH (25 to 35 sec.). Stir in caraway seed, salt, pepper and onion. Add tomatoes. Cover; microwave on HIGH, stirring every 2 min., until tomatoes are heated through (4 1/2 to 5 1/2 min.). Sprinkle with cheese mixture. Cover; let stand 1 min. Serve immediately.

Tomato Courgette Relish

6 servings
25 minutes

Serve this flavourful homemade relish as a menu accompaniment at your next barbecue or picnic.

30 g	(*1 oz*) sugar
45 ml	(*3 tbsp*) cider vinegar
15 ml	(*1 tbsp*) country-style Dijon mustard
1 ml	(*1/4 tsp*) salt
	Pinch of pepper
	Pinch of celery seed
	Pinch of mustard seed

1	med. red onion, sliced 3 mm (*1/8 in*), separated into rings
3	med. courgettes, cut into 1-cm (*1/2-in*) pieces
1	med. ripe tomato, cut into 1-cm (*1/2-in*) pieces

In 2-litre (*3 1/2-pt*) saucepan combine all ingredients *except* onion, courgettes and tomato. Cook over med. heat, stirring occasionally, until mixture comes to a full boil. Add vegetables; continue cooking, stirring occasionally, until vegetables are crisply tender (6 to 8 min.). Serve warm or at room temperature. Store refrigerated.

Microwave Directions: In 2-litre (*3 1/2-pt*) casserole combine all ingredients *except* onion, courgette and tomato. Cover; microwave on HIGH, stirring after half the time, until mixture comes to a full boil (2 to 3 min.). Add vegetables. Cover; microwave on HIGH, stirring after half the time, until vegetables are crisply tender (2 to 4 min.). Serve warm or at room temperature. Store refrigerated.

Buttery Crunch-Topped Tomatoes

How To: Buy Fresh Vegetables

Vegetable:	Peak Season:	Look for:
Asparagus	Spring	Tender green spears with closed tips.
Aubergine	All year	Firm, well-shaped, shiny purple skin.
Beans, Green	Summer	Bright green colour, firm crisp pods.
Beans, Lima	Summer and fall	Light green, crisp, full pods.
Beetroots	Summer and fall	Firm, smooth, round beetroots with deep red colour and fresh tops.
Broccoli	All year	Firm, tight, dark green clusters.
Brussels Sprouts	Fall and winter	Unblemished, firm, bright green sprouts.
Cabbage	All year	Firm, heavy heads of light green colour.
Carrots	All year	Firm, well-shaped carrots with good colour.
Cauliflower	Fall and early winter	Clean, compact flowerets with green outer leaves.
Corn	Summer	Bright green husks, fresh looking silk, plump, but not too large, kernels.
Courgette	Summer	Firm squash with shiny smooth skin.
Mushrooms	All year	Creamy white to light tan caps that are firm and plump.
Parsnips	Winter	Small to medium size, smooth, firm and well-shaped parsnips.
Peas	Spring and summer	Bright green, plump and tender pea pods.
Peppers, Green	Summer and Fall	Well-shaped, shiny, medium to dark green peppers with firmsides.
Spinach	All year	Tender, fresh, unblemished leaves of bright green colour.
Squash, Acorn	Fall and winter	Dark green colour and hard, tough rinds.
Squash, Butternut	Fall and winter	Good yellow or orange colour, hard, tough rinds.
Squash, Pattypan	Summer	Small, smooth-skinned, light green, flat, round, scalloped edge squash.
Squash, Summer, Yellow or Crookneck	Summer	Firm, bright yellow, blemish-free skin.

DESSERTS, CAKES & PIES

Whether held in the church basement, at a neighbor's house or in the local park by the river, the old-fashioned potluck dinner offered the best eating of the year. You could be sure that everyone would bring out their finest dishes. You had your favorites, of course. The desserts!

Apple pie with a crust so rich and flaky that you feared it would blow right off the top of the pie. Cherry pie with sugar-crusted strips of pastry criss-crossed atop the filling in a beautiful lattice pattern. Sometimes the pie pan would be so full that the filling would dribble over the edge, which made the pie even more tempting.

There was bread pudding, still warm from the oven. Cobblers and crisps with a pitcher of thick cream nearby. And for a light touch, fresh berries with custard sauce.

Next came the cakes. Dozens of them. Wedges of home-made carrot cake with a creamy smooth frosting. Chocolate cake, so rich that it glistened. Spicy gingerbread and old-fashioned blueberry buckle.

They were all so tempting. Who could fault you for slyly running your finger around the edge of the layer cake with its creamy frosting. Or trying every cake, pie and dessert on that table!

Apple Dumplings & Brandy Sauce

*A tender butter crust, baked to a golden brown,
surrounds these pecan-filled apple dumplings smothered in a rich sauce.*

Dumplings

300 g	(*11 oz*) plain flour
1 ml	(*¼ tsp*) salt
125 g	(*4 oz*) butter or margarine, cut into pieces
150 ml	(*¼ pint*) sour cream
6	med. tart cooking apples, cored, peeled
75 ml	(*5 tbsp*) sugar
75 ml	(*5 tbsp*) chopped pecans
30 g	(*1 oz*) butter or margarine, softened
	Milk

Sauce

90 g	(*3½ oz*) firmly packed brown sugar
30 g	(*1 oz*) butter or margarine
125 ml	(*4 fl oz*) double cream
15 ml	(*1 tbsp*) brandy*

Heat oven to 200 °C (*400 °F*) mark 6. In medium bowl stir together flour and salt. Cut in 125 g (*4 oz*) butter until mixture forms coarse crumbs. With fork, stir in sour cream until mixture leaves sides of bowl and forms a ball. On lightly floured surface roll dough into 48 x 30-cm (*19 x 12-in*) rectangle. Cut 2.5-cm (*1-in*) strip off 48-cm (*19-in*) end; reserve. Cut remaining dough into six (15-cm) (*6-in*) squares. Place apple in centre of each square. In small bowl stir together sugar, pecans and 30 g (*1 oz*) butter. Stuff 25 ml (*1½ tbsp*) into cored centre of each apple. Fold dough up around apple; seal seams well. Place seam side down on greased 38 x 25 x 2.5-cm (*15 x 10 x 1-in*) Swiss roll tin. Brush dough with milk; prick dough with fork. Cut leaf designs out of reserved 2.5-cm (*1-in*) strip of dough. Brush with milk; place on wrapped apples. Bake for 35 to 50 min. or until apples are fork tender. If crust browns too quickly, cover with aluminium foil. In 1-litre (*1¾-pt*) saucepan combine all sauce ingredients. Cook over med. heat, stirring occasionally, until mixture comes to a full boil (3 to 4 min.). Serve sauce over warm dumplings.

*5 ml (*1 tsp*) brandy extract can be substituted for 15 ml (*1 tbsp*) brandy.

Old-Fashioned Maple Apples

Old-fashioned baked apple goodness in a frying pan.

50 g	(*2 oz*) butter or margarine
75 ml	(*5 tbsp*) sugar
30 ml	(*2 tbsp*) cornflour
500 ml	(*17 fl oz*) single cream
50 ml	(*4 tbsp*) pure maple syrup
5 ml	(*1 tsp*) vanilla
3	med. tart apples, cored, cut in half crosswise

In 25-cm (*10-in*) frying pan melt butter; stir in sugar and cornflour. Stir in remaining ingredients *except* apples. Cook over med. low heat, stirring constantly, until thickened (6 to 8 min.). Place apples, cut side down, in cream mixture. Cover; continue cooking, spooning sauce over apples occasionally, until apples are fork tender (12 to 15 min.). Remove apples to individual dessert dishes. With wire whisk, whisk sauce until smooth. Serve sauce over apple halves.

Apple Dumplings & Brandy Sauce

Old-Fashioned Banana Bread Pudding

6 servings
60 minutes

A cozy kind of dessert that's comforting and scrumptious.

Bread Pudding

50 g	(*2 oz*) butter or margarine
125 g	(*4 oz*) cubed 2.5 cm (*1 in*) stale French or sourdough bread
3	eggs
100 g	(*4 oz*) sugar
500 ml	(*17 fl oz*) milk
2 ml	(*¹/2 tsp*) cinnamon
2 ml	(*¹/2 tsp*) nutmeg
1 ml	(*¹/4 tsp*) salt
10 ml	(*2 tsp*) vanilla
2	med. bananas, sliced 5 mm (*¹/4 in*)

Sauce

45 g	(*1¹/2 oz*) butter or margarine
30 ml	(*2 tbsp*) sugar
15 ml	(*1 tbsp*) cornflour
175 ml	(*6 fl oz*) milk
50 ml	(*4 tbsp*) light corn syrup
5 ml	(*1 tsp*) vanilla

Heat oven to 190 °C (*375 °F*) mark 5. In 2-litre (*3¹/2-pt*) casserole melt 50 g (*2 oz*) butter in oven (4 to 6 min.). Stir in bread cubes. In medium bowl slightly beat eggs; stir in remaining pudding ingredients *except* bananas. Stir in bananas. Pour over bread cubes; stir to coat. Bake for 40 to 50 min. or until knife inserted near centre comes out clean. Meanwhile, in 1-litre (*1³/4-pt*) saucepan melt 45 g (*1¹/2 oz*) butter over med. heat. Stir in sugar and cornflour; add remaining ingredients *except* vanilla. Continue cooking, stirring occasionally, until sauce comes to a full boil (3 to 4 min.). Boil 1 min. Stir in vanilla. Serve sauce over warm pudding.

Streusel Blueberry Buckle

9 servings
45 minutes

*A homespun dessert that's so good
you'll bake it for breakfast, brunch or picnics.*

Blueberry Buckle

300 g	(*11 oz*) plain flour
175 g	(*6 oz*) sugar
125 ml	(*4 fl oz*) milk
50 g	(*2 oz*) butter or margarine, softened
1	egg
10 ml	(*2 tsp*) baking powder
2 ml	(*¹/2 tsp*) salt
2 ml	(*¹/2 tsp*) nutmeg
150 g	(*5 oz*) fresh or frozen blueberries

Streusel Topping

100 g	(*4 oz*) sugar
75 ml	(*5 tbsp*) plain flour
2 ml	(*¹/2 tsp*) cinnamon
2 ml	(*¹/2 tsp*) nutmeg
50 g	(*2 oz*) butter or margarine, softened

Heat oven to 190 °C (*375 °F*) mark 5. In large mixer bowl combine all blueberry buckle ingredients *except* blueberries. Beat at low speed, scraping bowl often, until well mixed (1 to 2 min.). By hand, fold blueberries into batter. Spread into greased and floured 23-cm (*9-in*) sq. baking tin. In small bowl stir together all streusel ingredients *except* butter. Cut in butter until crumbly; sprinkle over batter. Bake for 30 to 35 min. or until wooden pick inserted in centre comes out clean.

Streusel Blueberry Buckle

Stars & Stripes Tart

6 servings
45 minutes

Grandma Ruth's Cherry Crumble

This country favourite gets its name from fruit being baked with a crumbly mixture on top.

Crumble

75 g	*(3 oz)* plain flour
40 g	*(1½ oz)* old-fashioned rolled oats
75 ml	*(5 tbsp)* firmly packed brown sugar
2 ml	*(½ tsp)* nutmeg
75 g	*(3 oz)* butter or margarine
50 g	*(2 oz)* sliced almonds

Filling

900 g	*(2 lb)* canned stoned tart cherries, drained
100 g	*(4 oz)* sugar
15 ml	*(1 tbsp)* plain flour
5 ml	*(1 tsp)* vanilla
	Vanilla ice cream

Heat oven to 180 °C *(350 °F)* mark 4. In large bowl stir together all crumble ingredients *except* butter and almonds. Cut in butter until crumbly; stir in almonds. Set aside. In medium bowl stir together all filling ingredients *except* ice cream. Fill each of 6 (175 ml) *(6 fl oz)* custard cups or ramekins about ⅔ full. Sprinkle each cup with about 50 ml *(4 tbsp)* crumble mixture; place cups on 38 x 25 x 2.5-cm *(15 x 10 x 1-in)* Swiss roll tin. Bake for 25 to 30 min. or until bubbly and lightly browned. Serve warm with vanilla ice cream.

Microwave Directions: Prepare crumble and filling as directed left. Fill each of 6 (175 ml) *(6 fl oz)* custard cups or ramekins about ⅔ full. Sprinkle each cup with about 50 ml *(4 tbsp)* crumble mixture. Arrange custard cups in circle in microwave. Microwave on HIGH, rearranging custard cups after half the time, until topping is set (10 to 13 min.). Serve warm with vanilla ice cream.

Tip: Grandma Ruth's Cherry Crumble can be baked in 1.5-litre *(2¾-pt)* casserole. Bake for 30 to 35 min.

12 servings
2 hours

Stars & Stripes Tart

A rich fruit tart.

Crust

225 g	*(8 oz)* butter or margarine, softened
100 g	*(4 oz)* sugar
375 g	*(13 oz)* plain flour
75 ml	*(5 tbsp)* milk

Filling

250 g	*(9 oz)* cream cheese, softened
90 g	*(3½ oz)* icing sugar
5 ml	*(1 tsp)* grated orange rind
15 ml	*(1 tbsp)* orange juice

Topping

325 g	*(11 ½ oz)* strawberries, hulled, sliced, or raspberries*
150 g	*(5 oz)* blueberries*
50 ml	*(4 tbsp)* apple jelly, melted

Heat oven to 200 °C *(400 °F)* mark 6. In large mixer bowl combine butter and sugar. Beat at med. speed, scraping bowl often, until light and fluffy (1 to 2 min.). Add flour and milk; beat at low speed until well mixed. Press dough on bottom and 1 cm *(½ in)* up sides of 33 x 23-cm *(13 x 9-in)* baking dish. Prick bottom with fork. Bake for 14 to 18 min. or until lightly browned. Cool. In small mixer bowl combine all filling ingredients; beat at med. speed, scraping

bowl often, until light and fluffy (1 to 2 min.). Spread over top of cooled crust. Refrigerate 1 hr. or until firm. Just before serving, arrange fruit on filling. Brush fruit and filling with melted apple jelly.

*Your favourite fruit (kiwi, mandarin orange segments, pineapple, etc.), arranged in any design, can be substituted for strawberries and blueberries.

375 ml (*13 fl oz*)
20 minutes

Caramel Rum Fruit Dip

Rich and creamy, this dip is an indulgent way to dress up fruit.

125 g	(*4 oz*) butter or margarine	15 ml	(*1 tbsp*) milk
400 g	(*14 oz*) caramels, unwrapped	15 ml	(*1 tbsp*) rum*
50 ml	(*4 tbsp*) chopped pecans		

In 2-litre (*3¹/2-pt*) saucepan melt butter and caramels over low heat, stirring occasionally, until caramels are melted (12 to 15 min.). Stir in pecans, milk and rum. Stir vigorously to incorporate butter. Keep warm; use as a dip for slices of apples, pears and bananas or serve over ice cream.

*5 ml (*1 tsp*) rum extract can be substituted for 15 ml (*1 tbsp*) rum.

Microwave Directions: In medium bowl melt butter and caramels on HIGH, stirring twice during time, until caramels are melted (3 to 4 min.). Stir in pecans, milk and rum. Stir vigorously to incorporate butter. Serve as directed left.

6 to 8 servings
15 minutes

Summertime Melon Melba

A favourite warm weather dessert that's simply delicious!

1	honeydew or cantaloupe melon Vanilla ice cream	175 g	(*6 oz*) raspberry preserves, melted

Cut melon in half crosswise and remove seeds. Slice melon into 2.5-cm (*1-in*) rings. Remove rind.

Fill each ring with scoops of ice cream. Top with melted preserves. Serve immediately.

Summertime Melon Melba

Granny's Peaches & Cream Cobbler

8 servings
60 minutes

This irresistible cobbler brings memories of visits to Grandma's house.

Filling

225 g	(*8 oz*) sugar
2	eggs, slightly beaten
30 ml	(*2 tbsp*) plain flour
2 ml	(*1/2 tsp*) nutmeg
4 to 6	med. fresh peaches, peeled and sliced*

Cobbler

225 g	(*8 oz*) plain flour
30 ml	(*2 tbsp*) sugar
5 ml	(*1 tsp*) baking powder
2 ml	(*1/2 tsp*) salt
75 g	(*3 oz*) butter or margarine, softened
1	egg, slightly beaten
45 ml	(*3 tbsp*) milk
45 ml	(*3 tbsp*) sugar
	Double cream

Heat oven to 200 °C (*400 °F*) mark 6. In large bowl stir together all filling ingredients *except* peaches. Stir in peaches. Pour into 33 x 23-cm (*13 x 9-in*) baking tin. In medium bowl stir together all cobbler ingredients *except* butter, egg and milk. Cut in butter until crumbly. Stir in egg and milk just until moistened. Crumble mixture over peaches; sprinkle with 45 ml (*3 tbsp*) sugar. Bake for 40 to 45 min. or until golden brown and bubbly around edges. Serve with double cream.

*900 g (*2 lb*) sliced frozen peaches can be substituted for sliced fresh peaches.

Pear Pandowdy

9 servings
1 hour 15 minutes

Pandowdy — a traditional favourite — features fresh fruit baked with buttery cinnamon-sugar and topped with biscuits.

175 g	(*6 oz*) firmly packed brown sugar
125 g	(*4 oz*) butter or margarine, softened
30 ml	(*2 tbsp*) plain flour
1 ml	(*1/4 tsp*) cinnamon
30 ml	(*2 tbsp*) lemon juice
5	med. pears, peeled, cored, sliced 3 mm (*1/8 in*)*

Biscuits

200 g	(*7 oz*) buttermilk baking mix
125 ml	(*4 fl oz*) milk
15 ml	(*1 tbsp*) sugar
1 ml	(*1/4 tsp*) cinnamon
	Vanilla ice cream or double cream

Heat oven to 200 °C (*400 °F*) mark 6. In large mixer bowl combine brown sugar, butter, flour, 1 ml (*1/4 tsp*) cinnamon and lemon juice. Beat at med. speed, scraping bowl often, until well mixed (1 to 2 min.). Add pears; toss to coat. Spoon into 2-litre (*3 1/2-pt*) casserole. Cover; bake for 25 to 35 min. or until pears are crisply tender. Meanwhile, in small bowl combine baking mix and milk; stir until just moistened. Drop dough by spoonfuls onto hot pear mixture to make 9 biscuits. In small bowl stir together sugar and cinnamon. Sprinkle sugar mixture over biscuits. Return to oven, uncovered; continue baking for 15 to 20 min. or until biscuits are lightly browned. Serve warm with ice cream or double cream.

*5 med. apple, peeled, cored, sliced 3 mm (*1/8 in*) apples can be substituted for sliced pears.

Granny's Peaches & Cream Cobbler

Berry Time Shortcake

9 servings
60 minutes

This strawberry shortcake is an easy summertime dessert.

Cake

175 g	(*6 oz*) plain flour
175 g	(*6 oz*) sugar
75 g	(*3 oz*) butter or margarine, softened
150 ml	(*¼ pt*) milk
2	eggs
12 ml	(*2½ tsp*) baking powder
2 ml	(*½ tsp*) salt
5 ml	(*1 tsp*) vanilla

Strawberries
Sweetened whipped cream

Heat oven to 200 °C (*400 °F*) mark 6. In small mixer bowl combine all cake ingredients *except* strawberries and sweetened whipped cream. Beat at med. speed, scraping bowl often, until well mixed (1 to 2 min.). Spread into greased and floured 23-cm (*9-in*) sq. baking tin. Bake for 20 to 25 min. or until lightly browned. Cool completely. Cut into squares. If desired, split each square in half horizontally. Serve with strawberries and sweetened whipped cream.

Lemon Picnic Cake With Berries

12 servings
1 hour 30 minutes

An old-fashioned butter cake, served with fresh berries, is the perfect dessert for a picnic or potluck.

Cake

4	eggs, separated
450 g	(*1 lb*) sugar
225 g	(*8 oz*) butter or margarine, softened
450 g	(*1 lb*) plain flour
10 ml	(*2 tsp*) baking powder
250 ml	(*8 fl oz*) milk
10 ml	(*2 tsp*) grated lemon rind
15 ml	(*1 tbsp*) lemon juice
5 ml	(*1 tsp*) vanilla

Glaze

75 ml	(*5 tbsp*) sugar
75 ml	(*5 tbsp*) lemon juice
15 ml	(*1 tbsp*) grated lemon rind

Fresh berries

Heat oven to 180 °C (*350 °F*) mark 4. In small mixer bowl beat egg whites at high speed, scraping bowl often, just until stiff peaks form (2 to 3 min.). Set aside. In large mixer bowl combine 450 g (*1 lb*) sugar and butter. Beat at low speed, scraping bowl often, until light and fluffy (1 to 2 min.). Add egg yolks; continue beating until creamy (1 to 2 min.). In small bowl stir together flour and baking powder. Gradually add flour mixture alternately with milk to butter mixture while beating at low speed. Add lemon rind, lemon juice and vanilla. By hand, fold egg whites into cake batter. Pour into greased and floured 25-cm (*10-in*) tube or ring mould. Bake for 50 to 65 min. or until wooden pick inserted in centre comes out clean. In 1-litre (*1¾-pt*) saucepan stir together all glaze ingredients *except* berries. Cook over med. heat, stirring occasionally, until sugar is dissolved (3 to 4 min.). With wooden pick poke holes in top of cake; pour glaze over cake. Cool 15 min.; remove from mould. If desired, leave cake in mould to transport. Serve with fresh berries.

Lemon Picnic Cake With Berries

Orange Pecan Delight

This tender, moist dessert bakes while you eat dinner.

8 servings
1 hour 30 minutes

50 g	(*2 oz*) butter or margarine
75 ml	(*5 tbsp*) crushed vanilla wafers
50 ml	(*4 tbsp*) plain flour
125 ml	(*4 fl oz*) milk
125 ml	(*4 fl oz*) orange juice
4	eggs, separated
30 ml	(*2 tbsp*) sugar

75 ml	(*5 tbsp*) sugar
2 ml	(*1/2 tsp*) vanilla
65 g	(*2 1/2 oz*) finely chopped pecans
250 ml	(*8 fl oz*) double cream
30 ml	(*2 tbsp*) sugar
10 ml	(*2 tsp*) grated orange rind

Grease bottoms only of 8 individual soufflé dishes or ramekins. In 2-litre (*3 1/2-pt*) saucepan melt butter over low heat. Stir in crushed vanilla wafers and flour; gradually stir in milk and juice. Cook over med. heat, stirring constantly, until mixture thickens and comes to a full boil (6 to 8 min.). Remove from heat; cool 20 min. Heat oven to 160 °C (*325 °F*) mark 3. In small mixer bowl beat egg whites at high speed, scraping bowl often, until soft peaks form (1 to 2 min.). Continue beating, gradually adding 30 ml (*2 tbsp*) sugar, until stiff peaks form (1 to 2 min.); set aside. In large mixer bowl combine egg yolks, 75 ml (*5 tbsp*) sugar and vanilla. Beat at med. speed, scraping bowl often, until thickened and lemon coloured (2 to 3 min.). Stir pecans and wafer mixture into yolks. Fold in egg

whites just until mixed. Spoon into prepared dishes. Place dishes inside two 23-cm (*9-in*) sq. baking tins; place in oven. Pour 2.5 cm (*1 in*) hot water into tins. Bake for 40 to 50 min. or until knife inserted in centre comes out clean. Meanwhile, in small chilled mixer bowl, beat chilled double cream at high speed, scraping bowl often, until soft peaks form. Gradually add 30 ml (*2 tbsp*) sugar and orange rind; continue beating until stiff peaks form. Serve hot dessert immediately with orange whipped cream.

Tip: 1.5-litre (*2 3/4-pt*) soufflé dish can be substituted for 8 individual soufflé dishes. Bake for 75 to 90 min. or until knife inserted halfway between edge and centre comes out clean.

To Prepare Orange Pecan Delight:

1. Cook over med. heat, stirring constantly, until mixture thickens and comes to a full boil (6 to 8 min.). Remove from heat; cool 20 min.

2. In small mixer bowl beat egg whites at high speed, scraping bowl often, until soft peaks form (1 to 2 min.). Continue beating, gradually adding 30 ml (*2 tbsp*) sugar, until stiff peaks form (1 to 2 min.); set aside.

Orange Pecan Delight

Sweetheart Cheesecake

10 servings

Sweetheart Cheesecake

Rich homemade cheesecake sweetened with a decorative ring of hearts.

Crust

175 g	(*6 oz*) crushed chocolate wafer cookies
50 g	(*2 oz*) butter or margarine, melted
30 ml	(*2 tbsp*) sugar

Filling

4	eggs, separated
125 g	(*4 oz*) butter or margarine, softened
450 g	(*1 lb*) cream cheese, softened
225 g	(*8 oz*) sugar
15 ml	(*1 tbsp*) cornflour
5 ml	(*1 tsp*) baking powder
15 ml	(*1 tbsp*) lemon juice

Topping

250 ml	(*8 fl oz*) sour cream
30 ml	(*2 tbsp*) sugar
5 ml	(*1 tsp*) vanilla
600 g	(*1¼ lb*) canned cherry pie filling
45 ml	(*3 tbsp*) cherry-flavoured liqueur

Heat oven to 160 °C (*325 °F*) mark 3. In small bowl stir together all crust ingredients. Press crumb mixture evenly onto bottom of 23-cm (*9-in*) spring-form tin. Bake 10 min.; cool. In small mixer bowl beat egg whites at high speed, scraping bowl often, until soft peaks form (1 to 2 min.); set aside. In large mixer bowl combine 125 g (*4 oz*) butter, cream cheese and egg yolks. Beat at med. speed, scraping bowl often, until smooth and creamy (2 to 3 min.). Add remaining filling ingredients *except* egg whites. Continue beating, scraping bowl often, until well mixed (1 to 2 min.). By hand, fold in beaten egg whites. Spoon filling into prepared tin. Bake for 60 to 80 min. or until centre is set and firm to the touch. (Cheesecake surface will be cracked.) Cool 15 min.; loosen sides of cheesecake from tin by running knife around inside of tin. Cool completely. (Cheesecake centre will dip slightly upon cooling.) In small bowl stir together sour cream, 30 ml (*2 tbsp*) sugar and vanilla. Spread evenly over top of cheesecake. Spoon out 30 to 45 ml (*2 to 3 tbsp*) of cherry sauce from pie filling; drop by teaspoonfuls onto sour cream topping. Carefully pull knife or spatula through cherry sauce forming hearts. Cover; refrigerate 4 hr. or overnight. In medium bowl stir together remaining pie filling and, if desired, liqueur. Serve over slices of cheesecake.

To Prepare Cheesecake:

1. Spoon out 30 to 45 ml (*2 to 3 tbsp*) of cherry sauce from pie filling; drop by teaspoonfuls onto sour cream topping.

2. Carefully pull knife or spatula through cherry sauce forming hearts.

Chocolate-Marbled Almond Cheesecake

Chocolate-Marbled Almond Cheesecake

12 servings
12 hours

*This rich, dark chocolate-marbled cheesecake, on an almond crust,
was meant for those with a passion for chocolate.*

450 g	(*1 lb*) sugar	10 ml	(*2 tsp*) vanilla
900 g	(*2 lb*) cream cheese, softened	5 ml	(*1 tsp*) almond extract
4	eggs	350 g	(*12 oz*) semi-sweet chocolate chips, melted
250 ml	(*8 fl oz*) sour cream		
15 ml	(*1 tbsp*) unsweetened cocoa	50 g	(*2 oz*) blanched almonds, finely chopped

Heat oven to 160 °C (*325 °F*) mark 3. In large mixer bowl combine sugar and cream cheese. Beat at med. speed, scraping bowl often, until light and fluffy (3 to 4 min.). Continue beating, adding eggs one at a time, until creamy (1 to 2 min.). Add remaining ingredients *except* chocolate chips and almonds. Continue beating, scraping bowl often, until well mixed (1 to 2 min.). By hand, fold in melted chocolate chips to swirl chocolate throughout batter for marbled effect. Lightly butter 23-cm (*9-in*) springform tin; press almonds firmly on bottom of tin. Pour batter into prepared tin. Bake for 65 to 75 min. or until set. Turn off oven; leave cheesecake in oven for 2 hr. Loosen sides of cheesecake from tin by running knife around inside of tin. Cool completely. Cover; refrigerate 8 hr. or overnight. Store refrigerated.

Apricot-Laced Cream Puffs

8 servings
2 hours

An apricot cream cheese filling provides an interesting twist to cream puffs, a heartwarming classic.

Cream Puffs

250 ml	(*8 fl oz*) water
125 g	(*4 oz*) butter or margarine
150 g	(*5 oz*) plain flour
4	eggs

Apricot Cream

125 ml	(*4 fl oz*) double cream
50 ml	(*4 tbsp*) icing sugar
225 g	(*8 oz*) cream cheese, softened
2 ml	(*1/2 tsp*) ginger
30 ml	(*2 tbsp*) apricot preserves
175 g	(*6 oz*) apricot preserves, melted
	Icing sugar

Heat oven to 200 °C (*400 °F*) mark 6. In 2-litre (*3 1/2-pt*) saucepan bring water and butter to a full boil. Stir in flour. Cook over low heat, stirring vigorously, until mixture forms a ball. Add eggs, one at a time, beating until smooth. Drop about 75 ml (*5 tbsp*) dough 8 cm (*3 in*) apart onto baking sheet. Bake for 35 to 40 min. or until puffed and golden brown. Cool completely. In chilled small mixer bowl, beat chilled double cream at high speed, scraping bowl often, until soft peaks form. Gradually add 50 ml (*4 tbsp*) icing sugar; continue beating until stiff peaks form (1 to 2 min.). Add remaining apricot cream ingredients *except* 175 g (*6 oz*) apricot preserves and icing sugar. Continue beating, scraping bowl often, until smooth (2 to 3 min.). Cut off cream puff tops; pull out any filaments of soft dough. Fill puffs with apricot cream; replace tops. Drizzle with melted apricot preserves; sprinkle with icing sugar.

Bananas Foster With Crepes

Buttery crepes served in a rich banana-rum sauce.

6 servings
45 minutes

Crepes

100 g	(*4 oz*) plain flour
7 ml	(*1 1/2 tsp*) sugar
1 ml	(*1/4 tsp*) baking powder
1 ml	(*1/4 tsp*) salt
250 ml	(*8 fl oz*) milk
1	egg
15 g	(*1/2 oz*) butter or margarine, melted
1 ml	(*1/4 tsp*) vanilla
5 ml	(*1 tsp*) butter or margarine

Sauce

125 g	(*4 oz*) butter or margarine
215 g	(*7 1/2 oz*) icing sugar
50 ml	(*2 fl oz*) milk
2 ml	(*1/2 tsp*) cinnamon
30 ml	(*1 oz*) rum*
3	med. bananas, sliced 5 mm (*1/4 in*)
30 ml	(*2 tbsp*) lemon juice

In small mixer bowl combine flour, sugar, baking powder and salt. Add remaining crepe ingredients *except* 5 ml (*1 tsp*) butter. Beat at med. speed, scraping bowl often, until smooth (1 to 2 min.). Melt 5 ml (*1 tsp*) butter in 15 to 20-cm (*6 or 8-in*) frying pan until sizzling. For each of 6 crepes, pour about 50 ml (*4 tbsp*) batter into frying pan; immediately rotate frying pan until thin film covers bottom. Cook over med. heat until lightly browned (2 to 3 min.). Run wide spatula around edge to loosen; turn. Continue cooking until lightly browned (2 to 3 min.). Place crepes on plate, placing waxed paper between each. Cover crepes; set aside. In 25-cm (*10-in*) frying pan

melt 125 g (*4 oz*) butter over med. heat. Stir in icing sugar, 50 ml (*2 fl oz*) milk, cinnamon and rum. In small bowl combine bananas and lemon juice; toss to coat bananas. Gently stir bananas into sauce in frying pan. Fold each crepe in half; fold in half again to form triangles. Arrange crepes in frying pan; spoon sauce over crepes. Cook over med. heat, spooning sauce over crepes occasionally, until heated through (4 to 6 min.). Serve immediately.

*5 ml (*1 tsp*) rum extract can be substituted for 30 ml (*1 oz*) rum.

To Prepare Bananas Foster:

1. Immediately rotate frying pan until thin film covers bottom.

2. Run wide spatula around edge to loosen; turn. Continue cooking until lightly browned (2 to 3 min.).

Bananas Foster With Crepes

Luscious Berries With Custard Sauce

Delightful custard sauce poured over sun-ripened berries.

500 ml (*17 fl oz*)
15 minutes

375 ml	(*13 fl oz*) double cream
100 g	(*4 oz*) sugar
15 ml	(*1 tbsp*) cornflour
4	egg yolks
10 ml	(*2 tsp*) vanilla

Fresh raspberries, strawberries and blueberries

In 2-litre (*3½-pt*) saucepan cook cream over med. heat until just comes to a boil (6 to 8 min.). Remove from heat. Meanwhile, in medium bowl gradually whisk sugar and cornflour into egg yolks. Whisk until mixture is light and creamy (3 to 4 min.). Gradually whisk hot cream into beaten egg yolks. Return mixture to same saucepan; stir in vanilla. Cook over med. heat, stirring constantly, until custard is thick enough to coat back of metal spoon (3 to 4 min.). (Do not boil because egg yolks will curdle.) Serve warm or cool over fresh berries.

Microwave Directions: In 1-litre (*1¾-pt*) casserole microwave cream on HIGH until just comes to a boil (2 to 4 min.). Meanwhile, in medium bowl gradually whisk sugar and cornflour into egg yolks. Whisk until mixture is light and creamy (3 to 4 min.). Gradually whisk hot cream into beaten egg yolks. Return mixture to same casserole; stir in vanilla. Microwave on HIGH, stirring after half the time, until custard is thick enough to coat back of metal spoon (1½ to 2½ min.). (Do not boil because egg yolks will curdle.) Serve warm or cool over fresh berries.

To Prepare Custard Sauce:

1. Gradually whisk hot cream into beaten egg yolks.

2. Cook over med. heat, stirring constantly, until custard is thick enough to coat back of metal spoon.

Luscious Berries With Custard Sauce

Best Ever Baked Custard

Best Ever Baked Custard

6 servings
1 hour 15 minutes

Each spoonful of custard is rich, creamy and so comforting.

100 g	(*4 oz*) sugar
6	egg yolks
375 ml	(*13 fl oz*) milk

125 ml	(*4 fl oz*) double cream
10 ml	(*2 tsp*) vanilla
	Pinch of nutmeg

Heat oven to 160 °C (*325 °F*) mark 3. In medium bowl gradually whisk sugar into egg yolks. Gradually whisk remaining ingredients *except* nutmeg into egg mixture. Pour into 6 (175-ml) (*6 fl-oz*) custard cups or ramekins. Place custard cups in 33 x 23-cm (*13 x 9-in*) baking tin; fill around custard cups with 2.5 cm (*1 in*) of warm water. Sprinkle top of custards with nutmeg. Bake for 50 to 60 min. or until knife inserted in centre comes out clean. Serve warm.

To Prepare Custard:

1. Place custard cups in 33 x 23-cm (*13 x 9-in*) baking tin; fill around custard cups with 2.5 cm (*1 in*) of warm water.

2. Bake for 50 to 60 min. or until knife inserted in centre comes out clean.

Chocolate Truffle Pudding

6 to 8 servings
3 hours

Indulge in this truffle-like pudding to satisfy chocolate cravings.

250 ml	(*8 fl oz*) milk		2	egg yolks, slightly beaten
250 ml	(*8 fl oz*) double cream		30 g	(*1 oz*) butter or margarine
100 g	(*4 oz*) sugar		5 ml	(*1 tsp*) vanilla
45 ml	(*3 tbsp*) unsweetened cocoa			
30 ml	(*2 tbsp*) cornflour			Sweetened whipped cream
125 g	(*4 oz*) semi-sweet real chocolate chips			Zest of orange rind
1	egg, slightly beaten			Unsweetened cocoa

In 2-litre (*3½-pt*) saucepan stir together milk and double cream. Cook over med. heat until warm (3 to 5 min.). In small bowl stir together sugar, 45 ml (*3 tbsp*) cocoa and cornflour. Gradually add to milk mixture. Add remaining ingredients *except* whipped cream, zest of orange rind and cocoa. Continue cooking, stirring constantly, until pudding just begins to thicken (5 to 10 min.). Pour pudding into 6 or 8 (125-ml) (*4-fl oz*) individual dessert dishes. Cool 30 min. Cover; refrigerate at least 2 hr. Pipe with sweetened whipped cream; top with zest of orange rind and sprinkle with cocoa.

Home-Style Rice Pudding

6 servings
2 hours

This creamy, old-fashioned pudding is topped with a delicious sweet meringue.

Pudding

100 g	(*4 oz*) sugar		**Meringue**	
15 ml	(*1 tbsp*) cornflour		2	reserved egg whites
2 ml	(*½ tsp*) salt		30 ml	(*2 tbsp*) sugar
1 ml	(*¼ tsp*) nutmeg			
600 ml	(*1 pt*) milk			
2	egg yolks, *reserve egg whites*			
2 ml	(*½ tsp*) vanilla			
325 g	(*11½ oz*) cooked rice			

Heat oven to 180 °C (*350 °F*) mark 4. In large bowl stir together 100 g (*4 oz*) sugar, cornflour, salt and nutmeg. Add milk, egg yolks and vanilla; with wire whisk, beat until smooth. Stir in rice. Pour into 1.5-litre (*2¾-pt*) casserole. Place casserole in 23-cm (*9-in*) sq. baking tin. Place in oven; pour hot water 2.5 cm (*1 in*) deep into sq. tin. Bake, stirring occasionally, until pudding is creamy and milk is absorbed (about 1½ hr.). Remove from oven; remove 1.5-litre (*2¾-pt*) casserole from sq. tin. Increase oven to 200 °C (*400 °F*) mark 6. In small mixer bowl beat egg whites at high speed, scraping bowl often, until soft peaks form (1 to 2 min.). Continue beating, gradually adding sugar, until stiff peaks form (1 to 2 min.). Spread over pudding, sealing around edges. Bake for 5 to 8 min. or until meringue is lightly browned. Serve warm or cold.

Chocolate Truffle Pudding

Steamed Cranberry Pudding

Old-fashioned, warmly spiced steamed pudding is sure to become a family holiday tradition.

Pudding

300 g	(*11 oz*) plain flour
225 g	(*8 oz*) sugar
250 ml	(*8 fl oz*) milk
1	egg
30 g	(*1 oz*) butter or margarine, softened
5 ml	(*1 tsp*) bicarbonate of soda
5 ml	(*1 tsp*) cinnamon
5 ml	(*1 tsp*) nutmeg
50 ml	(*4 tbsp*) plain flour
200 g	(*7 oz*) fresh or frozen whole cranberries

Sauce

100 g	(*4 oz*) sugar
90 g	(*3½ oz*) firmly packed brown sugar
125 g	(*4 oz*) butter or margarine
125 ml	(*4 fl oz*) double cream
5 ml	(*1 tsp*) vanilla

In large mixer bowl combine all pudding ingredients *except* 50 ml (*4 tbsp*) flour and cranberries. Beat at med. speed, scraping bowl often, until well mixed (1 to 2 min.). In small bowl toss together 50 ml (*4 tbsp*) flour and cranberries. By hand, stir cranberry mixture into batter. Pour into greased 1.5-litre (*2¾-pt*) metal mould or casserole. Cover tightly with aluminum foil. Place rack in flameproof casserole or roasting tin; add boiling water to just below rack. Place mould on rack. Cover; cook over med. heat at a low boil for about 2 hr. or until wooden pick inserted in centre comes out clean. Add boiling water occasionally to keep water level just below rack. Remove; let stand 2 to 3 min. Remove aluminum foil and unmould. Serve warm or cold with warm sauce. In 1-litre (*1¾-pt*) saucepan combine all sauce ingredients *except* vanilla. Cook over med. heat, stirring occasionally, until mixture thickens and comes to a full boil (4 to 5 min.). Boil 1 min. Stir in vanilla. Store sauce refrigerated.

To Prepare Steamed Cranberry Pudding:

1. Pour into greased 1.5-litre (*2¾-pt*) metal mould or casserole. Cover tightly with aluminum foil.

2. Place rack in flameproof casserole or roasting tin; add boiling water to just below rack.

Steamed Cranberry Pudding

Individual Fruit-Filled Meringues

6 servings
3 hours

*These heart-shaped meringues showcase a cloud of whipped cream
and a colourful arrangement of fresh fruit.*

Meringues

4	egg whites
10 ml	*(2 tsp)* cornflour
1 ml	*(¼ tsp)* cream of tartar
5 ml	*(1 tsp)* lemon juice
225 g	*(8 oz)* sugar
75 ml	*(5 tbsp)* icing sugar

Whipped Cream

250 ml	*(8 fl oz)* double cream
50 ml	*(4 tbsp)* sugar
5 ml	*(1 tsp)* vanilla
175 g	*(6 oz)* sliced fresh strawberries
175 g	*(6 oz)* 2.5-cm *(1-in)* pieces fresh pineapple
1	kiwi, cut into 6 slices

Heat oven to 140 °C (*275 °F*) mark 1. In large mixer bowl beat egg whites, cornflour, cream of tartar and lemon juice at high speed, scraping bowl often, until soft peaks form (1 to 2 min.). Continue beating, gradually adding 225 g (*8 oz*) sugar and icing sugar, until glossy and stiff peaks form (6 to 8 min.). On brown paper or parchment paper-lined baking sheet, shape or pipe 6 (about 10-cm) (*4-in*) individual heart-shaped or round meringues, building up sides. Bake

for 1 hr. Turn off oven; leave meringues in oven with door closed for 1 hr. Finish cooling meringues at room temperature. In chilled small mixer bowl, beat chilled double cream at high speed, scraping bowl often, until soft peaks form. Gradually add 50 ml (*4 tbsp*) sugar; continue beating until stiff peaks form (1 to 2 min.). By hand, fold in vanilla. Fill meringue shells with whipped cream; top with strawberries, pineapple and kiwi.

To Prepare Meringues:

1. Continue beating, gradually adding 225 g (*8 oz*) sugar and icing sugar, until glossy and stiff peaks form (6 to 8 min.).

2. On brown paper or parchment paper-lined baking sheet, shape or pipe 6 (about 10-cm) (*4-in*) individual heartshaped or round meringues, building up sides.

Individual Fruit-Filled Meringues

15 servings
6 hours 30 minutes

Chocolate Mousse Squares

Mousse-like dessert that's easy enough to prepare for a large group.

25	finely crushed chocolate sandwich cookies
75 g	(*3 oz*) butter or margarine, melted
225 g	(*8 oz*) icing sugar
225 g	(*8 oz*) butter or margarine, softened
225 g	(*8 oz*) cream cheese, softened
4	(30-g) (*1-oz*) sq. unsweetened chocolate, melted, cooled

4	eggs
10 ml	(*2 tsp*) vanilla
100 g	(*4 oz*) desiccated coconut
125 g	(*4 oz*) chopped walnuts
375 ml	(*13 fl oz*) double cream

In medium bowl stir together crushed cookies and 75 g (*3 oz*) melted butter. *Reserve 50 ml (4 tbsp) crumb mixture*; set aside. Press remaining crumb mixture on bottom of 33 x 23-cm (*13 x 9-in*) tin. In large mixer bowl combine icing sugar, 225 g (*8 oz*) butter, cream cheese, chocolate, eggs and vanilla. Beat at med. speed, scraping bowl often, until smooth and fluffy (2 to 3 min.). By hand, stir in coconut and walnuts. In chilled bowl, beat chilled double cream at high speed, scraping bowl often, until soft peaks form. Fold into chocolate mixture; pour over crumb crust. Sprinkle with reserved 50 ml (*4 tbsp*) crumb mixture. Cover; refrigerate at least 6 hr. Cut into squares. Store refrigerated.

8 servings
3 hours 30 minutes

Chocolate Mint Mallow Cups

A little extra time is needed for these individual mint delights, but everyone will praise the results.

175 g	(*6 oz*) semi-sweet chocolate chips
125 ml	(*4 fl oz*) milk
24	large marshmallows
	Pinch of salt
5 ml	(*1 tsp*) vanilla

	Pinch of peppermint extract
6	drops red food colouring
250 ml	(*8 fl oz*) double cream
75 ml	(*5 tbsp*) crushed starlight peppermint candy, *reserve 15 ml (1 tbsp)*

In 1-litre (*1¾-pt*) saucepan melt chocolate chips over *low* heat, stirring occasionally, until chips are melted (4 to 5 min.). Place 8 paper liners in a muffin tin. With pastry brush coat inside of each liner evenly with melted chocolate, about 3-mm (*⅛-in*) thick, bringing coating almost to top of liner, but not over edge. Refrigerate until firm (30 min.). Meanwhile, in 2-litre (*3½-pt*) saucepan combine milk and marshmallows; cook over *low* heat, stirring occasionally, until marshmallows are melted (9 to 12 min.). Remove from heat; stir in salt, vanilla, peppermint extract and red food colouring. Refrigerate until mixture mounds slightly when dropped from a spoon (about 1 hr.). Meanwhile, in chilled mixer bowl, beat chilled double cream at high speed, scraping bowl often, until stiff peaks form. Stir marshmallow mixture until smooth. Fold marsh-mallow mixture and crushed peppermint candy *except* reserved 15 ml (*1 tbsp*) into whipped cream. Spoon about 75 ml (*5 tbsp*) filling into each chocolate cup. Refrigerate at least 2 hr. Carefully remove paper liners from chocolate cups. To serve, sprinkle with reserved 15 ml (*1 tbsp*) crushed candy.

Microwave Directions: In small bowl microwave chocolate chips on HIGH, stirring every 30 sec., until chips are melted (1½ to 2½ min.). Prepare chocolate cups as directed left. In medium bowl microwave milk and marshmallows on HIGH, stirring every min., until marshmallows are melted (1½ to 2½ min.). Continue as directed left.

Chocolate Mint Mallow Cups

Fresh Strawberry Mousse Soufflé

Fresh Strawberry Mousse Soufflé

12 servings
6 hours 30 minutes

This cold soufflé has a mousse-like texture and the flavour of fresh strawberries.

225 g	(*8 oz*) sugar		250 ml	(*8 fl oz*) sour cream
15 g	(*1/2 oz*) unflavoured gelatin		7 ml	(*1 1/2 tsp*) almond extract
1 litre	(*1 3/4 pt*) double cream		5 ml	(*1 tsp*) vanilla
4	egg whites			
675 g	(*1 1/2 lb*) sliced 5 mm (*1/4 in*) strawberries			Strawberries

Make a 10-cm (*4-in*) strip of double layer aluminum foil 5 cm (*2 in*) longer than circumference of 2-litre (*3 1/2-pt*) soufflé dish. Collar soufflé dish with strip, securing strip around outside edge with string or tape. In 2-litre (*3 1/2-pt*) saucepan combine sugar and gelatin. Stir in 500 ml (*17 fl oz*) double cream; let stand 1 min. Cook over med. heat, stirring occasionally, until gelatin is dissolved (4 to 6 min.). Refrigerate, stirring occasionally, until mixture begins to thicken (about 1 hr.). In small mixer bowl beat egg whites at high speed until stiff peaks form (2 to 3 min.); set aside. In another chilled small mixer bowl, beat

500 ml (*17 fl oz*) chilled double cream at high speed, scraping bowl often, until stiff peaks form (3 to 4 min.). Set aside. In large mixer bowl combine 675 g (*1 1/2 lb*) strawberries, sour cream, almond extract, vanilla and thickened gelatin mixture. Beat at low speed, scraping bowl often, until strawberries are broken into pieces (2 to 3 min.). Fold in beaten egg whites and whipped cream. Pour into oiled and collared 2-litre (*3 1/2-pt*) soufflé dish. Cover; refrigerate until firm (5 to 6 hr.). To serve, remove collar and garnish with strawberries.

To Prepare Soufflé:

1. Make a (10-cm) (*4-in*) strip of double layer aluminum foil 5 cm (*2 in*) longer than circumference of 2-litre (*3 1/2-pt*) soufflé dish. Collar soufflé dish with strip, securing strip around outside edge with string or tape.

2. Refrigerate, stirring occasionally, until mixture begins to thicken (about 1 hr.).

Strawberry Trifle

8 servings
2 hours 30 minutes

Strawberry Trifle

Layers of fresh strawberries, pudding and double cream make this dessert as pretty as it is good to eat.

100 g	(*4 oz*) vanilla-flavoured instant pudding and pie filling mix
250 ml	(*8 fl oz*) sour cream
250 ml	(*8 fl oz*) milk
5 ml	(*1 tsp*) grated orange rind

500 ml	(*17 fl oz*) double cream, whipped
1/2	(25-cm) (*10-in*) sponge cake, cut into bite-size pieces
675 g	(*1 1/2 lb*) fresh strawberries, hulled, sliced

In large mixer bowl place instant pudding, sour cream, milk and orange rind. Beat at low speed, scraping bowl often, until thick and well mixed (1 to 2 min.). By hand, fold in whipped cream. In large serving bowl layer: 1/2 of cake pieces, 1/3 strawberries and 1/2 pudding mixture. Repeat layers. Arrange remaining strawberries on top. Cover; refrigerate at least 2 hr.

15 servings
8 hours

Banana Split Squares

Crowd-pleasing banana splits.

Crust

125 g	(*4 oz*) butter or margarine
250 g	(*9 oz*) graham cracker crumbs
50 ml	(*4 tbsp*) sugar

Filling

3	bananas, sliced 5 mm (*1/4 in*)
2 litres	(*3 1/2 pt*) vanilla ice cream, slightly softened
125 g	(*4 oz*) chopped walnuts

Sauce

225 g	(*8 oz*) icing sugar
125 g	(*4 oz*) butter or margarine
350 ml	(*12 fl oz*) canned evaporated milk
175 g	(*6 oz*) semi-sweet real chocolate chips
5 ml	(*1 tsp*) vanilla

Topping

250 ml	(*8 fl oz*) double cream
	Maraschino cherries

In 2-litre (*3 1/2-pt*) saucepan melt 125 g (*4 oz*) butter. Stir in crumbs and sugar. Press crumb mixture on bottom of 33 x 23-cm (*13 x 9-in*) tin. Layer banana slices over crumb mixture. Spread ice cream over bananas. Sprinkle with chopped nuts. Cover; freeze until firm (about 4 hr.). Meanwhile, in 2-litre (*3 1/2-pt*) saucepan combine all sauce ingredients. Cook over low heat, stirring occasionally, until mixture thickens and comes to a full boil (20 to 25 min.). Boil 1 min. Cool completely; pour evenly over ice cream. Cover; freeze until firm (about 3 hr.). In chilled bowl, beat chilled double cream at high speed, scraping bowl often, until soft peaks form. Spread over sauce. If desired, garnish with maraschino cherries. Serve immediately or freeze until served.

6 servings
5 hours 30 minutes

Maple-Nut Cream Cheese Cups

A creamy, rich dessert with the flavour of cheesecake.

50 ml	(*4 tbsp*) milk
75 ml	(*5 tbsp*) sugar
225 g	(*8 oz*) cream cheese, softened
1	egg
2 ml	(*1/2 tsp*) vanilla

50 ml	(*4 tbsp*) pure maple syrup or maple-flavoured syrup
30 ml	(*2 tbsp*) graham cracker crumbs
50 ml	(*4 tbsp*) chopped pecans

Line 6 muffin tins with paper liners; set aside. In large mixer bowl combine all ingredients *except* maple syrup, graham cracker crumbs and pecans. Beat at med. speed, scraping bowl often, until smooth (2 to 3 min.). Pour cream cheese mixture evenly into prepared muffin tins. Freeze until firm (4 to 5 hr.). In small bowl stir together maple syrup and graham cracker crumbs. Cover; refrigerate at least 2 hr. To serve, place each dessert upside down on dessert plate. Let stand at room temperature 10 to 15 min.; remove paper. Spoon 15 ml (*1 tbsp*) maple syrup mixture over each dessert; sprinkle with nuts.

9 servings
4 hours 30 minutes

Lemon Raspberry Ice Squares

A light, refreshing dessert for a warm summer day.

18	crushed lemon-flavoured sugar cookies
50 ml	(*4 tbsp*) sugar
45 ml	(*3 tbsp*) butter or margarine, melted
250 ml	(*8 fl oz*) raspberry-flavoured yogurt

250 ml	(*8 fl oz*) buttermilk*
75 ml	(*5 tbsp*) sugar
250 g	(*9 oz*) frozen raspberries
	Sweetened whipped cream

In small bowl stir together crushed cookies, 50 ml (*4 tbsp*) sugar and butter. Press on bottom of 23-cm (*9-in*) sq. baking tin; set aside. In medium bowl stir together remaining ingredients *except* raspberries and whipped cream. Fold in raspberries. Pour yogurt mixture over cookie crust. Cover; freeze until firm (3 to 4 hr.). To serve, let stand at room temperature 10 to 15 min. Cut into squares; garnish with sweetened whipped cream.

*15 ml (*1 tbsp*) vinegar plus enough milk to equal 250 ml (*8 fl oz*) can be substituted for 250 ml (*8 fl oz*) buttermilk.

Tip: Blueberry-flavoured yogurt and frozen blueberries or strawberry-flavoured yogurt and halved frozen strawberries can be substituted for raspberry flavoured yogurt and frozen raspberries.

Maple-Nut Cream Cheese Cups (top)
Lemon Raspberry Ice Squares (bottom)

Banana 'n Chocolate Chip Ice Cream Sandwiches

12 ice cream sandwiches
6 hours

Banana 'n Chocolate Chip Ice Cream Sandwiches

*Ice cream, bananas and coconut are sandwiched between chewy chocolate chip cookies
for frozen ice cream treats.*

24	(8-cm) (*3-in*) chewy chocolate chip cookies	50 g	(*2 oz*) desiccated coconut
1 litre	(*1²/₃ pt*) chocolate chip ice cream, slightly softened	1	med. banana, chopped

Prepare or purchase your favourite chewy chocolate chip cookies. In large bowl stir together ice cream, coconut and banana just until blended. Freeze mixture for 2 hr. Spread about 50 ml (*4 tbsp*) ice cream on each of 12 cookies. Top each with additional cookie; press together to form a sandwich. With metal spatula go around edges of each ice cream sandwich to remove excess ice cream. Wrap each ice cream sandwich with plastic wrap; freeze at least 4 hr.

Tip: A variety of cookies can be used. If smaller cookies are used, adjust measurement of ice cream proportionately. Leftover ice cream can be served as a milk shake.

9 servings
9 hours

Honey Peanut Butter Ice Cream Squares

This peanut butter ice cream dessert will quickly become a family tradition.

Crust

75 g	(*3 oz*) plain flour
75 ml	(*5 tbsp*) quick-cooking oats
50 ml	(*4 tbsp*) sugar
50 ml	(*4 tbsp*) butter or margarine
1 ml	(*¹/₄ tsp*) bicarbonate of soda

Ice Cream

125 g	(*4 oz*) crunchy-style peanut butter
75 ml	(*3 oz*) light corn syrup
30 ml	(*2 tbsp*) honey
2 litres	(*3¹/₂ pt*) vanilla ice cream, slightly softened
125 g	(*4 oz*) chopped salted peanuts

Heat oven to 180 °C (*350 °F*) mark 4. Line 23-cm (*9-in*) sq. baking tin with aluminum foil, extending excess foil over edges. In large mixer bowl combine all crust ingredients. Beat at med. speed, scraping bowl often, until crumbly (1 to 2 min.). Press on bottom of prepared tin. Bake for 12 to 20 min. or until lightly browned. Cool completely. In small bowl stir together peanut butter, corn syrup and honey. Spread half of peanut butter mixture over crust. Spread half of ice cream over peanut butter mixture. Drop by spoonfuls and spread remaining peanut butter mixture over ice cream; sprinkle with half of peanuts. Spread and swirl remaining ice cream over peanuts. Sprinkle with remaining peanuts. Freeze 8 hr. or overnight or until firm. To serve, lift ice cream square from tin, using aluminum foil as handles. Remove aluminum foil. Cut into squares; serve immediately.

Homemade Ice Cream

3 litres (*5 pt*)
1 hour 30 minutes

Everyone takes a turn cranking when making this creamy sensation.

1 litre	(*1¾ pt*) milk
1 litre	(*1¾ pt*) double cream
350 g	(*12 oz*) sugar

5	eggs
7 ml	(*1½ tsp*) vanilla
	Pinch of salt

In 3-litre (*5-pt*) saucepan combine milk and double cream. Cook over low heat until warm (6 to 8 min.). In large mixer bowl combine remaining ingredients. Beat at med. speed, scraping bowl often, until smooth (2 to 3 min.). Gradually stir into milk mixture. Cool to room temperature. Pour into ice cream canister. Freeze in ice cream maker according to manufacturer's directions.

Lemon Ice

3 litres (*5 pt*)
8 hours 30 minutes

The flavour of old-fashioned lemonade, frozen in a refreshing ice.

450 g	(*1 lb*) sugar
1 litre	(*1¾ pt*) milk
500 ml	(*17 fl oz*) double cream
150 ml	(*¼ pt*) lemon juice

3	eggs
2 ml	(*½ tsp*) salt
15 ml	(*1 tbsp*) lemon rind

In large mixer bowl combine all ingredients. Beat at low speed, scraping bowl often, until well mixed (1 to 2 min.). Pour into 33 x 23-cm (*13 x 9-in*) tin. Cover; freeze until firm (about 4 hr.). Spoon into large mixer bowl. Beat at med. speed, scraping bowl often, until light and fluffy but not thawed (2 to 3 min.). Return to tin; freeze at least 4 hr. or until firm.

Homemade Ice Cream

750 ml (*1¼ pt*)
20 minutes

Spiced Pears in Cider Sauce

Serve this flavourful sauce over gingerbread, spice cake or ice cream.

500 ml	(*17 fl oz*) apple cider	2	2 med. ripe pears, cut into 1-cm (*½-in*)
30 ml	(*2 tbsp*) cornflour		pieces
30 ml	(*2 tbsp*) firmly packed brown sugar	30 ml	(*2 tbsp*) lemon juice
	Pinch of allspice		
	Dash of ground clove		

In 2-litre (*3½-pt*) saucepan stir together all ingredients *except* pears and lemon juice. Cook over med. heat, stirring occasionally, until mixture is slightly thickened (5 to 7 min.). Stir in pears and lemon juice. Continue cooking, stirring occasionally, until pears are tender (3 to 5 min.). Serve warm sauce over gingerbread, spice cake or ice cream.

Microwave Directions: In 2-litre (*3½-pt*) casserole combine all ingredients *except* pears and lemon juice. Microwave on HIGH, stirring after half the time, until mixture is slightly thickened (5½ to 7 min.). Stir in pears and lemon juice. Microwave on HIGH until pears are tender (1 to 1½ min.). Serve warm sauce over gingerbread, spice cake or ice cream.

500 ml (*17 fl oz*)
15 minutes

Apricot Crème Sauce

This creamy apricot sauce brings a delightful touch to desserts.

400 g	(*14 oz*) canned apricot halves in their own juice, drained, *reserve juice*	125 ml	(*4 fl oz*) double cream
15 ml	(*1 tbsp*) cornflour	1 ml	(*¼ tsp*) nutmeg
175 g	(*6 oz*) apricot preserves	15 ml	(*1 tbsp*) lemon juice

Slice apricots into 5-mm (*¼-in*) slices; set aside. In 1-litre (*1¾-pt*) saucepan combine 150 ml (*¼ pt*) reserved apricot juice and cornflour; whisk to blend. Cook over med. heat, stirring occasionally, until thickened (4 to 6 min.). Stir in remaining ingredients and apricots. Continue cooking, stirring occasionally, until apricots are warm (4 to 5 min.). Serve sauce over pound cake, meringues, cream puffs or ice cream.

Microwave Directions: Slice apricots into 5-mm (*¼-in*) slices; set aside. In 1-litre (*1¾-pt*) casserole combine 150 ml (*¼ pt*) reserved apricot juice and cornflour; whisk to blend. Stir in remaining ingredients *except* apricots. Microwave on HIGH, stirring every min., until thickened (3 to 4 min.). Stir in apricots; microwave on HIGH until apricots are warm (1 to 2 min.). Serve sauce over pound cake, meringues, cream puffs or ice cream.

Spiced Pears in Cider Sauce

Dreamy Chocolate Mint Sauce

1 litre (1¾ pt)
15 minutes

Dreamy Chocolate Mint Sauce

A rich-tasting dessert sauce that's reminiscent of after dinner mints.

225 g	(*8 oz*) sugar
125 g	(*4 oz*) butter or margarine, cut into pieces
175 ml	(*6 fl oz*) water

50 ml	(*4 tbsp*) light corn syrup
350 g	(*12 oz*) semisweet real chocolate chips
50 ml	(*2 fl oz*) creme de menthe*

In 2-litre (*3½-pt*) saucepan combine sugar, butter, water and corn syrup. Cook over med. heat, stirring constantly, until mixture comes to a full boil (5 to 8 min.). Boil 3 min.; remove from heat. Immediately add chocolate chips; beat with a wire whisk or rotary beater until smooth. Stir in creme de menthe. Serve warm or cool over ice cream or cake.

*5 ml (*1 tsp*) peppermint extract can be substituted for creme de menthe.

Microwave Directions: In 2-litre (*3½pt*) casserole combine sugar, butter, water and corn syrup. Microwave on HIGH, stirring after half the time, until mixture comes to a full boil (4 to 7 min.). Boil 3 min. Immediately add chocolate chips; beat with a wire whisk or rotary beater until smooth. Stir in creme de menthe. Serve warm or cool over ice cream or cake.

550 ml (*18 fl oz*)
15 minutes

Homemade Caramel Sauce

Serve this rich dessert sauce over ice cream, gingerbread or pound cake.

130 g	(*4½ oz*) firmly packed brown sugar
175 g	(*6 oz*) sugar
75 g	(*3 oz*) butter or margarine

125 ml	(*4 fl oz*) light corn syrup
150 ml	(*¼ pt*) double cream

In 2-litre (*3½-pt*) saucepan combine all ingredients *except* double cream. Cook over med. heat, stirring occasionally, until mixture comes to a full boil (5 to 8 min.). Cool 5 min. Stir in double cream. Serve warm or divide sauce into 3 (175-ml) (*6 fl-oz*) portions and prepare variations as directed below. Store refrigerated.

Microwave Directions: In 2-litre (*3½-pt*) casserole combine all ingredients *except* double cream. Microwave on HIGH, stirring every min., until mixture comes to a full boil (4 to 5 min.). Cool 5 min. Stir in double cream. Serve warm or divide sauce into 3 (175-ml) (*6 fl-oz*) portions and prepare variations as directed below. Store refrigerated.

Variations:

Rum Raisin Sauce: While still warm, stir 50 ml (*4 tbsp*) raisins and 1 ml (*¼ tsp*) rum extract into 175 ml (*6 fl oz*) sauce.

Banana Sauce: Cool 175 ml (*6 fl oz*) sauce completely. Cut 1 banana into cubes; stir into cooled sauce.

Praline Sauce: While still warm, stir 50 g (*2 oz*) toasted pecan halves into 175 ml (*6 fl oz*) sauce.

Icebox Banana Cake With Chocolate Cream

Icebox Banana Cake With Chocolate Cream

This cake tastes great from the refrigerator or it freezes beautifully for a chilled treat.

12 servings
4 hours

Cake

225 g	*(8 oz)* sugar
150 g	*(5 oz)* butter or margarine, softened
10 ml	*(2 tsp)* vanilla
2	eggs
2	med. ripe bananas, mashed
50 ml	*(4 tbsp)* sour cream
225 g	*(8 oz)* plain flour
5 ml	*(1 tsp)* bicarbonate of soda

Chocolate Cream

375 ml	*(13 fl oz)* double cream
45 ml	*(3 tbsp)* icing sugar
5 ml	*(1 tsp)* vanilla
90 g	*(3 1/2 oz)* semi-sweet chocolate chips, melted
2	bananas
30 ml	*(2 tbsp)* chopped pecans

Heat oven to 180 °C (*350 °F*) mark 4. In large mixer bowl combine sugar, butter and 10 ml (*2 tsp*) vanilla. Beat at low speed, scraping bowl often, until light and fluffy (1 to 2 min.). Continue beating, adding eggs one at a time, until creamy (1 to 2 min.). By hand, stir in mashed bananas and sour cream. Fold in flour and bicarbonate of soda. Pour into 2 greased and floured 20-cm (*8-in*) round cake tins. Bake for 25 to 30 min. or until wooden pick inserted in centre comes out clean. Cool 5 min.; remove from tins. Cool completely. In chilled small mixer bowl, beat chilled double cream at high speed, scraping bowl often, until soft peaks form. Gradually add sugar and 5 ml (*1 tsp*) vanilla; continue beating until stiff peaks form (1 to 2 min.). Add melted chocolate; continue beating until well mixed (1 min.). (Do not overbeat.) On serving plate, place 1 cake layer. Spread with half of chocolate cream. Slice 1 banana; lay banana slices on top of chocolate cream. Top with remaining cake layer. Frost top of cake with remaining chocolate cream. Refrigerate or freeze cake 2 hr. or overnight. To serve, slice remaining banana; arrange banana slices around outside edge of cake. Sprinkle pecans in centre of cake. Serve immediately or freeze to prevent bananas from browning.

Tip: 2 (23-cm) (*9-in*) round cake tins can be substituted for 2 (20-cm) (*8-in*) round cake tins. Bake for 20 to 25 min.

Glazed Carrot Cake Wedges

10 servings
60 minutes

*No one can resist a wedge of this rich carrot cake
with an orange, cream cheese glaze.*

Cake

225 g	(*8 oz*) plain flour
225 g	(*8 oz*) sugar
7 ml	(*1½ tsp*) bicarbonate of soda
5 ml	(*1 tsp*) cinnamon
2 ml	(*½ tsp*) salt
175 ml	(*6 fl oz*) vegetable oil
2	eggs, slightly beaten
5 ml	(*1 tsp*) vanilla
3	med. carrots, finely shredded
100 g	(*4 oz*) desiccated coconut

Glaze

125 g	(*4 oz*) icing sugar
75 g	(*3 oz*) cream cheese, softened
15 ml	(*1 tbsp*) grated orange rind
15 ml	(*1 tbsp*) orange juice

Heat oven to 180 °C (*350 °F*) mark 4. In large bowl combine flour, sugar, bicarbonate of soda, cinnamon and salt. Stir in oil, eggs and vanilla until well mixed. Stir in carrots and coconut. (Batter is thick.) Spread into greased and floured 23-cm (*9-in*) round cake tin.

Bake for 40 to 45 min. or until wooden pick inserted in center comes out clean. Meanwhile, in small mixer bowl combine all glaze ingredients. Beat at low speed, scraping bowl often, until smooth (1 min.). Pour over warm cake. Cut into wedges.

Spiced Orange Gingerbread

9 servings
45 minutes

Gingerbread sweetly glazed with orange that is sure to warm your heart.

250 g	(*9 oz*) plain flour
75 ml	(*5 tbsp*) sugar
125 g	(*4 oz*) butter or margarine, melted
125 ml	(*4 fl oz*) light molasses
50 ml	(*2 fl oz*) water
50 ml	(*2 fl oz*) orange juice
1	egg
5 ml	(*1 tsp*) bicarbonate of soda
5 ml	(*1 tsp*) ginger
5 ml	(*1 tsp*) cinnamon
2 ml	(*½ tsp*) salt
2 ml	(*½ tsp*) cloves
175 g	(*6 oz*) orange marmalade
	Sweetened whipped cream

Heat oven to 180 °C (*350 °F*) mark 4. In large mixer bowl combine all ingredients *except* orange marmalade and whipped cream. Beat at low speed, scraping bowl often, until well mixed (1 to 2 min.). Pour into greased and floured 23-cm (*9-in*) sq. baking tin. Bake for 30 to 35 min. or until top springs back when touched lightly in center. In 1-litre (*1¾-pt*) saucepan place orange marmalade. Cook over low heat, stirring occasionally, until heated through (5 min.). Spread over warm gingerbread. Serve with whipped cream.

Spiced Orange Gingerbread (top)
Glazed Carrot Cake Wedges (bottom)

9 servings
40 minutes

Chocolate Chip Pound Cake Squares

A dessert that is reminiscent of old-fashioned pound cake with a sauce that is a chocolate dream.

Cake

225 g	(*8 oz*) sugar
150 g	(*5 oz*) butter or margarine, softened
3	eggs
175 g	(*6 oz*) plain flour
90 g	(*3½ oz*) mini semi-sweet chocolate chips
15 ml	(*1 tbsp*) vanilla

Sauce

175 g	(*6 oz*) semi-sweet chocolate chips
125 ml	(*4 fl oz*) double cream

Heat oven to 180 °C (*350 °F*) mark 4. In large mixer bowl combine sugar and butter. Beat at low speed, scraping bowl often, until light and fluffy (1 to 2 min.). Continue beating, adding eggs one at a time, until creamy (1 to 2 min.). By hand, fold in remaining cake ingredients. Pour into greased 23-cm (*9-in*) sq. baking tin. Bake for 30 to 35 min. or until wooden pick inserted in centre comes out clean. In 1-litre (*1¾-pt*) saucepan place 175 g (*6 oz*) chocolate chips and double cream. Cook over low heat, stirring constantly, until chocolate is melted (4 to 6 min.). Serve sauce over squares.

15 servings
1 hour 30 minutes

Chocolate Rocky Road Cake

Chocolate, marshmallows and peanuts top this moist chocolate cake.

Cake

300 g	(*11 oz*) plain flour
325 g	(*11½ oz*) sugar
50 g	(*2 oz*) unsweetened cocoa
125 g	(*4 oz*) butter or margarine, softened
250 ml	(*8 fl oz*) water
3	eggs
7 ml	(*1½ tsp*) baking powder
5 ml	(*1 tsp*) bicarbonate of soda
5 ml	(*1 tsp*) vanilla

Frosting

100 g	(*4 oz*) miniature marshmallows
50 g	(*2 oz*) butter or margarine
75 g	(*3 oz*) cream cheese
30-g	(*1-oz*) sq. unsweetened chocolate
30 ml	(*2 tbsp*) milk
375 g	(*13 oz*) icing sugar
5 ml	(*1 tsp*) vanilla
65 g	(*2½ oz*) coarsely chopped salted peanuts

Heat oven to 180 °C (*350 °F*) mark 4. In large mixer bowl combine all cake ingredients. Beat at low speed, scraping bowl often, until ingredients are moistened. Beat at high speed, scraping bowl often, until smooth (1 to 2 min.). Pour into greased and floured 33 x 23-cm (*13 x 9-in*) baking tin. Bake for 30 to 40 min. or until wooden pick inserted in centre comes out clean. Sprinkle with marshmallows. Continue baking 2 min. or until marshmallows are softened. Meanwhile, in 2-litre (*3½-pt*) saucepan combine 50 g (*2 oz*) butter, cream cheese, chocolate and milk. Cook over med. heat, stirring occasionally, until melted (8 to 10 min.). Remove from heat; stir in icing sugar and vanilla until smooth. Pour over marshmallows and swirl together. Sprinkle with peanuts.

Chocolate Chip Pound Cake Squares (top)
Chocolate Rocky Road Cake (bottom)

Pumpkin Pecan Layer Cake

Three layers of festive fall flavours create this memorable cake.

16 servings
45 minutes

Cake

250 g	*(9 oz)* crushed vanilla wafers
125 g	*(4 oz)* chopped pecans
175 g	*(6 oz)* butter or margarine, softened
525 g	*(18 oz)* spice cake mix
450 g	*(16 oz)* canned pumpkin
50 g	*(2 oz)* butter or margarine, softened
4	eggs

Filling

375 g	*(13 oz)* icing sugar
150 g	*(5 oz)* butter or margarine, softened
125 g	*(4 oz)* cream cheese, softened
10 ml	*(2 tsp)* vanilla
50 ml	*(4 tbsp)* caramel topping
100 g	*(4 oz)* pecan halves

Heat oven to 180 °C (*350 °F*) mark 4. In large mixer bowl combine wafer crumbs, chopped pecans and 175 g (*6 oz*) butter. Beat at med. speed, scraping bowl often, until crumbly (1 to 2 min.). Press mixture evenly on bottom of 3 greased and floured 23-cm (*9-in*) round cake tins. In same bowl combine cake mix, pumpkin, 50 g (*4 tbsp*) butter and eggs. Beat at med. speed, scraping bowl often, until well mixed (2 to 3 min.). Divide batter between tins. Spread batter over crumbs. Bake for 20 to 25 min. or until wooden pick inserted in centre comes out clean. Cool 5 min.; remove from tins. Cool completely. In small mixer bowl combine cream cheese, 150 g (*5 oz*) butter, icing sugar and vanilla. Beat at med. speed, scraping bowl often, until light and fluffy (2 to 3 min.). On serving plate layer 3 cakes (nut side down) with 125 ml (*4 fl oz*) filling spread between each layer. With remaining filling, frost sides only of cake. Spread caramel topping over top of cake, drizzling some over the frosted sides. Arrange pecan halves in rings on top of cake. Store refrigerated.

Tip: To remove cake easily from tin, place wire rack on top of cake and invert; repeat with remaining layers.

To Prepare Cake:

1. Press mixture evenly on bottom of 3 greased and floured 23-cm (*9-in*) round cake tins.

2. On serving plate layer 3 cakes, nut side down, with 125 ml (*4 fl oz*) filling spread between each layer. With remaining filling, frost sides only of cake.

Pumpkin Pecan Layer Cake

Chocolate Cherry Surprise Cake

Chocolate Cherry Surprise Cake

Two favourite taste treats combine to create a luscious cake.

16 servings
1 hour 30 minutes

Cake

575 g	(*1¼ lb*) canned maraschino cherries, drained, *reserve juice*
2	eggs, separated
450 g	(*1 lb*) sugar
150 g	(*5 oz*) butter or margarine, softened
2	(30-g) (*1-oz*) sq. unsweetened chocolate, melted
450 g	(*1 lb*) plain flour
10 ml	(*2 tsp*) bicarbonate of soda
2 ml	(*½ tsp*) salt
	Reserved cherry juice plus enough *buttermilk* to equal 500 ml (*17 fl oz*)

Frosting

175 g	(*6 oz*) sugar
75 ml	(*5 tbsp*) light corn syrup
45 ml	(*3 tbsp*) water
3	egg whites
7 ml	(*1½ tsp*) vanilla
100 g	(*4 oz*) desiccated coconut

Heat oven to 180 °C (*350 °F*) mark 4. Cut maraschino cherries in half; set aside. In small mixer bowl beat 2 egg whites at high speed, scraping bowl often, until soft peaks form (1 to 2 min.); set aside. In large mixer bowl combine 2 egg yolks, 450 g (*1 lb*) sugar, butter and chocolate. Beat at med. speed, scraping bowl often, until well mixed (1 to 2 min.). Add flour, bicarbonate of soda and salt alternately with cherry juice and buttermilk mixture. Continue beating until smooth (1 to 2 min.). By hand, fold in cherries, then egg whites. Pour into 3 greased and floured 23-cm (*9-in*) round cake tins. Bake for 30 to 35 min. or until wooden pick inserted in centre comes out clean. Cool 5 min.; remove from tins. Cool completely. In 1-litre (*1¾-pt*) saucepan stir together 175 g (*6 oz*) sugar, corn syrup and water. Cover; cook over med. heat until mixture comes to a full boil (3 to 5 min.). Remove cover; continue boiling until small amount of mixture dropped into ice water forms a firm ball or candy thermometer reaches 117 °C (*242 °F*) (8 to 12 min.). Meanwhile, in large mixer bowl beat 3 egg whites at high speed just until stiff peaks form (1 to 2 min.). Continue beating, pouring hot syrup mixture slowly into egg whites, until stiff peaks form (6 to 8 min.). Add vanilla; continue beating until well mixed. On serving plate layer 3 cakes with 125 ml (*4 fl oz*) frosting spread between each layer. Frost entire cake. Sprinkle top and sides of cake with coconut. Store loosely covered.

Tip: 3 (20-cm) (*8-in*) round cake tins can be substituted for 3 (23-cm) (*9-in*) round cake tins. Bake for 35 to 40 min. or until wooden pick inserted in centre comes out clean.

Tip: To cut cake easily, dip knife into water before cutting each slice of cake; clean knife if cake and frosting stick.

Chocolate Chip Macaroon Angel Food

16 servings
3 hours

Homemade angel food cake, light as a cloud and worth the extra effort.

Cake

200 g	(*7 oz*) icing sugar
130 g	(*4½ oz*) cake flour*
375 ml	(*13 fl oz*) (about 12) egg whites
7 ml	(*1½ tsp*) cream of tartar
225 g	(*8 oz*) sugar
1 ml	(*¼ tsp*) salt

5 ml	(*1 tsp*) almond extract
5 ml	(*1 tsp*) vanilla
175 g	(*6 oz*) mini semi-sweet chocolate chips
50 g	(*2 oz*) desiccated coconut
500 ml	(*17 fl oz*) sweetened whipped cream
100 g	(*4 oz*) toasted desiccated coconut

Heat oven to 190 °C (*375 °F*) mark 5. In small bowl stir together icing sugar and flour; set aside. In large mixer bowl beat egg whites and cream of tartar at med. speed until foamy (1 to 2 min.). Beating at high speed, gradually add 225 g (*8 oz*) sugar, 30 ml (*2 tbsp*) at a time. Continue beating, scraping bowl often, adding salt, almond extract and vanilla until stiff and glossy (6 to 8 min.). By hand, gradually fold in flour mixture, 50 ml (*4 tbsp*) at a time. Fold in just until flour mixture disappears. Fold in chocolate chips and 50 g (*2 oz*) coconut. Spread batter into 25-cm (*10-in*) tube tin. Cut gently through batter with metal spatula. Bake for 30 to 35 min. or until cracks feel dry and top springs back when touched lightly. Invert tin on heat-proof funnel or bottle; let cool 1½ hr. Remove from tin. Decrumb cake with fingertips. Place cake on serving plate. Pipe top and around bottom of cake with sweetened whipped cream; sprinkle with toasted coconut.

*150 g (*5 oz*) minus 30 ml (*2 tbsp*) plain flour can be substituted for cake flour.

Tip: 450 g (*16 oz*) angel food cake mix can be substituted for homemade cake.

To Prepare Cake:

1. By hand, gradually fold in flour mixture, 50 ml (*4 tbsp*) at a time.

2. Cut gently through batter with metal spatula.

3. Invert tin on heat-proof funnel or bottle; let cool 1½ hr.

4. Decrumb cake with fingertips.

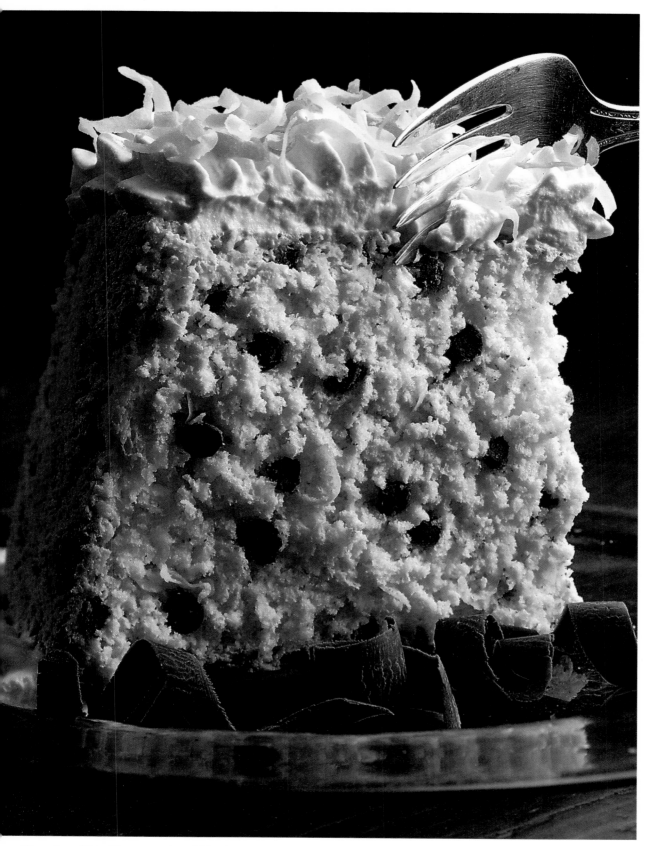

Chocolate Chip Macaroon Angel Food

Blue Ribbon Apple Pie

8 servings
2 hours

Blue Ribbon Apple Pie

Pour double cream into this delectable apple pie;
the cream thickens and settles around juicy apples.

Crust

300 g	*(11 oz)*	plain flour
5 ml	*(1 tsp)*	sugar
1 ml	*(¼ tsp)*	salt
1 ml	*(¼ tsp)*	cinnamon
1 ml	*(¼ tsp)*	nutmeg
75 g	*(3 oz)*	butter or margarine
75 g	*(3 oz)*	shortening
60 to 75 ml	*(4 to 5 tbsp)*	cold water

Filling

100 g	*(4 oz)*	sugar
50 ml	*(4 tbsp)*	firmly packed brown sugar
50 ml	*(4 tbsp)*	plain flour
2 ml	*(½ tsp)*	cinnamon
2 ml	*(½ tsp)*	nutmeg
675 g	*(1½ lb)*	peeled, cored, sliced 5 mm
	(¼ in)	tart cooking apples
15 g	*(½ oz)*	butter or margarine
5 ml	*(1 tsp)*	sugar
125 ml	*(4 fl oz)*	double cream

Heat oven to 200 °C (*400 °F*) mark 6. In large bowl stir together 300 g (*11 oz*) flour, 5 ml (*1 tsp*) sugar, salt, 1 ml (*¼ tsp*) cinnamon and 1 ml (*¼ tsp*) nutmeg. Cut in 75 g (*3 oz*) butter and shortening until crumbly. With fork mix in water until flour is moistened. Divide dough in half; shape into 2 balls and flatten. Wrap 1 ball in plastic wrap; refrigerate. On lightly floured surface roll out other ball into 30-cm (*12-in*) circle. Place in 23-cm (*9-in*) flan dish. Trim pastry to 1 cm (*½ in*) from rim of dish; set aside. In large bowl combine all filling ingredients *except* apples, 15 g (*½ oz*) butter, 5 ml (*1 tsp*) sugar and double cream. Add apples; toss lightly to coat. Spoon into prepared crust. Roll remaining pastry ball into 30-cm (*12-in*) circle;

cut 8 large slits in top crust. Place over pie; crimp or flute crust. Brush with melted 15 g (*½ oz*) butter; sprinkle with 5 ml (*1 tsp*) sugar. Cover edge of crust with 5-cm (*2-in*) strip of aluminum foil. Bake for 35 min.; remove aluminum foil. Continue baking for 10 to 20 min. or until crust is lightly browned and juice begins to bubble through slits in crust. Remove from oven; run knife through slits to open. Pour double cream evenly through all slits. Return to oven for 5 min. to warm double cream. Cool pie 30 min.; serve warm.

Tip: If desired, omit double cream for a traditional apple pie.

Cherry Orchard Pie

8 servings
1 hour 45 minutes

Grated orange rind spices this eye-catching lattice top cherry pie.

Crust

300 g	*(11 oz)* plain flour
1 ml	*(1/4 tsp)* salt
150 g	*(5 oz)* butter or margarine
60 to 75 ml	*(4 to 5 tbsp)* cold water

Filling

225 g	*(8 oz)* sugar
75 ml	*(5 tbsp)* plain flour
	Pinch of salt
900 g	*(2 lb)* canned red tart pitted cherries, drained
5 ml	*(1 tsp)* grated orange rind
	Milk
	Sugar

Heat oven to 200 °C (*400 °F*) mark 6. In large bowl stir together 300 g (*11 oz*) flour and 1 ml (*1/4 tsp*) salt. Cut in butter until crumbly. With fork mix in water until flour is moistened. Divide dough in half; shape into 2 balls and flatten. Wrap 1 ball in plastic wrap; refrigerate. On lightly floured surface roll out other ball into 30-cm (*12-in*) circle. Place in 23-cm (*9-in*) flan dish. Trim pastry to 1 cm (*1/2 in*) from rim of dish; set aside. In large bowl combine sugar, 75 ml (*5 tbsp*) flour and a pinch of salt. Add cherries and orange rind; toss lightly to coat. Spoon into prepared crust. With remaining pastry ball prepare lattice top. (See Desserts, Cakes & Pies page 471.) Brush strips with milk; sprinkle with sugar. Cover edge of crust with 5-cm (*2-in*) strip of aluminum foil. Bake for 50 to 60 min. or until crust is golden brown and filling bubbles in the centre. If desired, remove aluminum foil during last 5 min. If browning too quickly, shield lattice strips with aluminum foil.

Crumb Top Rhubarb Pie

8 servings
1 hour 30 minutes

Pecans and a crumb topping crown this delicious country favourite.

Crust

150 g	*(5 oz)* plain flour
	Pinch of salt
75 g	*(3 oz)* shortening
45 to 60 ml	*(3 to 4 tbsp)* cold water

Filling

275 g	*(6 oz)* sugar
45 ml	*(3 tbsp)* cornflour
2 ml	*(1/2 tsp)* cinnamon
1 ml	*(1/4 tsp)* nutmeg
500 g	*(1 lb)* sliced 5 mm (*1/4 in*) rhubarb
90 g	*(3 1/2 oz)* chopped pecans

Topping

150 g	*(5 oz)* plain flour
150 g	*(5 oz)* sugar
125 g	*(4 oz)* butter or margarine

Heat oven to 200 °C (*400 °F*) mark 6. In large bowl stir together 150 g (*5 oz*) flour and salt. Cut in shortening until crumbly. With fork mix in water until flour is moistened. Shape into a ball. On lightly floured surface roll into 30-cm (*12-in*) circle. Place in 23-cm (*9-in*) deepdish flan dish. Crimp or flute crust; set aside. In large bowl stir together all filling ingredients *except* rhubarb and pecans. Stir in rhubarb until well coated with sugar mixture. Spoon into pie shell. Sprinkle with pecans; set aside. In medium bowl stir together 150 g (*5 oz*) flour and 150 g (*5 oz*) sugar. Cut in butter until crumbly. Sprinkle mixture over rhubarb. Cover edge of crust with 5-cm (*2-in*) strip of aluminum foil. Bake for 50 to 60 min. or until topping is golden brown and filling bubbles around edges. If desired, remove aluminum foil during last 10 min.

Cherry Orchard Pie (top)
Crumb Top Rhubarb Pie (bottom)

8 servings
4 hours

Fresh Strawberry Almond Pie

Shortbread cookies and almonds create a delightful crust for this refreshing summer pie.

Crust

200 g	(*7 oz*) crushed shortbread cookies
50 ml	(*4 tbsp*) finely chopped blanched whole or slivered almonds
75 g	(*3 oz*) butter or margarine, melted

Filling

900 g	(*2 lb*) strawberries, hulled
225 g	(*8 oz*) sugar
45 ml	(*3 tbsp*) cornflour
75 ml	(*5 tbsp*) water
1 ml	(*1/4 tsp*) salt
2 ml	(*1/2 tsp*) almond extract

Sweetened whipped cream

Heat oven to 180 °C (*350 °F*) mark 4. In small bowl stir together all crust ingredients. Press on bottom and up sides of 23-cm (*9-in*) flan dish. Bake for 8 min. Cool completely. Mash enough strawberries to equal 250 ml (*8 fl oz*). In 2-litre (*3 1/2-pt*) saucepan combine sugar and cornflour. Stir in mashed strawberry mixture and water. Cook over med. heat, stirring constantly, until mixture thickens and comes to a full boil (8 to 15 min.). Boil 1 min.; remove from heat. Stir in salt and almond extract; cool 10 min. Fill baked crust with remaining strawberries; pour cooked strawberry mixture over strawberries. Refrigerate at least 3 hr.; garnish with sweetened whipped cream. Serve immediately.

8 servings
8 hours

Creamy Banana Pie With Lemon Zest

This banana cream pie is heavenly light and luscious.

23-cm	(*9-in*) baked pie shell
175 g	(*6 oz*) sugar
50 ml	(*4 tbsp*) cornflour
7 g	(*1/4 oz*) unflavoured gelatin
600 ml	(*1 pt*) milk
4	egg yolks, slightly beaten
30 g	(*1 oz*) butter or margarine

15 ml	(*1 tbsp*) vanilla
10 ml	(*2 tsp*) grated lemon rind
30 ml	(*2 tbsp*) lemon juice
3	med. bananas, sliced 5 mm (*1/4 in*)
175 ml	(*6 fl oz*) double cream
50 ml	(*4 tbsp*) apple jelly
15 ml	(*1 tbsp*) lemon juice
1	med. banana, sliced 5 mm (*1/4 in*)

In 2-litre (*3 1/2-pt*) saucepan combine sugar, cornflour and gelatin. Gradually stir in milk and egg yolks. Cook over med. heat, stirring constantly, until mixture comes to a full boil (10 to 12 min.). Stir in butter, vanilla and lemon rind until butter is melted; pour filling into large bowl. Cover; refrigerate until thickened (about 2 hr.). Place 30 ml (*2 tbsp*) lemon juice in small bowl; dip 3 sliced bananas into lemon juice. In chilled small mixer bowl, beat chilled double cream, scraping bowl often, until stiff peaks form (1 to 2 min.). By hand, fold whipped cream and bananas into pudding mixture. Pour into baked pie shell. Refrigerate at least 5 hr. or until firm. Just before serving, in 1-litre (*1 3/4-pt*) saucepan stir together apple jelly and 15 ml (*1 tbsp*) lemon juice. Cook over low heat, stirring occasionally, until apple jelly is melted (3 to 4 min.). Arrange remaining sliced banana 2.5 cm (*1 in*) from outside edge of pie to form a circle. Spoon or drizzle apple jelly mixture over bananas.

Creamy Banana Pie With Lemon Zest (top)
Fresh Strawberry Almond Pie (bottom)

8 servings
3 hours

Country Lemon Cream Pie

This refreshing lemon pie is creamy and rich.

23-cm	(*9-in*) baked pie shell	3	egg yolks, slightly beaten
		50 g	(*2 oz*) butter or margarine
Filling		50 ml	(*4 tbsp*) lemon juice
225 g	(*8 oz*) sugar	10 ml	(*2 tsp*) grated lemon rind
50 ml	(*4 tbsp*) cornflour	125 ml	(*4 fl oz*) sour cream
375 ml	(*13 fl oz*) milk		
	Pinch of salt		Sweetened whipped cream

In 2-litre (*3½-pt*) saucepan combine sugar, cornflour, milk and salt. Cook over med. heat, stirring constantly, until mixture comes to a full boil (10 to 12 min.). Reduce heat to low. Continue cooking, stirring constantly, 2 min. Remove from heat. In small bowl gradually stir 250 ml (*8 fl oz*) hot mixture into egg yolks. Return mixture to saucepan. Cook over med. heat, stirring constantly, 2 min. Remove from heat; stir in butter, lemon juice and lemon rind until butter is melted. Stir in sour cream; pour into baked pie shell. Refrigerate at least 2 hr. or until firm. Just before serving, garnish with sweetened whipped cream.

8 servings
3 hours

Chocolate Mint Silk Pie

Mint adds a refreshing touch to this delectable pie.

Crust		**Filling**	
18	crushed chocolate sandwich cookies	225 g	(*8 oz*) sugar
50 g	(*2 oz*) butter or margarine, melted	175 g	(*6 oz*) butter or margarine, softened
		3	(*30-g*) (*1-oz*) sq. semi-sweet chocolate, melted, cooled
		2 ml	(*½ tsp*) peppermint extract
		3	eggs
			Sweetened whipped cream

In medium bowl stir together crust ingredients. Press on bottom and sides of 23-cm (*9-in*) flan dish. Refrigerate 10 min. In small mixer bowl combine sugar and 175 g (*6 oz*) butter. Beat at med. speed, scraping bowl often, until well mixed (2 to 3 min.). Add chocolate and peppermint extract; continue beating until well mixed (1 to 2 min.). Add eggs; continue beating, scraping bowl often, until light and fluffy (5 min.). Spoon into prepared crust. Refrigerate at least 3 hr. or until set. If desired, garnish with sweetened whipped cream.

Chocolate Mint Silk Pie

Chocolate-Laced Pecan Pie

Chocolate-Laced Pecan Pie

8 servings
5 hours

Two all-time favourites — pecan pie and chocolate — come together in this extra rich pie.

	Single crust pie pastry*
150 g	(*5 oz*) sugar
75 g	(*3 oz*) butter or margarine, melted
250 ml	(*8 fl oz*) light corn syrup
3	eggs
2 ml	(*1/2 tsp*) salt

100 g	(*4 oz*) pecan halves
90 g	(*3 1/2 oz*) semi-sweet chocolate chips
	Pecan halves
	Semi-sweet chocolate chips, melted
	Sweetened whipped cream

Heat oven to 190 °C (*375 °F*) mark 5. Line 23-cm (*9-in*) flan dish with pastry; crimp or flute crust. Set aside. In small mixer bowl combine sugar, butter, corn syrup, eggs and salt. Beat at med. speed, scraping bowl often, until well mixed (1 to 2 min.). By hand, stir in 100 g (*4 oz*) pecans and 90 g (*3 1/2 oz*) chocolate chips. Pour into prepared pie shell; if desired, turn pecan halves right side up. Cover pie loosely with aluminum foil. Bake for 30 min. Remove aluminum foil; continue baking 10 to 15 min. or until filling is set. If browning too quickly, recover with aluminum foil. Cool; refrigerate at least 4 hr. or until ready to serve. If desired, dip additional pecan halves halfway in melted chocolate chips; refrigerate until set. Serve pie with sweetened whipped cream; garnish with dipped pecan halves.

*See Desserts, Cakes & Pies page 456 for single crust pie pastry recipe.

Tip: If desired, omit semi-sweet chocolate chips for a traditional pecan pie.

Maple Pecan Pumpkin Pie

8 servings
2 hours

A hint of maple in the filling, a drizzling over the pecans and a touch in the whipped cream makes traditional pumpkin pie extra ordinary.

	Single crust pie pastry*
450 g	(*16 oz*) canned pumpkin
50 ml	(*4 tbsp*) sugar
2	eggs, slightly beaten
250 ml	(*8 fl oz*) double cream
125 ml	(*4 fl oz*) pure maple syrup or maple flavoured syrup
5 ml	(*1 tsp*) cinnamon
2 ml	(*1/2 tsp*) nutmeg

1 ml	(*1/4 tsp*) ground ginger
1 ml	(*1/4 tsp*) ground cloves
50 g	(*2 oz*) pecan halves
30 ml	(*2 tbsp*) pure maple syrup or maple flavoured syrup
125 ml	(*4 fl oz*) double cream
15 ml	(*1 tbsp*) pure maple syrup or maple flavoured syrup

Heat oven to 190 °C (*375 °F*) mark 4. Line 23-cm (*9-in*) flan dish with pastry; crimp or flute crust. Set aside. In large bowl stir together pumpkin, sugar and eggs. Add remaining ingredients *except* pecans, 30 ml (*2 tbsp*) maple syrup, 125 ml (*4 fl oz*) double cream and 15 ml (*1 tbsp*) maple syrup. Pour into prepared pie shell. Cover edge of crust with 5-cm (*2-in*) strip of aluminum foil. Bake for 40 min. Remove aluminum foil. Bake for 15 to 25 min. or until knife inserted in centre comes out clean. Arrange pecan halves on top of pie; drizzle or brush 30 ml (*2 tbsp*) maple syrup over pecans. In chilled small mixer bowl, beat chilled double cream at high speed, scraping bowl often, until soft peaks form. Gradually add 15 ml (*1 tbsp*) maple syrup; continue beating until stiff peaks form (1 to 2 min.). Serve pie with whipped cream.

*See Desserts, Cakes & Pies page 456 for single crust pie pastry recipe.

Chewy Caramel Brownie Pie

8 servings
2 hours

*This brownie pie is exceedingly rich, chewy and irresistible
when topped with a scoop of ice cream.*

Brownie

125 g	(*4 oz*) butter or margarine
2	(30-g) (*1 oz*) sq. unsweetened chocolate
225 g	(*8 oz*) sugar
100 g	(*4 oz*) plain flour
2	eggs, slightly beaten
2 ml	(*1/2 tsp*) salt
2 ml	(*1/2 tsp*) baking powder
5 ml	(*1 tsp*) vanilla

Caramel

250 g	(*8 oz*) (30) caramels, unwrapped
45 ml	(*3 tbsp*) double cream
65 g	(*2 1/2 oz*) chopped pecans
50 ml	(*4 tbsp*) semi-sweet chocolate chips

Vanilla ice cream

Heat oven to 180 °C (*350 °F*) mark 4. In 2-litre (*3 1/2-pt*) saucepan combine butter and unsweetened chocolate. Cook over med. heat, stirring occasionally, until melted (4 to 6 min.). Stir in remaining brownie ingredients. Spread batter into greased 23-cm (*9-in*) flan dish. Bake for 20 to 25 min. or until brownie is firm to the touch. Meanwhile, in 1-litre (*1 3/4-pt*) saucepan cook caramels and double cream over med. low heat, stirring occasionally, until caramels are melted (5 to 6 min.). Remove brownie from oven; spread melted caramel mixture over entire baked brownie. Sprinkle with pecans and chocolate chips. Return to oven; bake for 3 to 5 min. or until caramel mixture is bubbly. Let stand 30 to 45 min.; cut into wedges. Serve warm with ice cream.

Celebration Ice Cream Pie

8 servings
9 hours

*This mile-high pie is snow-capped with a marshmallow cream meringue;
choose your favourite ice cream combinations for a celebration.*

23-cm	(*9-in*) baked pie shell
1 litre	(*1 3/4-pt*) praline pecan ice cream, slightly softened*
1 litre	(*1 3/4-pt*) chocolate almond fudge ice cream, slightly softened*
6	egg whites

500 ml	(*17 fl oz*) marshmallow cream

Chocolate sauce
Caramel sauce
Raspberry purée

In bottom of baked pie shell spread praline pecan ice cream. Freeze for 1 hr. Spread chocolate almond fudge ice cream on top of praline pecan ice cream. Freeze for 1 hr. Heat oven to 220 °C (*425 °F*) mark 7. Meanwhile, in large mixer bowl beat egg whites on high speed, scraping bowl often, until stiff peaks form (2 to 3 min.). Reduce speed to low. Gradually beat in marshmallow cream until smooth. Spread carefully onto frozen pie, sealing to edges of crust. Bake for 3 to 5 min. or until lightly browned. Freeze 6 hr. or overnight or until firm. Serve with chocolate sauce, caramel sauce or raspberry purée.

*Other Ice Cream Flavour Combinations:

Chocolate Chip and Rocky Road
Strawberry and Chocolate
Peppermint Bon Bon and Chocolate Chip
Strawberry Revel and Chocolate Revel
Vanilla and Chocolate

Tip: To prepare raspberry purée, place 250 g (*9 oz*) fresh raspberries or 275 g (*10 oz*) frozen raspberries, thawed, in 1.25-litre (*2 1/4-pt*) blender container. Blend on high speed until puréed. If desired, strain sauce to remove seeds. Sweeten with sugar to taste.

Celebration Ice Cream Pie

8 servings
6 hours 30 minutes

Chocolate Lover's Ice Cream Pie

Straight from the ice house, this is a chocolate lover's ultimate dessert.

18	crushed chocolate chip cookies
75 g	(*3 oz*) butter or margarine, melted
1 litre	(*1¾ pt*) chocolate ice cream, slightly softened

Chocolate-flavoured syrup
Sweetened whipped cream
Chocolate chip cookies, broken into pieces

In medium bowl stir together crushed cookies and butter. Press on bottom and sides of 23-cm (*9-in*) flan dish. Freeze until firm (10 min.). Spread ice cream over crust. Cover; freeze until firm (6 hr. or over-night). Just before serving, drizzle pie with chocolate syrup. If desired, garnish with sweetened whipped cream and pieces of chocolate chip cookies.

12 servings
13 hours

Blueberry-Peach Ice Cream Torte

Fresh peaches swirled in ice cream and topped with a blueberry sauce make an elegant presentation.

3	med. fresh peaches, peeled, sliced*
30 ml	(*2 tbsp*) sugar
12	sponge fingers, split
2 litres	(*3½ pt*) vanilla ice cream, slightly softened

Sauce

75 ml	(*5 tbsp*) sugar
30 ml	(*2 tbsp*) cornflour
250 ml	(*8 fl oz*) water
30 g	(*1 oz*) butter or margarine
30 ml	(*2 tbsp*) lemon juice
5 ml	(*1 tsp*) grated lemon rind
300 g	(*11 oz*) fresh or frozen blueberries (do not thaw)

In 1.25-litre (*2¼-pt*) blender container combine peach slices and 30 ml (*2 tbsp*) sugar. Cover; blend at high speed until well blended (30 to 40 sec.). Set aside. Place split sponge fingers upright (rounded side out) around edge of 25-cm (*10-in*) springform tin, fitting closely together. Place ice cream in large bowl. Swirl in peach mixture. Place, by spoonfuls, evenly into prepared tin, pressing gently to level ice cream. Cover with aluminum foil; freeze at least 12 hr. or overnight. In 2-litre (*3½-pt*) saucepan combine 75 ml (*5 tbsp*) sugar and cornflour; stir in water. Cook over med. heat, stirring occasionally, until mixture thickens and comes to a full boil (3 to 5 min.). Boil 1 min. Stir in butter, lemon juice and lemon rind. Cool 10 min.

Stir in blueberries. Just before serving, pour sauce over top of torte.

*375 g (*13 oz*) frozen sliced peaches, thawed, can be substituted for fresh peaches.

Tip: 23-cm (*9-in*) round cake tin can be substituted for 25-cm (*10-in*) springform tin. Line with aluminum foil, extending excess aluminum foil over edges. After torte is frozen, lift torte from tin, using aluminum foil as handles. Remove aluminum foil.

Tip: Fresh blueberries make a clear sauce; frozen blueberries make a blueberry-coloured sauce.

Blueberry-Peach Ice Cream Torte (top)
Chocolate Lover's Ice Cream Pie (bottom)

How To: Buy Fresh Fruits

Fruit:	Peak Season:	Look for:
Apples	All year	Firm, bruise-free apples. Choose specific varieties according to use.
Avocados	All year	Avocados which yield to gentle pressure, are bruise-free and do not have dark, soft, sunken spots.
Bananas	All year	Yellow or yellow tipped with green, bruise-free peel.
Blueberries	Summer	Round, firm, uniform dark blueberries with a silvery cast.
Cherries	Summer	Dark red coloured skins, green stems and plump cherries.
Cranberries	Fall	Shiny, firm, red, plump berries.
Grapes	All year	Plump, slightly soft grapes that are well attached to stems. Green grapes should be yellow-green; red grapes should be predominantly red.
Kiwi Fruit	Spring, summer and fall	Plump, blemish-free fruits.
Lemons, Limes and Oranges	All year	Smooth, blemish-free, thin-skinned, full-colour fruits.
Melons	Spring, summer and fall	Firm, heavy melons with good colour, aroma and smooth stem ends. Cantaloupes should have pronounced netting, green honeydew should have a waxy, white rind barely tinged with green. Watermelon should have symmetrical shape, a dull surface and an underside that's yellowish or cream coloured.
Peaches	Summer	Firm for slightly soft peaches with a creamy yellow background colour.
Pears	All year	Slightly firm pears. A minor scar or surface blemish does not affect the fruit's flesh.
Pineapples	All year	Plump, slightly firm fruit with green leaves and fragrant aroma.
Raspberries	Summer	Plump berries of medium red colour with no stems attached.
Rhubarb	Spring	Firm, crisp stalks with fresh looking leaves.
Strawberries	Spring, summer and fall	Plump, bright red berries with fresh green caps.

To Roll Out Pastry:

1.   Using a stockinet-covered or floured rolling pin, roll out pastry on lightly floured pastry cloth. For a uniform circle, roll pastry from centre to outside edge in four directions. For even thickness, lift rolling pin as you approach the edge.

2.   To keep circular, occasionally push edges in gently with sides of hands. Prevent sticking by gently lifting pastry occasionally and sprinkling cloth with flour, if necessary.

3.   To transfer pastry to flan dish, fold pastry into quarters. Place in flan dish with point in centre. Gently unfold and ease into flan dish, pressing pastry gently with fingertips to fit snugly into flan dish. This prevents stretching and shrinking of pastry.

To Prepare Decorative Pie Pastries:

Forked: Flatten pastry evenly on rim of flan dish. With kitchen shears trim pastry even with edge of flan dish. Dip tines of fork into flour. Press firmly into edge of pastry. Continue around entire edge.

Crimped: Fold and roll edge of pastry under — even with flan dish. Pinch pastry in V-shape between thumb and index finger on outside edge of pastry with other index finger on inside edge of pastry. Continue around entire edge.

Diagonally Fluted or Rope: Fold and roll edge of pastry under — even with flan dish. Press thumb at an angle into edge of crust. Pinch pastry between thumb and knuckle of index finger. Place thumb in groove left by knuckle and repeat. Continue around entire edge.

Decorative Leaf: With paring knife, cut leaf shapes from pastry scraps. With tip of knife, draw line down center of each leaf, creating a vein. Flatten pastry evenly on rim of flan dish. With kitchen shears, trim pastry even with edge of flan dish. Dampen edge of pastry and arrange leaves in overlapping pattern around entire edge.

Ruffle: Fold and roll pastry under — even with flan dish. With hand inside of pastry edge, place thumb and index finger 2.5 cm (*1 in*) apart on outside of pastry edge. With other hand on outside of pastry edge, place index finger on inside of pastry between thumb and index finger. Pull pastry toward outside. Continue around entire edge.

Simple Lattice Top: With kitchen shears, trim bottom pastry to 1 cm (*¹/2 in*) from rim of flan dish. Fill. Roll top pastry into 28-cm (*11-in*) circle. With sharp knife or pastry wheel, cut circle into 10 (1-cm) (*¹/2-in*) strips. Place 5 strips, 2.5 cm (*1 in*) apart, across filling in flan dish. Place remaining 5 strips, 2.5 cm (*1 in*) apart, at right angles to the strips already in place. With kitchen shears, trim strips. Fold trimmed edge of bottom pastry over strips; build up an edge. Seal; flute edge as desired.

COOKIES & CANDY

When Saturday was baking day, the big kitchen was abuzz with activity. Never mind that the heat of the stove made the room almost too warm to bear. If you stayed around long enough, and especially if you offered to help, you could win the first samples.

During the holiday season, baking became a marathon event that went on day after delicious day. There were gifts of sweets for everyone. A tin of cookies for the mailman. Sugar cookies that you helped decorate. Spicy drop cookies, plump with raisins. And chewy caramel nut bars.

But the best treats of baking day were the ones you got to eat. There were always special surprises in your lunchbox, like a gingerbread man with creamy white frosting, a crunchy piece of peanut brittle or brownies, unbelievably fudgy and rich with a cream cheese filling to add even more goodness.

And after every baking day, an assortment of sweets was packed away in boxes and tins so that friends and neighbors who dropped by could share in the sweet treasury of the kitchen.

3 dozen
45 minutes

Double Fudge Cream Cheese Brownies

Two kinds of chocolate and cream cheese make these
homemade brownies absolutely yummy.

Brownies

225 g	(*8 oz*) butter or margarine
4	(30-g) (*1 oz*) unsweetened chocolate
450 g	(*1 lb*) sugar
225 g	(*8 oz*) plain flour
4	eggs, slightly beaten
5 ml	(*1 tsp*) salt
5 ml	(*1 tsp*) baking powder
10 ml	(*2 tsp*) vanilla
175 g	(*6 oz*) semi-sweet chocolate chips

Heat oven to 180 °C (*350 °F*) mark 4. In 2-litre (*3¹/2-pt*) saucepan combine 225 g (*8 oz*) butter and unsweetened chocolate. Cook over med. heat, stirring occasionally, until melted (4 to 6 min.). Stir in remaining brownie ingredients *except* chocolate chips. Fold in chocolate chips. Spread half of batter into greased

Filling

50 ml	(*4 tbsp*) sugar
30 g	(*1 oz*) butter or margarine, softened
75 g	(*3 oz*) cream cheese, softened
1	egg
15 ml	(*1 tbsp*) plain flour
2 ml	(*¹/2 tsp*) vanilla

33 x 23-cm (*13 x 9-in*) baking tin. In small bowl stir together all filling ingredients. Spread over brownie mixture. Spoon remaining batter over cream cheese. (Batter will not entirely cover cream cheese mixture.) Bake for 30 to 35 min. or until brownies begin to pull away from sides of tin.

3 dozen
45 minutes

Caramel 'n Chocolate Pecan Bars

Popular candy flavours combined in an easy bar.

Crust

300 g	(*11 oz*) plain flour
175 g	(*6 oz*) firmly packed brown sugar
125 g	(*4 oz*) butter or margarine, softened
100 g	(*4 oz*) pecan halves

Heat oven to 180 °C (*350 °F*) mark 4. In large mixer bowl combine all crust ingredients *except* pecans. Beat at med. speed, scraping bowl often, until well mixed and particles are fine (2 to 3 min.). Press on bottom of 33 x 23-cm (*13 x 9-in*) baking tin. Sprinkle pecans evenly over unbaked crust. In 1-litre (*1³/4-pt*) saucepan combine 150 g (*5 oz*) butter and 90 g (*3¹/2 oz*) brown sugar. Cook over med. heat, stirring constantly, until mixture comes to a full boil.

Caramel Layer

150 g	(*5 oz*) butter or margarine
90 g	(*3¹/2 oz*) firmly packed brown sugar
175 g	(*6 oz*) semi-sweet chocolate chips

Boil, stirring constantly, until small amount of mixture dropped into ice water forms a firm ball or candy thermometer reaches 117 °C (*242 °F*) (about 1 min.). Pour evenly over pecans and crust. Bake for 18 to 22 min. or until entire caramel layer is bubbly. Remove from oven. Immediately sprinkle with chips; allow to melt slightly (2 to 3 min.). Swirl chips leaving some whole for a marbled effect. Cool completely; cut into bars.

Double Fudge Cream Cheese Brownies (right)
Caramel 'n Chocolate Pecan Bars (left)

Cheesecake Squares (top)
Lemon-Butter Bars (bottom)

16 bars
50 minutes

Cheesecake Squares

The flavour of cheesecake in an easy-to-make bar.

Crust

150 g	*(5 oz)* plain flour
90 g	*(3¹/2 oz)* firmly packed brown sugar
75 g	*(3 oz)* butter or margarine, softened
65 g	*(2¹/2 oz)* chopped walnuts or pecans

Filling

225 g	*(8 oz)* cream cheese, softened
50 ml	*(4 tbsp)* sugar
1	egg
30 ml	*(2 tbsp)* milk
30 ml	*(2 tbsp)* lemon juice
2 ml	*(¹/2 tsp)* vanilla

Heat oven to 180 °C (*350 °F*) mark 4. In large mixer bowl combine flour, brown sugar and butter. Beat at low speed, scraping bowl often, until mixture is crumbly (2 to 3 min.). By hand, stir in nuts. *Reserve half of mixture for topping*; press remaining mixture on bottom of 20-cm (*8-in*) sq. baking tin. Bake for 8 to 10 min. or until lightly browned. Meanwhile, in small mixer bowl combine all filling ingredients.

Beat at med. speed, scraping bowl often, until smooth (4 to 5 min.). Spread over hot crust. Sprinkle with reserved crumb mixture. Continue baking for 23 to 30 min. or until golden brown. Cool; cut into bars. Store refrigerated.

Holiday Squares: Stir 50 ml (*4 tbsp*) red and 50 ml (*4 tbsp*) green chopped candied cherries into filling mixture.

16 bars
50 minutes

Lemon-Butter Bars

Tangy lemon and creamy butter combine to make these classic bars.

Crust

200 g	*(7 oz)* plain flour
50 ml	*(4 tbsp)* sugar
125 g	*(4 oz)* butter or margarine, softened

Filling

150 g	*(5 oz)* sugar
2	eggs
30 ml	*(2 tbsp)* plain flour
1 ml	*(¹/4 tsp)* baking powder
45 ml	*(3 tbsp)* lemon juice
	Icing sugar

Heat oven to 180 °C (*350 °F*) mark 4. In small mixer bowl combine all crust ingredients. Beat at low speed, scraping bowl often, until mixture is crumbly (2 to 3 min.). Press on bottom of 20-cm (*8-in*) sq. baking tin. Bake for 15 to 20 min. or until edges are lightly browned. Meanwhile, in small mixer bowl combine all filling ingredients. Beat at low speed, scraping bowl often, until well mixed. Pour filling over hot crust. Continue baking for 18 to 20 min. or until filling is set. Sprinkle with icing sugar; cool.

Microwave Directions: Prepare crust as directed left. Press on bottom of 20-cm (*8-in*) sq. baking dish. Microwave on HIGH until top looks dry (4 to 5 min.). Meanwhile, in small microwave-safe mixer bowl combine all filling ingredients. Beat at low speed, scraping bowl often, until well mixed. Microwave filling on HIGH, stirring every min., until warm and slightly thickened (2 to 4 min.). Pour over hot crust. Microwave on HIGH, turning dish ¹/4 turn after half the time, until filling is just set in center (2 to 5 min.). Sprinkle with icing sugar; cool.

Glazed Apple Pie Bars

Glazed Apple Pie Bars

Apple pie — an all-time favourite crowd-pleasing treat.

Crust

375 g	*(13 oz)* plain flour
5 ml	*(1 tsp)* salt
225 g	*(8 oz)* butter or margarine, softened
1	egg, separated, yolk beaten with enough milk to equal 150 ml *(1/4 pt)*, *reserve white*

Filling

65 g	*(2 1/2 oz)* crushed cornflake cereal
8 to 10	med. cooking apples, cored, peeled, sliced
225 g	*(8 oz)* sugar
7 ml	*(1 1/2 tsp)* cinnamon
2 ml	*(1/2 tsp)* nutmeg
1	*reserved* egg white
30 ml	*(2 tbsp)* sugar
2 ml	*(1/2 tsp)* cinnamon

Glaze

125 g	*(4 oz)* icing sugar
15 to 30 ml	*(1 to 2 tbsp)* milk
2 ml	*(1/2 tsp)* vanilla

Heat oven to 180 °C *(350 °F)* mark 4. In medium bowl combine flour and salt; cut in butter until crumbly. With fork stir in egg yolk and milk until dough forms a ball; divide in half. On lightly floured surface roll half of dough into 38 x 25-cm *(15 x 10-in)* rectangle; place on bottom of ungreased 38 x 25 x 2.5-cm *(15 x 10 x 1-in)* Swiss roll tin. Sprinkle with cereal; layer apples over cereal. In small bowl combine 225 g *(8 oz)* sugar, 7 ml *(1 1/2 tsp)* cinnamon and nutmeg. Sprinkle over apples. Roll remaining half of dough into 39 x 26-cm *(15 1/2 x 10 1/2-in)* rectangle; place over apples. In small bowl beat egg white with fork until foamy; brush over top crust. In small bowl stir together 30 ml *(2 tbsp)* sugar and 2 ml *(1/2 tsp)* cinnamon; sprinkle over crust. Bake for 45 to 60 min. or until lightly browned. In small bowl stir together all glaze ingredients; drizzle over warm crust. Cut into bars.

Graham Cracker Caramel Crisps

Graham crackers are topped with marshmallows, buttery syrup and lots of almonds and coconut.

12	double graham crackers		5 ml	*(1 tsp)* cinnamon
100 g	*(4 oz)* miniature marshmallows		5 ml	*(1 tsp)* vanilla
175 g	*(6 oz)* butter or margarine		150 g	*(5 oz)* sliced almonds
130 g	*(4 1/2 oz)* firmly packed brown sugar		100 g	*(4 oz)* desiccated coconut

Heat oven to 180 °C *(350 °F)* mark 4. Line 38 x 25 x 2.5-cm *(15 x 10 x 1-in)* Swiss roll tin with graham crackers. Sprinkle marshmallows evenly over crackers. In 2-litre *(3 1/2-pt)* saucepan combine butter, brown sugar, cinnamon and vanilla. Cook over med. heat, stirring constantly, until brown sugar is dissolved and butter is melted (4 to 5 min.). Pour evenly over crackers and marshmallows; sprinkle with almonds and coconut. Bake for 8 to 12 min. or until lightly browned. Cool completely; cut into bars.

Frosted Orange Date Bars

Luxuriously moist, old-fashioned date bars are accented with orange rind
and a buttery orange frosting.

4 dozen
60 minutes

Bars

150 g	(*5 oz*) sugar
125 g	(*4 oz*) butter or margarine
125 ml	(*4 fl oz*) water
225 g	(*8 oz*) chopped dates
175 g	(*6 oz*) plain flour
125 g	(*4 oz*) chopped pecans
175 ml	(*6 fl oz*) milk
50 ml	(*2 fl oz*) orange juice
2	eggs
3 ml	(*3/4 tsp*) bicarbonate of soda
2 ml	(*1/2 tsp*) salt
15 ml	(*1 tbsp*) grated orange rind

Frosting

375 g	(*13 oz*) icing sugar
75 g	(*3 oz*) butter or margarine, softened
75 g	(*3 oz*) cream cheese, softened
15 ml	(*1 tbsp*) grated orange rind
30 to 45 ml	(*2 to 3 tbsp*) orange juice

Heat oven to 180 °C (*350 °F*) mark 4. In 3-litre (*5-pt*) saucepan combine sugar, 125 g (*4 oz*) butter, water and dates. Cook over low heat, stirring constantly, until dates are softened (5 to 8 min.). Remove from heat. By hand, stir in remaining bar ingredients until well mixed. Spread into greased 38 x 25 x 2.5-cm (*15 x 10 x 1-in*) Swiss roll tin. Bake for 15 to 20 min. or until wooden pick inserted in centre comes out clean. Cool completely. In small mixer bowl combine all frosting ingredients. Beat at med. speed, scraping bowl often, until light and fluffy (2 to 3 min.). Spread over cooled bars; cut into bars.

Old-World Raspberry Bars

Rich, moist bars filled with flavourful raspberry preserves.

2 dozen
60 minutes

350 g	(*12 oz*) plain flour
225 g	(*8 oz*) sugar
125 g	(*4 oz*) chopped pecans
225 g	(*8 oz*) butter or margarine, softened

1	egg
250 g	(*9 oz*) raspberry preserves*

Heat oven to 180 °C (*350 °F*) mark 4. In large mixer bowl combine all ingredients except raspberry preserves. Beat at low speed, scraping bowl often, until well mixed (2 to 3 min.). *Reserve 1/4 of mixture*; set aside. Press remaining mixture into greased 20-cm (*8-in*) sq. baking tin; spread preserves to within 1 cm (*1/2 in*) from edge. Crumble reserved mixture over preserves. Bake for 40 to 50 min. or until lightly browned. Cool completely; cut into bars.

*Your favourite flavour preserves can be substituted for raspberry preserves.

Old-World Raspberry Bars

Nutty Chocolate Chunk Cookies

3 dozen
45 minutes

Everyone loves these buttery cookies chock full of chocolate and nuts.

130 g	(*4¹/₂ oz*) firmly packed brown sugar	5 ml	(*1 tsp*) bicarbonate of soda
100 g	(*4 oz*) sugar	2 ml	(*¹/₂ tsp*) salt
225 g	(*8 oz*) butter or margarine, softened	125 g	(*4 oz*) coarsely chopped walnuts
1	egg	225 g	(*8 oz*) milk chocolate candy bar, cut into
7 ml	(*1¹/₂ tsp*) vanilla		5-mm (*¹/₄-in*) pieces
350 g	(*12 oz*) plain flour		

Heat oven to 190 °C (*375 °F*) mark 5. In large mixer bowl combine brown sugar, sugar, butter, egg and vanilla. Beat at med. speed, scraping bowl often, until well mixed (1 to 2 min.). Add flour, bicarbonate of soda and salt. Continue beating until well mixed (1 to 2 min.). By hand, stir in walnuts and chocolate. Drop dough by rounded tablespoonfuls 5 cm (*2 in*) apart onto baking sheets. Bake for 9 to 11 min. or until lightly browned. Cool 1 min. before removing from baking sheets.

Jumbo Candy & Nut Cookies

2 dozen
30 minutes

These oversized cookies are a family favourite.

225 g	(*8 oz*) sugar	125 g	(*4 oz*) quick-cooking oats
175 g	(*6 oz*) firmly packed brown sugar	5 ml	(*1 tsp*) bicarbonate of soda
225 g	(*8 oz*) butter or margarine, softened	2 ml	(*¹/₂ tsp*) salt
2	eggs	450 g	(*1 lb*) candy coated milk chocolate
15 ml	(*1 tbsp*) vanilla		pieces
300 g	(*11 oz*) plain flour	125 g	(*4 oz*) coarsely chopped peanuts

Heat oven to 180 °C (*350 °F*) mark 4. In large mixer bowl combine sugar, brown sugar, butter, eggs and vanilla. Beat at med. speed, scraping bowl often, until light and fluffy (2 to 3 min.). Add remaining ingredients *except* candy and peanuts. Beat at low speed, scraping bowl often, until well mixed (2 to 3 min.). By hand, stir in candy and peanuts. Drop dough by scant 50 ml (*4 tbsp*) 5 cm (*2 in*) apart onto greased baking sheets. Bake for 13 to 16 min. or until light golden brown.

Nutty Chocolate Chunk Cookies (left)
Jumbo Candy & Nut Cookies (right)

Old-Fashioned Oatmeal Cookies (right)
Chunky Peanut Cookies (left)

4 dozen
60 minutes

Old-Fashioned Oatmeal Cookies

These tasty, chewy cookies will remind you of Grandma's always-full cookie jar.

225 g	(*8 oz*) quick-cooking oats	5 ml	(*1 tsp*) cinnamon
350 g	(*12 oz*) firmly packed brown sugar	2 ml	(*1/2 tsp*) salt
225 g	(*8 oz*) butter or margarine, softened	10 ml	(*2 tsp*) vanilla
2	eggs	250 g	(*9 oz*) plain flour
5 ml	(*1 tsp*) bicarbonate of soda	250 g	(*9 oz*) raisins

Heat oven to 190 °C (*375 °F*) mark 5. In large mixer bowl combine all ingredients *except* flour and raisins. Beat at low speed, scraping bowl often, until well mixed (1 to 2 min.). Add flour; continue beating until well mixed (1 to 2 min.). By hand, stir in raisins. Drop dough by rounded teaspoonfuls 5 cm (*2 in*) apart onto greased baking sheets. Bake for 8 to 10 min. or until edges are lightly browned.

4 dozen
60 minutes

Chunky Peanut Cookies

A peanutty tasting lunchbox cookie.

250 g	(*9 oz*) plain flour	5 ml	(*1 tsp*) salt
100 g	(*4 oz*) sugar	2 ml	(*1/2 tsp*) bicarbonate of soda
90 g	(*3 1/2 oz*) firmly packed brown sugar	2 ml	(*1/2 tsp*) vanilla
125 g	(*4 oz*) butter or margarine, softened	300 g	(*11 oz*) salted peanuts
2	eggs		

Heat oven to 180 °C (*350 °F*) mark 4. In large mixer bowl combine all ingredients *except* peanuts. Beat at low speed, scraping bowl often, until well mixed (2 to 3 min.). By hand, stir in peanuts. Drop dough by rounded teaspoonfuls 5 cm (*2 in*) apart onto greased baking sheets. Bake for 8 to 12 min. or until lightly browned.

SugarTopped Butter Cookies

4 dozen
60 minutes

Old-fashioned crisp butter cookies — delicious served at 'tea time' or dipped in milk.

350 g	(*12 oz*) plain flour
225 g	(*8 oz*) sugar
225 g	(*8 oz*) butter or margarine, softened

1	egg
5 ml	(*1 tsp*) bicarbonate of soda
5 ml	(*1 tsp*) vanilla

Heat oven to 180 °C (*350 °F*) mark 4. In large mixer bowl combine all ingredients. Beat at med. speed, scraping bowl often, until well mixed (2 to 3 min.). Shape rounded teaspoonfuls of dough into 2.5-cm (*1-in*) balls; place 5 cm (*2 in*) apart on greased baking sheets. Flatten cookies to 5-mm (*1/4-in*) thickness with bottom of glass dipped in sugar. Bake for 8 to 11 min. or until edges are very lightly browned.

Chocolate Chip Butter Cookies: By hand, stir 175 g (*6 oz*) mini semi-sweet chocolate chips into dough.

Brickle Bit Butter Cookies: By hand, stir 175 g (*6 oz*) almond brickle bits into dough.

Holiday Thumbprint Cookies

3 dozen
60 minute

Make a beautiful cookie tray using one cookie dough with many variations.

Cookies

300 g	(*11 oz*) plain flour
90 g	(*3 1/2 oz*) firmly packed brown sugar
225 g	(*8 oz*) butter or margarine, softened
2	eggs, separated
	Pinch of salt
5 ml	(*1 tsp*) vanilla or almond extract

Suggested Coatings

200 g	(*7 oz*) finely chopped peanuts, almonds, pecans or walnuts
	Coloured sugars
	Cinnamon and sugar

Suggested Toppings

Chocolate stars
Candied cherries
Caramels, cut in half
Maraschino cherries
Fruit preserves

Heat oven to 180 °C (*350 °F*) mark 4. In large mixer bowl combine all cookie ingredients *except* egg whites. Beat at low speed, scraping bowl often, until well mixed (2 to 3 min.). Shape rounded teaspoonfuls of dough into 2.5-cm (*1-in*) balls. In small bowl beat egg whites with fork until foamy. Dip each ball of dough into egg white; roll in choice of nuts. (If using coloured sugars or cinnamon and sugar, do not dip balls of dough in egg white. Roll balls of dough in coloured sugars or cinnamon and sugar.) Place 2.5 cm (*1 in*) apart on greased baking sheets. Make a depression in center of each cookie with back of teaspoon. Bake for 8 min.; remove from oven. Fill centers with choice of suggested toppings; continue baking for 6 to 10 min. or until lightly browned.

Holiday Thumbprint Cookies

Melt-In-Your-Mouth Spritz

Melt-In-Your-Mouth Spritz

5 dozen
60 minutes

Perfect spritz cookies every time, plus five variations to create variety.

150 g	(*5 oz*) sugar		2 ml	(*¹/₂ tsp*) salt
225 g	(*8 oz*) butter or margarine, softened		10 ml	(*2 tsp*) vanilla
1	egg		350 g	(*12 oz*) plain flour

Heat oven to 200 °C (*400 °F*) mark 6. In large mixer bowl combine all ingredients *except* flour. Beat at med. speed, scraping bowl often, until mixture is light and fluffy (2 to 3 min.). Add flour. Reduce speed to low. Continue beating, scraping bowl often, until well mixed (2 to 3 min.). If desired, add the ingredients from one of the following variations. If dough is too soft, cover; refrigerate until firm enough to form cookies (30 to 45 min.). Place dough into cookie press; form desired shapes 2.5 cm (*1 in*) apart on baking sheets. Bake for 6 to 8 min. or until edges are lightly browned.

Variations:

Spiced Spritz: To dough add: 5 ml (*1 tsp*) *each* cinnamon and nutmeg, 2 ml (*¹/₂ tsp*) allspice, 1 ml (*¹/₄ tsp*) cloves. Glaze: In small bowl stir together 125 g (*4 oz*) icing sugar, 30 ml (*2 tbsp*) milk and 2 ml (*¹/₂ tsp*) vanilla until smooth. Drizzle over warm cookies.

Eggnog Spritz: To dough add: 5 ml (*1 tsp*) nutmeg. Glaze: In small bowl stir together 125 g (*4 oz*) icing sugar, 50 g (*2 oz*) softened butter, 30 ml (*2 tbsp*) water and 1 ml (*¹/₄ tsp*) rum extract until smooth. Drizzle over warm cookies.

Chocolate Flecked Spritz: To dough add: 50 ml (*4 tbsp*) coarsely grated semi-sweet chocolate.

Pina Colada Spritz: Omit vanilla in dough recipe above and add: 15 ml (*1 tbsp*) pineapple juice and 1 ml (*¹/₄ tsp*) rum extract; stir in 50 g (*2 oz*) finely chopped coconut. Frosting: In small mixer bowl combine 125 g (*4 oz*) icing sugar, 30 ml (*2 tbsp*) softened butter, 30 ml (*2 tbsp*) pineapple preserves and 15 ml (*1 tbsp*) pineapple juice. Beat at med. speed, scraping bowl often, until light and fluffy (2 to 3 min.). Spread on cooled cookies. If desired, sprinkle with toasted coconut.

Chocolate Mint Spritz: To dough add: 1 ml (*¹/₄ tsp*) mint extract. Immediately after removing cookies from oven place 1 chocolate candy kiss on each cookie.

Butter Pecan Tartlets

These mini tarts taste like pecan pie.

3 dozen
60 minutes

Tart Shells

125 g	(*4 oz*) butter or margarine, softened
100 g	(*4 oz*) sugar
1	egg
5 ml	(*1 tsp*) almond extract
250 g	(*9 oz*) plain flour

Heat oven to 200 °C (*400 °F*) mark 6. In large mixer bowl combine all tart shell ingredients. Beat at med. speed, scraping bowl often, until mixture is crumbly (2 to 3 min.). Press 15 ml (*1 tbsp*) mixture into cups of mini muffin tins to form 36 (4.5 to 5-cm) (*1¾ to 2-in*) shells. Bake for 7 to 10 min. or until very lightly browned. Remove from oven. Reduce oven to 180 °C (*350 °F*) mark 4. Meanwhile, in 2-litre

Filling

125 g	(*4 oz*) icing sugar
125 g	(*4 oz*) butter or margarine
75 ml	(*5 tbsp*) dark corn syrup
125 g	(*4 oz*) chopped pecans
36	pecan halves

(*3½-pt*) saucepan combine all filling ingredients *except* chopped pecans and pecan halves. Cook over med. heat, stirring occasionally, until mixture comes to a full boil (4 to 5 min.). Remove from heat; stir in chopped pecans. Spoon into baked shells. Top each with a pecan half. Bake for 5 min. Cool; remove from tins.

Butter Pecan Tartlets

Orange Spiced Gingerbread Cookies

4 dozen
2 hour 45 minutes

*Traditional cut-out gingerbread cookies are spiced with grated orange rind
for a subtle new taste sensation.*

Cookies

75 ml	(*5 tbsp*) firmly packed brown sugar
75 g	(*3 oz*) butter or margarine, softened
150 ml	(*1/4 pt*) light molasses
1	egg
10 ml	(*2 tsp*) grated orange rind
400 g	(*14 oz*) plain flour
5 ml	(*1 tsp*) ginger
2 ml	(*1/2 tsp*) bicarbonate of soda
2 ml	(*1/2 tsp*) salt

Frosting

500 g	(*17 1/2 oz*) icing sugar
125 g	(*4 oz*) butter or margarine, softened
45 to 60 ml	(*3 to 4 tbsp*) milk
10 ml	(*2 tsp*) vanilla

In large mixer bowl combine brown sugar, 75 g
(*3 oz*), molasses, egg and orange rind. Beat at med.
speed, scraping bowl often, until smooth and creamy
(1 to 2 min.). Add remaining cookie ingredients.
Reduce to low speed. Continue beating, scraping bowl
often, until well mixed (1 to 2 min.). Cover; refrigerate
at least 2 hr. Heat oven to 190 °C (*375 °F*) mark 5.
Roll out dough, 1/2 at a time (keeping remaining
dough refrigerated), on well-floured surface to 5-mm

(*1/4-in*) thickness. Cut with 8 to 10-cm (*3 to 4-in*)
cookie cutters. Place 2.5 cm (*1 in*) apart on greased
baking sheets. Bake for 6 to 8 min. or until no indentation remains when touched. Cool completely. In small
mixer bowl combine all frosting ingredients. Beat at
low speed, scraping bowl often, until fluffy (1 to
2 min.). If desired, colour frosting with food colouring.
Decorate cookies with frosting.

Homemade Caramel Corn 'n Nuts

4.5 litres (*8 pt*)
1 hour 25 minutes

This best-ever caramel corn is made extra special with the addition of mixed nuts.

225 g	(*4 oz*) popped popcorn
350 g	(*12 oz*) firmly packed brown sugar
225 g	(*8 oz*) butter
125 ml	(*4 fl oz*) dark corn syrup

2 ml	(*1/2 tsp*) salt
2 ml	(*1/2 tsp*) bicarbonate of soda
150 g	(*5 oz*) mixed salted nuts

Heat oven to 93 °C (*200 °F*) mark 1/4. In roasting
tin place popcorn; set aside. In 2-litre (*3 1/2-pt*) saucepan combine brown sugar, butter, corn syrup and salt.
Cook over med. heat, stirring occasionally, until mixture comes to a full boil (12 to 14 min.). Continue
cooking, stirring occasionally, until candy thermometer reaches 114 °C (*238 °F*) or small amount of mixture dropped in ice water forms a soft ball (4 to

6 min.). Remove from heat; stir in bicarbonate of soda.
Pour over popcorn; sprinkle nuts over caramel mixture. Stir until all popcorn is coated. Bake for 20 min.;
stir. Continue baking for 25 min. Remove from oven;
immediately place caramel corn on waxed paper. Cool
completely. Break into pieces. Store in tightly covered
container.

Orange Spiced Gingerbread Cookies

Aunt Emily's Soft Caramels

6 dozen
3 hours 30 minutes

This buttery caramel recipe has been enjoyed for generations.

450 g	(*1 lb*) sugar
175 g	(*6 oz*) firmly packed brown sugar
225 g	(*8 oz*) butter, softened
250 ml	(*8 fl oz*) milk

250 ml	(*8 fl oz*) double cream
250 ml	(*8 fl oz*) light corn syrup
5 ml	(*1 tsp*) vanilla

In 4-litre (*7-pt*) saucepan combine all ingredients *except* vanilla. Cook over low heat, stirring occasionally, until sugar is dissolved and butter is melted (20 to 25 min.). Continue cooking, without stirring, until candy thermometer reaches 120 °C (*248 °F*) or small amount of mixture dropped into ice water forms a firm ball (about 2 hr.). Remove from heat; stir in vanilla. Pour into buttered 33 x 23-cm (*13 x 9-in*) tin. Cool completely; cut into 2.5 x 3-cm (*1 x 1½-in*) pieces.

Tip: After cutting, wrap each caramel in plastic wrap.

Carnival Caramel Apples

10 to 14 apples
60 minutes

Reminiscent of carnivals and county fairs, these chewy treats are sure to please.

125 g	(*4 oz*) butter
350 g	(*12 oz*) firmly packed brown sugar
250 ml	(*8 fl oz*) light corn syrup
	Dash salt
400 ml	(*14 fl oz*) canned sweetened condensed milk

5 ml	(*1 tsp*) vanilla
10 to 14	tart apples, washed, dried
150 g	(*5 oz*) chopped salted peanuts

In 2-litre (*3½-pt*) saucepan melt butter. Add brown sugar, corn syrup and salt. Cook over med. heat, stirring occasionally, until mixture comes to a full boil (10 to 12 min.). Stir in sweetened condensed milk. Continue cooking, stirring occasionally, until candy thermometer reaches 118 °C (*245 °F*) or small amount of mixture dropped into ice water forms a firm ball (20 to 25 min.). Remove from heat; stir in vanilla. Dip apples in caramel mixture. Dip end of apples in chopped peanuts; place on greased waxed paper. Refrigerate until firm (10 min.).

Carnival Caramel Apples

Old-Fashioned Peanut Brittle

900 g (*2 lb*)
2 hours 30 minutes

A favourite during the holidays, this candy brings back memories.

450 g	(*1 lb*) sugar
250 ml	(*8 fl oz*) light corn syrup
125 ml	(*4 fl oz*) water

225 g	(*8 oz*) butter, cut into pieces
300 g	(*11 oz*) raw peanuts
5 ml	(*1 tsp*) bicarbonate of soda

In 3-litre (*5-pt*) saucepan combine sugar, corn syrup and water. Cook over low heat, stirring occasionally, until sugar is dissolved and mixture comes to a full boil (20 to 30 min.). Add butter; continue cooking, stirring occasionally, until candy thermometer reaches 138 °C (*280 °F*) or small amount of mixture dropped into ice water forms a pliable strand (80 to 90 min.). Stir in peanuts; continue cooking, stirring constantly, until candy thermometer reaches 152 °C (*305 °F*) or small amount of mixture dropped into ice water forms brittle strands (12 to 14 min.). Remove from heat; stir in bicarbonate of soda. Pour mixture onto 2 buttered baking sheets; spread about 5-mm (*1/4-in*) thick. Cool completely; break into pieces.

Microwave Directions: In 3-litre (*5-pt*) casserole combine sugar, corn syrup and water. Microwave on HIGH, stirring after half the time, until sugar is dissolved and mixture comes to a full boil (5 to 8 min.). Add butter; microwave on HIGH, stirring after half the time, until microwave candy thermometer reaches 138 °C (*280 °F*) or small amount of mixture dropped into ice water forms a pliable strand (15 to 20 min.). Stir in peanuts. Microwave on HIGH, stirring after half the time, until microwave candy thermometer reaches 152 °C (*305 °F*) or small amount of mixture dropped into ice water forms brittle strands (6 to 8 min.). Stir in bicarbonate of soda. Pour mixture onto 2 buttered baking sheets; spread about 5-mm (*1/4-in*) thick. Cool completely; break into pieces.

Buttery Chocolate Nut Toffee

575 g (*1 1/4 lb*)
45 minutes

One taste of this old-time favourite and you'll be back for more!

225 g	(*8 oz*) sugar
225 g	(*8 oz*) butter, cut into pieces

175 g	(*6 oz*) semisweet chocolate chips
50 ml	(*4 tbsp*) chopped walnuts

In 2-litre (*3 1/2-pt*) saucepan combine sugar and butter. Cook over low heat, stirring occasionally, until candy thermometer reaches 149 °C (*300 °F*) or small amount of mixture dropped into ice water forms brittle strands (25 to 30 min.). Spread on waxed paperlined 38 x 25 x 2.5-cm (*15 x 10 x 1-in*) Swiss roll tin. Sprinkle chocolate chips over hot candy; let stand 5 min. Spread melted chocolate evenly over candy; sprinkle with nuts. Cool completely; break into pieces.

Microwave Directions: In 2-litre (*3 1/2-pt*) casserole combine sugar and butter. Microwave on HIGH, stirring occasionally, until microwave candy thermometer reaches 149 °C (*300 °F*) or small amount of mixture dropped into ice water forms brittle strands (12 to 18 min.). Spread on waxed paperlined 38 x 25 x 2.5-cm (*15 x 10 x 1-in*) Swiss roll tin. Sprinkle chocolate chips over hot candy; let stand 5 min. Spread melted chocolate evenly over candy; sprinkle with nuts. Cool completely; break into pieces.

Old-Fashioned Peanut Brittle (top)
Buttery Chocolate Nut Toffee (bottom)

To Store Cookies for Short Term (1 Week):

1. Cool cookies completely.

2. Do not mix soft and crisp varieties in the same container or the crisp cookies will soon become soft.

3. Store soft cookies in a container with a tight-fitting lid.

4. Store crisp cookies in a container with a loose-fitting lid.

5. Store bar cookies in the tin in which they were baked; cover tin tightly with aluminum foil or plastic wrap.

To Store Cookies for LongTerm (6 Months):

1. Both frosted and unfrosted cookies can be frozen and stored up to six months.

2. Arrange cookies in a container lined with plastic wrap or aluminum foil. Separate with layers of aluminum foil or plastic wrap.

3. Tightly seal container, label and freeze.

4. Thaw cookies by allowing them to stand loosely covered on a serving plate for about twenty minutes.

For Mailing:

1. Bar, drop or fruit cookies can best withstand mailing. Tender, fragile cookies are apt to crumble when mailed.

2. Use a heavy cardboard box or empty coffee can as mailing container.

3. Line container with aluminum foil or plastic wrap.

4. Wrap four to six cookies of the same size together in aluminum foil, plastic wrap or plastic bags and seal securely with freezer tape.

5. Place the heaviest cookies in the bottom of the container and layer the wrapped cookies with crumpled paper toweling around them.

6. Seal container with freezer, plastic or adhesive tape.

7. Wrap container with an outer paper wrapper.

8. Print mailing address and return address on the package in ink. Mark the package 'Perishable Food' to ensure more rapid transit and careful handling.

To Make Candies:

1. Follow directions carefully.

2. Use the recommended size heavy cooking pan to prevent candy from boiling over.

3. Use a dependable candy thermometer! Stand it upright in the candy mixture, making sure the bulb is completely covered with liquid while not resting on the bottom of the pan.

4. If you do not have a candy thermometer, use the cold water test. Drop a small amount of the candy mixture into a cupful of very cold water. Remove candy drop from water and form into a ball with fingers. The firmness of the ball determines the candy temperature and is an indication of doneness.

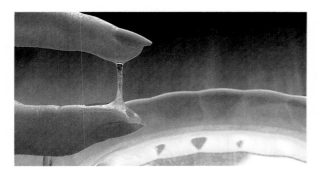

Thread: 106 ° to 112 °C (*223 ° to 234 °F*): Forms a 5-cm (*2-in*) soft thread.

Soft Ball: 112 ° to 115 °C (*234 ° to 240 °F*): Forms a soft ball which flattens when removed from water.

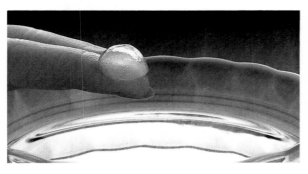

Firm Ball: 117° to 120°C (*242° to 248°F*): Forms a firm ball which does not flatten when removed from water.

Hard Ball: 121 ° to 131 °C (*250 ° to 268 °F*): Forms a hard, but pliable ball.

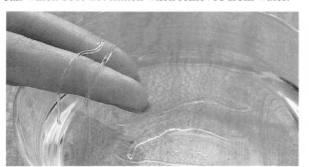

Soft Crack: 132 ° to 143 °C (*270 ° to 290 °F*): Separates into hard, but pliable strands.

Hard Crack: 149 ° to 154 °C (*300 ° to 310 °F*): Separates into hard, brittle strands.